DONALD B. ROSENTHAL, Professor of Political Science at the State University of New York, Buffalo, is the author of *The Limited Elite* and other studies of Indian and American politics.

The Expansive Elite

The Expansive Elite

DISTRICT POLITICS AND STATE POLICY-MAKING IN INDIA

Donald B. Rosenthal

UNIVERSITY OF CALIFORNIA PRESS

Berkeley · Los Angeles · London

036494

JQ
620
.M26 R67
1977

University of California Press
Berkeley and Los Angeles, California

University of California Press, Ltd.
London, England

Copyright © 1977 by
The Regents of the University of California

ISBN 0-520-03160-1
Library of Congress Catalog Card Number: 75-40665
Printed in the United States of America

Contents

Glossary

BAHUJAN SAMAJ: "the masses"

BAJRA: coarse grain grown in Maharashtra

BANDHARAS: small earthen dams

CRORE: 10,000,000

DADA: political boss

DALAL: commercial trader

DESHMUKH: high-status Maratha

DIWAN: prime minister

GADI: throne (literally: royal cushion)

GAT: group; faction

GOONDA: strong-arm man; thug

GRAM PANCHAYAT: village government council

GRAM SEVAK: village-level worker under community development scheme

GRAM SEVIKAS: women 'rural social service workers

HATTA: bargaining method used in determining prices in produce trade (literally: hand)

INAMDAR: traditional landholder whose rights derive from grant of superior person

JAGGERY: unrefined sugar; also referred to as *gul* or *gur*

JAGIRDAR: similar to *inamdar*

JANPAD: subdistrict revenue and governmental unit in some regions

JOWAR: coarse grain grown in Maharashtra

KULKARNI: traditional village secretary

LAKH: 100,000

MANDAL: lowest-level party unit; also, commitee or association

PANCHAYAT: traditional council

PANCHAYATI RAJ: term applied to contemporary form of rural local government; sometimes translated as "democratic decentralization"

PANCHAYAT SAMITI: intermediate level of contemporary rural local government

PATIL: village headman (traditional)

RUPEE (Rs.): unit of money equivalent to approximately one-seventh of a dollar

SARPANCH: village headman (under panchayati raj)

TAALIM SANGH: wrestler association

TALATI: revenue official serving several villages

TALUKA: subdistrict revenue and governmental unit in western Maharashtra

TALUKA SANGH: cooperative marketing society

TEHSIL: revenue and governmental unit (like *taluka*)

TEHSILDAR: revenue official for *tehsil* or *taluka*

VIDYA NIKETANS: schools for gifted rural children

WATAN: claim on land or other goods and services given to individuals performing services for a political authority

ZILLA PARISHAD: district government

Abbreviations

AICC: All-India Congress Committee
BDO: Block Development Officer
BPCC: Bombay Pradesh (State) Congress Committee
CEO: Chief Executive Officer
CPI: Communist Party of India
DCC: District Congress Committee
DCCB: District Central Cooperative Bank
DES: District Education Society
DLDB: District Land Development Bank
IAS: Indian Administrative Service
MLA: Member of the Legislative Assembly
MLC: Member of the Legislative Council
MP: Member of Parliament
MPCC: Maharashtra Pradesh (State or Regional) Congress Committee
PSP: Praja (People's) Socialist Party
PWP: Peasants and Workers Party
SSC: Secondary School Certificate
SSP: Samyukta (United) Socialist Party

Preface

One of the major themes of the study that follows is well summarized by Laxman, the *Times of India* editorial cartoonist, in the paper's issue of March 28, 1973. The cartoon shows the then-President of the Congress party at a microphone addressing a group of Congress members. The caption reads, "Like good Congressmen, I want you all to keep an eye on opportunists and careerists." In the foreground are a number of Congressmen glaring at each other; from their pockets protrude documents which carry the words *career* or *opportunity* on them.

This cartoon says as much about the state of political criticism in India as it does abut the condition of the Congress at the time. Unfortunately, events since June 1975 have made the expression of forthright criticism more difficult. Perhaps they have also made the necessity for that criticism less evident, but the grounds for doubt on that score are considerable.

Whatever the current state of political life and the suppression of political criticism, at the time the research reported in this volume was undertaken both politics and public commentary on it were lively and accessible to the foreign observer. It was possible for me to move with relative ease from my earlier interest in Indian municipal politics into a study of rural local elites and how elites based in two districts of the state of Maharashtra influenced the course of state and national politics and policy making. Initial field work was conducted during calendar year 1970, at a time when political arrangements at all levels were fairly fluid. Those actors whom I approached for interviews or data were, for the most part, friendly and eager to be helpful. While Indira Gandhi's dominating position had clearly improved by early 1973, when I revisited India for three months, I found most of the actors with whom I visited as accessible and informative as earlier. I wish to thank all of them for the assistance they provided. Some specifically requested that they not be cited by name; others are named in footnote references to interviews. It would be invidious to single out any of these actors in particular for thanks, since all contributed substantially to the work presented here.

Although events since 1975 have altered some of the terms on which the Indian political regime operates, much of the fundamental organization of social and economic life in the countryside goes on as it is described in the following pages. Thus, while some aspects of the present study are necessarily descriptive of patterns of behavior now characteristic only of the recent past, other parts are representative of current reality. Indeed, one of the arguments of the epilogue (written since the 1975 Declaration of Emergency) is that many of the basic features of the earlier regime remain, although the political system has been altered in significant respects. In particular, I would argue that much of the description and analysis of modes of institutional maintenance and the uses made of opportunity structures by the politically ambitious remains valid for an understanding of the contemporary scene.

In the course of my efforts I had the assistance of many organizations and individuals. Initial field work was supported jointly by the American Institute of Indian Studies and the American Council of Learned Societies—Social Science Research Council. I wish to thank both organizations. My visit in early 1973 was made possible by a sabbatical leave from the State University of New York at Buffalo.

Most helpful of those assistants with whom I worked were Milind V. Bahulekar, who provided enormous enthusiasm and energy in clearing hurdles in the way of data gathering, and Naresh Naik, who worked with me in 1973. During the process of assembling and analyzing those data, I have been aided at various times by Joseph Cavan, Judith Gentleman, Sidney Klein, and Arun Wagh. I want to thank them all for the contributions they have made to this study. Appreciation goes also to Professor Kurt Brassel, Ellen Mandel, and Diane Reeves for their excellent work on the three maps included in the text. Among the several typists who worked on various drafts of this manuscript, I wish to thank in particular Diane Biggins, Chris Black, Cynthia Breeden, and Bernice Poulton. They all approached the task with good humor despite the numerous problems that arose.

There are a number of persons whose insights into Maharashtrian political life have been especially helpful in shaping my understanding of events and personalities. In particular, I wish to thank Donald Attwood, Ram Joshi, Jayant Lele, Gail Omvedt,

V. M. Sirsikar, Robert Wirsing, and Eleanor Zelliot. Through their writings and through personal conversations, I have learned much from them about the people and politics of Maharashtra, including how much there remains still to be learned.

I hope no reader will be distressed by the lack of bibliography in this book. The citations in the footnotes, which are also cross-referenced in the index, provide complete bibliographical information, and I felt a bibliography would be an unwieldy and unnecessary appendage under the circumstances.

A portion of the material included in this volume has appeared in rather different form in pieces published in the following journals: *Comparative Education Review, Journal of Politics,* and *Economic and Political Weekly.* As indicated by the many citations of pieces in the *Economic and Political Weekly,* that journal was a particularly fruitful resource for research on Maharashtrian politics during the years encompassed by this study. The spirit of free enquiry encouraged by its editors was emblematic of the capacity for self-criticism which characterized the best in discourse about Indian public affairs among Indians and students of their political system from elsewhere. Indeed, if there is any broader purpose to which the present study is dedicated, it is to the spirit of serious and open enquiry which the *Economic and Political Weekly* and similar journals throughout India encouraged and represented so well before 1975.

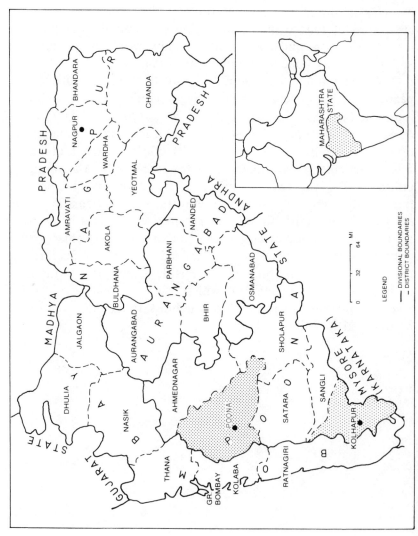

Maharashtra State

ONE

Introduction

The political system of India has been much admired (until recently) for its effort to combine political diversity with the pursuit of such societal goals as equality of opportunity and social equity. No doubt, political authorities moved with extreme caution in converting these abstract goals into meaningful public policies, but that caution reflected, at least in part, the difficulties involved in conducting the business of society out in the open where each proposal for action was subject to widespread debate and to the exercise of influence by a variety of opinion groups and organized interests. Inevitably in a society where inequality is engrained in social structure and economic relations, openness to diverse political influences compensated relatively deprived segments of society only in minor measure as compared with the advantages which flowed to those who controlled significant social or economic resources.

At first, the systemic problems that resulted from socioeconomic and political inequality were given only passing attention by students of Indian politics. Instead, they were concerned at the outset with the viability of a political system that sought to create a national identity out of distinctive cultural, linguistic, and regional interests.[1] This concern began to wane, however, as study after study pointed to the ways in which political and governmental institutions in the new system were serving not only to integrate but also to adapt pluralistic forces in society to the new political order. Among the most important institutions in this respect was the Congress party with its ability to incorporate a variety of local interests into an effective network of regional and national political organizations.[2] Even in those parts of the coun-

1. The classic statement of alarm is Selig S. Harrison, *India: The Most Dangerous Decades* (Princeton: Princeton University Press, 1960).

2. Among the more useful items dealing with the Congress at the state and national levels are Paul R. Brass, *Factional Politics in an Indian State: the Congress Party in Uttar Pradesh* (Berkeley and Los Angeles: University of California Press, 1968); Stanley A. Kochanek, *The Congress Party of India*

1

try where the Congress was not the only instrument of political integration, it generally was among the most significant in encouraging electoral participation by regional elites on terms acceptable to them.[3] The same may be said for the Congress role in encouraging their participation in other political arenas.[4] As a result of these processes of political integration and the political institutionalization associated with them,[5] it could well be claimed by the early 1960s that India, despite all of its economic problems, had a well-developed national identity and a pluralistic and reasonably participatory political system based on a national network of political activists who identified their own ambitions with the rewards that were available through the political system.[6]

(Princeton: Princeton University Press, 1968); Rajni Kothari, ed., *Party System and Election Studies* (Bombay: Allied Publishers, 1967); Richard Sisson, *The Congress Party in Rajasthan* (Berkeley and Los Angeles: University of California Press, 1972); and Myron Weiner, *Party Building in a New Nation* (Chicago: University of Chicago Press, 1967).

3. For a review of the integrative role of the *party system,* as contrasted with particular political parties, see the volumes by Kothari and Sisson.

4. A review of political experience in several of the Indian states points to the nation-building role of state governments as intermediaries in the federal system. See the contributions to Myron Weiner, ed., *State Politics in India* (Princeton: Princeton University Press, 1968); and Marcus F. Franda, *West Bengal and the Federalizing Process in India* (Princeton: Princeton University Press, 1968). The integrative role of democratic decision-making processes is suggested in Robert W. Stern, *The Process of Opposition in India* (Chicago: University of Chicago Press, 1970); and Myron Weiner, *The Politics of Scarcity* (Chicago: University of Chicago Press, 1962).

5. Following the lead provided by Samuel P. Huntington in his *Political Order in Changing Societies* (New Haven and London: Yale University Press, 1968), much of the present study is devoted to a review of the problems of creating and maintaining a stable organizational "infrastructure" in India. As Huntington elaborates the theme, "Institutionalization is the process by which organizations and procedures acquire value and stability. The level of institutionalization of any political system can be defined by the adaptability, complexity, autonomy, and coherence of its organizations and procedures" (p. 12). Our examination of the process of institutionalization at the local level in the Indian state of Maharashtra should not be read as concurrence in Huntington's personal commitment to institutional stability as a primary value. For an important corrective applied to the approach taken by Huntington and others, see Mark Kesselman, "Order or Movement?: The Literature of Political Development as Ideology," *World Politics* 26 (October 1973): 139-154.

6. In the language of the time, India appeared to have successfully weathered the "crises" of "nation building" (or "identity") and "legitimacy."

While India may have been successful in achieving a national political identity and in constructing and operating a set of political institutions through which that identity was expressed, it became clear in the years after Jawaharlal Nehru's death that the system was dealing only fitfully with serious strains introduced by a lack of effectiveness in handling problems of economic growth and social and economic distribution.[7] Regular affirmations by national leaders of support for "socialism" were rarely followed by actions; policies adopted were often more symbolic than substantive; verbal commitment to the poor relieved pressures for change temporarily but could not postpone indefinitely the need to identify policy goals clearly and to develop mechanisms appropriate for implementing those goals.

Unfortunately, the very success of the previous stage of political development may have contributed to the difficulties which the system later experienced. Indeed, it is the major thesis advanced in this study that the same institutional mechanisms which were created to integrate and harmonize the Indian political system eventually became counterproductive. The political leadership of the nation succeeded in attracting support from local elites and with their cooperation induced a measure of innovation and change in the countryside. However, in time those same local elites became barriers to further alterations in the economic and social structure.

This is not to assert that no benefits of government policy reached the vast majority of the rural population who tilled the land (many as day laborers, tenants, or sharecroppers) or provided their services as artisans or petty traders to the rural population. Rather, the claim is that the benefits of rural development in such

It also seemed well on the way to establishing that stability of political authority and popular support associated with surmounting "crises" of "participation" and "penetration." Where it was least successful was in matters of "distribution." For a review of these concepts, see Leonard Binder et al., *Crises and Sequences in Political Development* (Princeton: Princeton University Press, 1971), esp. Sidney Verba, "Sequences and Development," pp. 283-316.

7. One of the best statements of India's problems in this respect is contained in Rajni Kothari, *Politics in India* (Boston: Little, Brown, 1970), esp. pp. 338-382. He follows the approach of those analysts of political development included in the volume by Binder and his associates. Also see Gabriel A. Almond and G. Bingham Powell, *Comparative Politics: A Developmental Approach* (Boston: Little, Brown, 1966).

vital areas as agricultural investment, educational opportunity, and rural local government went principally to a relatively small segment of the rural population—those I have called the *expansive elite*.

To properly understand the recent problems and the future prospects of the Indian political system, then, one must go beyond an examination of the contours of the party system, the character of participation, and the organization of governmental and other politically relevant institutions to explore the processes by which the benefits of governmental actions have been distributed in the past and the consequences of those distributions. To do this, the emphasis should properly be on the formulation and implementation of public policy. Thus, the present work considers how proposals for action arose in the recent past in India, how policies were acted upon by authoritative decision-making agencies, and how those decisions were translated ultimately into functioning programs.[8]

Delimiting the Expansive Elite

It is the contention of this study that much that happens in district politics and in the politics and policy making of the Indian state of Maharashtra must be understood in terms of the exercise of influence by members of a relatively narrow political stratum. Members of that elite combine status and economic resources with control over political instrumentalities. In some instances, the possession of status and economic resources preceded entry into the political arena; in other instances, individuals have used opportunities in political life to gain control over other kinds of societal resources.

While most readily observed operating in district politics, members of the expansive local elite also have become actors in state

8. Concern with particular public policies has been fairly substantial in India. A good deal has been written about the problems associated with such policy areas as community development, language policy, population control, education, and agricultural innovation. However, only a few of those studies carefully have examined the political aspects of these policy processes. Among the more useful ones are those by Stern, *The Process of Opposition;* Franda, *West Bengal;* and Weiner, *The Politics of Scarcity.* For the most part, such policy studies accent policy formulation. One of the more useful efforts to examine problems of program implementation is Francine R. Frankel, *India's Green Revolution* (Princeton: Princeton University Press, 1971).

and national political and policy processes. Indeed, the line between "local," "state," or "national" politician is difficult to draw. Many members of the state legislature of Maharashtra (especially members of the popularly elected lower house)[9] and members of Maharashtra's parliamentary delegation to New Delhi would qualify for inclusion in this stratum; for the most part, these are rural-based politicians who have learned how to employ their private economic resources and the institutional infrastructure which has developed in rural Maharashtra to enhance their multifaceted political careers. They are oriented toward the personal rewards (both symbolic and material) of politics, though to gain those rewards they engage in political organizations and policy actions which do provide some benefits to their constituents.[10]

While this stratum will be treated as an elite with determinable boundaries (at least in principal), the use of the term *elite* should be understood in this particular case for both what it includes and what it excludes. Common usages of the term carry certain meanings. Among these are: (1) hierarchy; (2) stability; (3) consciousness; (4) exclusiveness; and (5) unity.[11] If each of these characteristics is visualized as one end of a continuum, it is probably arbitrary precisely where along that continuum one

9. The state legislature of Maharashtra has two houses. The upper house is the Vidhan Parishad or Legislative Council; despite the frequent use of the Indian term for the body, members are still known as MLCs (Members of the Legislative Council). Similarly, members of the more powerful lower house (the Vidhan Sabha) continue to be known as MLAs (Members of the Legislative Assembly).

10. An interesting discussion of the incentive systems which motivate individuals to participate in political life is contained in James Q. Wilson, *Political Organizations* (New York: Basic Books, 1973). For an earlier formulation of his approach see Wilson's *The Amateur Democrat* (Chicago: University of Chicago Press, 1962).

11. Useful reviews of elitist theories are contained in Peter Bachrach, *The Theory of Democratic Elitism* (Boston: Little, Brown, 1967); and T. B. Bottomore, *Elites and Society* (Harmondsworth, England: Penguin Books, 1966). A particularly relevant item for thinking about local political elites is Kenneth Prewitt, *The Recruitment of Political Leaders: A Study of Citizen-Politicians* (Indianapolis, Ind., and New York: Bobbs-Merrill, 1970). The literature of "community power" has been seriously concerned, of course, with the roles played by local elites. See, for example, the selections included in Willis D. Hawley and Frederick M. Wirt, eds., *The Search for Community Power*, 2d ed., (Englewood Cliffs, N.J.: Prentice-Hall, 1974) and the various approaches reviewed in David Ricci, *Community Power and Democratic Theory: The Logic of Political Analysis* (New York: Random House, 1971).

ought to place the behavior of particular actors in order to identify them as members of an elite.

In no case would I insist that the elites studied in Maharastra fall at the extreme end of the above continua. Thus, members of the expansive elite do not belong to a tightly integrated *hierarchical* structure. Still, I would hold that there exists in the two districts studied a relatively small group of men who stand higher than the mass of men and women in their exercise of influence or control over political, economic, and status resources. Who those individuals are remains fairly *stable* in the short run, although there is some circulation within the elite as new individuals advance and others recede within the political stratum. As we shall see, external events and new political opportunities introduced by outside forces have occasioned shifts in local political leadership over time. For the most part, those changes have taken place in an orderly fashion consistent with the value preferences and the social patterning acceptable to members of the local elite. In any event, it may be more accurate to speak of the stability of the elite system in rural politics in Maharashtra than of the stable positions of particular individuals within that system. Nevertheless, in both of the districts studied there has also been considerable continuity in the leadership structure during the twenty-five years reviewed later.

The suggestion that *consciousness* of group identity must be present for one to speak of individuals or families belonging to an elite is a troublesome one in the present case.[12] First, it should be noted that very few of the many rural political actors interviewed demonstrated what one might call a coherent set of ideological commitments. At one time, it may be argued, there were ideological overtones to the politics of Maharashtra. Some of the same persons whom one might now identify as members of the expansive elite took part in movements for national independence, for the creation of a distinct linguistic state, and for a larger voice for non-Brahmans in the affairs of that state. However, since Maharashtra emerged in 1960 as a separate state, the expansive elite has become the "establishment," both in party politics and in the

---

12. The problem of "subjective" and "objective" manifestations of elite group activity raised here is related to the conceptual difficulties discussed by Isaac Balbus in "The Concept of Interest in Pluralist and Marxian Analysis," *Politics and Society* 1 (February 1971): 151-177.

policy process, with very little inclination to state either a positive or a defensive ideology.

Yet implicit in both their statements about political life and their behavior has been a set of principles on which members of the expansive elite have proceeded.[13] Among these were the following features: (1) they professed a concern for equality of opportunity, but this concern generally took the form of resentment that urban people dominated the opportunity structures of Maharashtrian society rather than that rural people were distinguishable into the advantaged and the disadvantaged, and that they themselves belonged to the former group; (2) they uniformly opposed significant changes in the land tenure systems of their districts but supported government investments which favored the larger landholders; and (3) they saw very little need for a redistribution of available resources. Thus they looked to government for investment in rural development, but they strongly opposed increases in land revenues on agricultural holdings or the introduction of income taxes on the wealthier and more productive farmers.

There were a few dissident voices within the elite on these matters. Some individuals spoke the language of socialization of the means of production, but these views were unusual. Generally expressed by members of the minor opposition political parties, such attitudes were not effective in mobilizing popular support over the heads of the more stolidly status-quo groups within the rural elite. Even in the Congress, a few leaders did acknowledge the need for radical change. These individuals had, for the most part, moved somewhat out of the confines of district-level leadership. They had assumed roles in state and national politics which seemed to condition their political attitudes. Even these leaders did not go much beyond rhetorical commitment to radical socioeconomic change in actual pursuit of alterations in society.[14]

Like the other factors, *exclusiveness* is sometimes taken to be a measure of the existence of an elite. At the same time, those elites

13. Some of the difficulties involved in applying the language of "ideology" and "interests" to local politics in the United States are reviewed in J. David Greenstone and Paul E. Peterson, *Race and Authority in Urban Politics* (New York: Russell Sage Foundation, 1973), esp. pp. 99-162.

14. Ideological conflict is more evident at the state level than in rural local politics. In part this is a result of the addition of urban interests drawn from major Maharashtrian cities, such as Bombay, Poona, and Nagpur. Nevertheless,

in history that have been most successful have developed structures through which aspiring individuals may participate in some
measure in the direction of society. Much of the following study is
devoted to a description of some of the opportunity structures
which have been introduced into the Maharashtrian countryside in
the past two decades—opportunity structures which have provided
positions to men of talent and ambition. As a result, one finds a
mixture of persons in leadership positions: some have risen from
fairly humble beginnings; others have come from families of traditional social standing and wealth. Yet the seeming openness of the
political stratum has not meant an inundation of the political
process by mass influence nor a radical alteration in the terms of
trade of the expansive elite. Sharing many values with the older
leadership, the newly arrived appear to wish little more than to
join in the exploitation of economic benefits and prestige patterns
which already exist.

Finally, as I have indicated, an "ideal type" of elite might be
expected to display considerable personal and ideological *unity*.
The expansive elite reveals limited diversity on the ideological
dimension, but conflict over personal ambitions is extensive. Thus,
there is continuous contention among individuals within the elite
for priority in political influence and for superiority in the control
of important economic resources. In fact, a conflict which appears
to involve ideological differences may turn out, on closer examination, to involve tactical behavior employed by the ambitious to
maximize a political following in order to maintain or extend a
political career. New persons may be brought into the political
stratum or advanced in the system of opportunities and rewards
because they have shown skill in providing support to established
leaders in intrastratum conflicts. However, rarely does this conflict
within the elite lead to major alterations in the way relations are
articulated with the mass of citizens.

Other students of Indian politics have found in the situation I
have described the basis for an argument that a fairly closed

---

Maharashtra has been less marked on the whole by ideological conflict among
state politicians than are some other states, most notably West Bengal. In that
respect, see Marcus F. Franda, *Radical Politics in West Bengal* (Cambridge,
Mass.: MIT Press, 1971); and, for India generally, Paul R. Brass and Marcus F.
Franda, eds., *Radical Politics in South Asia* (Cambridge, Mass.: MIT Press,
1973).

system of power operates in the Maharashtrian countryside.[15] I am not prepared to go quite that far. What evidence I have been able to gather does suggest, however, that those factors which I have identified as characterizing the presence of an elite do exist in sufficient proportion in the Maharashtrian case to allow us to use the term.[16]

Several additional points need to be made in connection with the operations of an expansive elite in district politics. First, as we shall see in the following section, members of the local elite are not the only significant actors in important matters affecting public policy. Nor are the concerns of all district-based actors focused only on district affairs; some people move upward and outward from the district in trying to add to their stocks of personal and political resources.

Furthermore, when one shifts to an examination of state politics and policy, differences appear to exist among regions within a state and among interests which cross regions. These conflicts attenuate district elites' power and influence. For some purposes,

15. In particular, see Anthony T. Carter, *Elite Politics in Rural India: Political Stratification and Political Alliances in Western Maharashtra* (Cambridge: Cambridge University Press, 1974); and Jayant Lele, "Patriarchs, Patrons and Pluralists" (unpublished manuscript, 1974). Also see Donald W. Attwood, "Political Entrepreneurs and Economic Development" (Ph.D. diss., McGill University, 1974). For similar arguments applied to other regions of India, see David J. Elkins, *Electoral Participation in a South Asian Context* (Durham, N.C.: Carolina Academic Press, 1975); and John W. Gartrell, "Development and Social Stratification in India: The Structure of Inequality in Andhra Pradesh" (Ph.D. diss., University of Wisconsin-Madison, 1973).

16. I disagree, however, with the analysis developed by Mary C. Carras in her *The Dynamics of Indian Political Factions: A Study of District Councils in the State of Maharashtra* (New York and Cambridge: Cambridge University Press, 1972). Carras develops a model of competition among local political elites in Maharashtra which associates ideological conflict with distinctions in socioeconomic bases in a fashion that I find too mechanical. Furthermore, I believe there exists an ideological consensus within the elite where Carras finds cleavage. Similarly, where Carras sees highly institutionalized factions based upon ideological and economic distinctions, I find a good deal more fluidity in interpersonal relations among members of the district elites. For a detailed critique of the Carras study, see my "Sources of District Congress Factionalism in Maharashtra," *Economic and Political Weekly,* 19 August 1972, pp. 1725-1746. Both Carras and I looked at district politics in Poona, but our approaches resulted in rather different conclusions drawn from the same data.

it may be useful to think of district elites operating segmentally throughout the state of Maharashtra as part of a large stratum sharing certain interests when it comes to the formulation and implementation of state policy. On the other hand, there may be occasions when interests conflict among districts as when battles go on for investment of state resources or symbolic recognition of particular regional or district interests.

When raised to the level of national politics and policy, the problem of properly conceptualizing local influence becomes even more pronounced. Yet, it may be appropriate in some instances to speak of a series of regional and local elites exercising political influence on the central government of India to prevent the adoption of agricultural taxation or particular land reform policies. More positively, rural elites may cooperate to promote national programs of price supports, rural extension work, and investment in irrigation. In contrast, farmers in one state may come into conflict with farmers from another over such programs as grain procurement.

If this conceptualization of *elite* must necessarily remain arbitrary or ambiguous, the same may be said of the adjective *expansive*, with which I have characterized this elite at various places in the text. Employed throughout to describe an opportunistic group of local political actors who pursue personal ambitions through whatever social, economic, and political mechanisms come to hand, the term points to the essentially personal and amoral pursuit of power which characterizes many members of the rural elite.

Equally important, the notion of an expansive elite is intended to indicate the uses made of public institutions supported by societal resources. As we shall see in later chapters, many of these institutions were created by the national or state governments and introduced into the countryside without initial local support or demand. Once such institutions were set in place, however, they became opportunity structures which local political actors were more than willing to use in order to build their own stocks of political power and personal prestige. Thus, the externally induced institutions soon became a central part of the infrastructure of district life. In their operation these institutions sometimes had the general public in mind as beneficiary, as in the case of expanded educational opportunities. Sometimes benefits went directly to the elite group; for example, members of the elite held most of the positions in the new system of rural local government. In either case, these structures became important counters in the games of rural politics and the means by which the ambitious defined the character of their ambitions and the way in which a political career was to be either maintained or extended.

In another sense, the notion of an expansive elite is meant to contrast with the term *limited elite*, which I used in the title of a previous study of Indian municipal politics in the cities of Agra and Poona.[17] The use of the term at that time reflected my observation that elected members of the two municipal government bodies were highly constrained in their ability to direct municipal affairs. On the one hand, a municipal bureaucracy headed by a state-appointed professional administrator did not defer with any regularity to their preferences; on the other hand, they were limited by the narrow definition of municipal powers provided by state laws. I did not deal in any detail with the ambitions of municipal politicians outside the arenas of municipal politics and government. Thus, I excluded from examination how they might use non-municipal institutions as resources in building political careers. Recent studies suggest, however, that for some urban politicians a variety of opportunity structures exist through which political ambitions may be pursued, though the formal institutions of municipal government may be among the less important of these.[18]

Both studies are concerned with ambitious politicians moving through available opportunity structures, but where my earlier examination of municipal politics focused on the limitations that infringed on the ability of local political actors to use municipal institutions to advance their ambitions, the present study goes beyond the examination of rural local government institutions to include other rural opportunity structures which have provided scope for their political ambitions. To further complicate the comparison, however, institutions of rural local government do appear to give greater opportunities to political actors than do municipal governments.

17. *The Limited Elite: Government and Politics in Two Indian Cities* (Chicago: University of Chicago Press, 1970).

18. See, in particular, Rodney W. Jones, *Urban Politics in India* (Berkeley and Los Angeles: University of California Press, 1974); and Robert G. Wirsing, "Associational 'Micro-Arenas' in Indian Urban Politics," *Asian Survey* 13 (April 1973): 408-420.

It should be noted that the people who dominate rural politics and, through that domination, exercise considerable influence in state politics and policy making are not simply "rural politicians" in a tradition-bound sense. Rather, in the last two decades, processes have occurred in India which have had the effect of "deurbanizing" political life.[19]

There has been a considerable diffusion of modern values to the countryside at the same time as those political actors whose bases are in the villages and small towns have moved into positions of state and national power. Individuals who hold positions of local and state influence in contemporary Maharashtra have highly favorable attitudes toward the most modern sectors of Indian society. Indeed, they eagerly seek benefits for themselves and for their followers in the most forward-looking educational institutions, in commercial agriculture, and in the agro-industries which have been developed with the aid of the national and state governments. Many of the younger generation among them either have been educated in or have had considerable experience in urban areas. They interact easily with urban-based politicians and administrators. They are, however, an elite of local politicians who have chosen to build their political careers upon rural constituencies and whose concerns are oriented to problems of economic and political development in rural Maharashtra. In a nation where 80 percent of the population still lives in rural areas and where substantial societal resources have been invested in those areas—resources which can be turned to good political account—there are many incentives for the ambitious politician to identify himself with the interests of the rural population rather than to be one among many competitors for influence in an urban constituency.

OTHER ACTORS IN POLITICS AND POLICY

To argue that members of the expansive elite constitute a significant force in the policy process is not to assert that they have the

19. Donald B. Rosenthal, "Deurbanization, Elite Displacement and Political Change in India," *Comparative Politics* 2 (January 1970): 169-201. There I argued that at the same time as political power moved outward from the cities after independence, political men come to prominence in rural areas who exhibited the personal attitudes and behavior of the class of urban politicians whom they replaced in positions of state and national power.

field to themselves. Indeed, their role in public policy is often more reactive than initiatory. Yet they exercise a formidable veto over those who do initiate policy, either by constraining the alternatives which are raised or by making it difficult for effective actions to occur without their approval once legislation has been formulated or administrative plans have been put forward.

The interests and values of members of the expansive elite must contend with those who fill roles in the state and local political system. For the purposes of these introductory remarks, we may assign those actors to three categories: (1) functional specialists; (2) government bureaucrats; and (3) governmental and party leaders. In practice, the lines distinguishing such actors from one another and, in turn, from members of the expansive elite are not as clear-cut as one might like.

Functional specialists are persons who work in those many institutions which have developed since independence to provide a range of services to the countryside. They include individuals who operate the educational institutions of Maharashtra, others who manage specialized cooperative banking and agro-industrial organizations, and even some government employees who regard themselves as technical specialists in such areas as health, agriculture, and public works. Such specialists lay a claim to expertise and are tied into professional networks of national and sometimes international scope.

In contrast, *government bureaucrats* are generalists who have a strong conception of the prerogatives and duties of the governmental employee. Their bureaucratic commitments may not involve a great concern with the substance of public policy (so long as such policies do not threaten their own authority). Where the functional specialist may be an active contributor to the initiation of public policy, the bureaucrat is more likely to be involved in those problems of administrative management which accompany proposals for either substantive or structural reform. Thus, in the particular cases selected for this study, functional specialists played a major part in formulating proposals for educational change and contributed some ideas to the reforms proposed for the cooperative sector; only in discussions about structural reforms in rural local government did the bureaucrats' interests seem to be directly affected, and their interests, however muted in expression, may have been served by the way movement toward major change was prevented.[20]

We come full circle when we speak of *governmental leaders.* In the case of Maharashtra, the state government and the state Congress party have been intimately linked since 1960. Men who hold leadership positions in the government have risen from the districts and retain their state (and national) influence to the extent that their local bases remain strong. Where his own electoral constituency is concerned a state leader is also a local politician.

To be successful in a ministerial role, however, a politician must find ways of balancing the claims of the other three types of political actors: functional specialists, bureaucrats, and most importantly politically, members of the expansive elite. The result is that a subtle transition takes place in a person who becomes a state government leader. Office brings with it pressures not only to serve the political interests of one's territorial constituency but to serve the state as a whole. Even the most parochial of ministers or party leaders must accord attention to the demands of a wide range of local representatives if he is to retain political support within the state party. A reputation as an able leader also means establishing effective relations with the government bureaucracy, since the state leader ambitious to maintain or advance his career must rely on bureaucrats to administer the programs for which he is politically responsible. Finally, a leader who would like to develop a substantial personal standing must occasionally engage in policy innovations within his assigned sphere of work in order to gain public attention. This means appealing to certain functional specialists, if only to gain ideas which the leader can formulate into policy proposals. Thus, in accepting a policy role, the successful state political leader must of necessity move away from the narrower personal perspectives characteristic of many members of the expansive elite.

20. The distinction between functional specialists and government bureaucrats pursues a theme developed by Leonard Reissman more than twenty-five years ago when he suggested that different role conceptions may exist within the same organization. Thus, the Education Department of Maharashtra may provide places both to those Reissman called "job bureaucrats" (persons oriented primarily to the bureaucracy itself) and to "functional bureaucrats" (those oriented to reference groups outside the bureaucracy, particularly professional organizations). Leonard Reissman, "A Study of Role Conceptions in Bureaucracy," *Social Forces* 27 (March 1949): 305-310.

The expectations associated with the role of "successful" state leader are not fulfilled, of course, by every person appointed to a government position. Some individuals have risen beyond their natural capacities to respond to those role expectations and hold ministerial positions even though they are unable to demonstrate an ability to deal with the complex issues which regularly confront their offices. In contrast, some younger and frequently better educated individuals are still in the process of exploiting lower-order political opportunities in order to reach more inclusive areas of power and policy. These individuals may take an active part in the processing of policy issues even though their actual responsibilities may be circumscribed by more limited formal roles, perhaps as backbenchers in the state legislature. For most members of the expansive elite, however, a concern with policy proposals arises only when they see threats to their own localized interests or to the interests of those whom they feel they represent.

To further complicate matters, a government portfolio may not always measure accurately the power of the incumbent of an office. Thus, a person may hold a position on the basis of the support given to him by another more powerful national or state leader; he or she may have nothing in the way of institutional resources that can be brought to bear in securing a personal claim on that position or advancing further in political life. In contrast, some "local" politicians may actually have such substantial resources within their control that they may be counted as among the more significant participants in the state party and policy system of Maharashtra even when all their major institutional identifications are confined to a single district and they have no formal role in the state government.

At the highest levels of state and national responsibility, concern by top leaders with directing the activities of the three sets of political actors I have identified is joined to an interest in securing the support of a fourth, more general constituency—the electorate. Despite the fact that the Congress party has been in unquestioned political control of Maharashtra since the creation of the state, party and government leaders appear not only to feel themselves compelled to respond to the claims of the three sets of actors already mentioned but they also seem to behave as if they wish to attract the greatest possible support from the electorate. Recent studies suggest that a large proportion of the rural electorate in

Maharashtra is tied to the Congress by an elaborate system of
patron-client relations in which members of the expansive elite are
key actors.[21]

On the whole, state and national leaders have imbibed at least a
verbal commitment to popular democracy which leads them to act
as if the voters had an important role to play in politics and policy
making. This accounts for the egalitarian and "socialist" symbolism in which Congress electoral appeals are framed. Once
elections are out of the way, however, the several elite constituencies tend to reestablish their claims, and electoral promises are
only rarely converted into policy performances without those
interests being given considerable priority.

Whatever one may think of the character of appeals to the
general public, they have formed a source of constraint on the
behavior of state and national leaders. Such concerns have not
been as strong at lower levels of the elite structure where personal
ambition seemed to be pursued with reference to much narrower
personal and factional interests. Indeed, in rural local politics (at
least in the case of Maharashtra), concern with the fate of the
electoral base of the Congress was so weak that party identity
became an often irrelevant factor in the struggle for personal
opportunities. Since opposition parties were unusually weak in
rural Maharashtra (as contrasted to some other Indian states),
members of the expansive elite felt relatively free to put personal
ambition ahead of party loyalty without apparent concern for the
consequences to the *electoral* monolith that was the Congress
organization in the state.

ORGANIZATION OF THE STUDY

Although the study reported here involves an examination of
political conflict and policy-making processes in the state government of Maharashtra, it began as an examination of politics and
administration in the rural parts of two districts of the state.
During 1970, I spent the greater part of a year in India interview-
ing persons active in the politics of Poona and Kolhapur districts
about the structure of power in each. Only as I discovered the
extent to which those power structures implicated local actors in

21. See the items cited in n. 15.

institutions of cooperative finance, education, and local government did my exploration become more concerned with how such institutions had developed and what functions they were performing. This in turn led me to an examination of state-level policy disputes which had developed in each of the sectors. In the course of the study, interviews were held with many bureaucrats and functional specialists in the three policy sectors: education; cooperatives; and local government. Approximately three hundred interviews in all were conducted in 1970 with actors in the two districts and with persons who participated in the decision-making processes of the state government. In early 1973, an additional seventy persons were interviewed or re-interviewed during a three-month stay.

Although it would be possible to cite a variety of geographic, social, or historical differences between the two districts, the same could be said for any two districts included in such a study. The main purpose in presenting the district materials is to illustrate how political actors in those two districts operate in local politics and in the larger arenas of state politics and policy through their activity in policy-relevant institutions.

The familiarity that I had gained with urban Poona through my earlier study of that city led me to choose the rural part of that district as one base of operations for the present study. I was attracted to Kolhapur district for several reasons that stood in contrast to the Poona situation: it was formerly a princely state loyal to the British, whereas Poona had been a major center of British India and an early participant in nationalist activity; Kolhapur's agricultural production is favored by good rainfall and reliable river-based irrigation in a way that is alien to Poona's frequently drought-affected rural areas; Kolhapur district was well known for its cooperative organizations and for heavy commercial cultivation of sugarcane while Poona was not. In terms of research strategy, transportation connections to both Poona and Bombay from Kolhapur also allowed for relatively easy movement among the three research sites.

The selection of "policy" areas for study also involved a mixture of influences. First, it should be noted that my concern with policy took the form of examination of policy *sectors* and their ongoing organization and behavior as much as it did a specific concern with "issues" bounded in time and conforming to formalistic notions of stage of formulation and implementation.[22]

From the outset, I assumed that any sector of public policy that I selected would contain a number of conflicts over program goals and administrative means. The research question then became one of identifying *both* the characteristic operations of the sector and the kinds of conflicts within the sector that may have given rise to proposals for change. In taking this route, I tried to avoid some of the methodological issues raised by those who have criticized the decision-making approach to the study of community politics in the United States.[23] In each of the sectors studied in Maharashtra, I have attempted to ask such questions as: Whose interests do the sectors serve? What are the factors which give rise to proposals for change? How do existing political forces respond to such proposals? What effects do policy changes in the sectors have for the larger society?

An interest in modernization and the association of education with political life led me to select education as one area for examination. The rural cooperative movement has been promoted as another vehicle of social and economic change in India; the organization and operation of cooperative institutions seemed worthy of careful attention. Finally, I decided to look at the system of rural local government introduced into Maharashtra in 1962. While a theoretical literature and some descriptive materials existed on each sector, there was little more than passing attention given in that literature to the possible relationships between politics and policy.

It was only after I selected the three policy areas that I discovered how interesting a yield they were capable of producing, for each had been the subject of considerable conflict in recent years. All had undergone organizational changes promoted origi-

22. For a highly formalized model of the policy process, see Yehezkel Dror, *Public Policy Reexamined* (San Francisco: Chandler Publishing, 1968). Contrast that approach with Richard I. Hofferbert, *The Study of Public Policy* (Indianapolis, Ind., and New York: Bobbs-Merrill, 1974). Also see James E. Anderson, *Public Policy-Making* (New York: Praeger, 1975).

23. In particular, see Peter Bachrach and Morton S. Baratz, "Decisions and Nondecisions," *American Political Science Review* 57 (September 1963): 641-651. Also see the exchange between Raymond E. Wolfinger ("Nondecisions and the Study of Local Politics") and Frederick W. Frey ("Comment: Issues and Nonissues in the Study of Power"), *American Political Science Review* 65 (December 1971): 1063-1101.

nally by the central government: financial and political incentives had been provided by the national leadership in the 1950s to state governments to encourage the growth of educational institutions, the expansion of cooperative societies, and the renovation of local government structures. These stimuli and the political lead provided by the central government encouraged the creation of institutions which introduced a set of new opportunity structures into the countryside. If the original idea was to encourage equality of access to those institutions, that hope has been realized only in part. Instead, one major consequence of these innovations was to place new political resources, and control over access to those resources, into the hands of a rural elite emerging to positions of power in the 1950s. Members of this expansive elite turned the new institutions to their own ends and employed public resources not only to attain some of the nobler goals originally projected by national leaders—the opening of opportunities in education to a greater proportion of the population, modernization of agricultural production, bringing government closer to the people—but to enhance their holds on the political resources of the districts in which they operated.

Although some societal gains resulted from institutionalization of the new programs, by the 1960s complaints from various quarters also were being heard. The government of Maharashtra decided in each case to reconsider the goals or organization of the policy sector. As a result, each sector was subjected to a review by the responsible minister or by a government-appointed committee (in the case of local government). Thus, merely by chance, I had selected three areas of public policy which were intertwined with the character of political and economic change in the countryside; moreover, leaders of the state government had rather recently perceived that the performances of those sectors warranted some reconsideration of existing arrangements. As we shall see, the formal reexamination of each sector raised questions bearing not only on the ends and means of existing programs but on the distribution of political power in the state and the districts.

While some models of public policy making might regard political activity as little more than the energy applied to operate the policy system, I am arguing for a more complex conception of the relationship. In Maharashtra, policy is also the engine through which power distributions are altered among political activists and between elites and non-elites. In a broad sense, policies, and especially the operational decisions made in the course of policy implementation, permit some local groups rather than others to accrue benefits from public resource distributions; concomitantly, the existence of policy-related resources encourages political aspirants to come forward in order to enhance personal careers. Conflicts over policy alternatives among state leaders are also employed with some regularity as counters in quarrels over political power.

While individuals move easily among arenas of politics and policy, distinct state, district, and even subdistrict "political systems" may be said to exist at least to the extent that there are public institutions organized to collect and distribute resources and to carry on political activities within determinate geographical and institutional spaces. The political interests of individual actors regularly cross these formal boundaries. Thus, to speak of conflicts between "the political leadership of Kolhapur" and "of Maharashtra," as we shall do on occasion, is somewhat misleading. In Kolhapur, power conflicts have often involved a feverish war within the expansive elite; participants in that battle have been eager and willing on many occasions to employ resources from outside the district (including the help of state leaders and leaders of other districts) to advance their own positions in district affairs. At the same time, they have exchanged that outside support for their own support to combatants in the conflicts which go on in state politics and district politics elsewhere.

The following chapters attempt to impose some order upon this highly complex reality. To provide a general background to both the political and policy contexts in which the expansive elite and other policy actors operate, chapter 2 outlines some of the historical and social dimensions of political change in Maharashtra over the past century. The chapter also contains brief introductions to the three policy sectors we have selected for close attention.

In chapters 3 and 4 we examine the political organization of Poona and Kolhapur districts. It is in local arenas that we can most clearly see the way members of the expansive elite operate. We will be particularly concerned with struggles among members of that elite for control of those opportunity structures which have been opened to persons of ambition since independence.

With chapter 5 we turn to the arenas of state politics where we briefly review some of the conflicts within the state Congress party and state government which have shaped the way conflicts over state policy proceed. In chapters 6 through 9 we examine both the existing condition of the three policy sectors and the proposals for change which have been generated by local and state actors in the last several years. In chapter 10 we review the contribution of the expansive elite to the organization and operation of the state political system. Finally, in a brief epilogue, I attempt an examination of this system against the experience of recent events in India.

Politics and Policy in Maharashtra

The state of Maharashtra has its roots in a language (Marathi), a shared cultural identity (including a saint-poet religious tradition), a regionally distinctive social structure, and a common historical experience, which crystalized during the seventeenth and eighteenth centuries. For a time during that period, the region was the center of an empire which spread its influence throughout much of the subcontinent. Thus, while the state's emergence as a modern political entity in 1960 was the immediate product of national decision-making processes, both its creation and its character owe much to factors which long preceded that act.

Despite its distinctive heritage, Maharashtra has not experienced any conflict between national and regional identities. While leaders in states like Tamil Nadu and the Punjab have occasionally carried visions of regional autonomy to an extreme, Maharashtrians (like most Indians) have identified strongly with the idea of an Indian nation propounded by Mohandas Gandhi, Jawaharlal Nehru, and earlier nationalists, some of whom were Maharashtians. The demand for the creation of a distinct Marathi-speaking state within the Indian nation, therefore, did not involve any sense of separation from the larger Indian identity.

Yet, if the Maharastrians' identification as Indians is strong, a sense of Maharashtrian distinctiveness has continued to pervade the politics of the region during the past quarter-century. It was evident in the way agitations were organized around the issue of Maharashtra itself; more recently it has surfaced in the regional chauvinism of the Shiv Sena—a party based in the city of Bombay which has demanded greater economic opportunities and a larger voice in the politics of that city for the "sons of the soil" of Maharashtra.[1]

1. Ram Joshi, "Shiv Sena: A Movement in Search of Legitimacy," *Asian Survey* 10 (November 1970): 967-978; Mary F. Katzenstein, "Origins of Nativism: The Emergence of Shiv Sena in Bombay," *Asian Survey* 13 (April 1973): 386-399. Efforts to spread the Shiv Sena out of the city of Bombay, where Maharashtrians found themselves on the defensive economically, met with very little success.

A concern for economic and political opportunities and their linkage to regional chauvinism is not peculiar to Bombay and its hinterland. Indeed, it can be argued that a major part of the appeal of the many regional movements that have arisen in India has been the promise such movements have held out of greater opportunities in government and politics (and in government-related employment) for persons from the area.[2] From this perspective, the steps that led to the creation of Maharashtra can be viewed as part of a common process in India by which individuals and groups have been mobilized to promote collective advancement in relation to more established or institutionalized groups. This chapter emphasizes collective mobilization as a way of understanding Maharashtrian history, for much past political conflict in the region may be seen as part of a battle among collectivities for access to and control over economic and political opportunities. Conflicts over individual opportunities, no doubt, were as much part of the history of the region prior to 1947 as they are today. However, more recently, collective mobilization has been replaced in large part (though not entirely) by the politics of individual ambition.

The principal struggles with which we are concerned in the first part of the chapter are: (1) the emergence of the nationalist movement; (2) the rise of non-Brahman political activity in the region; (3) the demand for recognition of Maharashtrian identity; and (4) the rise to political power of rural non-Brahmans, particularly members of the Maratha community. We shall review those conflicts before indicating how the expansion of opportunities in education, in the cooperative sector, and in rural local government was tied to the achievement of political dominance by rural non-Brahmans in the new state of Maharashtra.

POLITICAL CHANGE PRIOR TO INDEPENDENCE

Prior to national independence in 1947, the Marathi speakers of India were separated into several distinct administrative jurisdictions, including both directly ruled British territory and areas

2. Katzenstein identifies some of these movements in her article. Conflicts in the past five years in Andhra—the first state created on linguistic lines— illustrate the extent to which agitations for regional autonomy can be stimulated by demands for guarantees in employment to persons from a particular region.

ruled indirectly by the British through Indian princes. The largest group of Marathi speakers was found within the multilingual state of Bombay, which included the city of Bombay (where they numbered only slightly more than 40 percent of the total population) and areas where Gujarati, Kannada, and other languages predominated. Thus, within the state of Bombay, Maharashtrians constituted a distinct minority. Marathi speakers were also found in the Central Provinces centered around the city of Nagpur (the region known as Vidarbha), where Hindi speakers were also to be found. Finally, a substantial number of Marathi speakers were included in the domain of the Nizam of Hyderabad, the largest principality in India before independence. (The Marathi-speaking districts in Hyderabad were known as Marathwada.)

Part of the distinctiveness of the Marathi-speaking area lay in its identification with the historical exploits of Shivaji, the warrior-king who founded the Maratha Empire in the late seventeenth century and used that empire as an instrument against the previously dominant Mughals. Though himself a member of the leading agrarian caste of Maharashtra (the Marathas), Shivaji's domain was ruled after his death by persons from a variety of communities. Indeed, conflicts among power wielders within the empire led to the creation of distinct provinces only loosely united by a series of Brahman *peshwas* (prime ministers) who gathered the powers of the descendants of Shivaji into their own hands. It was these peshwas who surrendered the last remnants of native power in western India to the British when they completed their conquest of the region in 1818.[3]

Indequately supplied with the European manpower necessary to service their bureaucratic machinery, the British turned to Indians for the purpose. Members of the Maharashtrian Brahman community were particularly eager to take to the new styles of Western education and to be absorbed into the opportunity structures opened in British service. They attended the educational institutions started by the British, including the Western-style colleges eventually consolidated under the University of Bombay in 1858. Some became lawyers and served in the legal system devised by the British.

3. For the Maratha period, see G. S. Sardesai, *New History of the Marathas,* 3 vols. (Bombay: Phoenix Publications, 1946-1948); for the early period of contact with the British, see Charles H. Heimsath, *Indian Nationalism and Hindu Social Reform* (Princeton: Princeton University Press, 1964).

At the same time that the British fired the ambitions of young men attracted into the new occupational structures, they pursued a carefully controlled policy of denying Indians access to the commanding heights of the administrative structure. They safeguarded the imperial power from the kind of challenge which might have followed upon a significant element of representative government. This cautious policy of mobilizing Brahman occupational ambitions, while at the same time frustrating ambitions insofar as political opportunities were concerned, provided part of the ground for the emergence of the nationalist movement. In Bombay State, as elsewhere in India, the movement took root first in the urban centers near the coast (principally Bombay City and Poona), but by the last two decades of the nineteenth century it spread to interior cities like Nagpur.

Maharashtrian Brahmans played leading roles in the nationalist movement before the turn of the century. Some, like G. K. Gokhale, argued for the direct application of British principles of government and politics to India; others, led by B. G. Tilak, constructed an indigenous nationalism based on elements of Indian culture and tradition, including appeals to the symbolic memory of Shivaji, whose anti-Mughal exploits were now given a more general anti-foreign complexion.[4]

When Mahatma Gandhi emerged as a major political leader in 1919 and Tilak died the following year, the position of the urbanized Maharashtrian Brahman in national and regional political life began to decline. Gandhi appealed to the less sophisticated classes of the cities and small towns of India. The moderates previously associated with Gokhale drifted into minor parties or abandoned politics; some of Tilak's followers rejected Gandhi's egalitarian and non-violent orientation for more militant upper-caste political groups like the Hindu Mahasabha. Nevertheless, a significant number of Maharashtrian Brahmans followed Gandhi in the 1930s. Some held major positions in the Indian National Congress, though their relative importance in the party declined as governmental and party reforms gave greater representation to rural areas and to the less advantaged segments of the population. These reforms signaled the increasing organizational importance of

4. One interpretation of the rise of the nationalist movement may be found in Anil Seal, *The Emergence of Indian Nationalism* (Cambridge: Cambridge University Press, 1968); also see Stanley A. Wolpert, *Tilak and Gokhale* (Berkeley and Los Angeles: University of California Press, 1962).

the numerically preponderant non-Brahmans. (Brahmans constitute less than 5 percent of the regional population.)

Though an attempt to mobilize non-Brahmans was initiated in
the late nineteenth century, active efforts at increasing Western
education and political participation among non-Brahmans began
seriously only in the second decade of the present century.[5] When
Gandhi took command of the Congress party in 1920, he attempted to spread the influence of that organization from the
urban elite and middle class, where it had its origins, to the urban
working class and to the peasantry. These efforts encountered
certain difficulties in areas where the Brahmans had the kind of
lead over the non-Brahmans that they did in what is now western
Maharashtra.[6] Some Brahman leaders in the region encouraged the
entry of non-Brahmans into the Congress, but others treated that
entry as a threat to their own power. However, when the Government of India Act of 1935 expanded the franchise, the die was
cast. The resulting increase in influence of non-Brahmans forced
the established Congress leadership to extend recognition to the

5. The first non-Brahman movement in the Bombay region during British
rule was stimulated by Jyotiba Phule in 1873 with the founding of the *Satya
Shodak Samaj* (Truth-Seeking Society). That organization waned with the
death of Phule in 1890. A stronger and more enduring movement emerged
and resurrected the Satya Shodak name around 1910. A major study of that
movement is contained in the writings of Gail Omvedt. See her "Jotirao Phule
and the Ideology of Social Revolution in India," *Economic and Political
Weekly,* 11 September 1971, pp. 1969-1979; "Non-Brahmans and Communists in Bombay," *Economic and Political Weekly*, 21 and 28 April 1973,
pp. 749-759 and 800-805; and her "Non-Brahmans and Nationalists in
Poona," *Economic and Political Weekly,* Annual Number, February 1974, pp.
201-216.

6. The non-Brahman movement was most meaningful in western Maharashtra, a term which I am using here to include the princely state of Kolhapur.
While nationalism was slow to enter Kolhapur, non-Brahmanism was actively
encouraged by the ruler. A major source for understanding the non-Brahman
movement in Kolhapur is A. B. Latthe, *Memoirs of His Highness Shri Shahu
Chhatrapati Maharaja of Kolhapur,* 2 vols. (Bombay: Times Press, 1924). Also
see Ian Copland, "The Maharaja of Kolhapur and the Non-Brahman Movement, 1902-1910," *Modern Asian Studies* 7 (April 1973): 209-225. In Vidarbha, political conflicts involved linguistic differences as well as cleavages
between non-Maharashtrian trading castes (Marwaris) and Maharashtrians. For
an examination of politics in that region earlier in this century, see David
Baker, "The Rise of Mahakoshal: The Central Provinces and Berar, India,
1919-1939," in B. R. Nanda and V. C. Joshi, eds., *Studies in Modern Indian
History,* no. 1 (Bombay: Orient Longman, 1972), pp. 19-39.

non-Brahmans lest the latter provide a base of support for British resistance to their own demands for political change.[7] The result was an uneasy alliance between Brahman and non-Brahman leaders, particularly in areas of western Maharashtra where non-Brahmans began to organize on their own to stake a serious claim to political power. Despite considerable distrust on both sides, this alliance allowed the Congress to gain strong support in the Marathi speaking portion of Bombay province in the elections of 1937. (That was the first pre-independence election extending significant provincial power to Indians.)

The Congress ministry that came to power after the elections provided only limited opportunities to non-Brahmans. In part, this simply reflected the fact that Marathi speakers constituted only one of the several major linguistic elements within the larger province of Bombay. A result of the frustration created by this blockage of ambition, however, was the emergence of a demand for the creation of a separate state of Maharashtra—a demand which became persistent only after independence. Such a demand was in consonance, however, with the general principle elaborated earlier by Gandhi that to be fully democratic politics and administration must be conducted in the language of the people.[8]

THE CREATION OF MAHARASHTRA

With the achievement of national independence, non-Brahman leaders pressed for greater recognition of their ambitions. The reluctance of the national and regional leadership of the Congress party to undertake major reorganization immediately was interpreted as an effort on their part to deny influence over powerful positions in the Congress to the leading non-Brahmans. As a result, major non-Brahman figures in the region, like Keshavrao Jedhe

7. During the period before 1930, non-Brahmans in western Maharashtra divided over the issue of seeking collective concessions from the British for themselves as against supporting the Brahman-led nationalist movement. The situation was similar to the one in Madras described by Eugene F. Irschick in his *Politics and Social Conflict in South India: The Non-Brahman Movement and Tamil Separatism: 1916-1929* (Berkeley and Los Angeles: University of California Press, 1969).

8. At Gandhi's suggestion, the Congress was reorganized in 1930 to take account of linguistic and territorial differences within India. Separate party units were created for Bombay City, western Maharashtra, and Vidarbha.

and Shankarrao More, men active in the Congress from the early 1930s, withdrew from the party in 1949 to form their own organization, the Peasants and Workers Party (PWP). The PWP appealed, as the earlier non-Brahman movement had, for the support of the *bahujan samaj* ("the masses"), as opposed to Brahmans and non-Maharashtrian business interests operating in the region. In the elections of 1952, however, the PWP received significant backing in only a few districts. These included the former princely state of Kolhapur, where the Congress had not established an effective political organization prior to independence but where, as we have already noted, non-Brahmanism was a strong sentiment propagated by the princely regime.

Independence brought with it issues of territorial reorganization throughout India. Under the plans of the national government the princely states were to be integrated with those parts of the subcontinent formerly under direct British rule. New states would be created. It soon became evident that part of the political viability of those states would depend on their acceptability to local populations. Still following the Gandhian principles adopted by the Congress party in the 1930s, the national leadership acceded to demands made by regional elites for linguistic states which would recognize the cultural and political aspirations of those regions.

While the principle of linguistic states was generally followed in the proposals put forward by the national States Reorganization Commission in 1956, it was compromised in the particular case of the Bombay region. There, the central government proposed to create a bilingual state which would place Gujarati and Marathi speakers together under a common government. The major stumbling block to separation of the two regions into distinct states was the disposition of Bombay City. Although Marathi speakers constituted the largest single language group in the city, the more prosperous Gujaratis played a significant role in the city's economic and political life. To safeguard that role, the Gujaratis (through their spokesmen in the regional and national Congress) sought to keep Bombay City within a bilingual unit.[9]

9. A study of the creation of Maharashtra that uses that case as an example of national policy making is contained in Robert W. Stern, *The Process of Opposition in India* (Chicago: University of Chicago Press, 1970). Also see Ram Joshi, "Maharashtra," in Myron Weiner, ed., *State Politics in India* (Princeton: Princeton University Press, 1968), pp. 177-212.

Thus, despite Maharashtrian resistance to the bilingual principle, the reorganized bilingual state of Bombay came into being in 1956. Opposition, which was concentrated in western Maharashtra, gathered together in a movement for a Samyukta (United) Maharashtra. For many of these political activists, a new state held out the promise of political office and other opportunities partially blocked by Gujarati claims.

There was considerable contention at this time among Maharashtrian Congress leaders over Samyukta Maharashtra. Some Congressmen, led by Bhausaheb Hiray, Minister for Revenue in the Bombay government, made their opposition to bilingual Bombay a vehicle for conflict with the national Congress leadership. In contrast, Yeshwantrao Balwantrao Chavan, Minister for Local Self-Government, assumed leadership of the faction within the Maharashtra Congress which placed its loyalty to the national Congress above provincialism.[10] At the same time, Chavan made it clear that he personally favored a separate state of Maharashtra. In a key vote taken in June of 1956, Hiray narrowly won support in the Maharashtra Pradesh (Regional) Congress Committee (MPCC)—the top Congress body in western Maharashtra—for a proposal stipulating that should the central government refuse to accept a formula favorable to Maharashtra on the Bombay City issue, the MPCC would authorize actions by Congressmen against the national party in support of the cause.[11] Chavan refused to back such a strong step. It was this affirmation of loyalty that contributed to Chavan's subsequent selection as the first chief minister of bilingual Bombay, succeeding Morarji Desai, the major leader of Gujarat, who had headed the multilingual state. Interestingly enough, little of Chavan's support in that inner-party election came from the districts of western Maharashtra, where his own power base should have been most evident.

Though the votes for Chavan for chief minister came from non-Maharashtrians in the Congress, he immediately set out to

10. Two biographies of Chavan are B. B. Kale, *Chavan: Man of Crisis* (Bombay: Sindhu Publications, 1969); and T. V. Kunhi-Krishnan, *Chavan and the Troubled Decade* (Bombay and New Delhi: Somaiya Publications, 1971). Though Chavan's older brother was active in the Satya Shodak movement, Chavan's earliest intellectual identifications were with the followers of M. N. Roy, who preached a "rationalist" and humanist variant of socialism in the late 1930s. Chavan was active in the revolutionary underground in his native Satara district after 1942.

11. Stern, *The Process of Opposition*, p. 126.

strengthen the position of Maharashtrians in state politics and to build a following for himself within bilingual Bombay State. However, popular feeling remained strong on the Maharashtra demand. The Samyukta Maharashtra movement polarized the 1957 state elections with the result that the Congress won only 33 of the 134 seats it contested in the districts of western Maharashtra for the Bombay State Assembly against the Samyukta Maharashtra Samiti (Committee), an electoral front of almost all opposition parties. Indeed, that front operated with either the open or tacit support of many Congressmen. The Samiti attracted the backing of all strata of Maharashtrian society from Brahmans to the Scheduled Castes (former untouchables) and received the support of ideological elements ranging the spectrum from left to right.

The setback to the Congress in Maharashtra actually strengthened Chavan's hand for further negotiations with the central government and the national Congress leadership. It also decimated the legislative strength of those within the Maharashtra Congress who might have opposed him as leader. Even as he fought for Maharashtra, Chavan was able to use the resources of his position to build a new Congress organization in the region more in keeping with the emerging realities of political power—a Congress organization based particularly on non-Brahman rural elites.

While they were not as aroused by the issue, leaders in Marathi-speaking Vidarbha agreed as early as 1953 to support the demand for Maharashtra after receiving assurances for their region of opportunities in any new state.[12] In the new state of Maharashtra, Vidarbha joined with a third Marathi-speaking area, Marathwada, which was economically and politically backward in comparison with the other two. The districts which constitute Marathwada usually provided a faithful following to the Maharashtra Congress leadership, both in the period of agitation over Samyukta Maharashtra (when electoral support to the Congress in western Maharashtra evaporated) and during much of the first decade after the birth of the state.

12. In September 1953, leaders from western Maharashtra formally agreed to a pact signed at Nagpur which extended various assurances to Vidarbha. For the terms of that pact, see Ram Joshi, in Weiner, *State Politics,* pp. 185-186. Nevertheless, demands for a separate Vidarbha state have regularly flared up since 1956 (including as recently as 1973).

Despite agitations by the opposition front and the discontent of Congress supporters, Chavan attempted to make a success of the bilingual state. As he gained in national stature through his display of administrative capacity and political acumen, however, he used these resources to press for a reopening of the Maharashtra issue. The matter was taken up again in 1959, and this time an agreement was achieved which allowed the new states of Gujarat and Maharashtra to emerge in early 1960 with Bombay City as the capital of the latter. With 39.6 million people, Maharashtra became the third largest of India's states.[13] (By 1971 the population had increased to 50.4 million.)

In securing his own base as chief minister, Chavan from the outset recognized the demands put forward by Vidarbha. Five of the fourteen ministerial positions in his first ministry (1956) went to persons from that region. After Chavan resigned in 1962 to become Minister for Defense in the national government, the two men who held the chief ministership (until early 1975) were from Vidarbha.[14] Such concessions were particularly vital at the outset of the new regime in 1960 because many of the seats in the legislative body reconstituted after the creation of the state were in the hands of opposition party members. Chavan had to rely on Vidarbha and Bombay City votes in the State Legislative Assembly to maintain his government in power. From 1960 on, however, he began to augment Congress strength by attracting to the party persons he personally wooed away from parties like the PWP and the Praja (People's) Socialist Party (PSP). Those parties had been at the forefront of the Samyukta Maharashtra movement. With the realization of the demand for Maharashtra and the tempting prizes Chavan now proffered in the form of political office or other items of governmental patronage, a number of opposition party members saw no reason to continue sitting with their earlier party groups.

13. Contemporary Maharashtra is divided into four administrative divisions. In the 1961 census, Bombay Division was the largest, with 13.7 million people (including 4.1 million in Bombay City and its immediately adjacent suburbs); Poona Division was second with 10.4 million. Together, the two divisions constitute what is generally understood to be western Maharashtra. Vidarbha followed with 9.2 million people, and Marathwada (largely coterminus with what is now Aurangabad Division) was fourth, with a population of 6.3 million.

14. Less attention was given to recognizing the interests of Marathwada, though some positions in the party and government were also extended to that region.

Many who came to the Congress were non-Brahmans, especially Marathas. They helped solidify the Maratha character of the party,
particularly in the countryside.[15] (In Bombay City, non-Marathas
continued to play a major role in the Congress.[16]) The process of
change from urban to rural political dominance in the state had
already been well under way when Chavan came to power, but he
promoted policies favoring the countryside in a more vigorous
fashion than had been the case earlier. Thus, while he and his
successors continued to conciliate the Gujaratis and other minority communities living in major urban centers, the state government was increasingly concerned with serving rural interests,
especially the well-off Maratha peasantry.

POLITICS IN THE NEW STATE

Chavan and the Congress organization have consistently denied
any intention to represent one caste alone among Maharashtrians.
The peculiarities of Maharashtrian social structure make it possible, however, to appeal to the landed sections of society without
giving that appeal an openly "casteist" expression. Brahmans remain a distinct stratum of Maharashtrian society engaged primarily
in urban occupations, including government service (in white-
collar positions), education, business, and the professions. Western
Maharashtra lacks a trading community in the traditional sense of
a Vaishya (merchant) caste, but much petty trade is conducted by
Gujaratis or by those generally designated as Marwaris (persons

15. For an excellent review of the "Maratha-ization" of the Congress in
Maharashtra, see Ataram Ganesh Kulkarni, "A Study of Political Parties in
Maharashtra" (Ph.D. diss., University of Poona, 1968). Kulkarni traces the
composition of the MPCC from 1923 to 1966. Of twenty-two members on
the party executive in 1957, five were Brahmans and eleven were Marathas;
by 1966, there were no Brahmans and thirty-two Marathas on a body which
had increased to forty-four. These changes in caste composition were also
reflected in the All-India Congress Committee (AICC). In 1946, there were
thirty Maharashtra representatives in that national party body, of whom
fourteen were Brahmans and six Marathas; of sixty-three representatives in
1966, five were Brahmans and thirty-eight were Marathas.
16. After the creation of Maharashtra, regional Congress units outside
Bombay were molded into a single Congress organization—the Maharashtra
Pradesh Congress Committee (MPCC). Bombay City was permitted to operate
through a Bombay Pradesh Congress Committee (BPCC) as a concession to
the non-Maharashtrian interests active in the Congress in that city.

from Hindi-speaking areas like Rajasthan and Uttar Pradesh). Considerable business, as we shall see in the next chapter, is also in the hands of Maratha merchants.

Among the Marathas, who number perhaps 40 percent of the state population (an unusually high figure for any single "caste" in an Indian state), there are individuals who identify themselves as part of a traditional warrior caste. Until the early part of the present century, only such individuals were known as Marathas. Among them were persons with inherited claims to village economic and political leadership *(patils)* and those who held economic and political control over a wider area *(deshmukhs)*. The bulk of the rural population were classified as Kunbis. Where the former were the large landholders, sometimes claiming hereditary grants of land for services rendered to the Maratha Empire, the latter were petty peasant cultivators and tenants with no great claim on either economic or social status. In the course of the non-Brahman movement, however, there occurred a political consolidation of the two strata. As a result, for many purposes, the distinction is no longer significant.[17]

While the Maratha "community," as we shall see, is given to considerable political factionalism, Chavan's leadership has provided the Congress with most of the benefits of the caste's support since 1960. Men like Keshavrao Jedhe and Shankarrao More had played a major part in bringing Marathas into the Congress in the 1930s. When they left the Congress to form the PWP in 1949, the political solidarity of the Marathas was temporarily shattered. The death of Jedhe, the return of More to the Congress in 1954, and the splintering of the PWP into a number of fragments during the 1950s spelled the end to what chance the PWP might have had to establish itself as a serious competitor to the Congress by basing

17. A leading Indian anthropologist has written, "The politically conscious and progressive leaders of the Maratha community have, during the past few decades, striven to diminish and ultimately to abolish the distinction between Marathas and Kunbis. The distinction has remained even today as regards marriage etc., but the term 'Kunbi' has as good as vanished and every Kunbi now calls himself a Maratha." Irawati Karve, "Maharashtra—Land and People," *Maharashtra State Gazetteer* (Bombay: Directorate of Government Printing, Maharashtra State, 1968), p. 30. None of my respondents identified themselves as Kunbis. Indeed, several respondents whose antecedents were traditionally distinct from either Marathas or Kunbis had come to label themselves members of one or another "subcaste" of the larger Maratha "community."

itself in certain sections of the Maratha community. It continues to demonstrate a capacity on occasion to capitalize on lapses in the performance of the Congress. This was most evident in the period of Samyukta Maharashtra when the PWP was one of the leading forces in that movement. Since 1960, however, the Maharashtra Congress has shown a consistent capacity to recover from such setbacks and to outbid the PWP for the sustained support of both the Maratha political elite and the mass of Marathas who accept the leadership of that elite.[18]

Chavan has been more than a competent political leader to members of the Maratha community. He has become a symbol of political achievement. He was the first Maratha to hold a chief ministership and the first to attain a major national position. As Defense Minister, he boosted the Maratha self-image, both by his role in the national party leadership and by the way he represented them as a "martial" people in the national Cabinet—an image derived from the exploits of Shivaji and sustained by the claims of generations of higher-status Marathas.

By his identification with the aspirations of the Marathas, Chavan not only cut the ground from under the PWP but denied mass support, especially in the rural areas, to other parties. Thus, the Socialists and the Communists (in the various transmutations and splinterings both have gone through) remained largely urban-based parties. Rightist parties, like the Jan Sangh and the Hindu Mahasabha, have been Brahman-dominated and oriented toward protecting the status interests of the Brahmans.

The control of a secure following among members of the Maratha community allows the leadership of the Congress to reach out selectively for the support of other communities. In cities like Bombay, Poona, and Nagpur, the party gives considerable weight to non-Marathas. In the rural areas also, which still constitute about 70 percent of the population of the state, Chavan and the subordinate leadership of the Congress have tried to gain the support of non-Marathas. In 1967, for example, the Congress forged an alliance for local government elections with the Republican Party, which represents a section of the major ex-untouch-

18. In her study of Akola district in Vidarbha, Mary Carras reports a similar pattern of shifts in the power base of the Congress after 1960, but in that case the shift was from urban-based communities (especially the Marwaris) to rural Maratha leaders. Mary Carras, "Congress Factionalism in Maharashtra," *Asian Survey* 10 (May 1970): 410-426.

able community of Maharashtra, the Mahars.[19] The service from 1963 to 1975 of Vasantrao P. Naik as chief minister, a man who is a member of a tribal community from Vidarbha (married to a Brahman wife), also contributed to the image of the party as an inclusive non-Brahman party appealing to smaller communities as well as to Marathas.

Indeed, Chavan has gone further and has selectively included in his group of personal advisors a number of urban Brahmans who, as a result, have held important national and state positions in the party and government. As one example, Mohan Dharia represented Poona City in the Lok Sabha (the lower house of the Indian Parliament) after 1971. Dharia was a leading member of the Praja Socialist Party until Chavan won him over to the Congress in 1960. Subsequently he served as a secretary of the MPCC, as a member of the Rajya Sabha (the upper house of Parliament) and then, as Minister of State for Planning in the national cabinet.

Another case of a career raised to national stature by Chavan is that of V. N. Gadgil, who replaced Dharia in the Rajya Sabha after the latter moved to the more powerful lower house. Gadgil had also served as one of the secretaries of the Maharashtra Congress party for a time. He was the son of N. V. Gadgil, who had held leading roles in the Congress for many years and was one of the few prominent Brahmans in the state party organization during the 1930s to encourage the political rise of the non-Brahmans. V. N. Gadgil's own career (like Dharia's) advanced more because of the support Chavan gave him than because of any personal following he was able to develop within the party organization.

By 1960 Chavan was clearly alone at the top of a political system which was the culmination of the historical processes to which we have already referred: a successful fight for national independence, which had given considerable weight to regional identifications; the "deurbanization" of political participation, which shifted influence from urban elites to elites based on the greater numbers prevailing in the countryside; and achievement of

19. On the growth of the Republican Party as one aspect of the modernization of the Mahar community, see Eleanor M. Zelliot, "Buddhism and Politics in Maharashtra," in Donald E. Smith, ed., *South Asian Politics and Religion* (Princeton: Princeton University Press, 1966), pp. 191-212; and her "Dr. Ambedkar and the Mahar Movement" (Ph.D. diss., University of Pennsylvania, 1969).

a secure following for the Congress among both the Maratha elites and masses.

The problem that faced Chavan and the state Congress leadership in the late 1950s and especially after 1960 was how to further institutionalize its base of support. Here the developmental goals of the national government during the Nehru years and the political and social purposes of the national and state Congress organizations combined. One major vehicle for gaining and keeping a political following was the pattern of public investment in the rural infrastructure. We shall concentrate our attention on the evolution of policy and the development of institutions in three sectors: education; the cooperative organization of the rural economy; and the reorganization of rural local government. Activity in all these areas was already under way by 1960. Indeed, some of it was being encouraged before Chavan came into office in 1956, or Chavan began in 1956 to give administrative force to national policy goals which had been enunciated earlier. Nevertheless, the full effects of institutionalization in those sectors were not felt until the 1960s. At first, the effects were purely beneficial to the growth of support for the existing political order; later in the decade, the seeds implanted through institutionalizing activities began to be perceived by some of the top state leadership as causing major problems. In the rest of this chapter, we will provide brief introductions to the three sectors. Later in the study, we will discuss recent efforts to introduce reforms.

THE EXPANSION OF EDUCATIONAL OPPORTUNITIES

For the most part, education in India under the British was directed toward supplying a set of personnel to assist in operating British-dominated governmental and commercial structures. Liberal homilies to the contrary notwithstanding, very little was done by the British in the early nineteenth century either to expand the educational system beyond the immediate needs of the rulers or to provide the means by which opportunities might be opened in education to the less privileged segments of the native population, particularly those residing in rural areas.

While the British did extend some financial assistance to the system of Western-style education that had begun gradually to emerge during the second quarter of the nineteenth century, many of the costs had to be borne by the upper-middle-class residents who fell within the jurisdictions of various local government boards and municipalities. Those gentlemen were not particularly eager to tax themselves to make education accessible to the larger population. As a result, in 1886 only 17 percent of the males of school age in India were in primary schools; even fewer opportunities in education were made available to females. By 1901, the figure for primary education had increased merely to 18.5 percent for boys.[20]

In many places in India, the dominant mode of education was through primary schools supported by private societies or individual patrons. In the province of Bombay, privatization of educational support was less common than elsewhere. Tinker estimates that three-quarters of the educational institutions in the province were operated through local governmental bodies and only about a quarter through private institutions, most of which received financial assistance from local governments.[21] Although education at the primary level was nominally under local control, supervision of educational activities by provincial educational authorities was fairly strict.

As a concession to rising nationalism, the provinical government (reorganized in 1921 under a system of dyarchy which extended some power to Indian ministers in certain areas, such as education) moved in 1923 to give municipalities and rural local government boards larger roles in the field of education. This was done through the creation of local school boards partially dependent on local government bodies for finance and direction. Nevertheless, they were still subject to the control of the Department of Education in many respects.

While the following period saw a considerable increase in the number of boys attending primary schools—from 23.5 percent of the potential group in 1902 to 59 percent in 1937[22]—there were many complaints from those who felt that appropriate standards

20. Hugh Tinker, *The Foundations of Local Self-Government In India, Pakistan and Burma* (London: Athlone Press, 1954), p. 249. A. R. Kamat, in his *Progress of Education in Rural Maharashtra* (Bombay: Asia Publishing House for the Gokhale Institute of Politics and Economics, 1968), p. 11, indicates what seems to be a more substantial increase in enrollments in Bombay State: from 149,298 in 1870-1871 to 513,211 in 1901-1902. Unfortunately, he does not provide an appropriate base figure for the eligible population.

21. Tinker, *Foundations of Local Self-Government*, p. 250.

22. Ibid., p. 257

had been sacrificed in the name of greater local control. They insisted that "politics" had entered into the running of local educational affairs with consequences harmful to education. The first popularly elected Congress government of Bombay, which came to power in 1937, was sufficiently responsive to these charges of local mismanagement to see fit to withdraw some jurisdiction over education from local governments. Complaints involved, in particular, charges of growing laxity and politicization among teachers. Where previously teachers had been responsive to direction by provincial inspectors and clearly were in accord with the British-oriented curriculum they were expected to teach, they were now less likely to pay strict attention to their bureaucratic superiors and more inclined to turn to local political authorities for support. As Tinker has written:

> Promotion of teachers was too often by favouritism or bribery and teachers were encouraged to spend a large part of their time in waiting upon members. There was little incentive to improve one's teaching methods and produce better examination results when a teacher's record was frequently ignored. The disregard for discipline which spread through the teaching staff infected pupils also and was stimulated by political campaigns bringing authority into contempt.[23]

It may well be that the politicization of education reduced the quality of educational performance. However, such politicization was part of a larger shift in social values away from education by and for a narrow elite and toward principles of mass education, a point Tinker does not emphasize.

The success of the nationalist movement brought to power at the local level men who were committed, at least in principle, to greater opportunities in education for all strata of society. Thus, the nationalist leadership which took office in Bombay in 1946 wrote a new education act in 1947, which encouraged the growth

---

23. Ibid., p. 273. Though the specific reference is to the situation in Uttar Pradesh, it also describes the kinds of complaints heard at the time in Bombay. Tinker seems to assume that overt involvement by politicians in education is inappropriate, whereas the covert political consequences of a bureaucracy-dominated educational system are more acceptable. It is typical of this view that he appears to treat as illegitimate the issues raised by the Gandhians. To the extent that they brought "authority into contempt" in the operation of the existing educational pattern, fundamental issues *were* being raised about the nature of the authority structure then being operated in education (as elsewhere) in the interests of the British.

of education by assuming much of the actual cost of primary education. Indeed, the new government announced its intention to provide universal free primary education (for the first four years) within the following decade.

That goal remains to be fulfilled. Still, there has been an enormous growth in the educational facilities available in Maharashtra since 1947. In 1950 there were only 22,423 primary schools offering classes in state-prescribed subjects for the first to seventh standards. By 1969 the figure had grown to 44,223.[24]

Various measures were taken by Chavan's government after 1956 to accelerate the development of rural education. In 1959, elementary education became virtually free for all students; the only exceptions were in those cases where schools were run by private societies. (Many of these received grants-in-aid from the state government, which allowed them to lower the fees they charged their students.) In the same year, the grounds for granting educational concessions to students at the secondary level and in colleges were also changed. Previously, provision had been made out of central and state funds to encourage education among students from traditionally backward communities. In Maharashtra, such grants had gone to members of the ex-untouchable Scheduled Castes, to members of tribal communities, and to members of certain other communities designated as Other Backward Classes.

The administration of such grants became politically awkward after 1956. In that year many Mahars, who formerly had accepted consignment to Scheduled Caste status, began to convert to Buddhism following the lead of Dr. B. R. Ambedkar. In order to qualify for educational grants, students from the community would need to declare they were still Mahars even though their religious conversion was itself premised on a desire to discard the insignia of the caste system. The crisis of identity within the community; the desire of Chavan to promote support among the Mahars for the Congress; an interest on the part of the state Congress leadership in assuming a socialist garb at relatively low social cost—all led to a decision to premise educational concessions

24. Data for 1950-1951 are drawn from the Government of Maharashtra, Education and Social Welfare Department, *Educational Development in Maharashtra State (1950-51 to 1965-66)* (Bombay, 1968), pp. 2-5. The data for 1969 were graciously provided by the Directorate of Education, Government of Maharashtra, Poona, in 1970.

on income rather than caste. At first, the income level was set at Rs. 900 for parents of any student eligible; in 1960, the amount was raised to Rs. 1,200, and more recently to Rs. 1,500. This change in definition had the beneficial effect not only of removing the stigma of caste associated with such concessions; it also had the political advantage of bringing within the purview of educational benefits poorer Marathas and members of other communities who had not qualified under previous caste-based formulas. [25]

While rural primary education has become almost entirely a governmental responsibility since 1950 (primary schools financed by government but operated by local voluntary groups were taken over in that year [26]), the overwhelming majority of secondary schools (grades eight through eleven) and colleges are run by private societies which receive substantial grants-in-aid from the state government.

As a result of the interest shown by private societies and the financial support of the governments first of Bombay State and more recently of Maharashtra, the number of secondary schools increased from 765 in 1950 to 5,476 in 1971. [27] During the same period, enrollments in primary education went from 2.7 million to 6.5 million; they increased in secondary schools from 244,042 to 1.9 million. Recently, however, the growth rate of higher education—principally in colleges offering courses in liberal arts and business—has been even more remarkable. In 1969 there were something more than 286,000 students attending 343 colleges in the state as contrasted with only 43,384 in the 98 colleges which were functioning in 1950-1951. Quantitatively, if not qualitatively, the expansion of educational opportunities at all levels has been impressive.

25. Some abuses allegedly occur in the operation of the system. In particular, it is common for students whose family income exceeds the stipulated amount to qualify by misreporting such income. Since certificates of verification are supplied by leading local politicians designated by the state government to perform that function, the process is politicized. Some politicians are willing to grant them to anyone who approaches them.

26. Rural and urban local governments operate the majority of primary schools, but major urban centers, such as Bombay, Nagpur, and Poona, also have primary schools run by sectarian groups or by elite-sponsored private societies.

27. The latter figure is from the *Times of India,* 25 February 1972.

As one might expect from these figures, education has moved outward from the cities, where most early institutions were located, and downward from the upper and middle classes to include larger segments of the population. Despite the various subsidies and concessions to what are now called the "economically backward classes," there is considerable "wastage"—dropping out of school at an early stage—and only a small proportion of those who ever enter a classroom manage to advance to secondary education. Education is still a luxury item for the majority of the population, though there is a quickening sense of its potential among all classes.

The actual administration of education has remained largely in the hands of functional specialists and the educational bureaucracy. The design of curriculums and the imposition of educational standards is mainly a responsibility of the state's Department of Education with only minor involvement by elected officials. Such "local control" of education as exists relates more to matters like the location of primary schools and the assignment of teachers to particular schools than to the content of education. Educational performance criteria are not essentially subject to direct interventions by the local population.

As we shall see in chapter 6, the administration of education has become implicated in the Maharashtrian political system because of the very successes associated with its rapid growth. The debates of the 1960s involved not only questions of educational organization but serious issues about the content of education as well.

GROWTH OF THE COOPERATIVE SECTOR

In the last fifteen years, there has been a rapid growth in cooperative institutions in the rural areas of Maharashtra.[28] This growth has been the direct result of an interest on the part of the national government and the state leadership in promoting the develop-

28. There has also been a growth of certain kinds of urban cooperatives, particularly housing societies. On that particular form of organization, see Robert A. Wirsing, "Associational 'Micro-Arenas' in Indian Urban Politics," *Asian Survey* 13 (April 1973): 416-418. Urban economic activity in the cooperative sector has not attracted, on the whole, the same investment of political energy.

ment of agricultural investment, for cooperative societies in Maharashtra are used primarily to distribute loans to farmers which enable them to invest in the technology associated with modern agriculture: improved seeds; fertilizers; pesticides; irrigation facilities; and machinery. Not only has agricultural credit been organized principally on a cooperative basis, but there has been a significant growth in Maharashtra in agro-industries which are organized as cooperatives. The most notable of these are factories processing sugarcane and producing textiles.

The cooperative movement in western Maharashtra had its origins in the late nineteenth century in the efforts of Brahman social reformers and British officials to improve the economic position of the peasant and, particularly, to decrease his dependence on the rural money-lender.[29] Despite the good intentions involved, the credit and marketing facilities that were created—with a few notable exceptions—were difficult to maintain. By the 1950s, the cooperative infrastructure in most districts of Maharashtra was short of funds and operated only fitfully. Around 1955, the state government of Bombay undertook a thoroughgoing reorganization. Part of the spur to this action was provided by the financial investment of the central government.[30]

The principal local channels for short-term agricultural credit in Maharashtra are the district central cooperative banks (DCCBs). Prior to the reorganization of cooperatives, a DCCB might operate in parts of a district while branches of the state-level Bombay (now Maharashtra) State Cooperative Bank functioned in other places. Since reorganization, a federal structure has been introduced. Below the district banks, primary credit societies were organized or refinanced in most of the larger villages. Some few of these village societies had existed for many years, but most were newly created. Membership in these primary societies involves the purchase of shares by farmers, but most societies are dependent on

29. I. J. Catanach, *Rural Credit in Western India* (Berkeley and Los Angeles: University of California Press, 1970).

30. Reserve Bank of India Committee of Direction, *All-India Rural Credit Survey,* vol. 1 (1956), vol. 2 (1954) (Bombay: Reserve Bank of India). The findings of that study should be contrasted with the more recent *Report of the All-India Rural Credit Review Committee* (Bombay: Reserve Bank of India, 1969), pp. 247-253, which reports a doubling of short-term loans between 1960-1961 and 1966-1967. At the same time, however, overdues increased from 20 percent of outstanding loans to 37.3 percent.

the financial backing provided by the DCCBs. The district banks are given responsibility for extending loans to primary societies (not to individual members) for distribution to their members.

Although credit societies follow the theory of cooperative participation by encouraging the membership of producers in each village, effective control over the financing and operation of most cooperative institutions resides finally in the hands of the political leadership of the state and central governments. That such institutions do have political ramifications is indicated by the fact that until 1972 a key figure in Maharashtra politics combined the office of president of the MPCC with that of chairman of the Maharashtra State Cooperative Bank; a number of other members of the board of that agency were also leading figures in the state Congress organization.

In addition to the DCCBs, the government of Maharashtra has helped to build other cooperative institutions. For the purpose of distributing long-term credit to farmers for capital investment in machinery and land improvement, district land development banks (DLDBs) were introduced in each district. As in the case of the Bombay State Cooperative Bank, a Bombay State Land Mortgage Bank had operated in some places prior to reorganization in the 1950s, but the institution was underfinanced and not functioning with much effectiveness at the time Chavan came to power. The state government moved to invigorate the system. The extent of its success has varied considerably from district to district, but the DLDBs became centers of increasing importance in encouraging long-term agricultural investment during the 1960s.

Characteristically, reorganization of the major cooperative credit institutions has involved alterations in their political character. Boards of the DCCBs and DLDBs were "deurbanized" as an older generation of urban (often Brahman) "social workers" were replaced by avowed political activists from the countryside. The state government encouraged this process by requiring that a majority of seats on these boards be elected in the various *talukas* (subdistrict administrative units) by village societies (in the case of the DCCBs) or by borrowers (in the case of the DLDBs). [31] The result was that the top positions in cooperative institutions were

31. The practice of electing representatives to the land development banks by borrowers in good standing caused considerable debate and contributed to complaints which accumulated about the way in which those banks functioned.

assumed by men with considerable political standing in the rural areas. Offices in the credit structure came to be seen as major prizes in the political wars of most districts; almost by definition, the successful rural politician was likely to hold a seat in a major credit institution or to maintain close relations with those who did.

The state government also encouraged the development of marketing societies at the taluka level. Called "purchase and sales unions," or *taluka sanghs,* these societies were created with the expectation that they would contribute to the collection and sale of the farmer's goods, thus short-circuiting the role of the private middleman. In practice, however, they have developed more as vehicles for the distribution of agricultural "inputs" required by the farmer than as marketing agents for goods produced by the farmer. Such goods and services are provided to the village credit societies, which then supply them to their memberships. In some districts, including both Poona and Kolhapur, district-level marketing societies also exist to play a role in handling certain goods produced by the farmer and to provide him with items unavailable from other sources.

As a result of the government's financial inducements and the ambitions of local political activists, a major network of credit and service societies has developed within each district and taluka in Maharashtra which exercises considerable influence over economic resources. Those resources also can be employed for political purposes, as when "arrangements" are made to forgive outstanding loans or defer repayments, or when services are made available to politically supportive farmers but not to others.

In addition to the three principal forms of credit and marketing facilities already outlined—short-term credit available through the DCCBs; longer-term credit through the DLDBs; marketing services through the purchase and sales unions—there are many other cooperative activities under way in Maharashtra. Perhaps the most important of these are the processing cooperatives. In the districts of western Maharashtra this means especially cooperative sugar factories, though some districts also have been developing cooperative spinning and weaving mills, oil presses, and other agro-industries. Until the 1950s, most sugar production in the state was in private hands. A few cooperative factories were founded before 1956, but the great movement toward the introduction of cooperatives in sugar was not undertaken until that year. The central government has played a major role in designating areas for factories and in financing their development. It also sets national prices for sugar and regulates the operations of the industry. Though farmers in a designated area contribute share capital to the operations of the factories, financing of construction would be impossible without governmental support. Backed by central government loans and by guaranteed market prices, the cooperative-based sugar industry has expanded rapidly in Maharashtra.

Since these are large enterprises directly affecting the lives of hundreds of farmers in a given territory, the sugar factories necessarily play an important role in the politics of the sugar-growing districts. Along with the cooperative banks, they have become major arenas for the expression of political ambition. Not only do their managements—elected by the farmer members of a factory—work with large resources, which can effect the economic lives of many individuals, but through this economic influence they can and do have an impact on the course of political life in one or more talukas. Leadership of such bodies has come to be seen as a major source of political power in district and state politics. If that leadership is secure, it is difficult for political opposition based in the Congress or in governmental positions to undermine it. Indeed, it is commonly said in western Maharashtra that every MLA (Member of the Legislative Assembly) would like to have his own sugar factory in order to assure his continued political power.

In chapters 3 and 4, we shall detail some of the battles for control of particular cooperative institutions in Poona and Kolhapur districts. Such conflicts are common throughout the state.[32] We will provide a state-level review of the politics of the cooperative sector and proposals for reform in chapters 7 and 8.

OPPORTUNITIES IN LOCAL GOVERNMENT

The creation of Maharashtra opened up a few additional chances for persons ambitious to hold state-level posts. Opportunities increased particularly for Marathas. Still, the number of positions available in the reorganized state party and in the state govern-

32. For a review of the politics of sugar factory elections typical of the state see "Maharashtra: Battle for Sugar Co-Operatives," *Economic and Political Weekly,* 8 December 1973, pp. 2165-2166.

ment were limited. A decision to expand opportunities at district and, especially, taluka levels by enhancing rural local government was therefore significant to the structuring of ambitions in the new state of Maharashtra.

A system of representative local government for the districts of rural India was initiated under the British, but the powers given those bodies were limited. Significantly, the government of India bypassed those bodies in the 1950s when it began to finance schemes for "community development." Such schemes were intended to improve the lives of the rural population by promoting agricultural innovations, public health measures, adult literacy, and other steps to be taken by the rural population under the guidance of a bureaucracy of village and subdistrict ("block") development officials appointed for the purpose.[33]

Developmental schemes tended to be directed by the bureaucracy with only minimal participation by the general public. At the district level in Maharashtra, for example, the head of the revenue collection and law and order departments—the district collector—was placed in charge of new district development boards. Other members were appointed by the state government. Though developmental activities might conceivably have been routed through the existing district local boards, they were not. During the years prior to the creation of Maharashtra, there were some political advantages to this procedure. At a time when the Samyukta Maharashtra movement had a strong following in the countryside, the appointment of non-officials to sit with the district development boards allowed the state government to choose men loyal to the Congress party, who would participate in making developmental decisions and distributing resources in ways which might ultimately benefit the party. Thus, in Poona district, the top non-official positions on the board went to two individuals who were emerging as the "boss" of the district Congress and his chief lieutenant.

Experiences with the community development scheme were less than happy. Developmental targets were not met; government employees became more deeply involved in bureaucratic details and paperwork than in promoting rural involvement in planning and implementation; the interest of the rural public in the plans

33. A pilot program for the improvement of village life was launched in 1952 with the aid of the Ford Foundation.

initiated by the bureaucracy was limited. The national government undertook a reevaluation of its work in the mid-1950s and in 1957 produced a set of recommendations for *panchayati raj* (rural local government) in which developmental activities covering a wide range of subjects would be brought together under units of local government responsible to the public. The spirit of the report put forward for adoption by the states was one imbued with Gandhian ideals of "democratic decentralization."[34] In his many years of national leadership, Gandhi frequently spoke of the need to make the village the central unit of the Indian political order. The plan for panchayati raj, therefore, advocated a devolution both of powers of decision making and of significant resources to the lowest possible levels of government and administration. In practice, this was not so much to be the village as the "block"—the taluka in western Maharashtra and its equivalent, the *janpad,* in Vidarbha—with the district body acting merely as a coordinating agency.

Though panchayati raj was promoted by Gandhian elements in the national government, state governments responded to the proposal with a certain reserve. Most adopted variants of the structures recommended, though some have still not acted. However, few state governments were willing to relinquish their supervisory roles in local decision making, and they were even less anxious to devolve meaningful financial control. In Maharashtra, the functions of the development boards were combined with those of the older district local boards. Furthermore, district school boards were consolidated into the newly created district bodies. On the whole, Maharashtra proceeded rather cautiously in responding to the other recommendations of the central government. Thus, in a report issued in 1961 by a committee headed by Vasantrao Naik, who later became Chief Minister of the state, several structural deviations from the national pattern were proposed.[35] Instead of centering power at the taluka level, the report

34. The recommendations for panchayati raj were produced by a national committee appointed by the central government and headed by Balwantray Mehta. The first state to initiate the new scheme was Rajasthan, in October 1959. Sugan Chand Jain, *Community Development and Panchayati Raj in India* (Bombay: Allied Publishers, 1967). For a briefer overview, see Iltija H. Khan, *Government in Rural India* (Bombay: Asia Publishing House, 1969).

35. Government of Maharashtra, Cooperation and Rural Development Department, *Report of the Committee on Democratic Decentralization*

made district-level bodies the significant foci of local government. Thus, where the notion had been propagated by the national government that members of the highest district body—the *zilla parishad*—should be indirectly elected from among members of the taluka-level *panchayat samitis,* Maharashtra provided for direct election of its zilla parishad members from small single-member constituencies. At the same time, each panchayat samiti was to consist of all the members of the zilla parishad from the particular taluka, and twice that number of representatives selected in electoral colleges made up of elected village officers formed into electoral clusters within each taluka. A further linkage from the village government councils (*gram panchayats*) to the district was to be provided by making presidents of panchayat samitis exofficio members of the zilla parishad in those cases where they were not already directly elected to those bodies.[36]

Unlike several other states, Maharashtra also decided to exclude MLAs from membership in either the district or taluka governments. It was recognized that such memberships might provide linkages to the state government, but the Naik Committee thought there would also be a tendency for these more experienced legislators to dominate the local bodies and to prevent local leadership from blossoming. During the discussion on panchayati raj in the Maharashtra Assembly, MLAs were particularly unhappy with this provision. Previously, they had been the most prominent popular representatives in their territories; now they were being provided with potential rivals—the members of the zilla parishad and the panchayat samitis in their home areas. The leaders of these bodies, in particular, might be able to deal directly and frequently with the public on the day-to-day minutiae of service deliveries, thereby rendering less important the activities of the MLAs. Checking their fears in this respect, Congress MLAs followed the state leadership's preferences for direct election of zilla parishad members and for the non-participation of MLAs.[37]

(Bombay: Government Central Press, 1961). Excerpts from the Committee report are included in M. Pattabjiram and M. Venkatarangaiya, eds., *Local Government in India,* (Bombay: Allied Publishers, 1969), pp. 338-349.

36. While individuals may sit on both bodies, they may not hold official positions in the zilla parishad and a panchayat samiti at the same time.

37. On the first reactions to panchayati raj in Maharashtra, see Lawrence L. Shrader and Ram Joshi, "Zilla Parishad Elections in Maharashtra and the District Political Elite," *Asian Survey* 3 (March 1963): 143-155.

Despite the structural changes and the verbal commitment to decentralization made by the state government, the actual powers exercised by the zilla parishads represented only a marginal advance over the cumulative powers exercised by their three predecessors. Indeed, in some respects, their powers were reduced. Mobilization and allocation of resources at the local level is still dominated to a considerable extent by the state government; budgetary decisions are heavily circumscribed by state rules; and the administrative cadre of the district is headed by a bureaucrat appointed by and largely responsible to the state government. (Previously, district local boards were empowered to choose their own administrative officers.) Thus, the verbal commitment to devolution of power has amounted to little more than administrative decentralization in practice. Nevertheless, the political weight of those who fill major leadership positions in the zilla parishads has become such that state government ministers and administrators are increasingly sensitive to the demands for action which emanate from such district bodies.

If the decision-making and fiscal powers granted to the zilla parishads are highly circumscribed, those extended to the taluka panchayat samitis are even narrower. In districts like Poona and Kolhapur, with total rural populations in 1971 of 1.6-1.8 million, about a dozen such taluka-level bodies existed to provide services to the countryside.[38] While the functions given to the panchayat samitis are minor, their elected officers (like the officers of the zilla parishad) are paid and have a limited amount of patronage at their command. Finally, in the three-tier system of panchayati raj, village governments are connected more clearly to the hierarchy of political influence and decision making. One consequence of the strengthened linkages from village to district, whether intended or not, was to clarify and structure the ambitional route to district and state power.

While the economic capacities of local government bodies in Maharashtra barely touch the basic needs of the general population, those bodies do have certain restricted powers in education, road construction, irrigation, and other developmental areas. Given a tendency among Indian politicians to contend over even

38. Most districts in western Maharashtra have ten to a dozen talukas; districts in Vidarbha have half that number. However, sparser population concentrations in Vidarbha result in talukas which are only marginally larger in population than good-size talukas in the western part of the state.

the most limited expenditures and powers, local government bodies have become important foci of political activity and major vehicles for building political careers.

OVERVIEW

Observers of Y. B. Chavan's political style over the past fifteen years suggest that part of his technique for remaining the most durable state-based political leader in India was his great ability to orchestrate the personal rivalries and factional conflicts within the Congress. I would carry this assertion one step further and suggest that Chavan succeeded in doing this by skillfully manipulating the extension of opportunities to ambitious men. The system of panchayati raj, with its promise of influence in the distribution of societal resources in a district or taluka; the pattern of educational expansion, with the opportunities it provided for institutional leadership to many local politicians; and the rural cooperative institutions, with their control over substantial economic re-sources—all contributed to the construction of a political system in Maharashtra that proved remarkably stable during a period of political flux elsewhere in India. Indeed, Chavan and the other principal leaders of the Maharashtra Congress succeeded in de-veloping a set of interlocking institutions which integrated the political demands of village, taluka, and district elites with the ambitions of state and even national leaders.

The state Congress acted as a major instrument for operating this system of power, but the effectiveness of the party as an organizational weapon was hardly impressive. It succeeded as much by not asking a great deal of local political elites as it did because of the material benefits it extended to them. Indeed, it might well be argued that maintenance of the Congress organiza-tion was an end which the activation of other opportunity struc-tures served. The Congress was rarely a career route in itself except for those whose opportunities were restricted elsewhere.

In any case, it was part of an ambitional system which served the interests of Y. B. Chavan and his followers throughout the state very well. Chavan's unchallenged hold on this power struc-ture allowed the Maharashtra Congress to display what passed for organizational coherence when challenged from the outside.

Nevertheless, personalistic factionalism pervaded the district and state Congress party in Maharashtra. This factionalism made Chavan's position dependent, at least in part, on his ability to supply a steady stream of rewards to other leaders; at the same time, it made it possible for him to employ his personal skills to capitalize upon intraparty conflicts to maintain his own standing.

THREE

Poona District: Maratha Merchants and Rural Politicians

In this chapter and the next, we will review the recent political histories of Poona and Kolhapur districts in some detail. Conflicts for control of rural political resources are common to the two districts, but those in Poona have appeared to be qualitatively less severe. In part, this was made possible by the assumption of leadership during the period from 1960 to 1971 of a man, N. S. Mohol, who attempted to act as an arbiter among individuals and groups seeking ascendancy within the Congress and other key economic and governmental institutions in the district. He was not completely successful at this role, as we shall see, for one particular family (the Kakades) with control over a major set of institutional resources never accepted the way in which Mohol and other political actors in the system withheld opportunities for enhanced political power from them.

With the retirement of Mohol in 1971, a brief period of interregnum occurred in which a three-man group emerged to operate the Congress party in the district and to play a major role in other institutions. By 1973, however, another leader, S. G. Pawar, was clearly beginning to emerge from among the three; Pawar was bolstered by the prominence he had gained in the state government. When first interviewed in 1970, Pawar was simply a young MLA with a promising but uncertain future. His rise was a product of factors common to political achievement in India: some talent, some luck, and some well-honed contacts with key people in state politics.

However one views the political life of Poona district—as a high-conflict system only slightly modulated by the presence of a few key personalities, or as a system of moderate conflict in comparison with Kolhapur—it is necessary to stress that much of the contention for political dominance recorded in this chapter was carried on by members of a fairly narrow stratum of Indian society. Furthermore, these individual and group struggles for ascendancy had only the most limited of implications for societal

change in terms of potential redistribution of economic and political opportunities to the great majority of the population of the
district.

THE POLITICAL ECONOMY OF POONA DISTRICT

Some understanding of Poona politics may be gained by a brief
introduction to the economic geography of the district. Poona
City lies roughly at the center of the district (see map 2) and is
approximately 120 miles southeast of Bombay City. A major
railway system and the principal highways of the district running
east-west and north-south pass through the city. In the last two
decades Poona has developed into a major industrial center; its
easy access to Bombay by road and rail provide part of the
explanation for its initial industrial growth. Radiating from the
city are other population centers, which have become subcenters
for Poona City and, to some extent, for Bombay.

The agricultural economy of the district is deeply affected by
the pattern of rainfall associated with the Sahyadri mountain
range in the western section of the district. Western Poona district
receives substantial rainfall, while the east is a chronic scarcity
area, for the rain clouds deposit much of their content in the west
and are prevented by the mountains from reaching eastern Poona.
As a result of this pattern, the western talukas (Mulshi, Mawal,
Bhor, and Velhe) are capable of producing such rain-dependent
crops as rice. Unfortunately, much of this area is also hilly and
rocky and the actual extent of commercial cropping (except for
some rice in Mawal) is limited. To the northeast of this rainy zone,
rice-growing areas shade off into territory where nuts, potatoes,
and coarse grains (*jowar* and *bajra*) are grown; some of that crop is
marketed. These are the western parts of the talukas of Ambegaon, Junnar, and Khed. As one moves east even in these
talukas, the effects of an unreliable water supply become quickly
apparent. Though various irrigation projects are regularly discussed, few major schemes have been completed in this area.
Further east, the situation is even bleaker. Indeed, this part of the
district and the neighboring section of Ahmednagar district are
regularly affected by severe drought conditions. Thus, the eastern
talukas (Dhond and Sirur, in particular) present a picture of
largely unrelieved desolation and rural poverty.

While the taluka surrounding Poona City (Haveli) and the
other eastern talukas (Purandhar, Baramati, and Indapur) are as

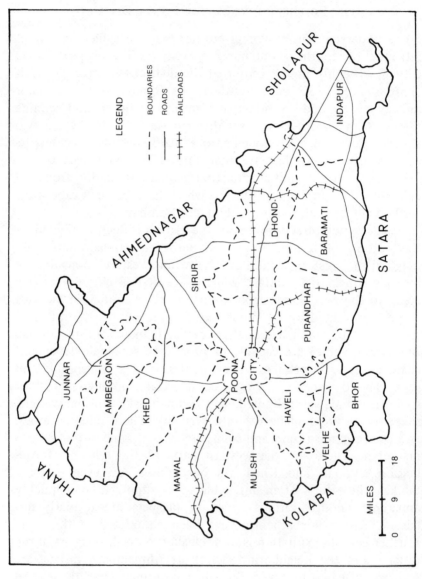

Map 2. Poona District, Maharashtra

affected by limited rainfall as are Sirur and Dhond, parts have been benefited by irrigation. The soils in these talukas are potentially quite rich, but it is only in those areas where the Nira Canal system was built, in the early twentieth century, that the better-placed farmers have been in a position to take advantage of commercial cropping on a significant scale. Haveli is in an especially favorable position. As the major hinterland for the city, industry has moved into the area. Farmers have the advantage of immediate access to a growing urban market made up of a relatively prosperous population in need of a steady supply of fruits, vegetables, and other commercial crops. Haveli agriculture prospers in Poona's shadow, even drawing some of the water supply for its agricultural needs from the sources tapped in the western part of the district to keep the urban population from going thirsty. To a lesser extent, Mulshi taluka on the west also benefits from its location in relation to the city.

Where access to irrigation is available in Haveli taluka or along the branches of the Nira Canal in Purandhar, Baramati, and Indapur, there has been an interest among market-oriented farmers in growing sugarcane, a crop which is highly profitable but requires a substantial water supply. In recent years, too, the more "progressive" farmers have diversified into such specialized crops as grapes. Farmers of this kind are increasingly tied into a network of communications about price conditions in Poona, Bombay, and other cities in western and central India, with the result that they can ship their goods to those markets where prices are most favorable.

For the commercial farmer, the structure of his market position is obviously a crucial economic and political issue. Until recently, the trade was dominated by the commodity wholesaler *(dalal)*, who was often a Maratha with substantial personal and commercial ties to the rural parts of the district. Only a few really large producers were in a position to bargain effectively with the wholesaler or to market their products directly to the urban consumer;[1] the many smaller producers who marketed only a limited supply of goods were individually at the mercy of the wholesaler. The latter would bargain to his own advantage with

1. It should be stressed that most production in the district, as elsewhere in India, is for home consumption or for sale at small village or town markets. Trading in the markets of Poona City, like politics, is the activity of a relatively small proportion of the total agricultural population.

the farmer in the field through agents who visited the village at various times of the year or, in some cases, agents who themselves lived in the rural areas. The dalal was generally well positioned in the operations of the city's centralized fruit and vegetable markets to have control over access by the farmer to the urban consumer. In a society where the eating of meat is devalued, and particularly for a city like Poona with its large Brahman population, a location in the commercial fruit and vegetable market has been and continues to be of both economic and political importance.

The Congress party has long been sustained in Poona City from the coffers of the dalals. Indeed, as Omvedt shows, part of the finance for the earlier non-Brahman movement in both Bombay and Poona came from Maratha merchants in these markets.[2] This political connection still has some importance. Thus, several of these merchants have been mayors of Poona City in recent years. Still, the political influence of the Maratha dalals seems to be declining as a younger generation of members of merchant families enter the professions and other kinds of businesses— engineering and industrial activity, urban entertainment and dining facilities.[3] These activities also reflect a self-conscious diversification of investment. Many dalals who feared greater governmental regulation of their businesses have invested in rural property in which they have sunk considerable capital. Others have protected themselves against the fortunes of economic change and threats of land reform by maintaining an economic interest in urban enterprises.

In any case, there continues to exist in the public life of Poona district a class of people with connections both to the market system of the city and to the commercial farmers of the countryside. Many of these men maintain a personal interest in

2. Gail Omvedt, "Non-Brahmans and Nationalists in Poona," *Economic and Political Weekly*, Annual Number, February, 1974, pp. 201-216; and "Non-Brahmans and Communists in Bombay," *Economic and Political Weekly*, 21 and 28 April 1973, pp. 749-759 and 800-805.

3. In recent years, there has been a rapid expansion in restaurants and hotels in Poona City. Many of these activities have been financed by successful Maratha merchant families or by commercial farmers seeking outlets for investment. Like the American saloon earlier in the century, such facilities provide public meeting places for local politicians and the politically influential, including those farmers visiting the city on governmental, political, or farm-related business.

cultivation of land. Either they own inherited family property or have invested in additional lands which they have turned to commercial crops. Since schools in the rural areas are still considered inferior to those in the city, the merchant's children generally live in the city while they are being educated. The result is that the Maratha merchant and his family may be rural and urban at the same time.

It might be tempting to contrast the life style of the dalal with that of the big farmer firmly planted in his rural environment. Unfortunately, such an ideal contrast is increasingly meaningless, for the large commercial farmer has either become urbanized or is bringing up his own sons to emulate the life style of the merchant. Like the merchant, he encourages the education of his children, though he may support the financing of rural colleges to allow his sons to become educated nearer to home. Many of these men have also established residences in the city to be nearer the seats of governmental and political power, as well as to enjoy the social life of the city.[4]

It is from this class of commercial farmers that the support base for the cooperative movement has come, though it may well be (as several informants suggested) that the largest commercial farmers do not make use of cooperative credit, since they have financial resources of their own and would rather remain aloof from the tangled politics of cooperative institutions. Still, even the biggest landholders occasionally use cooperative devices when it suits their purposes. Thus, two of the most prominent families in the district have operated their own "cooperative" sugar factories in a fashion that has made them virtually family enterprises.

If the really large-scale commercial farmer in Poona district has options about his involvement in politics, the middle-sized commercial farmer may feel himself under greater constraint to make use of cooperative facilities both for credit and for supplies of the agricultural "inputs" he requires. Because these resources, as well as such factors as his supply of water, the size of his landholdings, and his marketing practices, may all come in for governmental scrutiny—under government procurement programs, for example, the farmer is required (at least in theory) to turn

4. The political attractions of the city are enhanced by the fact that the headquarters of the zilla parishad, most district cooperative institutions, and the District Congress are all located in the city. The same is true for Kolhapur City in that district.

much of his marketable surplus in food grains over to the state government—the farmer must pay constant attention to his relations with the political system. Some choose to protect themselves by supporting political activists in their area; others assume local leadership themselves or aspire to it.

Though he may not welcome too-close governmental supervision of his own activities, the commercial farmer seeks a stable market where he can make a good profit. It is for this reason that such farmers have favored the cooperative sugar factory with its centrally fixed "remunerative" price, guaranteed market, and limited risk. Maharashtra is a deficit state in wheat and rice, and relatively little of each is produced around Poona, with the result that the intervention of government is not of much significance there; state-trading in coarse grains, which started in 1965 in Maharashtra, caused some debate initially, but chronic shortages in the state have permitted the trade to be shifted to state agents without great opposition. Conflicts did arise in the 1960s, however, between the merchants and the farmers of Poona district over the regulation of the wholesale market in fruits and vegetables. We shall reserve our discussion of that conflict until chapter 8, since it involved state policy and resulted in an uneasy compromise effected by state actors.

Even though that conflict involved a drawing of battle lines between the dalals of Poona City and the commercial farmers, particularly from Haveli taluka, the outcome of the battle itself suggests that differences between the urban merchants and the agricultural leaders are not irreconcilable. Save for that one issue, there have been few divisions in the busy factional life of Poona district that seem to coincide with such an obvious potential economic cleavage. Rather, most political conflicts in the district center around attempts by individuals to advance their ambitions through the existing institutional framework. Such ambition is only rarely expressed through the nuances of economic debates or, indeed, with reference to any ideological concerns. Nor is the evidence clear that the conflicts owe much to objective differences among the actors involved. To understand the conflicts which do occur, we turn to an exploration of the power structure of Poona district.[5]

5. Some of the materials in the remainder of this chapter have been utilized in my "Sources of District Congress Factionalism in Maharashtra," *Economic and Political Weekly*, 19 August 1972, pp. 1725-1746. These data

THE POLITICAL LEADERS OF POONA

To speak of a "power structure" in Poona district is not to suggest the existence of a monolith in which a rank can be assigned to each participant in some neat fashion.[6] Yet I would argue that a large portion of the politics of Poona during the period from 1960 to 1973 could be understood by focusing on the interlocking network of institutional affiliations and personal relationships which existed among perhaps no more than a dozen individuals or families in the district. I do not mean that these dozen persons dominated *all* institutional positions in rural Poona, nor that other politicians or members of the public had no voice in what happened; in a broader sense, each of the dozen men "represented" a larger group in his home territory and in some instances responded to those others in the way he played the games of district politics. Furthermore, there was some porosity to the power structure because rivalries among the leaders of the district, and among the followers of each leader, created some openings through which individuals with sufficient ambition and adequate political resources (including both economic and skill resources) could move into positions from which they were able to exercise influence over the fates of great numbers of people.[7]

The Older Generation

The prime leader of Poona during the decade from 1962 to 1972 was N. S. (Mamasaheb) Mohol. He was born in 1904 into an impoverished rural family farming four to five acres of not particu-

---

bring into question the interpretations advanced by Mary C. Carras in her study of rural politics in four districts of Maharashtra (including Poona); see *The Dynamics of Indian Political Factions: A Study of District Councils in the State of Maharashtra* (New York and Cambridge: Cambridge University Press, 1972).

6. In the debate over community power structures during the late 1950s, non-pluralists left more room for conflicts among local elites than pluralists were willing to concede they had. For the standard approaches, see Floyd Hunter, *Community Power Structure* (Chapel Hill: University of North Carolina Press, 1953); Robert A. Dahl, *Who Governs?: Democracy and Power in an American City* (New Haven: Yale University Press, 1961). Also see Peter Bachrach and Morton S. Baratz, *Power and Poverty* (New York: Oxford University Press, 1970).

7. The situation in Poona, as in Kolhapur, accords well with what Peter Bachrach has called "democratic elitism." See his *The Theory of Democratic Elitism* (Boston: Little, Brown, 1967).

larly good land in what was then the tiny princely state of Bhor (within Poona district). Mohol received no more than a sketchy fourth-grade education. As a youth he became involved in wrestling and gained a considerable local reputation in that sport.[8] With the money he earned from his wrestling, Mohol invested in a traveling film theater. He eventually built this into a group of theaters, which he and his sons now manage.

Active in the Congress from the 1930s, Mohol was elected to Bhor's local assembly in 1940. In 1952, Mohol ran for MLA from what had become Bhor taluka. He did so at the urging of Bhausaheb Hiray, state Congress leader from Nasik district. It was only natural, therefore, that Mohol should support Hiray on the Samyukta Maharashtra issue and in the contest with Chavan for Chief Minister in 1956. Indeed, in that vote Poona district stood with Hiray. Given the strong feeling on the issue in Poona district in 1957, however, only one of the twelve seats for MLA contested in rural or semirural Poona was won by the Congress. The rest went to persons associated with the Samyukta Maharashtra Samiti or to independents. Among those defeated was Mohol.

The sole seat won by the Congress in 1957 was the one contested by S. B. Patil. Born in a village in Indapur taluka in 1924 but educated through LL.B. in Poona City, Patil was one of a small number of well-educated Marathas in Indapur and came from a family of local political prominence. (Both his father and grandfather had been members of the Poona District Local Board.) Patil's first public activity involved a nomination to the Poona District School Board in 1949. First elected MLA in 1952, he has continued to play a major (but often relatively quiet) role in district politics. Patil's ambitions have been more state-oriented. He has held ministerial posts for the greater part of the last decade, though until 1974 only at the subcabinet level.[9] As long as his own political interests were secure—and this has meant, in

8. Wrestling is a very popular sport in rural Maharashtra and continues to be a vehicle for building a following in village politics. For a few individuals, it is a means of social mobility akin to sports in the United States. Wrestlers also constitute a useful set of followers for politicians because the line between purely verbal political solicitation and strong-arm techniques is not observed with great delicacy in rural Maharashtra.

9. In a ministerial reorganization late in 1974, Patil was promoted to ministerial rank and placed in charge of the ministry for rural development—the portfolio responsible for supervising panchayati raj. *Times of India*, 9 November 1974.

particular, that no one has come forward to challenge his domination of Indapur taluka and his ability to place his followers in positions of influence in district institutions—Patil has usually allowed others to take the lead in running the machinery of the District Congress organization.

One incumbent defeated along with Mohol in the 1957 elections was Annasaheb Magar. Magar was from a wealthy rural family operating agricultural lands located just outside Poona City in Haveli taluka. As in the case of Patil, his father had been a member of the District Local Board. After receiving a degree in agriculture in 1944 (the only important Poona or Kolhapur politician interviewed who had done so), he entered politics in 1946 and was elected MLA in 1952. From 1947 to 1957 he also served as a secretary of the District Congress Committee (DCC).

Shivajirao Kale was another MLA candidate in 1957 but he was then a member of the Praja Socialist Party (PSP) and was elected as a candidate of the Samyukta Maharashtra Samiti. Like Patil and Magar, he came from a family with local political involvements, but his father had never been more than a leader of his own village. Like them, too, he was in his mid-forties in 1970. Unlike those two leaders, however, Kale was educated only through the eighth standard at the small taluka headquarters in Junnar taluka.[10] As a young man, Kale had joined the youth wing of the Socialist Party and also became involved in cooperative activities in his village. By 1953, he was chairman of his taluka's purchase and sales union. Working his way up through the cooperative system, he became a director of the DCCB in 1955 and subsequently vice-chairman of that body (in 1957) and vice-chairman of the District Purchase and Sales Union. On the basis of his reputation as a major cooperative leader in his taluka (as well as an unsuccessful contestant for MLA in 1952) the Samyukta Maharashtra Samiti made him its candidate for MLA in 1957. After the realization of Maharashtra in 1960, Kale was attracted to the Congress by Y. B. Chavan. In return, Chavan promised Kale that he would be given a Congress nomination for MLA in 1962.

For much of his political career, Shankarrao Bhelke acted as Mohol's leading lieutenant. Like Mohol, Bhelke came from Bhor

10. The amount of education for all persons is self-reported. There may be a tendency for the less educated to inflate the amount of schooling, just as there is probably a tendency for most respondents to understate the amount of land they own.

and had engaged in Congress politics since the 1930s. Bhelke, however, emerged from a middle-class background: his father had been in government service; the family owned thirty acres of land; and Shankarrao had received a B.A. In 1949 he was nominated to the District School Board and about the same time began to serve as a secretary of the DCC, a pattern of activity similar to Patil's. In 1952, the first post-independence elections were held for the District Local Board. Bhelke was elected and assumed the presidency of that body, a position he held until new elections in 1956, when the Congress was defeated by the Samyukta Maharashtra Samiti. Bhelke then became leader of the opposition.

It was during these years in opposition that a District Development Board was organized separately from the District Local Board. Though the District Collector was the official head of the Local Board, the working political responsibility fell on leading Congressmen. Mohol was appointed vice-chairman while Bhelke became secretary of the Development Board. These positions strengthened their claims on major roles in the local Congress party; those who wished to gain access to developmental funds needed to approach the board members for assistance. Mohol thus became an important channel to the state government from the district and vice versa.

The two men were also active in the early phases of renewed stimulation of the cooperative field. When the district land development banks were reorganized in 1960, Bhelke was asked by state leaders to assume the position of chairman of the Poona DLDB. He held that position until 1966. Thus, during those years, he was holding responsibilities not only in the DLDB and the District Local Board but in the Congress, on the District Development Board, and (after 1962) as an MLA.

The wealthy Kakade family, with their substantial landholdings (some informants suggest that as many as one thousand acres of productive land are controlled either directly or indirectly by this very large family), are exceedingly proud of their family history. They claim deshmukh (high Maratha) status. They have also played an active role in cooperative institutions organized in the Nira Canal area since the canal was completed in the second decade of the century.

A special service district running through the three talukas which lie along the banks of the Nira Canal was organized around 1910 into a cooperative Purchase and Sales Union to provide farmers within the irrigated tract with marketing facilities and a regular supply of inputs. From the late 1920s until 1952 the technical staff of the union was headed by a man named Pawar, who served as managing director. The important families of the area, including the Kakades, held official positions in the Union, but much of the day-to-day management was in Pawar's hands.

During the five years immediately after independence, however, conflicts among factions within the Union led to instability and contributed to a general deterioration in the organization's financial position. The Kakades, who were party to the conflict, sought to take direct control of the Union. In that conflict, the Kakades were the victors; unfortunately for him, Pawar was on the side of the minority group, and when the Kakades established their predominance in 1952, he retired to cultivate his lands.[11]

Though Pawar had not engaged in politics himself, he encouraged his family to become active. His wife was given a seat on the District Local Board about 1940 and later was nominated to the District School Board. One of his sons was quite active in the PWP and served as leader of the Samyukta Maharashtra Samiti in the district until his accidental death. After that, the Pawars seemed to be relatively inactive politically, though the father did maintain some interest in cooperatives and was one of the founder-members and an early director of one of the district's first cooperative sugar factories.

In the years that followed their assumption of control of the marketing organization in the canal area, the Kakades strengthened its financial position and extended their own influence to incorporate other institutions. Control of scarce agricultural inputs, like fertilizers and cement, through the marketing cooperative gave the Kakades important economic resources which they were able to exchange for political influence. For the most part, however, their activities were confined to the cooperative sector. Because of their control of the most important marketing society in the canal area, they were able to gain predominance in the Purchase and Sales Union for the district as a whole. Both organizations have remained reliable parts of their economic barony during the last fifteen years. A representative of the family has

11. Some of the information about the Kakades and the Pawars comes from data collected by Donald W. Attwood for his "Political Entrepreneurs and Economic Development: Two Villages and a Taluka in Western India" (Ph.D. diss., McGill University, 1974).

also generally sat on the board of the DCCB. Indeed, they have usually had an important voice in the operation of that body. Similarly, when a cooperative sugar factory was proposed for the Nira Canal area, they managed to win governmental recognition away from potential rivals, successfully organize the farmer membership, and pick the directors. The result was that ever since the factory began operating in the late 1950s, it has been in the control of the Kakades.

Something should be said of the family itself. It consists of seven brothers, who divide responsibilities for different parts of the family's activities. In 1970 one brother (Mugatrao) was chairman of both the District Purchase and Sales Union and the sugar factory; another (Babulal) sat on the boards of both; and a third (Sambhaji) was managing director of the district marketing organization. The latter assumed that position in 1958 at the age of twenty-four shortly after receiving his LL.B. Another legally trained brother, Ramrao, has occasionally run for public office.

Because their activities were largely confined to the cooperative field and the cooperatives did not become a major arena for political involvement until after 1960, the Kakade family was able during the late 1950s to maintain a fairly cordial relationship with the dominant group in the District Congress—Mohol, Bhelke, Patil, and Magar. Minor political claims were recognized by the DCC but not major ones. Significantly, the territorial spaces were different. None of the four top Congress leaders except Patil had developed political bases in the talukas where the Kakades were strongest and a modus vivendi between Patil and the Kakades allowed direct conflict to be avoided. At the time, Baramati taluka—where the Nira Canal's effects are most immediately felt and where part of the Kakades' interests lie—was marked by continuous factionalism within the local Congress party unit and within the small municipality that serves as taluka headquarters; but the Kakades did not seek dominance over those institutions.

The Second Generation of District Politicians

As major figures in the District Congress, Mohol, Patil, Bhelke, and Magar played the leading roles in designating candidates for MLA in 1962. All had strong bases in their own talukas and easily obtained nominations for the Assembly for themselves; they were subsequently elected without much difficulty. Most of their recommendations for the other nominations also were accepted at the state level. When district leadership is unified in such matters, it can often have its way at the state level.

In two instances, however, opposition from within the Congress did arise after the nominations were made. As we noted earlier, Shivajirao Kale had just left the PSP. Although he had been elected chairman of the DCCB prior to the MLA elections and though his nomination for MLA had been assured by Y. B. Chavan, he lost the seat by a narrow margin. It went to a PSP nominee who was really a rebel Congressman disappointed by his own failure to receive the Congress ticket.[12] While it is generally agreed that Mohol supported Kale's nomination and election, if only to please Chavan, Kale from that time forward maintained that Magar had been less than enthusiastic about both. It set the stage for a continuing conflict between the two men.

The basis for another rivalry was laid with the nomination of Dnaneshwar Khaire for MLA in Purandhar taluka. Khaire was then only thirty, but he belonged to a wealthy dalal family engaged in the Poona wholesale market and more recently involved in running a hotel in Poona City. Despite his background, his early public work (1949 to 1952) was in the youth wing of the Socialist Party and his political sympathies have been more frequently expressed in terms of support for socialist principles than is common among Poona politicians. After receiving a law degree, Khaire was employed for a time (1958-1960) in Bombay. While there, he established contact with Chavan and apparently impressed him with his organizational and verbal ability. As a result, when Khaire returned to Poona in 1961 and began to cultivate his political connections, he was offered the ticket for MLA in Purandhar, where his family owned some land.

Khaire won easily in a six-way contest in 1962, receiving 40 percent of the vote to his leading opponent's 24 percent. However, his ability to build an institutional base in the taluka was regularly inhibited in the following years by rivals both from outside and from within the Congress. On the latter score, his main rival was Shankarrao Ursal.

12. Kale lost by 127 votes out of more than 40,000 cast. A major issue in the campaign was the location of a road through the taluka which would connect it with Bombay City through some rather difficult mountain passes. Kale favored one plan, whereas many leading Congressmen in another section of the taluka and elsewhere in the district supported another.

Like Khaire, Ursal came from a wealthy family of fruit merchants settled in Poona but maintaining ties in their native Purandhar. After receiving a B.A. and working for a time in the family business, Ursal entered municipal politics in 1952. In 1954-1955, he served as the youngest mayor in Poona City history up to that time. He set his sights on a higher post in 1957 when he sought the MLA ticket for Purandhar, but he was denied that ticket and, instead, was nominated to the District Development Board. That marked his formal entry into rural politics. Equally important, he served a term as General Secretary of the Maharashtra Youth Congress from 1959-1961. He sought the MLA ticket again in 1962 but was told by the local leaders of the DCC to wait for the first elections of the zilla parishad. Ursal, when interviewed, insisted that no one had given him assurances of any future posts in the zilla parishad, but he was willing to support Khaire in the 1962 MLA election on the expectation that his own interests would be served. Despite the common economic backgrounds of the two men and the somewhat different career patterns, the foundations for a bitter rivalry were laid during this time. It should be noted, however, that there is no readily available evidence that this rivalry led either man to be disloyal to the DCC or to the state Congress when the rivalry was not itself involved.[13]

Shivajirao Kale was the only Congress nominee for MLA defeated in rural Poona in the elections held in February 1962; most MLA candidates of the Congress won by impressive margins. The DCC's Election Committee—often called its "Parliamentary Board" in imitation of the inner group of the national Congress party which is responsible for giving final approval to parliamentary candidates—then turned to the selection of candidates for the first zilla parishad and panchayat samiti elections scheduled for mid-1962. Among the Congress candidates named were Ursal, Kale, and a member of the Kakade family (Ramrao).

13. The conflict was complicated by the prominence in the taluka of other political actors in addition to Khaire and Ursal. One element was associated with a deshmukh family which played a role in district cooperatives (sometimes in association with the Kakades). They and others regularly intervened in the Khaire-Ursal rivalry and benefited politically from efforts of one to weaken the other. Thus, in 1972, the high-status family provided the winning rival to Khaire in the contest for MLA. Allegedly, Ursal's followers worked to defeat Khaire in that contest.

Among those to whom Congress tickets were denied was Vasantrao Sanas. Although Sanas came from a leading political family in the Poona City area, which was also highly influential in Haveli taluka, he was new to politics and quite a young man, only twenty-five at the time. Nevertheless, he stood as an independent candidate and was elected. Some informants suggest that he was denied a ticket because of the potential challenge he might have been able to mount against Annasaheb Magar in Haveli taluka and in the Congress had he seriously sought to build a political career. Clearly, his own independent economic and political base (or rather that of his family) could have provided the initial resources to organize a challenge.[14]

Among the nominations over which Magar clearly did exercise influence was the decision to give a party ticket to V. V. Satav, a relative of his from Haveli. Satav was a very successful lawyer in urban Poona, a large landholder in both the urban and rural areas, and a long-time participant in the work of several major non-Brahman education societies in the district. He also had served as a member of the District Land Development Bank since 1950.

The Affirmation of Mohol's Leadership

Of fifty-eight seats in the zilla parishad filled by election in 1962—other members were added on an ex-officio basis or were co-opted to the body—forty-three went to Congressmen and ten others to "independents." (Some of the latter had sought Congress tickets but were passed over when party nominations were made.) The dominant Congress leadership group had worked reasonably well together during the MLA elections and the elections for panchayati raj institutions, but there was some conflict among them with respect to the choice of candidates for positions in the zilla parishad: the president, vice-president, and the two chairmen of subject committees.[15] On these matters, Magar attempted to

14. Sanas's uncle was "boss" of the Poona City Congress at that time and a leading dalal; his father was a major agricultural leader in Haveli taluka. The family had been involved in politics for over thirty years and had helped finance the non-Brahman movement in the district. The situation was complicated at the time, however, by a family quarrel between the two older men.

15. The committees to be apportioned were Education, Finance, Works, Cooperatives, Agriculture, and Health. The vice-president usually presides over two of these and two other members are designated to chair two others. The president chairs only general body meetings and the Standing Committee of the zilla parishad.

mount a direct challenge to Mohol by contesting his choices. For president, Mohol stated a preference for Ursal; he had long been a family friend of the Ursals and he respected Ursal's education and past experience as mayor of Poona City. Magar wanted Satav, his cousin, to fill the new post. For vice-president, Mohol felt the party should designate Kale, since the latter was a recent MLA and a major leader in his own taluka, an area that he felt should be represented in the distribution of leadership posts. Magar, apparently reaching out for allies, supported Ramrao Kakade for the position.[16] While this situation threatened at first to create serious conflict within the local party organization, matters did not come to a serious break.

On the key vote in the party caucus, Ursal defeated Satav twenty-eight to twenty.[17] Kale was selected over Ramrao Kakade by a closer margin. Having tested and proven his strength in direct combat, Mohol then moved to achieve a compromise with Magar; Satav was designated for one of the two chairmanships of subject committees. While not significant in itself, this contest set the tone of district politics for nearly a decade. Magar bowed to Mohol's leadership of the local party thereafter, for there was no subsequent occasion of an overt challenge by him. However, as we shall see, Magar did manage to gradually strengthen his own position, in part by continuing to weaken the claims of prospective rivals to the position of second-most important leader in the district.

Rivalries at Subordinate Levels

Mohol's leadership of the district party and Bhelke's importance to him as a reliable lieutenant were confirmed in 1964, when

16. The two contests emphasized social similarities rather than differences between the rivals. Ursal and Satav were highly urbanized men of great wealth. Though Satav had been involved in cooperative activities in the past, he was no more ideologically inclined to the left than Ursal, despite suggestions by Carras that this was the case. Carras, *Dynamics of Indian Political Factions,* esp. pp. 80-103. For vice-president, the contest was between men who either personally or as family representatives (in the case of Kakade) represented major cooperative interests. Indeed, Kale and the Kakades have been allies in the cooperatives on a number of occasions since 1962.

17. The vote involved the forty-three members elected as Congressmen and the five taluka panchayat samiti chairmen who sat on the zilla parishad ex-officio. It is significant that the matter was not pressed in the full body by either leader, even though the dissidents might have won if they had solicited support from the small group of opposition party members and independents in the zilla parishad.

the man who had been designated for those committee chairmanships which had not gone to Satav was removed. Actually, it was
the position of Bhelke rather than Mohol that was at issue in this
conflict. The rivalry between Bhelke and the Chairman of the
Works and Cooperatives Committees was stimulated, in part, by
efforts by the two men to gain the leadership of an internationally
funded dairy cooperative scheme. The head of the scheme would
profit at least politically, and Bhelke (with Mohol's support) did
not want the benefits to flow to a potential rival. It is alleged that
Magar lent support to the action taken against the incumbent
Chairman because he hoped that his own supporters would gain
from changes in local government positions.[18] Under increasing
political pressure, the Chairman was forced to resign in April
1964. Interestingly, Mohol himself assumed the chairmanship of
the dairy cooperative federation.

Other than this case, the years that followed saw a general
harmony within the district leadership. Patil took very little active
interest in the working of local institutions, and much of the final
authority on such matters was in Mohol's hands, though an increasingly large role was given by the latter to Magar both formally
and informally. For example, Magar was president of the DCC
during the period leading up to the MLA elections of 1967 and,
therefore, had a significant share in the designation of candidates,
though state party leaders played a major (and, some would say, a
growing) role in the designation of such candidates.

Typical of the smooth functioning of district politics at the
time were the changes made in the choice of leadership of the
major district cooperative banks. The party leaders decided to
designate Vasantrao Sanas as chairman of the Poona DLDB in
Bhelke's place in 1966. There was apparently no opposition to this
from Bhelke since he had party work and his own campaign for
reelection with which to concern himself. Despite Sanas's family's
involvements in Congress politics and his associations with Congress leaders, he had remained an independent until 1966; but at
the urging of Mohol and Magar, he joined the Congress in that
year.[19]

18. And, in fact, Satav assumed the position of chairman of the powerful
Works Committee (with its influence over construction activity) in addition
to his already important chairmanship of the Education Committee.

19. One of the reasons cited for this encouragement was the fear in
Congress circles that Sanas might be tempted to contest for MLA against
Mohol or Magar.

By 1966, Kale had also served five years as chairman of the DCCB. The leaders of the DCC asked him to give someone else an opportunity to hold that post. He acceded to this request with only a minor fuss, and Mohol himself became chairman, a position which he held until late 1967. Kale continued to serve as a director of the bank and to play an active role in its operations.

For the dozen MLA seats available in 1967, incumbents were renominated in six cases—Mohol, Patil, Bhelke, Magar, Khaire, and one lesser figure with no real influence in district politics. Despite growing conflict within Purandhar district between Khaire and Ursal, the latter was willing to settle for a second term as president of the zilla parishad. Perhaps reflective of an appreciation of the political capital that could be built up through participation in the zilla parishad, Kale also chose to remain in that body rather than contest for MLA. Instead, he reluctantly supported for the seat in Junnar a man who had become a rival in that taluka.

Among the new Congress candidates was Sharad Pawar, a newcomer to electoral politics. He stood in Baramati taluka where the Kakade family had part of its power base. Pawar, as a reader interested in kinship rivalries might note, was the son of the former managing director of the Nira Canal Purchase and Sales Union. His selection, like the choice of Khaire in 1962, partly represented an effort of the *state* leadership to bring promising young people into the party. To some observers it also involved an attempt to develop new leaders in an area where factional quarrels were weakening the party.

Parts of Baramati taluka are at the most advanced stage of economic development in the district. Prosperity, however, provided a "free" resource base for the playing of a particularly complex brand of local politics. Rivalries of all varieties existed within the taluka for control of cooperative institutions (including one of the two sugar factories), the local party organization, and the municipality. Because of these conflicts, the MPCC had decided in 1962 to designate a token woman candidate for MLA rather than trying to select among the local contenders. In 1967, Pawar was selected. As might have been expected, there was some resentment among local party workers against the choice. Indeed, one informant close to Pawar suggested that opposition was voiced even in the DCC (allegedly by Magar and Patil). Though the taluka organization backed Pawar, Magar and Patil originally preferred to give the ticket to an older man. However, the MPCC Parliamentary Board, operating with the direct involvement of Chavan, chose Pawar.

Despite his older brother's involvement in the PWP, Pawar had become active in the State Youth Congress in 1958 while studying in Poona City; by 1962 he was president of the district unit, and in 1964 he was chosen secretary of the state body, a position which brought him into regular contact with the MPCC leadership. Even while studying in Poona City (up to 1963), he built up political contacts in Baramati taluka through an association of students from the taluka then in college in the city. Many of these returned home and were beginning to become involved in taluka institutions when Pawar ran for MLA in 1967.

The Kakade family apparently saw Pawar's nomination as a direct challenge to its role in the area and decided to stand one of the brothers (Babu Lal) as Pawar's opponent for MLA. Though much dissidence existed in the taluka, Pawar was elected easily over Kakade (63 to 33 percent) with two minor candidates also in the field. Having started at the top, Pawar proceeded to consolidate his strength. After the elections, he established firmer relations with the board of one of the sugar factories and with the taluka panchayat samiti. At the state level, he was immediately appointed one of the secretaries of the Congress legislative party in the Assembly and one of three secretaries of the MPCC, positions of considerable opportunity for a young politician. Certainly he was an ambitious young man with considerable prospects in state politics. This made him a useful rallying point for opposition to the Kakade family both in Baramati and in district politics.

Despite these subordinate quarrels within the District Congress organization, the ultimate measure of the party's solidarity was the outcome of the 1967 elections. All of the Congress candidates for MLA were elected except for one incumbent. This is particularly striking when it is recalled that the election took place at a time when the Congress did badly in many parts of India and even in some districts of rural Maharashtra (including Kolhapur).

Shortly after the general elections, new elections were held for the zilla parishad. The Congress proved itself as strong as it had in 1962. Not only did party candidates win forty-three seats outright (the same number as in 1962), but one Republican was

elected with Congress support.[20] The remaining members included ten "independents" (among whom were ex-Congressmen
and some soon-to-be Congressmen). Only four members were from
other parties: one each from the PWP and Jan Sangh; two from
the Samyukta Socialist Party (SSP).

While the zilla parishad elections passed off rather easily, the
selection of top office holders raised a few new difficulties. Mohol
continued to favor Ursal, Magar was again interested in giving the
position to Satav, and it is said that S. B. Patil made a halfhearted
attempt to get a man of his own selected. However, a compromise
was effected among these top leaders with Bhelke's weight, as
usual, being placed behind Mohol. Ursal was retained as president
but Satav was promoted to the position of vice-president over
Kale. A Patil supporter was made chairman of the Finance and
Health Committees. In the reshuffle, Kale was replaced as vice-
president, but he continued to chair two of the zilla parishad's
lesser committees (Agriculture and Cooperatives).

This was obviously not a decision regarded with equanimity
by Kale; yet he had little alternative but to go along with the
change since the other leaders had reached an understanding in the
matter.[21] Full-scale conflict broke out later in 1967, however,
when Mohol asked Kale to support Magar for the chairmanship of
the DCCB in succession to himself. Given the continuing causes
for emnity between Magar and Kale, this proved too much for the
latter to accept. Allegedly, he had aspired to the presidency of the
zilla parishad. Now he found himself first demoted in that body
and then asked to retreat from a major position in the DCCB
vis-à-vis a long-time rival; to acquiesce would only accentuate his

20. In 1967, state Congress leaders reached an understanding with the
Republicans in Maharashtra for the zilla parishad elections. In Poona district
the Congress did not contest six seats so that these might be left vacant for
Republican candidates. However, the Republican candidates won only one of
the six seats, largely because local Congressmen did not favor the electoral
understanding reached at higher levels. The inability of the state party
leadership to convince local party workers of the correctness of their policy
(or simply to impose their will upon local workers) is another indication of
how tenuous party discipline actually is in Maharashtra when it comes into
conflict with other interests.

21. A local paper reported at the time that when members of the DCC
met, Mohol actually indicated a personal preference for the retention of Ursal
and Kale in their posts. After private discussions, however, Ursal and Satav
were selected, unopposed, as the candidates. Kesari, 12 August 1967.

weakness and imply his acceptance of a position of possibly permanent inferiority. He, therefore, decided to stand his ground in the DCCB. The directors of the DCCB, most of whom had been elected in 1966 while Kale was still serving as chairman, had accepted Mohol's succession without much dispute.[22] This time, however, Kale's men broke with Mohol, and Kale swept to victory over Magar by a margin of fourteen to seven. As a result, Kale regained his former position as chairman of the DCCB and temporarily reasserted his status in local politics. In this contest, Kale was backed by the Kakade family. Indeed, from that point on the Kakades began to work openly with Kale in the various arenas of politics to weaken the local party leadership.[23]

In response to his failure to carry out what they regarded to be a directive from the party leadership, the Magar group (reluctantly supported by Mohol) pressed for the removal of Kale from his chairmanships in the zilla parishad. Top state party leaders tried to intervene to prevent an open break that could weaken the party. It was only in October 1968, after complex maneuvering, that Kale was formally deprived of his local government position.[24] The punishment handed out to Kale was accompanied by action on the part of the DCC to cancel Mugatrao Kakade's party membership for "anti-party behavior."[25]

The following year, the leadership of the DCC again found itself engaged in a battle with the Kakades and Kale for maintenance of its authority in the district cooperative banking structure. In 1969, seats were contested on the bank boards from each

22. Prior to 1966, there were one-year terms for membership on the DCCB. Since then, three-year terms have been in effect. Chairmen are elected annually from among the members.

23. Mohol still insisted in mid-1970 that Kale was a member in good standing of the DCC Executive, and others suggested that Kale might even get an MLA ticket in 1972. Strangely enough, this almost happened. In the accommodative style of politics characteristic of Poona, friends of Magar insisted that Mohol had always shown a certain "softness" toward Kale and that he was not entirely unhappy to see Magar defeated in the DCCB election.

24. *Kesari,* 4-15 October 1968. He remained an ordinary Congress member of the body. Kale's successor was a man personally close to Mohol, possibly as compensation to Mohol from Magar.

25. *Kesari,* 14 October 1968, reported that the elder Kakade had lost his primary membership in the Congress for working against official Congress candidates, not only in elections for the zilla parishad but in the elections for taluka panchayat samitis and for MLA in 1967.

taluka, as well as among non-borrowing members (in the case of the DLDB) and non-society members (in the DCCB case). Previously such contests had been relatively low-keyed, but because of the attempt by the Kakade-Kale group to mount a major display of power in the cooperative sector—the sector where their strength was greatest—contests took on the character of major political warfare. Considerable money was spent to win the support of the narrow electorate involved. Legal disputes occurred at each step of the way with respect to the qualifications of candidates, the manner in which the contests were being conducted, and, ultimately, the seating of those supposedly elected. Though the Kakade-Kale group originally seemed to have a DCCB majority in their grasp, the victory was denied them by the sudden disqualification of one of their members. The DLDB had also seemed likely to fall to that group, but the chairmanship was maneuvered out from under them by the issuance of a court order postponing the election for chairman. By the time elections were finally held for the chairmanships of the two district banks, a Mohol-Magar nominee was chosen to head the DCCB, and Bhelke took over again as chairman of the DLDB.[26]

As a result, by early 1970 the Kakade-Kale group was rendered a close minority on the two major cooperative credit agencies in the district. Their position in the Congress party and governmental structure was considerably weaker. When the national Congress split came, however, the Poona Congress was barely affected. Both the majority group and the various local dissidents continued to support Y. B. Chavan. The only major local figure in the rural area to directly identify himself with the anti-Indira Congress ("the Syndicate") was Sambhaji Kakade, but this was not until late 1970. Even then, his older brothers continued to call themselves either independents or supporters of Indira Gandhi. When their economic interests were involved, however, the family was sure to band together.

District Leadership to 1970: An Overview

It may be useful to summarize some of the characteristics of the men whose backgrounds and political activities have been described in this chapter. Collectively, these leaders' and families'

---

26. *Kesari,* 14 October 1969. Quarrels over seats in the two bodies continued into 1970 as various legal suits were pressed on both sides. The *Maharashtra Times,* 3 February 1970, reports one Kale-Kakade man being

political involvements radiate into almost every village in the district. Since there is an element of geographical representation in almost every district institution, one result is that some individual from each taluka is necessarily assigned a role in district affairs even when the taluka's own internal political processes have not generated leadership with strong district-wide capabilities. Once chosen to fulfill the territorial obligations of a taluka, however, an individual may build further connections in district-level institutions.

In any case, it is noteworthy that the eleven men treated by name in this chapter (plus one other leader, Sahebrao Satkar, who faded rapidly from power after 1970[27]) included persons from eight of the district's thirteen rural talukas. Among them were ten of the twenty-four members of the Poona District Congress Committee (DCC) Executive selected in 1968 and continuing to serve through mid-1970.[28] These included the president, vice-president, and treasurer of the District Congress. Among them, too, they held seven of the eleven MLA seats which fell within the jurisdiction of the Poona DCC.[29] A third source of influence in the district—the zilla parishad—was represented by Ursal, who served as president of that body from 1962 to 1972; by Kale, who was vice-president from 1962 to 1967; and by Satav, who succeeded Kale in 1967 (and in 1972 became president of the body). Satkar was chairman of two zilla parishad committees prior to his election as MLA in 1967.

With respect to the cooperative movement, these same men played prominent roles in district and taluka cooperative institu-

---

removed by an action of the DCCB directors on the grounds that the man's opponent had been declared off the ballot illegally.

27. Although he has not figured in the narrative, Satkar was active in the cooperatives of Khed taluka and held a prominent position in the zilla parishad before being elected MLA in 1967. Before his sudden political eclipse in 1972 (partly because charges had been raised about his financial manipulation of some cooperative societies and partly because of the changes in the top political leadership of the district), he also served for a time as chairman of the DCCB and as vice-president of the DCC.

28. Not everyone on the DCC can be counted a major leader. Some members represented a taluka where no one predominated; others held offices which commanded respect (MLA; zilla parishad committee chairmen), though the men holding those posts did not.

29. Three other MLAs sat on the DCC Executive; only one Congress MLA did not. The latter was selected in 1967 because the MPCC saw fit to reward

tions. From 1962 to 1970 three of the men served as chairmen of the District Central Cooperative Bank (DCCB): Kale (1962-1966, 1968-1969), Mohol (1966-1967), and Satkar (1969-1970). Two served as chairmen of the District Land Development Bank (DLDB): Bhelke (1960-1966, 1969-1970) and Sanas (1966-1969). Satav has been a director of the DLDB for more than twenty years. At one time or another during those years, therefore, eight of the dozen men served as directors on one or both of these major district cooperative credit institutions.

Furthermore, of the four cooperative sugar factories in the district, three were implicated in the activities of these politicians.[30] One of the three factories is controlled by the Kakade family. Another factory was more open to contests for control before 1970, but Pawar has taken an increasing interest in that factory since his election as MLA in 1967. Though he was not himself a director, the factory is increasingly identified as part of his support structure. Magar was the "promoter" of a third factory located in Haveli taluka that entered into operation in 1970; despite Sanas's political opposition to Magar, Sanas's father was one of the directors of the new factory.[31] In addition to these three factories in Poona, Patil is influential in a sugar factory located in a neighboring district; that factory draws some sugarcane from Patil's taluka. Finally, in identifying the leadership of the major cooperative institutions of the district, it should be recalled that the Kakade family has controlled the District Purchase and Sales Union for at least the last twenty years.

---

an unassuming party worker of a minor community (Lingayat Kumbhar) in a taluka where there was no outstanding leader for the post.

30. A fourth factory was described by some respondents as being "owned" by a less politically active but prominent family. Family members held three of the dozen seats on the board of directors, and since the family allegedly owned or indirectly controlled as much as 25 percent of the land that came under the factory, there was no political challenge to them within the body. For the most part they remained outside of local politics. One informant remarked that "In Indapur taluka, they support Patil; in Baramati taluka, they support Kakade." In the factional struggles of Poona district, Patil and the Kakade family were on opposing sides, of course, but that does not mean the informant's comment was incorrect.

31. Another director of the factory was an important private trucker and dalal. He was elected deputy mayor of Poona City in 1970. Since Magar was a leading figure in the anti-dalal campaign, this indicates how narrow differences really were between dalals and commercial farmers for many practical purposes.

In terms of personal characteristics, the men represented here ranged in age in 1970 from thirty (Pawar) to sixty-six (Mohol). Seven of the men fell within the thirty-five to forty-five age decile. Despite the rural communities they represented and with which they maintained close contact, they were almost all fairly urbanized in demeanor, with the possible exceptions of Mohol, Satkar, and Kale. All twelve were Marathas. Eight of the twelve had B.A.s or their equivalents, and five held law degrees. Furthermore, though almost all claimed some land holdings, only three admitted to holding really substanial acreage (Kakade, Sanas, and Satav). Many of those who mentioned ownership of land also had business interests: Khaire, Ursal, and Sanas came from dalal families; their families also had invested in various urban businesses, including restaurants and hotels. Mohol owned five cinemas; Bhelke was a contractor; Satkar had been a trucker of produce. Satav continues to be a very successful practicing attorney. Only Magar, Kale, and Satkar claimed to be fully dependent on farming in 1970, though others insist that Magar had various business interests.

Underlying the fluctuations in individual power resources during this period was the consistent role of Mohol as arbiter of the local political system. Once he had established his priority as a result of his victory over Magar in the contest for zilla parishad president in 1962, his own political ambitions appear to have been sated. Thus, he seemed to concede to Patil the role of district representative in the state government.

He did assume the chairmanship of the DCCB for a time— partly as a way of heading off a direct confrontation between Kale and Magar; he also took over the chairmanship of the dairy federation from Bhelke's rival and continued to head that body through 1972. On the whole, however, Mohol did not pursue additional opportunities. Rather, he attempted to moderate the ambitions of others. At various times, for example, he intervened to prevent rivals from taking that extra step which might have disabled the Congress-directed system as a whole. No doubt, his very mediation of such rivalries helped in a certain sense to keep matters simmering and, therefore, preserved Mohol's own superiority, but this is not to argue that Mohol either consciously created such rivalries or enhanced them.

The one compromise Mohol and other local leaders were not willing to make was to cede significant political power to the Kakades. The reasons for this are by no means clear. Mohol assumed a populist garb when speaking of the Kakades: they were described as selfish big landowners exploiting the masses, men whom the public had never supported in a general election. In his attacks on them he was again the poor village youth of fifty years ago, rather than the wealthy movie-theater owner and investor in agricultural lands. At the same time, no doubt, there was an indication in his remarks that the Kakades might be tolerated within the cooperative field, but to allow them opportunities to expand into direct control of other political institutions would mean that a party requiring at least the public aura of mass concern would lose its image. (Whether there has been much reality behind that image is another question.) With the image might go crucial electoral support from the mass of poor farmers and landless laborers who look to the Congress for hope (a hope not necessarily substantiated by economic achievement). It is important to retain this electoral constituency even if it is not the functional constituency upon which the Congress depends at times when popular elections are not being held.

At best, therefore, perhaps all we can suggest is that Mohol was capable of leading the Congress in a fashion which allowed both its electoral constituency and its smaller functional constituency to work together. This argument does not imply any real ideological commitment by local party leaders. Indeed, the primacy of their ambition and their organizational loyalties allowed the leaders of the Poona Congress to follow Chavan with relative ease as he changed sides during the inner-party conflicts within the Congress in 1969-1970. The support of local leaders like Mohol was unquestioning, their reasons (except for trust in Chavan's abilities) difficult to identify. More articulate local leaders like Sharad Pawar clothed their shifting commitments in terms of socialist rhetoric. The end result was the same: the maintenance of an organization grounded in the broad spectrum of the Maharashtrian population but owing much of its character to the dominant rural elite which provided its activist stratum.

THE CONTEST FOR MLC

Although particular instances have already been indicated where state party or government leaders intervened in Poona affairs to influence the choice of candidates, the relative harmony of Poona district leadership, as compared to some other districts in Maharashtra, necessitated a minimum of such interventions. However, in late 1970 a contest for member of the Maharashtra Legislative Council (MLC) precipitated a major dispute not only within the district but in the top ranks of the state party leadership. This occurred when a seat for a local bodies constituency fell vacant. Voters for this functional constituency were limited to the elected members of the Poona Municipal Corporation, the smaller municipalities in the district (including the army-supervised cantonment boards), and all the members of the zilla parishad.

There were three aspects to the conflict which may be seen as operating together, although in combination they might be described as "overdetermining" the election results. First, there was a conflict internal to the state ministry and to the MPCC leadership. Second, there was major dissidence within the Poona City Congress. Third, there was some minor dissatisfaction in the rural DCC that bolstered the creation of an expedient alliance of opposition party members with dissidents in the DCC.

The incumbent MLC from Poona district was an ex-Jan Sangh leader from a municipality in western Poona where the Jan Sangh had its greatest following (other than in Poona City itself). He had joined the Congress in 1959 and by 1970 had served a term as MLC to the general satisfaction of the District Congress. However, when decisions were being made by the MPCC leadership on nominees for a number of seats for MLC (including one for Kolhapur, as we shall see in the next chapter), an understanding allegedly was reached between D. S. (Balasaheb) Desai, Minister for Revenue, and Vasantrao (Dada) Patil, President of the MPCC, by which Balasaheb's "man" in Poona, the president of the City Congress, was given the Poona ticket in place of the incumbent in return for Patil's nominee being selected in Kolhapur.

Within the Poona City Congress, this decision was greeted with particular distaste. Two groups had emerged within the City Congress in 1968, and though they had compromised at the time of municipal elections, the leader of the dominant group in the municipal corporation had sought the MLC ticket for himself.[32] This was probably the crucial division, as we shall see. Not only was the Congress party in the city bitterly divided but opposition party groups in the corporation were in a position to swing the

32. For a discussion of Poona City politics, see my *The Limited Elite* (Chicago: University of Chicago Press, 1970).

vote of that body against the Congress if Congress party ranks broke, since the Congress had only a bare majority in the municipal government.

Most of the municipalities outside of Poona City elected their members in nonpartisan elections. Many of these local bodies were dominated by non-Maharashtrian merchant and minority communities (Gujaratis, Marwaris, Jains)—groups not actively represented in the leadership structure of the DCC or in zilla parishad politics. Politicians based in these municipalities had lost political power over the years, both in the Congress and in district affairs, to interests more closely in contact with rural life. There were some exceptions, like the municipalities in two of the most scarcity-affected talukas (Sirur and Dhond), where the marked deprivation of rural life seemed to make the role of the municipalities more crucial to political action in the talukas. Another notable exception was the municipality in Baramati, but here Maratha farmers from the nearby countryside had settled in town and were playing an active role in municipal politics.

The MLC contest demonstrates the role that short-term interests play in Maharashtrian politics, as opposed to any alignment of political forces on ideological bases. In a sense, Sambhaji Kakade, who emerged as the candidate in opposition to the unpopular Congress nominee, was a man of the political right, yet his base was in the cooperatives. Kakade received the backing of all the opposition parties, including the leftist groups in urban Poona. Furthermore, he gained the support of a motley group of Congress dissidents and local independents, men who were concerned principally with advancing their own interests in opposition to the Congress rather than with the outcome of the race as such.[33]

The notable lack of enthusiasm displayed by some leaders of the rural DCC for the city-based Congress candidate imposed on them by the MPCC also may have confirmed the dissidents in their action. Some DCC leaders felt a candidate from the rural area or from one of the smaller municipalities should have been chosen; others resented the fact that the candidate was not even native to the district and that he had profited in the past from appointments given out by state leaders.

---

33. Many interviewees insisted that the Kakades used large cash inducements to win several votes but I have no hard evidence on this.

TABLE 1: POONA MLC ELECTION, 1970

	Eligible	*Kakade*	*Congress Nominee*
Poona Zilla Parishad	68	20	46
Poona Municipal Corporation	73	44	27
Cantonment Boards (3)	40	21	14
Municipalities (12)	202	108	88
Totals	383	193	175

When the votes were counted, Kakade was the winner by a margin of 193 to 175. (The pattern of voting is summarized in table 1.[34]) Given all the plausible explanatory factors working against the Congress nominee, it is surprising Kakade did not win by a larger margin. As the table shows, the Congress nominee lost most decisively in the Poona City corporation. He also did badly in certain of the smaller municipalities. (Kakade received a majority in six of the dozen municipalities including the one in his home taluka.[35] He tied in two others.)

This political victory had no long-term effect on the Congress. It provided temporary encouragement for political activity on the part of the Kakades. However, when they decided· to run Ramrao for Parliament in 1971 against R. K. Khadilkar of the Congress, they experienced a crushing defeat.[36]

34. The sixty-eight persons eligible to vote from the zilla parishad included the fifty-eight elected members and ten panchayat samiti presidents who were ex-officio members of the body. (Three others held both offices by election.)

35. Members of the municipal government in Baramati voted twelve to nine in favor of Kakade, much to the embarrassment of Sharad Pawar, who was responsible for overseeing the election in the district on behalf of the MPCC.

36. Khadilkar won with 185,637 votes to Ramrao Kakade's 54,677, while a third man drew only 9,815 of the 267,635 votes cast. There were three other minor candidates. This confirms a point made by several interviewees:

CHANGING THE LOCAL GUARD: 1970-1973

Between 1970 and 1973, politics in Poona district underwent major changes in personnel, though not in the fundamental character of local leadership. Gone or sharply reduced in authority by the end of the period were Mohol, Bhelke, Ursal, and Kale. If any shift was most remarkable, however, it was the rise of Sharad Pawar. He now shared with Magar and S. B. Patil the reins of power in the Congress party. Together they held a large part of what local influence was exercised in selecting MLA candidates in 1972. (District influence in these processes generally had been reduced in recent years because of increased intervention from the state and national party Congress leaderships.) The same three men had a major voice in the selection of zilla parishad nominees later in the year and of the persons to fill the major positions in that body. Their influence in the cooperative sector was less certain, for the Kakades and their allies by no means had been obliterated.

Two things are notable about the shift in leadership. First, there occurred a change in image, albeit only a slight one, with the replacement of a few major leaders: the new image was somewhat more youthful, better educated, and more urbanized. Second, the new leadership seemed to employ the language of socialism and of attachment to the reformist ideals of the national leadership more easily than had its predecessor. In reality, however, the District Congress remained strongly in tune with the state leadership group associated with Chavan.

The transition in leadership involved (at least temporarily) a certain narrowing of participation as even fewer men than in the past played with the major counters of local political power. This may have been a function of the transition itself, as new men were placed in positions of potential authority and others declined in influence. What is perhaps more striking is that the process of change was relatively routinized, though it did involve a small measure of conflict and accounted for some of the losses the Congress party temporarily experienced in the State Assembly elections of early 1972. By the time of the zilla parishad elections in mid-year, however, the Congress had not only recovered but

---

the Kakades were effective in bringing their resources to bear on small electorates but were incapable of building more substantial popular bases.

managed to win an even more substantial rural majority than it had in the past.

The greatest single stimulus for change within Poona district was the result of a personal choice—the decision by Mohol to retire from politics at the age of sixty-eight. As a parting gesture, he attempted to hand on his own MLA seat to his son. This proposal was accepted halfheartedly by other members of the DCC and forwarded to the MPCC as a recommendation, but the MPCC chose instead a major figure in the vegetable and fruit market of Poona City who was a former mayor of Poona City and influential in the Poona City Congress. (He did have a connection to the rural constituency because his family held some land there.) Once the choice was made, Mohol showed no inclination to oppose it.

Mohol's retirement not only resulted in his own withdrawal from the field of political influence, but it meant that his support was no longer available to others. Opponents of Bhelke, for example, used the opportunity to raise charges against him for allegedly misusing funds in connection with the construction of a number of small irrigation schemes in his home taluka. When these charges were followed with court cases, his nomination was withdrawn. The Congress nomination was then given to a woman from Poona City whose major claim to political activity was membership in the Poona municipal council and past associations with R. K. Khadilkar. Khadilkar, though the Member of Parliament (MP) from Poona, had little following in the district. However, his influence with Mrs. Gandhi and his status as a member of the national government—he was at the time Minister of State for Rehabilitation, the department responsible for maintaining the Bengali refugee camps in the period before the Indo-Pakistan war of December 1971—gave Khadilkar a claim to recognition in local politics. The DCC had recommended two names for the seat, neither of them a supporter of Khadilkar. However, the MPCC granted the ticket to Khadilkar's follower. Not surprisingly, given the antipathy of the DCC, Khadilkar's nominee was beaten soundly by a young and educated former government servant running as an independent. (His was one of the two names originally recommended by the local party organization.)

This time around, Ursal, the retiring president of the zilla parishad, actively sought the MLA nomination from Purandhar. Khaire, the incumbent MLA, had the support of leading figures in the MPCC and gained the nomination. Ursal did very little to support Khaire's election, and some of Ursal's followers allegedly worked against him. Khaire was defeated by a high-status Maratha—a long-time opponent of both Khaire and Ursal—who ran as a candidate of the Socialist Party.

While these seats were being lost, the influence of other leaders was confirmed or enhanced elsewhere in the district. Pawar, Patil, and Magar were all easily renominated for MLA even though the last two considerably exceeded a supposed state party stipulation (asserted during preparations for the election) that two-term MLAs should not be renominated. These three top leaders of the DCC also agreed to the renomination (along with Khaire) of incumbents in Ambegaon and Mawal constituencies. None of the three top leaders had a personal base in those western sections of the district. Like Khaire, the two incumbent nominees were defeated. The incumbent in Ambegaon lost to an ambitious young sometime-Congressman who had previously been active in the zilla parishad; the Mawal incumbent was defeated by a Jan Sangh candidate in the only taluka in the district where the Jan Sangh has a strong position in the cooperative movement and an active following among non-Brahmans.

Other nominations reflected an attempt on the part of the MPCC (rather than the DCC) to bring "new blood" into the party. In one case, the nomination went to a woman who had served as president of a small municipality; she won creditably. A second seat involved the only case where the Congress did not have an incumbent. The sitting member from the constituency had been elected by the PSP, but he was no longer interested in electoral politics. At the insistence of the MPCC, a ticket was given to a member of the Dhangar caste (a low-status shepherd community), a man who had previously served in the zilla parishad. While the nominee was not recommended by the DCC as a whole, he was personally favored by Sharad Pawar, who exercised direct influence with the MPCC. In a third instance, an incumbent was dropped in favor of a young lawyer from a wealthy rural family. Like the other two new people, he won.

Finally, in the case of Junnar, the DCC could not agree on a single candidate but recommended the names of Shivajirao Kale and a prominent member of the zilla parishad. The MPCC originally gave the ticket to the second man, then reversed itself and sent Kale's name to the Parliamentary Board of the All-India

Congress Committee (AICC), the national decision-making body for the Congress. There a further change was made. The major veto at the national level allegedly came from Khadilkar, who had been actively opposed by Kale when MP nominations were being made in 1971. Kale did not contest the AICC decision either directly or indirectly during the election, and his local rival was elected.

On the whole, the Congress did not do as well in Poona district in 1972 as in 1967. While the party was winning 222 of the 267 seats in the Maharashtra Assembly in the wake of the Bangladesh triumph, in Poona the Congress lead in rural seats slipped from ten to one to only seven to four. However, the state and local leadership were reasonably satisfied that they had brought a more appealing group of young people into district politics and that they were now in a better position to take advantage of future opportunities than had been possible under the older generation of Mohol-connected politicians.

The evolving power situation in the district was more clearly defined following the elections for MLA. Sharad Pawar, who had already emerged as an energetic young district leader after 1967 and had exercised state-wide responsibility from 1967 to 1972 as one of the secretaries of the MPCC, was given the important post of Minister of State for Home Affairs, a position responsible for overseeing the law and order situation in the state.[37] This new state authority enhanced Pawar's influence within the district. While he had been influential but not authoritative at the time of the elections for the Assembly, with his new stature he was able to play a more prominent role when zilla parishad elections were held in mid-1972.

Thus, in the selection of candidates, the DCC, led by the triumvirate of Pawar, Magar, and Patil, apparently agreed among themselves on candidacies without too much difficulty, and the

37. Although this was not full ministerial status, it involved major responsibility for Pawar. The portfolio was nominally held by the Chief Minister, but the latter was able to exercise only marginal personal authority over it because of his other duties. In May 1973, the mishandling of food supplies in the state led to further responsibility for Pawar. The Food and Civil Supplies Minister, who was then under heavy public attack, was retained in his position, but Pawar was assigned the additional responsibility of Minister of State in those areas. Pawar's double responsibility reflected the close connection that existed between food supply and police at the time. In a Cabinet reorganization in late 1974, Pawar was made Minister for Education.

campaign was not hard fought either in the party or during the subsequent election. Few contests for nominations were referred to the MPCC. The Congress, which had won forty-three of fifty-eight seats in 1967, increased its margin to forty-nine seats.[38]

In the selection of officers for the zilla parishad, the former vice-president (Satav) was elevated to the presidency. This confirmed the continued importance of Magar in district affairs. The vice-presidency went to a Chambhar (an ex-untouchable) member from Baramati taluka; the man selected had little personal following, but he was the choice of Pawar. His selection had two useful side-benefits for Pawar: it placed in that office a man of relatively little personal ambition who was almost entirely dependent on the dominant leadership group for his position; at the same time, it had the symbolic utility of affirming the concern of the Congress for the general plight of the ex-untouchables and the party's continuing interest in providing opportunities to representatives of all communities.

One of the other two major positions was filled in a way that also reflected Pawar's rising political influence. The man selected as chairman for two subject committees had been Pawar's original choice for an MLA nomination. For the other set of chairmanships, the incumbent (a protégé of S. B. Patil) was renamed.

Agreement was also easily reached on major positions within the DCC Executive Committee at the end of the year. Magar was reinstalled as president, succeeding Bhelke, and as vice-president the leaders agreed on Khaire. Like Pawar, Khaire spoke the language of socialism and radical change, but he was above all a proven Chavan loyalist. He also had shared an association with Pawar during service in the Assembly when they were two of the handful of young non-ministerial Congress MLAs to take an active interest in legislative affairs.[39]

While this small group of men played the major roles in district politics and government in early 1972, they still did not

38. Some of the gain in seats should be counted against the fact that this time there was no alliance with the Republican Party. In that connection, see n. 20.

39. Since Khaire no longer held an MLA seat and his organizational base in Purandhar taluka was not strong, his selection as vice-president of the DCC was more a gesture toward his verbal facility and socialist-leaning credentials than to his political stature in the district. Pawar is said to have had an important role in this choice.

fully control the cooperative sector. In those talukas where they were MLAs, Magar and Patil had a substantial corner on cooperative institutions. Magar largely dominated one sugar factory, and Patil another, though it was not located in Poona district. Pawar had a major voice in one of the two sugar factories in his taluka. Still, Pawar had to contend with the Kakades in other Baramati institutions. In other talukas, individuals not aligned with the top leaders still had political resources. Thus, Kale remained an influential figure in the cooperatives of Junnar.[40] Indeed, in late 1971, the majority group in the DCC lost control of the DCCB to the Kakades. Through a switch of two votes, a Mohol supporter was replaced by Babu Lal Kakade as chairman of the DCCB. Thus, the Kakades managed to hold onto and even slightly enhance their standing in the cooperative sector, though they demonstrated little ability to move beyond that sector to capture influence in governmental and party affairs.

OVERVIEW

In this chapter, I have described the pattern of political relationships in one district of Maharashtra: Poona. We have seen something of how a relatively small group of men dominated the major institutional structures in the district and how, despite some recent changes in the leadership, such a pattern continued to characterize the institutional life of the district. The newer leadership provided greater recognition to a generation of younger men who were not actively involved in the political field before independence. It was a political stratum with roots in the rural area but at ease with an urbanized style of rural life. There is little evidence that the new leadership represented a major deviation from the direction pursued in the past by the Congress party in Poona district. Individuals like Sharad Pawar may speak as if they seriously believe that major changes are necessary in societal organization, but in practice theirs is a moderate leadership more often concerned with the practicalities of maintaining party advantage or advancing personal careers than with bringing about radical societal change.

40. Though the newly elected MLA from Junnar was seated on the DCC Executive in Kale's place, Kale held on to one token of political recognition: he was selected the Junnar taluka representative to the general body of the MPCC.

As we shall see in chapter 8, Pawar and Khaire participated in attempting to limit the power of the cooperative barons while they were fairly young MLAs; Magar took the initiative in trying to reduce the advantages of the Maratha merchants in the Poona City market; Patil was Minister of State for Cooperatives and publicly supported the reforms introduced under two different ministers. Nevertheless, none of the changes these men advocated involved a radical restructuring of cooperative-based power in Maharashtra. Insofar as possible, all have employed the instrumentalities that have evolved in the past fifteen years—the cooperative movement, positions of influence in state and local government, authority in the district party organization— essentially to maintain or advance their political careers and only marginally to redirect public policy. Deeply implicated as they are in the institutions created to serve the countryside, none is in a position to alienate the crucial support base of the Congress: that stratum of big- and medium-size farmers oriented to commercial agricultural production. As political leaders, however, they have recognized a possible hiatus between their two constituencies—the rural elite, which dominates the new institutions of politics and government (including the cooperatives) at the village and taluka levels; and the mass electorate, which has provided continuing support to the Congress and helped maintain that party in office. It is the recognition of the existence of some tension on this score by a few key people in Maharashtra politics and their attempt to cope with it through the evolution of policy changes, or at least the appearance of receptivity to change, that has made the Maharashtrian political system one of the most durable in India. In fact, the party has made the effort to give the appearance of a commitment to bettering the life of the average Maharashtrian. For this, the greatest credit must go to Chavan and to the generally underrated Chief Minister of Maharashtra, Vasantrao Naik.

Kolhapur District:
Sectarianism, Personal Ambition,
and Political Routinization

The princely state of Kolhapur was relatively aloof from the nationalist currents that affected other parts of western Maharashtra in the late nineteenth century.[1] In contrast, Chhatrapati Shahu Maharaj, who ruled the state from 1894 to 1922, did provide an important source of personal legitimacy to the non-Brahman movement in Kolhapur and in Bombay State more generally. After Shahu's death, his successor, Rajaram, displayed little of his father's personal commitment to the non-Brahman movement, and the state experienced a recession in importance as a center of non-Brahman activity. In the last years of his reign, which lasted until 1940, Rajaram began to encounter internal opposition from a growing middle class, which sought greater representation in the public life of the state, but this opposition was only tangentially connected to the greater movement for national independence.

Upon the death of Rajaram in 1940 and the adoption of a child into the royal family, Kolhapur entered a period of regency. The heir's death in 1946 created new uncertainties within the ranks of the ruling elite of the state. The selection of a successor by the British—Rajaram's sister's son—met with a good deal of opposition from members of Rajaram's court. This division in the ranks of the nobility also encouraged middle-class activists to renew their demands for a major role in government. Maneuvers for political leadership between and among the nobility and the urbanized middle class contributed to disputes which subsequently surrounded the integration of Kolhapur into independent India.

1. For a brief history of the district before independence, see my "From Reformist Princes to 'Cooperative Kings,'" *Economic and Political Weekly,* 19 May 1973, pp. 903-910. Some materials for the present chapter are drawn from that issue and from two later installments which appeared in the same journal on 26 May and 2 June 1973, pp. 951-956 and 995-1000.

We shall consider these matters and more recent aspects of Kolhapur politics after we have briefly identified some of the socioeconomic features of the district which bear on politics and policy
making.

THE GEO-POLITICS OF KOLHAPUR

In 1971 Kolhapur district had slightly more than 2 million people.
Only about four hundred thousand of these resided in urban
places, the chief one being Kolhapur City with a population of
259,050.[2]

Kolhapur district's western section, like Poona's, includes a
portion of the Sahyadri mountain range and is similarly affected
by those mountains in terms of rainfall distribution. The western
part of the district experiences heavy rainfall and is separated by
forests from the upland of the coastal district of Ratnagiri. In
contrast, eastern parts of Kolhapur bordering on Sangli district
and on Karnataka (formerly the state of Mysore) regularly share
with those areas marked shortages in rainfall (see map 3).

While the rainfall of the district is distributed in somewhat
the same fashion as in Poona, Kolhapur has a more substantial
network of rivers, and those eastern talukas which have relatively
low rainfall benefit from the river systems which originate in the
western part of the district. Indeed, in a normal year the agricultural yields seem to be greatest in those talukas—Gadhinglaj,
Hatkanangale, and Shirol—where the rainfalls are lowest. The
district's farmers developed extensive lift-irrigation facilities on a
collective basis to cope with this situation long before such efforts
became a subject for governmental activity.[3] Irrigation works
encouraged the growth of sugarcane—one of the major crops of

2. The second largest city is Ichalkaranji, which had a population of
87,731 in 1971. Prior to independence, Ichalkaranji was the seat of a
Brahman feudatory state owing formal allegiance to Kolhapur but frequently
in conflict with that state. After Ichalkaranji, none of the other municipal
areas of Kolhapur district has a population of over 20,000.

3. When questioned about a demand of Kolhapur politicians that more
money be invested by the state government in irrigation facilities, the Minister for Power and Irrigation of Maharashtra responded, "It is said that
Kolhapur is not receiving enough money on irrigation projects, but that is
because so many irrigation schemes were previously taken up in the district
under private or government resources." Interview, Vasantrao (Dada) Patil,
17 February 1973.

Map 3. Kolhapur District, Maharashtra.

the district—and predated governmental support for cooperative activities to promote economic development. Such agricultural development organized on a collective basis may explain why Kolhapur district has taken so readily to the various cooperative structures encouraged by the state government in the past twenty years. Indeed, the district is one of the most cooperative-oriented in Maharashtra.

Ironically, while Kolhapur politicians have often felt themselves mistreated in the distribution of political rewards by the state government, the district has one of the strongest rural economies in the state. Not only are its governmentally supported cooperative sugar factories centers of economic prosperity, returning assured profits to farmer-members, but its more prosperous farmers are engaged in other agro-industries like fertilizer plants, weaving and spinning mills, and factories producing oil engines to drive agricultural machinery. Sometimes these activities are organized as private ventures, sometimes as cooperative schemes. Those who prosper either as private entrepreneurs or as leaders of the cooperative sector are from the same "class"; in some cases, they are the same individuals.

The prosperous agricultural talukas of Shirol, Hatkanangale, and Gadhinglaj share more than a rain problem with the Kannada-speaking hinterland of Karnataka on which they border. They share certain social structural similarities. Thus, whereas the western ridge of Kolhapur district and much of central Kolhapur (around the capital city) are populated by Marathas, the three eastern talukas (and particularly Gadhinglaj) contain a large number of Lingayats; the other two eastern talukas (Kagal and Chandgad) and Kolhapur City also have substantial numbers of Jains. Although both of these religious communities are Marathi-speaking and indigenous to the region, they have provided an added dimension to the social life of Kolhapur that is important for understanding politics in the district.[4] The two religious sects reject Brahmanism; they contributed important sympathizers to the non-Brahman movement organized locally under Shahu. Indeed, some of the most prominent figures in Shahu's government came from these smaller communities and from the even smaller CKP (Chandrasenya Kayastha Prabhu) caste. Despite their minority positions in even those talukas where they are concentrated, the Jains and Lingayats have been among the most prosperous and substantial farmers of the district; they have taken to commercial farming with great élan.

An influential stratum emerged from among these communities, which was activated earlier than the majority of Marathas for participation in modern political and economic life.

4. The two communities number only approximately 5 percent each of the district's total population.

Though literacy rates for the two communities were not substantially higher than for Marathas at the turn of the century, they seemed better able to make immediate use of those economic and educational opportunities made available through Shahu's reforms. Perhaps, too, religious contacts with Kannada-speaking Lingayats in those areas under British rule adjacent to the eastern talukas provided a spur to nationalist activity and sympathies among these non-Brahman minorities; it is notable that some of the older politicians interviewed in this part of the district refer to the influence Gandhi had on them, whereas older Marathas from the western and central Maratha-dominated talukas are less likely to tie their personal histories to Gandhi and the nationalist movement. Instead, their associations are with the political history of the princely regime.

Not only did the social structure of the region open the district to a variety of external contacts in the past, but Kolhapur's geo-economic structure orients the several parts of the district in rather distinct directions today. The western talukas are blocked from easy access to the seacoast by mountains and forest areas. Much of their marketing activity is directed to the central part of the district, focusing on Kolhapur City. On the other hand, the more favorable topography of the eastern talukas results in that territory being interspersed with a number of commercial centers in Karnataka and other districts of Maharashtra. Finally, the backward, Marathi-speaking taluka of Chandgad in the southeastern part of the district was added to the former princely state only in 1956, when the rest of what was then Belgaum district was included in the new Mysore State after reorganization of the Indian states. Chandgad still looks to Belgaum for its principal urban market.[5] The northeastern talukas are less Belgaum-oriented, but they distribute their marketing activities among Kolhapur City, Ichalkaranji, towns in Karnataka like Nipani, and nearby Maharashtrian cities, like Miraj and Sangli in Sangli district.

5. The intimate links of Chandgad with the city of Belgaum account for the high level of concern found in that taluka for a favorable resolution of a border dispute between Maharashtra and Karnataka over Belgaum district. Recognition of Maharashtra's demands would result in the incorporation of the Marathi-speaking city of Belgaum into Maharashtra. The situation is complicated by the fact that the city is surrounded by rural areas which are Kannada-speaking.

Thus, social structure, geography, and economic history have collaborated to produce a district marked by distinct interests in economic and political development. The talukas most implicated in modern commercial agriculture are those in the northeastern part of the district. As one moves west and south the farmers appear to be involved in a less market-oriented, less productive series of agricultural activities. To some extent, the politics of the past quarter-century has reflected an attempt on the part of the less progressive talukas of the west and center to catch up with the achievements of the northeast. This situation has been complicated by the fact that the distinction sometimes has been perceived in terms of caste—Marathas versus Lingayats and Jains.

Maratha politicians spent more than a decade after independence seeking to gain dominance in the Congress and access to the rewards of local government bodies and cooperative institutions which went with such dominance. Success sated their *collective* ambition when Marathas gained most of the symbolic and material rewards of politics in the district after 1962, but that success merely opened the way to a decade of pursuit of *individual* ambition by Maratha politicians. Strangely enough, the very extravagance of their behavior in the course of pursuing those ambitions has resulted more recently in creating the ground for a unified leadership structure (akin to the one developed in Poona) which represents the class interests of the market-oriented farmer and agro-industrial entrepreneur without great regard for earlier caste distinctions.

THE STRUCTURE OF POST-INDEPENDENCE LEADERSHIP

Demands for greater public participation in shaping the behavior of the princely regime began to appear in Kolhapur only in 1937, when an agitation was organized which demanded a lowering of land revenue collected from the farmer, restrictions on the conversion of farm land by the royal family to private use (for hunting grounds), and a measure of responsible government.

This agitation was led by Madhavrao Bagal, a Maratha journalist and artist, then in his early forties. Bagal's father had been employed in the princely service and his family actively supported Shahu's local variant of the Satya Shodak movement (see chapter 2, n. 5). Bagal, himself, had gained a reputation (which he held throughout his long life) for being a fiery anti-Brahman. His anti-Brahmanism included attacks on the Brahman priesthood, an attack many middle-class non-Brahmans accepted. But Bagal went on to question Hinduism itself—a position that few "respectable" non-Brahmans shared with Bagal.

Associated with Bagal from the start of the local agitation was Ratnappa Kumbhar, a rural-born youth from a Lingayat family. While Bagal was a highly effective public speaker, Kumbhar gained a reputation as a political organizer. When the two men converted the popular agitation of 1937 into a more institutionalized form in 1939 as the Kolhapur Praja Parishad (People's Organization), Bagal became its president and Kumbhar, general secretary.

Both men, plus many others who had their start in the Praja Parishad, came out of those institutions which Shahu had founded to advance non-Brahman education. Members of the nobility were casual about their concern with education, but upwardly mobile Marathas and non-Brahmans from smaller communities took advantage of those educational opportunities opened by Shahu. Thus, Kumbhar, who was the son of a potter and small farmer, received his B.A. in 1933 in Kolhapur; Bagal, who continued to devote part of his time to painting, was sent to study art in Bombay under Shahu's patronage. When they formed the Praja Parishad in 1939, they were representatives of a class of ambitious non-Brahmans who had imbibed the effects of Western education and had some sense of the stirrings for political change which were occurring on a larger scale elsewhere in India.

Both Bagal and Kumbhar were imprisoned by Rajaram for their leadership of the 1939 movement, but they were released in a general amnesty in 1940 at the time of the birth of a daughter, Padmaraje, Rajaram's first (and only) child. A ban continued on the Praja Parishad, however, until early 1942. The sympathy of the Congress with that organization is indicated by the fact that the former Congress Chief Minister of Bombay State, B. G. Kher, presided at the first public session of the Parishad held later in the year. The nationalist movement, which entered its most militant phase in 1942, attracted Kumbhar; he left Kolhapur in order to work underground against colonial rule in British India.[6] Mean-

---

6. The Congress reinforced the distinction between British and princely India by not organizing party units in the princely states. As in Kolhapur, however, they did indicate their support or sympathy for certain local

while, the Praja Parishad, now primarily under Bagal's leadership, continued to constitute a presence in Kolhapur politics, though mainly in municipal affairs. Since it was essentially a movement for state reform and not for national independence, it was allowed to function even during the period when the Congress was under a ban elsewhere.

In conjunction with preparations for independence in 1946 and early 1947, a political situation emerged in Kolhapur which placed the Praja Parishad on one side—with its complement of support from the urbanized middle class of Kolhapur City and from the rural talukas of the northeast—and the princely regime and its supporters on the other. Many of the latter group had their landed estates in the central and western parts of the state. The memory of the great Maratha prince, Shahu, and the general reformism of his regime shored up the position of the Maratha nobility in this contest and made it difficult for Bagal and Kumbhar to build a successful following throughout the state.

After the death in 1946 of an adopted male heir to the throne, an unpopular ruler, Shahji, came to power in Kolhapur. Rajaram's widows were bitterly opposed to the selection of Shahji,[7] but they accepted it with the understanding that the succession would provide recognition to the interests of the late Rajaram's daughter, Padmaraje, particularly if she had a son. Popular support, insofar as it is known, seemed to reflect sympathy for Padmaraje and, through her, for the preservation of the revered Shahu's direct male line.

The fact that the new ruler was popular neither among the local Maratha nobility nor among the public made the task of organizing the demand for popular participation easier than it had been in the past. Bagal and his co-workers were able to come forward during the last years of the regency and at the time of

---

movements in these states. See, for example, Richard Sisson, *The Congress Party in Rajasthan* (Berkeley and Los Angeles: University of California Press, 1972), especially pp. 43-72.

7. Rajaram had two wives: Tarabai, the mother of Padmaraje; and Vijayamala, the younger wife. Tarabai acted as regent during the minority of the adopted male heir. Her opposition to the selection of Shahji involved a fear that the interests of Padmaraje would not be recognized in any further succession. There were also personal quarrels between Shahji's mother and Rajaram's widows which embittered their relationship. For a view of Shahji as a youth, see E. M. Forster, *The Hill of Devi* (New York: Harcourt Brace, 1953).

Shahji's accession and solidify a wider following for their organization, especially in the city of Kolhapur. Maratha leaders of the Congress organization in Maharashtra, like Keshavrao Jedhe and Shankarrao More, gave considerable encouragement to Bagal. Kumbhar, who did not reenter Kolhapur politics until 1947, thus found himself in a weakened position vis-à-vis Bagal and his own former followers in the Parishad when he returned.

Lacking any political base of his own, Shahji turned to the Praja Parishad in 1947 when he sought to construct a ministry with greater popular support than the one he had formed at the time of his accession. It is alleged that he hoped to fend off merger of the state into what was formerly British India by gaining the backing of the Parishad.[8] In the original understanding about the ministry, Bagal was to be Prime Minister (Chief Minister) of the state, and Kumbhar and an associate of his were to hold major portfolios. However, a dispute, which had apparently been smoldering for some time, came to the surface when Kumbhar demanded the critically important post of Minister for Home Affairs in the new cabinet. The two principal leaders of the Parishad split on this issue. Rather than concede or compromise, neither man entered the ministry. Instead, Vasantrao Bagal (Madhavrao's brother)—a lawyer who had been a supporter of the Parishad[9] —assumed the Prime Minister's post. The new ministry was a mixed group. It included several who were loyal to Shahji or to no one group, as well as a few representatives from the Praja Parishad.

Part of the dispute between Kumbhar and Bagal flowed from the fact that the two men had different points of social and political access to regional and national political leadership. Kumbhar's work in the Praja Parishad was oriented to the national Congress party. He received special encouragement from leaders like Sardar Vallabhbhai Patel, B. G. Kher, and Morarji Desai, prime figures in the Bombay City and Gujarati wing of the Congress in Bombay State, and from reformist Brahmans, like N. V. Gadgil and Shankarrao Deo, in the Maharashtra Congress. On the other hand, Bagal was closer to men like Jedhe and More, leaders of the Maratha section of the party. Such alignments conformed both to

8. Shahji's reluctance to merge Kolhapur into India is mentioned in V. P. Menon, *The Story of the Integration of the Indian States* (Bombay: Orient Longman, 1956), pp. 199-200.

9. Vasantrao had served as president of the Kolhapur municipality in 1941.

their conceptions of where the real interests of Kolhapur lay as well as to notions of where their own chances for personal political advantage were likely to be greatest.

A series of events in 1947-1948—none of which were internal to the district—brought local, regional, and national politics together in a way that was to affect district politics in Kolhapur for the next two decades. Three of these "events" are particularly notable: (1) conflict over the merger of Kolhapur into India; (2) the assassination of Mahatma Gandhi; and (3) the creation of the PWP in Maharashtra.

Although negotiations over the entry of Kolhapur into Bombay State began even before independence, Shahji temporized. Pressures from the Kumbhar section of the Parishad in favor of the merger worked in the direction sought by the national government and, particularly, by Sardar Vallabhbhai Patel, Home Minister in the national government. As independence approached, Bagal evidenced increasing reluctance to support Kolhapur's entry into a Bombay State which he feared would be dominated by Bombay City and Gujarati interests. This position was made clear in early 1948 when Bagal's group held a special meeting at which a resolution was passed indicating that the Parishad wanted merger with a separate state of Maharashtra but not with Bombay State. They proposed the continuation of Kolhapur's distinctiveness as a separate political entity until Maharashtra was created. (Though it may now be too long after the fact for memories to be trustworthy, Kumbhar's supporters claim that his demand for the Home Ministry in Shahji's government had grown out of his desire to prevent Bagal from obstructing the efforts of the national government to bring about a merger of Kolhapur with Bombay.) Something of the character of this dispute can be seen in Bagal's attacks on Kumbhar at the time. He was quoted in a local newspaper as having said, Kumbhar "could not get power in [Kolhapur] state . . . and therefore he is trying to achieve the merger. . . . If he . . . would have gotten some powers he would not have started an agitation for the merger of Kolhapur state. He is communal minded. Jains and Lingayats hate the masses."[10]

With the assassination of Gandhi by a Brahman from Poona, arson and looting on a large scale occurred in Kolhapur (as in other parts of western Maharashtra), directed against the small

10. *Pudhari,* 1 January 1948.

Brahman community. Vasantrao Bagal and most leading Maratha politicians were not directly implicated, but Madhavrao Bagal and some outspoken non-Brahman figures were imprisoned. They were later released and formal charges were never brought against them.[11] However, these events provided the central government with the opportunity to abolish the prince's government in Kolhapur and to impose direct rule from New Delhi.[12] It was during this interim period that steps toward full integration of Kolhapur into Bombay State were completed. The series of events connected with the merger, and particularly the manner in which the arrests were carried out, left a bitterness that lingered for years among Maratha political activists in Kolhapur.[13]

The third "event" of the 1947-1948 period was the attempt of Patel's forces within the national Congress and in Bombay to gain control over the party organization at the national and state levels. Resistance in Maharashtra to this attempt at dominance by regional leaders associated with Patel came from Jedhe and More, who had organized their Peasants and Workers League within the Congress by 1947. When, in 1948, the national party promulgated a new constitution which called for an end to all autonomous "parties" within the Congress (a move aimed particularly against the Socialists[14]), Jedhe's League also came in for criticism. Rather than abolish the League, Jedhe and More withdrew from the

11. The reasons for holding Bagal and some of his co-workers in preventive detention have never been disclosed. They deny any complicity in the anti-Brahman violence.

12. Central rule was declared on March 19, 1948. A few days later, the administrator appointed by the central government to oversee the state banned all *taalim sanghs* (wrestlers associations) from operating because they were seen as "dangerous to the peace" of Kolhapur. It is widely intimated that some of the taalim sanghs which were backed by non-Brahman political leaders were particularly active in the anti-Brahman violence.

13. One informant active in politics at the time recalled how members of the municipality upset the centrally appointed administrator by passing a resolution in 1948 opposing merger of Kolhapur with Bombay. The administrator then superseded the municipality and called for new elections. He was surprised to see thirty-eight of the forty seats in the municipality go to members of the Praja Parishad. Despite this strong local opposition, plans for merger went ahead. Announcement of the final decision was made in February 1949, and Kolhapur was formally merged into Bombay State in August of that year.

14. Myron Weiner, *Party Politics in India* (Princeton: Princeton University Press, 1957), pp. 52-58.

Congress and formed the Peasants and Workers Party (PWP). Despite its leftist verbiage, that party took on some of the coloration of the earlier non-Brahman movement. In Kolhapur, as one might expect, the PWP received the backing of Bagal and his followers.[15]

Bagal's affinity for the PWP cleared the way for Kumbhar to become the chief leader of the Congress in the district. Kumbhar's personal friendships with Patel and Kher (by that time, again Bombay Chief Minister) made the task of gaining recognition for his leadership all the easier. As a result, upon formal merger of the state with Bombay in early 1949 and Kolhapur's conversion into a district, a District Congress Committee (DCC) was established with Kumbhar as its president. Since Kolhapur had not been part of India when national and provincial elections were held in British India in 1946, the national government nominated members to the Constituent Assembly (which doubled as a Provisional Parliament). In January 1950, Kumbhar was selected as one district representative to that body. Some informants contended that he also had a major voice in the selection of other MPs and MLAs. Among the latter was M. R. Shresti, then a close associate of Kumbhar's.[16]

Though Kumbhar gained control of the DCC and access to the Bombay State government, the emerging Maratha leadership of the regional Maharashtra Congress (particularly Bhausaheb Hiray, who became president of the MPCC in 1948) sought to establish a stronger Maratha base for the Congress in the predominantly Maratha district of Kolhapur. Since Bagal had taken with him to the PWP that section of the Praja Parishad consisting particularly of middle-class and urbanized Marathas (as well as a few non-Maratha sympathizers), Hiray turned to the political leadership he could find from among certain landlord and high-status Marathas in the state who had previously been associated with the princely regime. In V. T. Patil, for example, he had a prosperous lawyer who had served as president of the Kolhapur municipality from

15. In the statement calling upon his followers to enter the PWP, Bagal also encouraged supporters to work for Samyukta Maharashtra. *Pudhari*, 20 February 1949.

16. In addition to being nominated an MLA, Shresti served on the nominated District Local Board which replaced the Kolhapur Assembly. The centrally appointed administrator served as chairman and Shresti as "non-official" president of the Local Board. *Pudhari*, 30 July 1949.

1933-1938, as a member and then president of the Kolhapur State
Assembly from 1939 to 1948, and as a confidante of Rajaram.
Identified with V. T. Patil was Ganpatrao Jadhav, editor of the
leading local newspaper (founded in 1938 by persons associated
with the princely regime, including Patil) and a political activist in
his own right for the non-Brahman cause.[17] Jadhav was among
those nominated to represent Kolhapur in the Bombay State
Assembly.[18]

By the time of the first general election in 1952, therefore,
three major political groups had crystallized in Kolhapur politics.
One group appealed especially to lower-middle-class Marathas
(Maratha petty landowners in rural Kolhapur; the working-class
and lower white-collar non-Brahmans in the city). This group
formed the core of the following for the PWP.[19] The Kumbhar
group dominated the local Congress organization and maintained
its greatest following among the small-town and rural Lingayats
and Jains in the northeastern part of the district. The third major
group consisted of those non-Brahmans (mainly Marathas) formerly identified with the princely regime who were now politically
"available" to the state Congress party, though their relations with
the local Congress were cool.

While Kumbhar nominally controlled the DCC, when it came
to distributing party nominations for MLA and MP in 1952
pressures were exerted by top Maratha leaders in the MPCC on
behalf of the members of what we shall call the "princely"
Maratha group. Thus, when decisions about nominees for the
eleven MLA seats from the district were completed, a majority
were associated with Kumbhar, but several tickets went to men
who were not Kumbhar's allies, including V. T. Patil and Ganpatrao Jadhav. In the subsequent election both Jadhav (running

17. For a time, Jadhav had been associated with leaders of the non-
Brahman movement in Bombay like Bhaskarrao Jadhav, Keshavrao Jedhe,
and, particularly, Dinkarrao Javalkar. In this connection, see Gail Omvedt,
"Non-Brahmans and Nationalists in Poona," *Economic and Political Weekly,*
Annual Number, February 1974, esp. pp. 205-209.

18. Jadhav insists, however, that he, Shresti, and a prominent local lawyer
were nominated to the Bombay Assembly by the district administrator
without the matter being referred to Kumbhar. Interview, Ganpatrao Jadhav,
26 September 1970.

19. Factionalism within the PWP was evident as early as 1950. In 1951
Bagal resigned from the party ("in disgust with groupism"). *Pudhari,* 4 July
1951.

for MLA from Kolhapur City) and Kumbhar (running for MP) were defeated, the latter by a noted educator running as an independent with PWP support.[20] Informants suggest that these defeats reflected groupism within the Congress, but it should also be recognized that: (1) the Congress was still searching for an electoral base in the district; (2) the PWP continued to have a large following; and (3) the administrative regime which had operated after Gandhi's assassination had rendered the Bombay and national governments distasteful to many local political activists, particularly in Kolhapur City.

Despite electoral setbacks in 1952,[21] the Kumbhar group continued securely in control of the district's Congress machinery. Kumbhar himself remained president of the DCC until 1956, and when he stepped down he chose Shresti as his successor. For the most part, Kumbhar's nominees were recognized by the MPCC in 1957 but, as elsewhere in western Maharashtra, the Congress suffered a rout at the hands of the Samyukta Maharashtra Samiti, losing all of the MLA seats in Kolhapur district. Samyukta Maharashtra was a cause to which the PWP could rally an enormous following. Indeed, Bagal reemerged at the forefront of those supporting the movement in the district.

In 1957, curiously enough, the Congress, which had not been strong enough previously in the rural area to capture power in the District Local Board,[22] managed to obtain control of that body. Kumbhar's choice for president was an elderly Maratha associated with his group; the man chosen as vice-president was a young, well-educated Maratha from a princely background, Udaisingh Gaikwad. Gaikwad was encouraged to enter politics in the contest for the local body by D. S. (Balasaheb) Desai, a figure of growing importance in Maharashtra politics.[23]

20. A third candidate was Vasantrao Bagal, who stood as a Socialist, a party with little following in the district.

21. In all, the Congress, with approximately 38 percent of the vote in the district, won five of the eleven MLA seats. PWP candidates were elected in four contests, and two seats went to independents.

22. In 1952, the PWP had put together a majority which enabled it to control the District Local Board for most of the term of that body.

23. Gaikwad came from a family of *inamdars* with hereditary claims on the revenues of five villages. His grandfather had served in Rajaram's ministry about 1927. When Balasaheb Desai, who came from neighboring Satara district, was a student in Kolhapur he had served as a tutor to the children of the Gaikwad family. Desai's personal contacts with the family continued in the years thereafter.

THE EXTENSION OF COOPERATIVE INSTITUTIONS

It is from about this time, or even a little earlier, that one can date the emergence of cooperative institutions as major arenas of political as well as economic activity in Kolhapur district. The character of the soil and the agricultural traditions of the region lent themselves particularly well to heavy investment in the commercial development of sugarcane. In the early 1950s, Bhausaheb Hiray took a leading role in encouraging locally prominent people in Kolhapur and elsewhere to interest themselves in starting cooperative sugar factories. As a result, the ground was laid for the creation of five cooperative sugar factories in the years from 1955 through 1960. (A private factory already operated near Kolhapur City.) The pattern followed in some cases (though not all) was to recognize established political leaders as the organizers of these factories.

Kumbhar was one of the first to establish a factory, the Panchaganga. It was registered in 1955 but did not begin actual operation until 1959 because difficulties were encountered in raising local share capital.[24] Since its establishment, Panchaganga has provided an important economic and political base for Kumbhar. Kumbhar also extended his political support to the Kore family, merchants in the raw sugar market in Kolhapur City, who established a factory on the Warna river.[25] (Like Kumbhar, the Kores are Lingayats.) Although there have been occasional contests for seats on the board of the latter factory and intermittent efforts from political leaders outside the territory of the

24. While share capital might be raised from any sugar-growing landowners in the territory designated as the base for the factory, only a portion of the potential suppliers in an area can be accommodated as members. The allocation of memberships to some farmers but not to others allows favoritism to be shown toward friends or supporters of the organizers of the factory. It is charged, for example, that Kumbhar's factory relied disproportionately on Jain and Lingayat landowners in the designated area. This charge should be balanced against the fact that there was considerable difficulty in the very early years eliciting membership interest from any quarter. That situation changed dramatically as the factories proved to be profitable to farmers.

25. Before the introduction of cooperative sugar factories, most local production of cane went into *jaggery* (unrefined sugar) processed in a more primitive fashion than the various grades of sugar available through modern cooperative facilities. Kolhapur has been one of the long-time centers of western India for marketing jaggery.

factory to affect the outcome of its elections, the family and its associates have continued to play the predominant role at Warnanagar.

Those two factories are generally identified with Kumbhar in political terms, though the Warna factory is not so much a personal political base as is Kumbhar's own Panchaganga. On the other hand, the Bhogawati factory, which was registered at about the same time as Warna and began crushing operations in 1957, was associated from the outset with the former princely wing of the Congress. The factory is dominated by a highly urbanized but rural-based family, the Kaulaukar-Patils. The elder brother has been chairman of the factory board for many years; the second brother, Balasaheb, was a major organizer of the factory. He also has been active in the Congress since he received his LL.B. in 1949. (Balasaheb entered the Congress with V. T. Patil, served on the District Development Board from 1952 to 1957, contested unsuccessfully for MLA in 1952 and 1967, served as a member of the DCC Executive from 1952 to 1962, and was an MPCC member from 1952 to 1970.[26])

After these first three factories were organized, efforts were initiated to establish two others: Bidri and Kumbhi-Kasari. V. T. Patil played a crucial role in establishing the former and was its first chairman. The factory soon became embroiled in factionalism. The factory's cane area, which spans four politically and socially diverse talukas, provided a crucial testing ground for the Kumbhar group against its Maratha opponents within the Congress. In the process, it was not unusual to find alignment of the Kumbhar group with persons who were PWP sympathizers, even though from the past histories of the two groups one might not have expected them to be drawn together as allies. Since 1962, when the first elections to the board of management of the factory were held, regular changes have followed from a "multiperson" game of constantly shifting alignments. In Kumbhi-Kasari, the contest has not involved the Kumbhar group so much as it has been a struggle for domination of factory resources between what might be called a "nonpartisan" group of Maratha sugar growers

26. Along with his other cooperative activities, Balasaheb is chairman of the Maharashtra Engineering Society Ltd. of Kolhapur, a statewide organization which acts as a cooperative marketing agent for various engineering products, including Yamaha power tillers.

against warring Maratha leaders within the Congress who have attempted to play a major role in the factory.[27]

In addition to the sugar factories and ancillary enterprises which some of them run, like dairies, poultries, and colleges,[28] Kolhapur has an active infrastructure of primary (village) agricultural credit societies and district and taluka cooperative organizations. The most important cooperative marketing institution in the district is the Shetkari Sahakari Sangh (the Farmers' Cooperative Organization). Started with the encouragement of the princely regime in the late 1930s, the Sangh during much of its formative life was dominated by Tatyasaheb Mohite, a dedicated man who kept the organization's operations out of politics.[29] The Sangh handles such inputs as fertilizers, pesticides, seeds, and oil engines, which are marketed either directly to farmers or through credit arrangements with village or taluka-level cooperative credit societies. As in Poona district, taluka purchase and sales unions are not subordinate to the district body but operate autonomously. In addition, the Sangh maintains branches of its own throughout the district and functions either through those branches or as a middleman for the taluka sanghs on a strictly commercial basis.

Institutions like the district's DLDB and DCCB have been much more directly involved than the Sangh in politics. The DLDB was created in 1960. Prior to that time, the Bombay State Land Mortgage Bank maintained two branches in the district, which were operated directly from Bombay City for the purpose

27. The private factory and the five cooperatives are not the only ones presently having an impact on Kolhapur district. A sixth cooperative factory located in Sangli district includes territory (and members) from Kolhapur. Two more factories were also authorized subsequently by the state and national governments. In one case, as we shall see, the active interest of Kumbhar in starting the factory was short-circuited in favor of a rival political leader; in the other instance, V. K. Chavan-Patil, chairman of the Kolhapur DLDB and then MLA, was designated the official "promoter" of the factory.

28. Warna runs a college and Bidri also has proposed opening one. In the latter case, there was a disagreement between the factory management and a major educational institution founded by V. T. Patil over the location of the college and the managerial auspices under which the college should operate.

29. This does not mean that several politicians have not served on the board (including a member of the leading Communist party family in the district), but it does mean that the Sangh has not been involved as a political arena in district politics nor have politicians used the Sangh as a major

of granting long-term loans to farmers for capital investment in their land. Leaders of the district started the Kolhapur body to get around the problem of constant referral to Bombay. In recent years, the DLDB has been a base for the activities of one major political faction within the Maratha wing of the Congress, a faction which allegedly turned the bank's resources to its own personal and political benefit.

A DCCB was established in Kolhapur in 1938, but it served only four of the state's talukas. The Bombay State Central Cooperative Bank served the nine others through its branches. It was not until 1958-1959 that authority for short-term agricultural finance was transferred to a reorganized DCCB. While that reorganization was taking place, a nominated board was placed in authority and directors were appointed by the state government to represent local interests. In making the nominations, Y. B. Chavan (then Chief Minister) gave many of the positions to Congressmen, though the first chairman was an ex-judge. From among the other members, Udaisingh Gaikwad was selected as vice-chairman, and in the following year V. K. Chavan-Patil, a Congressman from Chandgad, became chairman. Chavan-Patil not only dominated the cooperative and political structures in his home taluka during the next decade, but he came to hold a range of other important positions in the district. He served as chairman of the DLDB for a time as well as being MLA from his taluka from 1962 to 1972. Counted a Kumbhar supporter at the start, he was one of several Kumbhar associates nominated to the DCCB board. However, in 1960, at the time of the first regular elections to the board (by representatives elected from eligible primary credit societies), the Kumbhar and anti-Kumbhar factions were about equal in size in that body. The anti-Kumbhar faction was ultimately successful in winning over Chavan-Patil to their side. As the price of their "control" of the board, they made him chairman of the bank.

What should be stressed here is that by 1962 to speak of the bases of political power in Kolhapur district (as in Poona) meant to refer not only to those persons with formal power in state or local legislative bodies, or to men with a voice in the District Congress party, but also to those most active in the economic institutions of the district—institutions which drew upon governmental financing organized under the guise of cooperative economic activity. At the same time, it should be emphasized that the

opportunity structure. Informants insist that this was the result of the "non-partisan" traditions built up by the previous management.

introduction of these new institutions into district political life both opened the district to new channels of political opportunity and had the consequence of linking local political ambition to national and state policies with respect to rural investment. While public resources have been wasted in some cases—for example, when an unnecessarily large number of employees are recruited by a sugar factory in order to win electoral support for the incumbent board, or when credit is extended to poor credit risks to gain political leverage—the changes wrought in rural life in Kolhapur during these years also have been significant.

An Era of Unchecked Ambition

As we noted earlier, the Congress won the election for the District Local Board in 1957. The post of vice-chairman went to Udaisingh Gaikwad, who, though from the Maratha elite, had entered Congress with Kumbhar's acquiescence and had served a term as secretary of the DCC. By late 1960, however, with the creation of Maharashtra, the strength of the Maratha section of the Kolhapur Congress was being reinforced by the accretion to the party of persons who formerly had been members of opposition parties, most notably the PWP.

The issue of how to deal with these new elements in the party contributed to Kumbhar's difficulties not only at the local level but with Y. B. Chavan, among others. For some time, while Kumbhar's associate Shresti was serving as DCC president, a quarrel had been simmering between the two men over the kinds of opportunities which should be provided to new entrants into the party. Shresti reportedly advocated an "open door" policy, while Kumbhar insisted on the need to stick with "tested" party workers. Similar views were expressed by Kumbhar toward what he regarded as the "opportunistic" strategy advocated by Chavan in state politics. His strongly held views brought Kumbhar into conflict with the state leadership, represented locally by Balasaheb Desai. Desai held a special role in the state Congress with respect to Kolhapur because he was charged by Chavan with looking after the interests of the state Congress organization in the district. On occasion, he served as a rallying point in opposition to Kumbhar, particularly for Maratha Congressmen.[30]

30. It has been the practice of the MPCC to assign a person of ministerial stature to look after the organizational problems of each district. Since Kolhapur did not have a minister of its own, Desai, from neighboring Satara,

With the passage of time, the importance of the caste dimension began to fade. What had been at the heart of earlier caste-related conflicts that had alienated Kumbhar from other Congress members was the understanding that people had had of the appropriate support base for the party and the political advantages likely to flow to individual political leaders under different recruitment patterns. Once the goal of maximizing support from all sections of the population had been established, caste was no longer so direct a source of conflict, though political actors still used caste-based appeals on occasion. Indeed, after 1960, individual non-Maratha Congressmen continued to exercise considerable influence in some parts of the district and, consequently, in the politics of the District Congress as a whole. For example, Shresti and B. B. Khanjire, a prominent Jain from Ichalkaranji, became actively identified with the opposition to Kumbhar, and they did so not merely as pawns of Maratha leaders but as powerful figures in their own right. Until his voluntary retirement from politics in 1965, in fact, Shresti was sometimes identified as the premier leader of the heterogeneous political group opposed to Kumbhar.

The conflict over qualifications for important party and government positions was at least as much a matter of personal ambition as a concern with ethical, caste, or organizational issues. Kumbhar's continued insistence that recognition be given to "old party workers" meant, in practice, granting special weight not only to non-Marathas but also to those few northeastern talukas where the Congress had a longer history. It was those areas, of course, where Kumbhar had his own electoral support base and his cooperative institutions.

By promoting representation from other talukas and from Marathas in the northeastern talukas, Kumbhar's opponents in the state and district party may have had the greater and more immediate interests of the party at heart. As late as 1960, they claim, the Congress organization was still relatively weak in the majority of talukas and it was necessary to establish a more effective organizational base throughout the district. In the process of doing so, however, any pretense of maintaining party discipline was soon abandoned. Instead, the Congress became a

---

played that role. As it turned out, Desai's interventions were by no means of a purely disinterested character.

gathering place for every ambitious individual in the district. Many of those who took advantage of opportunities offered by the state and national governments and by the party were interested in their own personal gain rather than in any benefits or costs their activities might bring to the party or to the larger political system.

Despite growing tension in the party, Kumbhar was still able to elect one of his own men as president of the DCC as late as 1959. The vote in that case was fifty-eight for Kumbhar's candidate as against thirty-one for the candidate of the opposing group, Balasaheb Kaulaukar-Patil. A Kumbhar supporter became treasurer of the DCC, and Chavan-Patil (still a Kumbhar man at the time), party secretary. When dissident elements in the DCC called for the replacement of Kumbhar's man as president of the District Local Board in 1960, Kumbhar publicly went along with their desire to promote Gaikwad to the presidency, but he or some of his key lieutenants threw their support covertly to Gaikwad's opponent. As a result, though Congress leaders thought they could count on thirty-nine of the fifty-four members, Gaikwad, the party's official candidate, lost the election twenty-eight to twenty-five. [31] Shortly thereafter, a complaint was lodged with the MPCC by Shresti, Gaikwad, and their associates against Kumbhar, demanding that the DCC be dissolved and that an ad hoc body be established in its place. No action was taken at the state level, however, to punish the Kumbhar forces. Nevertheless, from that point on, Kumbhar's grasp on local party leadership clearly began to decline.

Since the Kumbhar forces had won the Congress organizational elections of 1959, they managed to retain nominal control of the District Congress through 1962. This de jure control was vitiated by the increasing refusal of the MPCC leadership (apparently under pressure from Balasaheb Desai) to recognize the electoral recommendations of the Kolhapur DCC. Thus, only a minority of Kumbhar's suggestions for MLA and MP were conceded in 1962. Instead, those identified with "the Shresti group" received a majority of party endorsements for the new Maharashtra State Legislative Assembly. Despite such conflicts within the local party, the flood of popular enthusiasm for the Congress in the wake of the creation of Maharashtra and the resultant disorganization of the opposition made it possible for Congress candi-

---

31. Six former Samyukta Maharashtra Samiti members had crossed over to the Congress just before those elections. *Pudhari,* 26 October 1960.

dates to win all but one seat in the district. The exception was the MLA seat from Kolhapur City, which the Congress has not yet captured in the five state legislative elections since independence.[32]

In the elections for the new zilla parishad in June 1962, a major conflict emerged between Shresti and Kumbhar over the distribution of tickets. Kumbhar persisted in his demand that only old workers of the Congress be recognized, while Shresti advocated a strategy of pursuing likely winners. Given the conflicting recommendations of the two groups, the MPCC was in a position to assert its own preferences, which coincided mainly with Shresti's. Only about a quarter of the Congress nominees were Kumbhar's choices. Although a few Kumbhar men proceeded to stand as independents, and several were elected, the Kumbhar group as a whole (both those elected on Congress tickets and those who ran as independents) constituted little more than a dozen members of the approximately sixty-one eligible to vote for zilla parishad officials.[33] Rather than press their claims, the Kumbhar forces agreed to support Dinkarrao Yadav for president and Balasaheb Kaulaukar-Patil for vice-president of the zilla parishad and they were easily elected. The latter had been active in the Congress since 1952. Yadav, the choice for president (a choice made, in large part, by Balasaheb Desai), was a newcomer to the Congress.

Unlike Kaulaukar-Patil, whose association with the princely Maratha group was clear, Yadav was from a lower-status urbanized Maratha family. His father had served as a clerk in the service of the princely regime and also had farmed the family's thirteen acres. Yadav joined Bagal's Praja Parishad in 1944. His personal style was very much in keeping with Bagal's populist Maratha approach.[34] Along with Bagal, Yadav was implicated in the anti-Brahman riots following Gandhi's assassination and was jailed for more than a year at the time. He subsequently became a leader of the PWP in the district; he served a term as a member of the District Local Board (1952-1957) and as chairman of the District

32. For most of the past twenty years, the seat has been held by T. S. Karkhanis, a CKP associated with Bagal's Praja Parishad in the 1940s. He had been with the PWP since its organization in the district.

33. Of the sixty-one, forty-two were listed as Congress members at the time of the vote, eight as independents and eleven from the Samyukta Maharashtra Samiti (mainly the PWP). *Sakal,* 12 August 1962.

34. Yadav's populist attitudes may have struck a responsive chord in Balasaheb Desai, who had established a reputation for exploiting such appeals himself.

School Board (1953-1955). Yadav took a leading role in the Samyukta Maharashtra agitations in 1957 but by 1960 was attracted to the Congress by the increasing openness of the party to Marathas of his inclinations. Yadav's detachment from past Congress party controversies was an advantage to him at the time of the 1962 elections, as was his well-known compassion for the lower classes. In addition, the fact that he came from Shirol taluka, an area where Kumbhar was dominant in the cooperative field and from which he had just been elected MLA, was seen as an advantage to the anti-Kumbhar group. Yadav's supporters hoped that he would serve as a magnet for the taluka-level political opposition to Kumbhar.

The anti-Kumbhar effort was carried forward in late 1962 when new DCC elections were held. Both factions submitted lists to the MPCC of members they claimed to have enrolled. On the basis of what the Kumbhar group later insisted were inflated membership figures, the anti-Kumbhar faction elected B. B. Khanjire, the Jain leader from Ichalkaranji, as District Congress president. The Kumbhar group insisted that the procedures of their opponents had been improper, and they appealed the action to the MPCC president, Vinayakrao Patil. When that appeal brought no results, they turned to the All-India Congress Committee (AICC). Again, at the national level, no action was taken. After this failure to elicit support from within the party, the matter was taken to court. Following a period of legal maneuver which lasted well over a year, the court found in favor of the Kumbhar group. Rather than conform to the court ruling and accept the continuation of major Kumbhar influence in the party, the MPCC simply abolished the old DCC and designated an ad hoc DCC in its place. Chavan-Patil was installed as president of that body and Gaikwad as vice-president. With the painfully slow processing of complaints and the drawn-out legal procedures involved, the appointed body was not officially installed until May 1965. It remained in office for about three years.

For all practical purposes, then, the Kumbhar group ceased to be a major force within the Congress after 1963, but its decline came at a time when the Congress was no longer a central source of political power in the district. Kumbhar and his followers continued to play important roles in cooperative institutions and to have a major place in the local government institutions of two or three important talukas. From these bases, henceforth, they could assure themselves a continuing voice in district politics. Even more than in Poona, the Congress had been converted from a directive force in the affairs of the district into simply one among many political arenas where local power wielders might iron out their differences or struggle for additional political resources.

The retreat of the Kumbhar faction from the local Congress organization did not spell the end of factionalism within the majority group; it merely provided the occasion for opening each political event within the party to a series of purely personal quarrels for ascendancy among individual leaders. Furthermore, to play the political game within the majority group, contestants were frequently in need of displaying their strength in non-party arenas. Ironically, this sometimes meant cooperation in those arenas with Kumbhar and with persons from other non-Congress party groups, including the PWP. Because of growing rifts among District Congress leaders, for example, a supporter of Kumbhar was actually elected to the DCCB chairmanship for a year in 1966. By late 1969, however, only two of the twenty-one seats on that bank board were held by persons easily identifiable as Kumbhar men. Yet the quarrels continued. In that year, the other members of the majority group agreed, without too much dissent, to the selection of Udaisingh Gaikwad as chairman, since he was president of the DCC (a position assumed by him in 1968) and a long-time director of the DCCB. But by 1971 he, too, had been ousted.

The DLDB has operated under even more heavily politicized circumstances than the DCCB. Organized in 1960, it was chaired by three men during the next decade, including Chavan-Patil, who served in 1960-1961 and again in 1970-1972. Its elections were manipulated in such a way as to minimize opposition. They were postponed on various excuses and when they were held the style of conducting elections came in for severe criticism from the opponents of those who dominated the board.[35]

While these battles within and between cooperative institutions went on, other organizations, which elsewhere in Mahara-

---

35. In fact, there was disagreement among interviewees over whether scheduled elections even had been held for the board of the bank in 1969. Members of the board insisted such elections had been held, but opponents (both inside and outside the Congress) asserted that they had not. The discrepancy arises from the charge that nomination procedures were so engineered as to prevent opposition candidates from challenging the incumbents.

shtra were marked by levels of high conflict (for example, the zilla parishad), were operating rather placidly. This was possible because each arena seemed to stimulate its own particular set of personal conflicts. The DCC occasionally tried to direct the flow of traffic among these various arenas but was very cautious about intervening because of its own organizational difficulties. Where one leader dominated a taluka, that area was relatively peaceful, and this increased the leader's flexibility at the district level, but such cases were exceptional. Most leaders seemed to be maneuvering constantly just to maintain their political and economic positions within the ever-shifting balance of power among the district's political elite.

THE 1967 ELECTIONS AND AFTER

Into this cauldron of personal quarrels and fights for economic dominance a "traditional" issue was injected in the early 1960s. While he still was Chief Minister of Maharashtra, Y. B. Chavan had rekindled the wrath of the people of Kolhapur against the Maharashtra and national governments by allowing Shahji, who had faded from public sight since the merger of Kolhapur into Bombay State, to adopt an heir (his own grandson). This was contrary to the agreement that allegedly had been made with the widow of Rajaram at the time of Shahji's accession. Demonstrations were organized when this happened, and Chavan made a critical mistake in remarking that the dispute over a "torn *gadi*" (royal seat) was of little moment. In his view, princes were no longer important, particularly since the national government had declared its intention to abolish their privy purses.

Opposition groups led by the PWP skillfully seized upon Chavan's comments and organized a campaign in 1965 that focused on the demand that "justice be done" to Padmaraje, the daughter of Rajaram. The women of Kolhapur City, in particular, were drawn into the cause, and embers of Kolhapuri nationalism long dormant were rekindled. Chavan's earlier remarks were played up by leaders of the campaign and held to constitute a slur on the history of the state and particularly on the memory of Shahu Maharaj. Chavan's personal popularity—which had never been high in the district because of a feeling that Kolhapur had been inadequately recognized in state politics—fell even further, and along with it fell the fortunes of the Congress. The opposition capitalized on the issue by making Vijaymala (Rajaram's second wife) its candidate for Parliament in 1967 in one of the two seats assigned to the district. The Congress countered by choosing as its nominee a previously non-political army general whose family came from the district. The contest received considerable publicity and substantial resources were put into it by the state Congress, but the party was not able to overcome its defensive posture.

Under these special circumstances and given Kumbhar's institutional strength in parts of the district, the MPCC was cautious about ending its association with him altogether.[36] As a sop to Kumbhar, therefore, MLA seats were extended to him and to a supporter (for a seat reserved to the Scheduled Castes). One of Kumbhar's top men, Shankarrao Mane, was also made the nominee for Parliament from the area centered around Kolhapur City. The remaining Congress MLA nominations went to persons in good standing with the anti-Kumbhar group.

Because of the Vijaymala factor, the equivocal position of the Kumbhar group, and the conflicts within the Congress, as well as rising prices and a general dissatisfaction with the prevailing economic situation, the Congress lost the MP seat from the rural area (to Vijaymala), and four MLA seats went to PWP candidates. One of these was the seat held by Udaisingh Gaikwad, whose defeat was blamed in part on the intervention of the Kore family, which allegedly resented attempts on Gaikwad's part to gain personal influence in the operation of "their" cooperative sugar factory.

For the zilla parishad elections, which followed later in 1967, few Kumbhar supporters received Congress tickets. Among the fifty-four persons elected were twenty-two non-Congressmen— eleven independents (not all of whom were Kumbhar sympathizers[37]) and eleven from a PWP-dominated electoral front. When

36. Until the 1969 split in the national Congress, Kumbhar was helped by his ties to Morarji Desai, a prominent figure in the national government, and to Congress President, Nijalingappa (a former Chief Minister of Mysore and a Lingayat). One state politician suggested that even after 1969 reluctance to move against Kumbhar reflected a fear on the part of the state Congress leadership that they would offend Lingayats both in Kolhapur and elsewhere in Maharashtra. It is interesting that the Lingayat MLA from Poona district who served from 1967 to 1972 viewed Kumbhar with considerable admiration.

37. Few Kumbhar supporters even tried to get Congress tickets. Indeed, one who did wrote directly to the MPCC and was rather surprised when the ticket was given to him, even though he was a long-time party worker and had held prominent positions at the district level.

the election for president was held in August, Dinkarrao Yadav was reelected, but only by a margin of twenty-eight to twenty-four over a Kumbhar lieutenant, Dinkarrao Mudrale, who received the support of opposition groups and independents as well as a few dissident Congressmen. The men selected for vice-president and committee chairmen were all from the anti-Kumbhar group, but none was an especially prominent figure at the district level in either the Congress or the cooperative movement. As a matter of course, however, when the DCC was reconstituted in 1968, after years of contention over the legality of the 1962 elections, all four of the zilla parishad's main office-holders (president, vice-president, and the two committee chairmen) were included on the DCC Executive Committee along with the non-Kumbhar Congress MLAs and a sprinkling of taluka-level leaders who had advanced their careers principally through cooperative institutions.

The continued conflict in the DCC was evident in the election for Member of the Legislative Council (MLC) held in 1970 from the Kolhapur local bodies constituency. As in Poona, this election was a major test of the state organization during the period of national division within the Congress. The incumbent, who came from Satara district, had established a good personal reputation in Kolhapur since his first election in 1964, but his candidacy blocked the ambitions of others. Some of these employed the claim that he was an "outsider" as a means of enhancing their own opportunities for office and as a way of stirring feeling against the manner in which non-Kolhapurians (and particularly persons from neighboring Satara and Sangli districts) regularly intervened in the politics of the district from their positions in the state government or in the MPCC.

As we noted in the last chapter (see pp. 78-81), the 1970 contest for MLC from Kolhapur was allegedly involved in a bargain struck between Balasaheb Desai and Vasantrao Patil that involved Poona district as the other piece in the exchange. The arrangement was supposed to assure Desai's support to the Kolhapur incumbent—a man linked to Patil. However, a group of Kolhapur men friendly to Desai did not accept this arrangement. Instead, they encouraged the vice-president of the Kolapur municipality (a member of the tiny Samyukta Socialist Party unit in the city) to defect from his party and enter the contest with their support as well as the backing of the PWP. In addition to these two candidates, there were three others: the SSP's own official candidate; a Kumbhar candidate (who was a former MLA);

and a dissident from the PWP. Since no nominee received a majority of the first preference votes, the second preferences of persons choosing the lesser candidates were counted and the official Congress nominee scraped through by a margin of 118 to 109 over the unofficial Desai candidate.[38]

Until this time, the Balsaheb Desai group seemed to be on the ascendancy in the district. The group included the president of the zilla parishad, the leader of the relatively ineffectual party unit in Kolhapur City (a relative of Desai's) and, somewhat less clearly, Udaisingh Gaikwad. However, when Desai fell into disfavor with Y. B. Chavan after these events, local Congressmen quickly disassociated themselves from him.[39]

TOWARD ROUTINIZATION OF DISTRICT POLITICS

The state and national leadership of the Congress moved in the period after 1967 to neutralize the effects of the Padmaraje movement in Kolhapur. Their major action was to choose the son of the leader of the Padmaraje movement as one of the party's candidates for the two parliamentary seats from Kolhapur district in 1971. The nominee had spent a decade out of India (mainly in Germany), returning to Kolhapur only in 1964; he had no previous political credentials. In selecting this relatively young man (he was forty-two), Chavan, who played a key role in the decision, passed over the incumbent MP, Shankarrao Mane.[40]

If the choice in this case was a man with little political history, the nominee for the other MP seat, Dattajirao Kadam, was of a very different stripe. His emergence may have signaled the start of a basic change in the style of Kolhapur politics. Operating essentially from the prosperous textile mill town of Ichalkaranji (where his cooperative institutions literally face those of Ratnappa

38. In addition to Desai, this contest allegedly saw the involvement of a minister from Sangli district who had an interest in seeing his rival in that district (the MPCC President) suffer a personal setback.

39. For further details on the aftermath of these incidents, see chapter 5, p. 00.

40. Mane had voted for V. V. Giri, Mrs. Gandhi's candidate, in the Presidential election of 1969. Mrs. Gandhi's leadership position in early 1971 was too uncertain to allow her to intervene successfully with the MPCC on Mane's behalf, but she subsequently brought him back to New Delhi as Commissioner for Scheduled Castes and Scheduled Tribes.

Kumbhar), Kadam had become a major force in that city's cooperative movement in the previous decade. Whereas Kumbhar drew his strength from rural activities—his sugar factory, his rural cooperative bodies, and those local government institutions in Hatkanangale and Shirol talukas which his men ran—Kadam's influence was rooted in Ichalkaranji's urban institutions. He and his associates had initiated a large-scale cooperative weaving and spinning mill as well as an urban cooperative bank during the preceding fifteen years.

Equally significant, however, was the political style of the municipal group with which Kadam was associated. It included a Brahman member of the Rajya Sabha, A. G. Kulkarni. (Kulkarni was based mainly in Sangli district, where he was associated with Vasantrao Patil, but he also had a long-term economic and family interest in the development of Ichalkaranji.[41]) B. B. Khanjire, the Jain MLA from Ichalkaranji, was also a prominent figure in the cooperatives there and worked closely with Kadam.

In a manner that is an interesting case of contemporary institutionalization, Kadam and his associates had put together an economic and political "power structure" in Ichalkaranji that was formalized locally under the title of "the Civic Board." That Board assigned positions in urban cooperative institutions, in the local unit of the Congress party, and in the municipality. These positions were allocated on a rotational basis, which tended to reduce conflict and moderate ambition.[42] The Board remained relatively aloof from the internal quarrels of the District Congress. They protected their own economic interests when such interests could be affected by the DCCB, but because of the urban and industrial nature of those interests, their activities were directed principally at exercising influence in state and national politics

41. Kulkarni's father had been *diwan* (Prime Minister) of the feudatory state of Ichalkaranji for about twenty-five years before his retirement in 1935. The father encouraged his four sons to take an interest in industrial development, particularly in the spinning and weaving industry. The Kulkarni brothers made investments in such industries both in Ichalkaranji and in the city of Sangli, which was capital of another Brahman princely state before independence.

42. That moderating aspect also may have been a function of the thriving economic situation of the city, for the opportunities available in the economy allowed many people to share in the economic expansion which the city was experiencing. It is not clear that such a political strategy would have been as successful in a less expansionary context.

(concerning policies with respect to such matters as industrial licensing procedures) rather than in district politics.

In the late 1960s, Kadam began to expand his ambitional sphere into the rural area by helping to organize a sugar factory in Shirol taluka. He received the help of key leaders at the state and national levels against Kumbhar, who had been trying to organize a factory in the same area for a number of years. Kadam's selection in 1971 as a parliamentary candidate by the MPCC, at a time when Indira Gandhi was publicly avowing a commitment to greater equalization of wealth, actually served instead to demonstrate the growing strength of economic interests concentrated in a few hands in the region.

It is not surprising that Kumbhar worked against the two official Congress candidates for MP in 1971. What may be surprising is that the MPCC was so slow to punish his behavior. Leaders of the DCC brought complaints to the MPCC leadership, but the MPCC took considerable time to go through the formal motions of requesting an explanation from Kumbhar. Rather than dissimulating, Kumbhar argued openly that the quality of candidates offered by the Congress was not worthy of his support. Final action was still pending against him at the time MLA nominations were made in early 1972. By that time events had again conspired to continue, and actually to improve, Kumbhar's political standing in Kolhapur.

Indira Gandhi had been too weak in 1971 to force her choices upon the MPCC, but her national stature was so great by early 1972 that it was rather difficult for the MPCC leadership to resist her determined support for particular candidates. By then, a degree of division had also surfaced in the MPCC which allowed the national Congress leadership to intervene more easily in state and local choices. The state factions which were beginning to emerge made themselves felt only indirectly in Kolhapur, but their activation elsewhere did provide an opening which forced a number of decisions about MLA tickets to be raised to the national level. In the case of Kumbhar and a second ticket (from Gadhinglaj taluka), the MPCC left the seats open pending a decision about the action to be taken against Kumbhar because of his behavior in the 1971 parliamentary elections. However, with the help of some of Mrs. Gandhi's party lieutenants and with the intervention of Shankarrao Mane, Kumbhar and a long-time associate were given the tickets for the two MLA seats in question.[43] This did not restore harmony elsewhere in the district, for three Congress nominees were subsequently defeated by dissidents (including a man backed as an independent by Balasaheb Kaulaukar-Patil, who himself had been denied a ticket).[44]

Oddly enough, a new spirit of compromise seemed to arise after the elections among a few leaders, such as Udaisingh Gaikwad, Kumbhar, and Kadam. In that spirit and also possibly as part of an effort to wield greater state power, Vasantrao Patil in his role as MPCC President abolished the old DCC and created an ad hoc party body in Kolhapur in early 1972. He appointed as its president Anantrao Bhide, chairman of the Deccan Spinning and Weaving Mills in Ichalkaranji. (Bhide, like Kulkarni, is a Brahman.[45])

In preparation for the zilla parishad elections of 1972, a District Election Committee was created which gave substantial weight to the Kumbhar forces. Some of the anti-Kumbhar activists subsequently expressed dismay at the extent of favor shown by Bhide to Kumbhar and his followers. Not only did Kumbhar receive a substantial bloc of nominations for the zilla parishad, but when the time came to select officers Dinkarrao Mudrale was made vice-president of the body. One set of committee chairmanships was also given to a man inclined to the Kumbhar group.

Furthermore, in party organization elections held later in 1972, the spirit of compromise was carried forward by setting a rule that no one who was an office-bearer in other major institutions should hold posts in the DCC. As a result, Bhide was

43. While the national leadership accommodated Kumbhar, V. K. Chavan-Patil was dropped as the MLA from Chandgad by the MPCC. In large measure, this action was taken against him because of pending charges about his mismanagement of several cooperative societies and a bitter dispute over the organization of the sugar factory proposed for his constituency.

44. This show of strength resulted in Kaulaukar-Patil's being welcomed back to the Congress later in 1972. He continued to regard himself as a loyal Congressman.

45. The appointment of Bhide involved consultations by Vasantrao Patil with Kadam and A. G. Kulkarni, but few other local politicians were apparently involved in these deliberations. Bhide's selection and continuing role in Kolhapur politics strengthened Patil's own position in the various arenas of state politics by adding important Kolhapur support to his resource base within the party.

installed as president, an ironic choice in Kolhapur, that most non-Brahman of districts. Yet, in the circumstances, Bhide's selection held out the promise of pacifying quarrels among contending local groups and bringing to the Congress some of the routinized behaviors characteristic of Ichalkaranji's orderly political life.

Similarly, in elections for the DCCB held in March 1973, a compromise candidate, Dadasaheb Nimbalkar, was chosen without opposition. A member of the princely elite and long associated with the Padmaraje movement, Nimbalkar had become more sympathetic to the Congress since the election of his son as MP in 1971. The harmony in the bank election was in marked contrast to the situations during earlier elections. In 1971, as noted earlier, the incumbent, Udaisingh Gaikwad, not only had been backed by local party leaders but by the MPCC President. The president of the Satara DCCB, who is a leading Chavan lieutenant in that district, had been on hand to rally support on Gaikwad's behalf, and Vasantrao Patil sent Sharad Pawar (then an MPCC secretary) to oversee the elections. Yet, from within the ranks of the majority group in the Congress came a challenge to Gaikwad that was supported by the Kumbhar men and the single Communist Party of India (CPI) member of the bank. As a result, Gaikwad was defeated by a vote of ten to nine. In that election, the vice-president of the District Congress, who had sought to become president of the DCC, voted against Gaikwad.[46]

The question of representation of the district at the state level was one of the sources of emerging unity in the Kolhapur Congress organization after 1972. Almost every Congressman from Kolhapur interviewed in early 1973 commented bitterly on the fact that the district had never been represented either in a major governmental or state party post. After the elections of 1972, delegations of local leaders met with Chief Minister Vasantrao Naik to seek assurances on this point. Promises were made of opportunities at the time of a future expansion of the ministry, but the question of representation (and ultimately of fair treatment to the district in the distribution of resources by the state) continued to rankle local leaders. It was only in late 1974 that the

46. In making the appointment of a president for the ad hoc DCC in 1972, Patil pointedly passed over the vice-president. The latter claims this was due to his failure to support Gaikwad in the 1971 DCCB election at a time when Patil, as MPCC President and also as head of the Maharashtra State Cooperative Bank, had backed Gaikwad for reelection.

Chief Minister made good on his promises by appointing *both* Ratnappa Kumbhar and Udaisingh Gaikwad to sub-cabinet positions. It remains a question what effects these appointments may have upon unity in the district and upon latent rivalries between these two men and other leaders.[47]

KOLHAPUR IN PERSPECTIVE

To review the outlines of the previous story: prior to independence, the Maratha ruling house of Kolhapur encouraged social reforms and educational opportunities for non-Brahmans in the state but resisted pressures for greater political participation by the "new class" that was created as a result of those reforms. This gave rise in the 1930s to a movement for greater political participation; however, that movement was never able to rally powerful opposition to the regime. Conflicts between the Maratha nobility and the movement for responsible government were complicated in the period after 1946 by (1) the ascension to the *gadi* of a ruler unpopular with the princely elite and (2) the emergence within the Praja Parishad of divisions between Marathas, on the one hand, who made appeals to localism and to populist ideas, and a second, more Congress-oriented, group of non-Marathas (principally, Lingayats and Jains) with nationalist orientations. Part of the conflict within the Parishad was conditioned by the personal character of its leaders and the nature of their ambitions.

With the formation of the PWP, a segment of the populist Maratha element moved into a political party of its own. Maratha leaders of the Congress organization in Bombay State then turned for help to members of the princely elite in Kolhapur. By seeking to mobilize the rural Marathas behind the Congress, the state party leadership downgraded those non-Marathas who were holding positions of influence in the party and in local government institutions.

47. Kumbhar replaced Sharad Pawar as Minister of State for Home, Information, and Publicity; Gaikwad was appointed Minister of State for Public Health, Energy, Electricity, Food, and Civil Supplies. When asked why a senior Congressman like Kumbhar had been given a subCabinet position, Chief Minister Naik responded that the national party leadership had decided that new entrants into the ministry should not be appointed Cabinet ministers immediately. *Times of India,* 9 November 1974.

The introduction of cooperatives functioning under government auspices in the mid-1950s further complicated the local situation by providing an alternative set of arenas in which conflicts among the various political groups might be worked out. While the introduction of cooperative bodies promoted the extension of inter-individual conflicts into new territories, it actually had the effect of cushioning the process by which the influence of non-Marathas declined in governmental and party affairs. For those who, like Ratnappa Kumbhar, were perceptive enough to see the importance of these new opportunity structures, early entry provided them with the means for continued political influence, though on a smaller scale than previously.

Upon the creation of Maharashtra in 1960, the "populist" Marathas increasingly entered the Congress and came into conflict with the older elite Maratha group. These locally grown conflicts were exacerbated by conflicts among state political actors for influence in Kolhapur politics. A few individuals, like Chavan-Patil, Kumbhar, and Udaisingh Gaikwad, managed to become the apex leaders in a pyramid of political and economic power within their home areas and, consequently, were able to have considerable impact on the public life of the district from those bases. In the course of accumulating the power necessary to become district influentials, such men had to dominate the choice of persons to fill responsible positions not only in the State Legislative Assembly (often a post they reserved for themselves), in the zilla parishad, and in taluka governmental bodies, but in the array of cooperative institutions and ancillary organizations relevant to local political life.

In this situation, a man might be able to dominate one taluka by holding the major power positions himself or by entrusting some of those positions to a few lieutenants. However, if he had aspirations in district or state politics this could well raise a set of dangers to himself. First, there was the "span of control" issue. How far could a single man really dominate a taluka without either antagonizing other ambitious people within the taluka or closing himself off from vital information about pretenders to his position? Lieutenants might lie in wait for errors on his part, or he might have to spread himself too thin in overseeing every relevant institution. In the 1960s, the possibility of one-man domination even in a single taluka became more remote and the voices for sharing the fruits of power more persistent as the number and variety of institutions grew.

If the organization of power on a personal basis was difficult in a single taluka, the possibilities for individual ascendancy in the district were being rendered even more remote. No individual was in a position to rise above the immediate battles as we have suggested was occasionally possible for Mohol in Poona. In Kolhapur, the more common phenomenon was that as a man pursued his aspirations upward, those who played major roles at the district or state levels would reach out to create or support institutional rivals in order to undercut any reach for power which might threaten their own interests.

Thus, for nearly a decade, politics in Kolhapur was an almost unrelieved conflict of individual wills seeking to gain control of established or new opportunity structures. That style of politics operated in a context of laissez-faire assumptions about the propriety of personal ambitions and the acceptability of fluid personal alliances for the achievement of economic and political benefits. Events since 1970 suggest this situation may have been only a transitional stage. What we may be seeing in the recent compromises among powerful local interests is an effort to "depersonalize" or, more positively, to routinize the operation of various institutional sectors, and political life more generally. This may mean redefining the terms on which participants in the political order can benefit directly and personally from their participation. The willingness and ability of state leaders to discard previously major local leaders, like V. K. Chavan-Patil, when some of the personal economic activities of such men became too unsavory, may point in the direction indicated. In contrast, some men, like Kumbhar, have presided over their personal cooperative empires in a style that has kept both themselves and their organizations free of public condemnation.

The model for the future, however, may be neither of these types, the individual "cooperative king" or the local political entrepreneur. Rather, it may be the Ichalkaranji Civic Board with its collective leadership and corporate structure in which highly urbanized men like Kadam, Bhide, and Khanjire participate with others in the setting of limits to personal ambition through the use of schemes of rotation in office and rewards based on bureaucratic skills. Systems of politics based purely on personal ambition are essentially unstable in character. At some point, men seeking to preserve the personal gains they have made may attempt to reach understandings among themselves about the best ways to create and maintain political order, so that they can reduce the uncertainty normally attendant on a politics of open personal conflict. In a fashion reminiscent of the early decades of this century in the United States, local politics in Kolhapur after 1970 may be turning away from a contest among individual entrepreneurs and political machines to a search for those managerial skills appropriate to the administration of a society marked by an increasingly complex institutional infrastructure.[48]

48. Robert H. Wiebe, in *The Search for Order* (New York: Hill and Wang, 1967), describes how such a process of change occurred in the United States beginning in the last quarter of the nineteenth century. Also see Martin Shefter, "The Emergence of the Political Machine: An Alternative View," in Willis D. Hawley, Michael Lipsky et al., *Theoretical Perspectives on Urban Politics* (Englewood Cliffs, N.J.: Prentice-Hall, 1976), pp. 14-44.

FIVE

The Congress as
a Linkage System

The preceding two chapters have focused on the political organization of two districts. In the course of the presentation, I have occasionally indicated how actors, events, and policies from outside those districts have affected local politics. However, the emphasis has been on the operation of selected institutions within the districts as arenas for the advancement of individual political ambition. In this chapter and the ones that follow, the horizon broadens to include a more systematic examination of the currents of national and state politics as they interact with the policy-making process in the state of Maharashtra.

In moving from district politics to an examination of state politics and policy making, my concern with actors based in the local institutions of the countryside is not diminished. Rather, I hope to show in the following chapters how past policies have influenced political behavior in the districts of Poona and Kolhapur and how political actors from Poona, Kolhapur, and other districts in Maharashtra have joined together to influence the way state policies are made and, equally important, the way those policies are implemented.

THE CONGRESS "SYSTEM"

A key problem in understanding the relationship between district politics and the arenas of state and national political life is assigning a proper weight to the role played by the Congress party. This problem took on different forms in the various states of India prior to 1975.[1] In the case of Maharashtra, cities like Bombay, Poona, and Nagpur experienced competitive party politics, and the Congress had to be selective both in its electoral appeals and in the

---

1. For some of the relevant items on state politics, see chapter 1, n. 1.

interests to which it sought to accommodate itself.[2] In the Maharashtrian countryside, however, the Congress had the field almost entirely to itself.

Because of the party's great following in rural Maharashtra, the state was the most consistently pro-Congress in India after 1962. It returned large electoral and legislative majorities for the party in state and national elections; and in each of the last three local governmental elections, the Congress captured all but one of the zilla parishads in its twenty-six districts.[3] However, Congress identification among rural politicians was so pervasive that it took on a certain ambiguity. It was analogous in the sphere of politics to what Hinduism is in the case of Indian religion—an umbrella under which one can pursue personal goals to self-realization by one of many paths chosen largely according to one's own lights.

Thus, on closer examination, the Congress in rural Maharashtra was both stronger and weaker than one might expect from electoral results. It was so pervasive that only a few politicians completely alienated themselves from it by identifying with other political organizations. Yet, because it was so much part of the rural political scene, no one worked very hard to maintain it as an organization based either on principles or more than superficial

2. Poona municipal politics is examined in my *The Limited Elite* (Chicago: University of Chicago Press, 1970). For Nagpur, see Philip K. Oldenburg, "Indian Urban Politics with Particular Reference to the Nagpur Corporation" (M.A. thesis, University of Chicago, 1967); and Robert G. Wirsing, "Socialist Society and Free Enterprise Politics" (Ph.D. diss: University of Denver, 1971). The available studies on Bombay include Henry C. Hart, "Urban Politics in Bombay," *Economic Weekly*, 12 June 1960, pp. 987-992; idem., "Bombay Politics: Pluralism or Polarization?" *Journal of Asian Studies* 20 (February 1961): 267-274; and B. A. V. Sharma and R. T. Jangam, *The Bombay Municipal Corporation: An Election Study* (Bombay: Popular Book Depot, 1962). For an examination of one aspect of Bombay political life, the rise of the Shiv Sena, see Ram Joshi, "Shiv Sena: A Movement in Search of Legitimacy," *Asian Survey* 10 (November 1970): 967-978; and Mary F. Katzenstein, "Origins of Nativism · The Emergence of Shiv Sena in Bombay," *Asian Survey* 13 (April 1973): 386-399. For a collection of essays dealing with urban politics in various parts of India, see Donald B. Rosenthal, ed., *The City in Indian Politics* (Delhi: Thomson, 1976).

3. In 1972, the official Congress nominees did not gain control of the Nasik zilla parishad; a dissident Congress group was elected. The Congress was in a minority position in 1967 in Kolaba, where the PWP had a majority. In 1962, Dhulia was the only district without a Congress majority.

symbolic loyalties. Even those who held "active" memberships in the party seemed to evidence loyalty to the organization only when it served their own carefully calculated self-interests.[4]

This meant, for example, that the absence of strong non-Congress opposition in Maharashtra did not cut the electoral system off from alternatives to the party's official nominees. Instead, the Congress usually generated such alternatives from among its own local factions. Ambitious local politicians were only too eager to seize every opportunity to gain more power, and they were frequently willing—as we have seen in the last two chapters—to act in ways that harmed official party candidates for public (and quasi-public) office if it advanced their own careers. In so doing, they might justify their independent candidacies as involving loyalties to the Congress just as true as those advanced by officially identified party nominees. Since state and national leaders themselves occasionally encouraged such dissident behaviors—the most notable example being the support Mrs. Gandhi gave to the "independent" candidacy of V. V. Giri for president of India in 1969—it is difficult to describe the Congress as a "disciplined" organization.

Given the studied vagueness with which Congress goals were defined and operationalized over the years, the party was neither an instrument of mobilization nor one of implementation of government policies. Rather, the Congress government of Maharashtra was rendered electorally secure because the party was effective in maintaining an appropriate balance among interests in the various local constituencies. It was a security which partook of accommodation to localistic interests at every step of the way. This accommodation provided members of the local elite with leverage in the political system that they exploited not only to advance the political careers of particular local leaders but to influence the scope of public policies.

The pervasiveness of the Congress and the looseness of discipline associated with party membership made the party a weak instrument for any effort to overcome the inertia of locally based

4. Two classes of Congress membership exist: "active" and "ordinary." The ordinary member pays a nominal fee and agrees to support the party; the active member pays a higher membership fee and is eligible to participate in inner-party elections. For an examination of the Congress organization prior to the 1969 split, see Stanley A. Kochanek, *The Congress Party of India* (Princeton: Princeton University Press, 1968).

political forces. One might have expected it to be otherwise, for Maharashtra (at least until recently) gave the appearance of domination by a single personality. Y. B. Chavan, during his seven years first as Chief Minister of Bombay State and then as Chief Minister of Maharashtra, seemed to dominate both the party and the government in the Maharashtra region. Even when he relinquished his position in the state government to become Defense Minister of India in 1962, he maintained an active involvement in Maharashtra affairs. That activity level continued at least through 1971, although some of the responsibility for integrating state and party matters was shared with the man who headed the government as Chief Minister of Maharashtra from 1963 to 1975, Vasantrao Naik. Until the 1970s, the MPCC and the state government frequently overlapped in personnel with the result that Maharashtra experienced very little of the conflict between Congress party organization and Congress government which marked politics in some of the other Indian states.

Yet, despite this integration of party and government, state and national government leaders showed little inclination to use the party to serve policy-related goals. In this they differed significantly from the behavior observed in some one-party nation-states. Instead, at each level the party was little more than an electoral instrument, involved sometimes in bitter wrangling over the designation of candidates for public office but participating only to a limited extent in the policy-making process.

That situation was accentuated by the character of those persons who were recruited to public office. They were designated because of their standing in local affairs or because of functional interests which state or national leaders wished to represent rather than because they spoke for any coherent set of principles bearing on the character of Indian society or its economy. Very few legislative members saw themselves as playing a major role in formulating public policy. Beyond members of the state ministry, only a very thin layer of legislators took an active interest in policy making, and these were usually individuals who used their participation in the legislature to stake claims to future governmental roles. For the most part, Congress legislators in Maharashtra saw themselves primarily as spokesmen for constituency interests pursuing material benefits for those constituents in the form of dams, irrigation systems, roads, and other tangible rewards. They did not think seriously about policy issues.

The situation, as we shall see in subsequent chapters, was somewhat different at later stages of the policy process. Once policies emerged from the State Cabinet, rural politicians were interested in identifying threats to their interests or ambitions. They became actively involved, therefore, in the way legislative principles were converted into policy actions. Furthermore, they had the capacity through the local political arena to convert proposals for change into little more than symbolic gestures on the part of the state government. It was this ability to render ineffective legislative pronouncements that we shall see demonstrated in a number of cases reviewed in later chapters.

In this chapter, however, I would like to set the political context for understanding state policy-making processes by describing in detail some of the characteristics of the Congress system and how that system was associated with the operation of government in the state for the fifteen years prior to 1975. In simplest terms, the Congress system in Maharashtra resembled until recently the operation of Congress party politics in Poona district except that the arbiter role played by Mamasaheb Mohol in Poona was assumed in the state by Y. B. Chavan.

Before the emergence of the institutional infrastructure described in previous chapters, several generations of politicians had built political bases in the party organization itself, but this was during the period when the party, as embodiment of the nationalist movement, constituted the prime vehicle for political activity and personal political advancement in the country. During the period of greatest nationalist activity, a few individuals, like Y. B. Chavan of Satara, established themselves as district leaders through their nationalist exploits and then moved into state politics when opportunities were made available to young men with the proper party and personal credentials (e.g., education, caste). Some of those belonging to the nationalist generation have faded from view because of age or an inability to convert nationalist activity into organizational resources. Others, however, used their earlier positions in the party organization to stake claims for sharing the rewards of institutional development. We have seen several cases of this kind in Kolhapur and Poona, quintessentially in the instance of Ratnappa Kumbhar.

THE ARBITER ROLE

Much like Mohol in Poona district, Chavan established a pivotal place for himself in his native Satara district and then later in Maharashtra politics by assuming the role of arbiter among conflicting interests. He did this by displaying unusual political skill and moderation in personal character. To assign the label of "arbiter" to either of these men is perhaps to tag them more as political neuters than they really have been. For, like the more effective "bosses" of urban machines in the United States, the Indian arbiter (whether consciously or not) is concerned with assuring his own power by maintaining an equilibrium among other contestants for power. In the Poona case, Mohol was one of the few politicians whom one might identify as a preserver and defender of the Congress party as an organization. Because others recognized that he held organizational values so high, they turned to him when conflicts arose in order to help maintain balances in the various institutional arenas where Congress party members vied for political support. Other local leaders did not regard him as particularly concerned with his own further advancement; indeed, he had reached a plateau of ambition, and they felt they could trust him to distribute both the tangible and intangible benefits of power (most notably, party nominations and support for local government office) among members of the party rather than trying to hoard such resources for himself.

All these features were commonly ascribed to Chavan's behavior in state politics. He was seen as slightly above the common quest for self-aggrandizement (at least at the local and state levels) and, therefore, fit to play an arbitrational role among those whose behavior was more self-seeking. Of course, many rewards do flow to such a political leader, both in terms of the psychic deference paid to him and the ability to influence those decisions about which he feels strongly enough to intervene. He also is likely to be accorded an important role as a link between the arena in which he is recognized as the leader and the next more extensive arenas of politics and government. In the case of national politics, this meant that Chavan was the principal representative of Maharashtra in national Congress circles and had a major voice in national government policies affecting the state.

The arbiter maintains an important part of his following by being concerned not only to resolve, or at least to moderate, conflicts which arise among those who hold power already but to bring others who aspire to power into the leading institutions. We have seen, for example, how Sharad Pawar gained from association with Chavan.

A large number of informants described Chavan in terms which conform to this general arbiter model. The extent of his involvement in the minutiae of state and district politics was sometimes surprising, though it was apparently in decline in the 1970s as compared to a decade earlier. He was still frequently called upon personally to moderate conflicts among factions in different institutional arenas or to designate others to arbitrate such contests. Most contestants to a quarrel came away feeling that some justice had been received or, at least, that their positions had been heard. Even where people grumbled at the outcome of decisions, that grumbling was directed more frequently at the manipulations of their rivals than at Chavan.

His harshest critics argued, however, that Chavan maintained himself as the dominant figure in Maharashtrian politics by never allowing those below him to reach positions of power from which they could challenge him; as these persons would have it, Chavan actually encouraged institutional rivalries in order to maintain himself as the final arbiter. However, to give even small justice to each side of the many factional disputes which color the public life of Maharashtra is, of necessity, to help maintain those quarrels. At the same time, the feeling that somebody in the Congress could be approached on matters of vital importance and that a fair hearing would be given was an important consideration in sustaining the Congress as a major vehicle for all those with political ambitions. It prevented the kind of alienation from occurring which had created persistent cleavages in the highest ranks of the Congress in several other states or had led to the formation of new political organizations made up of dissident Congressmen.

Where an arbiter did not exist in district affairs, as in Kolhapur district for much of the period covered by this study, factionalism constantly plagued the operations of the various centers of power in the district. Not only did instability in local politics make relations among institutional leaders uncertain, but it rendered the district weaker in dealing with external forces. In contrast, the availability of an arbiter in Poona district provided fewer opportunities for external actors to intervene.

Similarly, Chavan, as arbiter for the Maharashtrian system, so placed himself within the politics of that system as to make it difficult for actors in national politics from outside Maharashtra to challenge him directly through appeals to dissident groups in the state. This became more feasible after 1971, however, as Mrs. Gandhi launched an effort to establish herself as the dominant force in Indian national politics and, in so doing, increasingly assumed the role of arbiter of the national political system.

While the arbitrational role was crucial to the success of the Congress organization in sustaining a wide following within the politically active stratum in Maharashtra, it worked against the development of a Congress party organization capable of exercising control over local activists—control that might be associated with enunciating a consistent set of goals and developing means for implementing those goals. Instead, the Congress party leadership merely accommodated itself to the factions which it helped to spawn within numerous state and local institutions, and arbiters intervened largely to effect reconciliations among contenders for claims in those arenas. Not all such interventions were successful, but that, in part, reflected the influence of local elites within the political system, for dissidents were quite willing to label some actions as "meddling" by outsiders or as serving the personal interests of the intervener.

Indeed, it is a comment on the defects of the party organization that it was dependent on arbiters like Chavan, for that dependence constituted recognition that the party had failed to develop a more coherent bureaucratic structure. Even if the performance of units of the Congress may not be accorded high marks in bureaucratic terms, however, such units tried to perform reconciliation or arbitrational functions. In doing so, they drew together many of the leading actors in the territory and attempted to coordinate the increasingly diverse set of institutional interests which developed in rural Maharashtra.

Ironically, the very institutionalization encouraged by government policy contributed to weakening the party organization upon which that government was based. Thus, the autonomy exercised by the "cooperative kings" in resisting attempts to change the cooperative system in the state or by rural backbenchers in opposing proposals for reform in the educational patterns of the state (matters that will be considered in subsequent chapters) would not have been possible if state and district party leaders had been more firmly in control of such institutionalized sectors.

To better understand the situation of the Congress and the way the weakness of the Congress impinged on the policy-making process in the state, the remainder of this chapter will review the organizational condition of the party in district and state political life and then briefly examine some of the state-level quarrels which both enhanced Chavan's role as arbiter and weakened the Congress as an instrument of mobilization and policy direction. In the course of doing so, it will also be useful to examine the eclipse in Chavan's influence engineered by Mrs. Gandhi.

DISTRICT AND SUBDISTRICT CONGRESS ORGANIZATION

Prior to the politicization of cooperatives and the development of panchayati raj institutions as major vehicles for the advancement of ambition, district Congress units may have had a larger voice in setting the terms on which participants in local politics might prosper. With the development of new opportunity structures, however, party units appear to have lost ground.[5] Thus, below the district level, one found a few party workers who were engaged in seemingly intense but unproductive factional quarrels—quarrels which often had more to do with institutions other than the party than with the party itself. Very little effective activity was carried on by such "party workers" except at election time, and even then most political campaigns seemed to be conducted by individual candidates who exploited personal networks of kin, friends, and neighbors rather than depending on the party organization. This is a situation familiar to students of American party organizations in a post-machine "reform" era.

5. The historical comparison hypothesized here may be unwarranted. While the Congress has deep roots in the symbolic identifications of an older generation, it is by no means clear how substantial its roots have ever been in an organizational sense, particularly since independence. More recently, the ease with which Indira Gandhi defeated the leadership of men presumably grounded in the party organization (in states other than Maharashtra) suggests that the party as a popular symbolic orientation to politics has been more meaningful than the party as one among various concrete political institutions.

The Congress party, as such, had very little public salience in non-electoral periods, especially at the subdistrict level.[6] What accounted for the greater vitality of the DCCs was the role they were supposed to play in the designation of candidates for district and state offices. In practice, as some local politicians complained, the MPCC had increasingly bypassed the recommendations of district party leaders in selecting MLA and parliamentary candidates, with the result that local politicians feared the DCCs might also be developing into political units of limited influence except perhaps in local government elections.

Aside from participation in the performance of electoral functions, the DCC was the meeting place for major political and socioeconomic interests in a district.[7] In Poona, where one leadership group clearly prevailed, decisions were taken in the DCC Executive about the party's candidates not only for zilla parishad elections, but about nominees for bodies of the cooperative movement, including the DCCB and the DLDB. Of course, the absence of the powerful Kakade family, with their control over important

6. Under the rules of the Maharashtra Congress, taluka party units have no official standing. The basic units are *mandals* (blocks), which are supposed to consist of one person for each 2,000 population up to a total block Congress membership of thirty. A rural taluka may average two or three mandals; while unofficial, many talukas in Poona and Kolhapur seemed to have skeletal taluka party organizations.

Neither they nor the mandals were particularly vigorous bodies. According to the office secretary of the Kolhapur District Congress, the party had an enrollment of 60,000 primary members in 1970. However, many were paper members recruited (and sometimes paid for) by active members who attempted to use their votes to influence intraparty contests and party nominations. My informant estimated that there had been about 1,300 "active" members in the district in 1968 but this had increased to 2,400 in 1970 as the result of a special effort that had preceded elections for party office. In one taluka, where conflicts between factions were particularly bitter, the ranks of active members swelled from 165 to 526 between 1968 and 1970.

7. A DCC consists of four members elected by each mandal plus the president of the mandal Congress. From this large general body, a smaller executive committee is chosen which operates as the effective leadership body within the DCC. It is this executive committee with which we are particularly concerned when describing the activities of the "district leadership." At least in Poona and Kolhapur districts, leadership of the DCC Executives did not arise so much from factors internal to the local party membership as from recognition of territorial factors and the need to represent major cooperative and local government leaders, as well as MLAs and other prominent district politicians.

resources in the cooperative sector, inhibited the DCC in its capacity to effect compliance with its preferences for cooperative offices.

In Kolhapur, the DCC was a much less decisive body. For those in the DCC it did furnish a place where local barons—leaders of the zilla parishad, heads of the major cooperative institutions of the district (except for Kumbhar and his followers), representatives of the various talukas (usually the MLA, where that office was held by a Congressman)—could come together to reconcile conflicts. Since the body was not sufficiently authoritative without the presence of the Kumbhar forces or certain dissident Maratha leaders, its efforts at reconciliation often failed. Thus, as we have noted, in elections to the DCCB it was common for Congressmen who did not receive support from the DCC to seek non-DCC allies and to win major positions.

One of the chief weaknesses of the DCCs flowed from the fact that one no longer built a political career through the party, particularly at the district and subdistrict levels. Rather, one legitimated the success already achieved in some other sphere by being chosen for a seat on the DCC or the DCC Executive and participating in its operations, with the ultimate benefit being a nomination for MLA or special access to governmental leaders. Furthermore, successful performance of party work by such persons as Pawar or Dharia meant advancement out of the party organization. It may reflect the weaker position of the MPCC vis-à-vis the state government of Maharashtra that two of the most recent presidents of the MPCC left that position to take up ministries, though the reverse was the case with the most recent president.

In sum, the Congress continued to be the premier electoral organization in Maharashtra, but in non-electoral periods its chief activities revolved around the reconciliation of quarrels which developed within district and sub-district units. These units existed increasingly to reconcile or manage conflicts which arose among various individuals and interests in an increasingly differentiated rural situation. The dynamics of performance of this function required the inclusion of senior figures in the locality in the DCC. It is indicative of the relative importance of the DCCs in Poona and Kolhapur, however, that fights to get on to the DCC Executive were mild in comparison to contests for governmental office or for control of cooperative institutions. Certainly, a position in a

DCC Executive bore witness to a successful political career, as well
as constituting a means of enhancing that career, but it did not in
itself call for peculiar dedication to the care and feeding of the
party. Much more often, it merely reflected a person's claims to
individual recognition in district political life, quite independent
of an interest in the maintenance of the party as an instrument of
state and national power and policy.

THE STATE PARTY ORGANIZATION

In recent years, the MPCC Executive consisted of forty-four members. In addition to a president, vice-president, and treasurer, there
were four secretaries (nominated by the president), who attended
to the regular organizational work. In 1967, there were no contests for officers. Choices were agreed on among state party
leaders. The 1969 split in the national Congress caused little
disruption in the Maharashtra organization. As we shall see in the
next section, greater conflict occurred in 1972 when new organizational elections were held.

The four secretaries of the MPCC generally represented different regions of Maharashtra and divided the party's work among
themselves, both regionally and functionally. Thus, in 1970, when
there were two secretaries from western Maharashtra (Sharad
Pawar and V. N. Gadgil, both from Poona district), they divided
responsibilities in that region, while the other two secretaries dealt
with Vidarbha and Marathwada. Functionally, Pawar was responsible for overseeing the activities of such groups as the Youth
Congress (a body in which he had gotten his own start) and party
matters bearing on the zilla parishads, whereas Gadgil had some
responsibility for looking after party headquarters in Bombay City
and party conferences. Another secretary maintained contacts
with Congress unions and the party's social service wing, the
Congress Seva Dal. One of the primary functions of party secretaries and others designated by the president was to keep track of
local conflict situations. This function was performed in several
instances of quarrels within Poona and Kolhapur districts when
state party officials were sent to arbitrate local conflicts.

Membership in the general body of the MPCC has been based
on one representative for each 100,000 of population plus the
presidents of the DCCs, and up to 10 percent co-opted members

drawn from such groups as women and minorities (Scheduled Castes, tribals, Muslims). In addition, all ex-MPCC presidents were automatically members, and the MLAs of the party elected fifteen members from their ranks to sit on the MPCC. As a result, there were about five hundred individuals who constituted the general body of the Congress party in Maharashtra (outside Bombay City).

In theory, the party executive was chosen from the general body, but the choices were actually made in the 1960s by Chavan, Naik, and a few close associates. They also took the leading part in the selection of the State Election Committee (Parliamentary Board). There were fourteen members of this pivotal agency, which acted as the organ for processing applications and recommendations from lower-level bodies for nominations to seats for the state legislature, the national Parliament, and for district offices. The president and vice-president of the MPCC were members of the Parliamentary Board on an ex-officio basis. As one MPCC informant described the process of becoming a party nominee in Maharashtra:

> When an election is announced for MLA or MP, the MPCC invites applications and people apply directly. The DCC may also pass a resolution at that time recommending a particular person but an application does not need to come through the DCC. The Parliamentary Board meets and selects candidates. These are recommended to the AICC in the case of MLA and MP elections. The MPCC itself is the final decision maker in the case of candidates for the zilla parishads. They invite candidates to appear before them for these various posts but in many cases decisions are already made. . . . All fourteen members are supposed to sit together in reviewing candidates but in the case of zilla parishad elections, they may delegate their authority to a smaller group. Sometimes decisions really are left to the president of the MPCC and the Chief Minister. In the case of MPs, the final word usually is with Chavan and this is sometimes the case with MLAs. However, Chavan has been intervening less in these matters in recent years.

RIVALRIES FOR STATE LEADERSHIP

As the leader of the Maharashtra government, Chavan established a practice of making sure that the party organization could not or would not challenge his authority. This was done, in part, by designating as president of the MPCC a series of men whose personal political followings were quite limited.[8] Even when Vasantrao Patil from Sangli district became president in 1966, his personal loyalty to Chavan and his reputation as an organizer in the cooperative sector, rather than as a leader with governmental ambitions, were factors taken into account. At the same time, party secretaries were generally young or otherwise immediately unsuited for major governmental roles. Important positions on the MPCC Executive went to individuals who also held governmental positions and were likely to put their governmental activities ahead of party careers.

Within this framework of a party and governmental system under the leadership of Chavan and Naik, individuals jockeyed for personal political advantage in state politics. The situation was similar to the one in Poona district where Mohol presided over quarrels among secondary leaders. It may be useful to illustrate how two particular conflicts worked themselves out. In some of its characteristics, the conflict between Yeshwantrao J. Mohite, Minister for Cooperation, and D. S. (Balasaheb) Desai, Minister for Revenue, was a classic example of how such quarrels both serve the interests of higher-level leaders and contribute to occasional convulsions within the Congress system. A second set of conflicts bears more directly on the eventual succession to Naik as Chief Minister in 1975 of Shankarrao B. Chavan of Marathwada.

The Desai-Mohite Rivalry

In western Maharashtra, Balasaheb Desai and Y. J. Mohite, both from Y. B. Chavan's own Satara district, have figured prominently in the party politics and government of the region and of the state. Indeed, it can be argued that the recent politics of the state of Maharashtra can be understood, at least in part, by an understanding of the backgrounds and ambitions of these and other men based in various parts of Satara district. For, below the level of Chavan, Satara politics has been marked by a series of intra-taluka and inter-leader conflicts that sometimes make the conflicts of Poona and Kolhapur districts seem mild by compari-

8. This may be described as the "Nehru strategy," since it replicated the approach to the national party organization that Nehru took in order to insure his own autonomy as leader of the government of India. In that connection, see Kochanek, *The Congress Party.*

son.[9] Two of the key leaders have been Desai and Mohite. Their careers have followed rather different paths.

Desai was born about sixty-two years ago into a family with high-status claims but little land. Forced to operate largely on his own from an early age, he went to Kolhapur for an education and lived there from 1924 to 1937. In 1937, he completed his degree in law and returned to Satara district. He started what became a thriving practice both in his native taluka and in the town of Karad. In 1941, he decided to enter politics and was elected to the District Local Board as an independent; he served as president of that body from 1941 to 1952. During the earlier years, while the local Congress leadership was in jail or underground, Desai was leader of one of the two major factions in the district, but he was not associated with the Congress until he was encouraged to join the party by Chavan in 1945. Some observers have seen Desai as a faithful lieutenant to Chavan; others have viewed him as a potential rival always seeking his own advantage.[10]

Despite the ambiguity of his loyalties, Desai became one of the MPCC secretaries around 1954; and then, in 1957, when Chavan reconstituted his cabinet, Desai was chosen to be Minister for Public Works. Later, he served terms as Minister for Education and Home Minister. It became increasingly clear, however, that Chavan's favor would never be shown toward Desai as a nominee for Chief Minister. As a result, relationships between them and also between Desai and the incumbent Chief Minister, Vasantrao Naik, became more difficult. These ambitional difficulties occasionally showed up in the posture on policy matters that Desai took in the Cabinet, though such differences also reflected the two men's personal orientations: Desai, the occasionally demagogic Maratha man of the "masses"; Naik, the non-populist pragmatist.

9. Some of the complexities of recent Satara politics are suggested in V. M. Sirsikar, *The Rural Elite in a Developing Society* (New Delhi: Orient Longmans, 1970), pp. 177-184; and Jayant K. Lele, "Politics and Social Structure in India" (Paper presented at the 1968 Meetings of the American Political Science Association, Washington, D.C., September 2-7). For an examination of the politics of one taluka in Satara district and the linkages of taluka leaders to district and state politics, see Anthony T. Carter, *Elite Politics in Rural India: Political Stratification and Political Alliances in Western Maharashtra* (Cambridge: Cambridge University Press, 1974).

10. Lele, "Politics and Social Structure," p. 11.

Desai's relations with Naik became particularly difficult after 1967 when Desai was replaced as Home Minister by the Chief Minister himself. Though Desai remained in the Cabinet as Minister for Revenue and as one of two deputy leaders of the Congress legislative party, he harbored personal grievances against the Congress leadership. In turn, they disliked his populist style, and its appeals to Maratha chauvinism, and his administrative approach, which often exceeded the bounds of bureaucratic propriety in order to exercise personal discretion.

At the district level, Desai constantly experienced political opposition from other Chavan associates. Thus, in 1966 one local leader regularly backed by Chavan on other matters captured control of the Satara DCCB away from Desai and himself replaced Desai's cousin as the chairman of that body. Desai's position in the district was further clouded by the rise of Y. J. Mohite.

Like Chavan, Yeshwantrao Mohite was born in Karad taluka, but unlike Chavan he was born (in 1920) into a wealthy and high-status agricultural family. After college education in Kolhapur, he joined the PWP as soon as it was organized in 1948. Mohite was first elected to the Assembly in 1952. Despite his patrician upbringing (or perhaps just because of it), he was attracted to the more leftist element in the PWP, represented by men like R. K. Khadilkar and D. R. Chavan. When the PWP split in 1953 along ideological lines, D. R. Chavan and Mohite left to help form the short-lived Mazdoor Kisan Party. Like other groups, that party was swept up in the Samyukta Maharashtra movement. It was under the banner of that movement that Mohite was reelected in 1957 to the MLA seat in the constituency bordering on Y. B. Chavan's.

At the time Chavan was seeking possible entrants to the Congress, he approached Mohite. Mohite responded by crossing over to the Congress in 1960 and was rewarded with the position of Deputy Home Minister, a position he held for four years.[11]

11. Mohite, like his former associates, D. R. Chavan and R. K. Khadilkar, managed to remain relatively independent of Y. B. Chavan. D. R. Chavan, who entered the Congress about the same time, held the second parliamentary seat from Satara district—the one not held by Y. B. Chavan himself—and filled various ministerial positions in the central government for a decade until his death. The independent emergence of Mrs. Gandhi in 1971 provided politicians like D. R. Chavan, Khadilkar, and Mohite with alternative routes for advancing their careers other than their earlier dependence on the good will of Y. B. Chavan.

During those years, Mohite managed to build a strong personal following in his home area centered around a sugar factory controlled by his family. This base allowed him to follow a relatively independent course in both state and Satara politics, marked by a taste for what one observer has characterized as "patrician socialism." Mohite's career has advanced more than it might otherwise have done—given his slender personal following in Satara district outside his home taluka and his general detachment from Chavan and Naik—because of his strategic position at the time of various conflicts among other local and state leaders.

Thus, Lele suggests that Mohite gained considerably when he temporarily joined with Desai in 1967 against Rajaram (Bapu) Patil, then a junior minister from Sangli district, who was a protégé of Naik's; Patil was a rival to Mohite among those junior ministers from western Maharashtra seeking future ministerial status.[12] Mohite came out of that affair as Minister for Housing and State Transportation, a position he held until late 1969, when he assumed the even more prestigious position of Minister for Cooperation, a position he continued to hold into 1975. As the only two men holding full ministerial portfolios from Satara district after 1967—a third Satara man, D. H. Jagtap (Y. B. Chavan's son-in-law), held a junior position in the ministry—the rivalry between Mohite and Desai became more pronounced. It came to a head, however, as Desai moved more vigorously to challenge the position of Vasantrao Naik.

Certain strains in Congress party leadership became evident in elections to the Rajya Sabha, the lower house of Parliament, from the Maharashtra Assembly in March 1970. Prior to that election, Shankarrao B. Chavan, Minister for Irrigation and Power and leader of Marathwada, had threatened to resign as one of the two deputy leaders of the party. In part, S. B. Chavan's threat was a response to charges by publicly unidentified Cabinet colleagues (allegedly including Desai) that more funds were being spent on the development of the Marathwada region than on other regions.[13] Congress MLAs from Marathwada rallied to S. B. Cha-

12. Lele, "Politics and Social Structure," p. 12. Rajaram Patil had previously served a term as president of the MPCC. He continues to be a major figure in Sangli district and is the leader of the Congress faction opposed to Vasantrao Patil there. After a temporary setback in 1967, he reemerged as Minister for Industries, a position he filled until 1972.

13. *Times of India*, 13 March 1970.

van's support, and Naik smoothed their feelings by assuring them of continued government concern with the development of the economically backward Marathwada region.[14]

In the subsequent elections to the Rajya Sabha, candidates supported by the Congress should have won five of the six seats being contested. Instead, one of the candidates went down to defeat. The man excluded was a sitting member of the Rajya Sabha from Marathwada. His defeat was coincident with the election of an Organization Congress candidate, even though the Organization Congress (the opposition splinter against the Congress led by Mrs. Gandhi) held only thirteen seats in the Assembly and had received the additional public support of no more than the six Jan Sangh MLAs.[15] Despite the protest of some members of the MPCC Secretariat, Vasantrao Patil, President of the MPCC, and Naik refused to act against those who were known to have defected or encouraged defection.[16]

Shortly thereafter, communal riots at Bhiwandi and Jalgaon occurred, and the Chief Minister came in for severe criticism for the state government's handling of those riots.[17] That criticism surfaced within Congress party circles with the circulation of a pamphlet at a meeting of the AICC in Delhi in May which accused Naik of failure to deal effectively with the law and order situation in the state. The same pamphlet also raised questions about the MPCC's attitude toward the Shiv Sena in Bombay City.[18] Though Desai publicly dissociated himself from these charges, several interviewees insisted that those who had circulated the statement included persons close to Desai. Tensions in the relationship between Desai and Naik increased.

This embarrassment to the Chief Minister was subsequently compounded by defeats to the Congress in Poona (and Nasik

14. *Times of India,* 14 March 1970.

15. *Indian Express,* 26 March 1970; "Cracks in MPCC Fort," *Link,* 5 April 1970, pp. 19-20.

16. Sharad Pawar resigned as secretary of the Congress legislative party in protest against their inaction on the matter. However, he retained his position as an MPCC secretary. He was succeeded in his legislative post by Dnaneshwar Khaire of Poona.

17. For coverage particularly critical of the behavior of the Naik government, see *Link,* 17, 23, and 31 May and 7 June 1970.

18. Weeklies of the left, like *Link* and *Blitz,* have regularly attacked Naik for allegedly giving encouragement to the rise and development of the Shiv Sena. *Current,* a right-wing journal, also has joined this attack on occasion.

district) and a poor performance in Kolhapur in the elections to the local bodies constituencies for MLC (which we reviewed in the last two chapters). There followed a grim MPCC meeting in early July, 1970, at which charges and counter-charges were exchanged. The conflict between Mohite and Desai became the center of attention when a prominent Marathi-language paper published in Bombay accused Mohite of being behind the victory of Kakade in Poona district.

As one prominent MPCC figure narrated the events leading up to the confrontation: the MPCC was to meet on the fifth of July; in preparation for that meeting, there were discussions with Y. B. Chavan about the possibility of taking firm action against those who had defected in the Rajya Sabha and MLC elections. Despite arguments made in favor of action, Chavan (in a manner typical of the Chavan "style") preferred to take no steps that would directly antagonize anyone. However, the published story led Mohite to deny the charges at the MPCC meeting. He asserted that he was ill during the period of the campaign and, therefore, inactive. His statement led others (particularly from Poona and Kolhapur) to demand firmness with party dissidents. Without Desai's name being mentioned, it was clear they were talking about him; but when Desai turned to Chavan for help, Chavan made it clear that he would leave the matter entirely to the Chief Minister. Having lost Chavan's personal support, Desai chose to resign rather than remain in his ministry. [19]

The dispute attracted national political attention, especially because the Congress in Maharashtra had proven itself more loyal to Chavan than to Indira Gandhi in the national presidential elections of 1969. From both the left and right came intimations that Mrs. Gandhi might use Desai as a vehicle for weakening Chavan in Maharashtra. [20] For whatever reason, these rumors came to nothing. Desai's personal strength in the party proved limited. In Kolhapur, where Desai was thought to be particularly popular, ceremonies were organized by a few local Congress leaders to greet him on a visit he made immediately after his resignation. When "inquiries" into these welcoming activities were made by MPCC leaders, however, expressions of local support for Desai rapidly

19. On the public story, see *Times of India*, 5 July 1970; *Link*, 12 July 1970.
20. *Current*, 18 July 1970; *Blitz*, 1 August 1970.

waned. By the end of 1970, Congressmen were insisting that Desai was a "spent force" in Maharashtra politics. [21]

Mrs. Gandhi and Maharashtra Politics: Round I

In August 1969, when the Congress divided over the selection of a candidate for President of India, Mrs. Gandhi backed the candidacy of V. V. Giri, the incumbent Vice-President, while the President of the Congress and other party leaders supported Sanjiva Reddy of Andhra Pradesh. In this conflict, Chavan sided with the party leadership and took most Congressmen in Maharashtra along with him. [22] Although Chavan stood with Mrs. Gandhi in the open break within the party that followed the presidential vote and continued to serve in the national Cabinet, a certain distance surfaced in their relationship.

These differences, though unavowed publicly, were reflected in negotiations for parliamentary candidacies in 1971. Mrs. Gandhi's personal following in Maharashtra was too weak for her to offer attractive incentives to potential dissidents from the MPCC leadership. As a result, the MPCC made several decisions which attempted to undercut Mrs. Gandhi by denying nominations to the handful of individuals from Maharashtra who had backed Giri despite Chavan's orders. By coincidence, these decisions affected the selection of candidates in Poona and Kolhapur districts most severely. The MPCC denied a ticket to an incumbent MP, Shankarrao Mane, in Kolhapur; in Poona, both R. K. Khadilkar and Tulshidas Jadhav—incumbents with national reputations for association with leftist groups and known as personal supporters of Mrs. Gandhi—came under fire. Neither man had a substantial personal following in the district. Indeed, many local politicians would have been happy to be rid of them, particularly if opportunities were opened for themselves. [23] Despite pressures from Mrs. Gandhi's

21. Both Desai and Mohite were renominated in 1972 for MLA from their long-time constituencies. Intense efforts went on by supporters of each man to defeat the other, but both managed to win. For a report of the efforts of Desai's people to defeat Mohite, see *Times of India*, 4 March 1972.

22. On the division of the Congress, see Basant Chatterjee, *The Congress Splits* (Delhi: S. Chand, 1970); and M. M. Rahman, *The Congress Crisis* (New Delhi: Associated Publishing House, 1970).

23. In addition to his associations with Y. J. Mohite, which went back to their days in the PWP, Khadilkar occasionally identified himself with local dissidents like the Kakades. Despite this personal association, Khadilkar was regarded as a leftist in Congress circles. As a leader of the Poona DCC

followers in the AICC, the MPCC refused to grant a ticket to Jadhav anywhere in Maharashtra. An offer was finally made by means of the national party leadership to find him a place in the list of party nominees from the state of Madhya Pradesh. The matter became so embarrassing to Jadhav, however, that he left the Congress and ran unsuccessfully with the backing of the PWP as a candidate from another Maharashtra district. [24] Khadilkar, who had been even closer than Jadhav to Mrs. Gandhi and had some national visibility as a leftist within the party, was retained by the MPCC, but his constituency was altered to what might have been expected to be a less favorable one.

In the election itself, opposition parties were so disunited and Mrs. Gandhi's personal appeal so effective that Congress candidates in Maharashtra swept to victory in forty-three of the forty-four contests in the state. Thus, Maharashtra, despite the ambivalence of her politicians about Mrs. Gandhi's leadership, contributed hand-somely to her overwhelming parliamentary majority.

The results of this election were something of a Pyrrhic victory for the Maharashtra Congress and for certain other state party groups which did nearly as well. The very size of her majority encouraged Mrs. Gandhi to use the year following the national elections and prior to elections for many state legislatures (including Maharashtra's) to attempt to build a national party organization more in keeping with her own search for national authority. Her ambition, if we can characterize it as such, was to create a national Congress more sensitive to direction from above. In pursuit of that goal she gave her search for strengthened personal authority the cloak of an egalitarian struggle. In the course of doing so, she appeared willing to weaken autonomous units of political authority such as the one Chavan had con-structed so skillfully, even though leaders like Chavan professed to support social goals much like her own.

---

remarked in 1973, "Khadilkar is really close to the communists. He is a spokesman for Dange [leader of the CPI] and such. It is true that he has a few contacts with people like the Kakades but it is not a major factor in his views."

24. The Poona DCC originally recommended V. N. Gadgil, Mohan Dharia, and A. V. Patil for the MP seats in Poona district. Dharia and Patil were nominated, but Khadilkar was given the third party nomination instead of Gadgil. *Times of India,* 2 and 3 January 1971. On Jadhav's resignation from the Congress, see *Times of India,* 6 February 1971.

Unlike states like Andhra and Rajasthan, where she was able to place her own men in charge of state governments, Mrs. Gandhi encountered considerable resistance to her power-building activities in Maharashtra. Chavan's mass following, his reputation for humanitarianism, and the socialist language in which he had long clothed himself, both in state and national politics, made it very difficult for Mrs. Gandhi to find an entering wedge to employ against him. There were only a few Congress politicians of any stature in the state who stood to the left of Chavan and they were not viable alternatives to him. At the same time, her own socialist credentials were bound to be questioned if Mrs. Gandhi supported persons with decidedly more conservative views than Chavan's.

From about 1956, there had existed a Congress-related intellectual group, the Congress Forum for Socialist Action. That group had received encouragement from Mrs. Gandhi even before her parliamentary victory in 1971. The Forum was useful to Mrs. Gandhi as a prod to the larger Congress organization to move in a leftist direction, which would presumably have more appeal to the mass electorate. When an attempt was made in 1971 to revitalize a unit of the Socialist Forum in Maharashtra, where it had had little following previously, Chavan saw this as an Indira-inspired challenge and so arranged matters that he emerged as the patron of the state unit and his men, Sharad Pawar and Mohan Dharia, were placed at the forefront of the organization. (Pawar served as president of the state body during 1971.[25]) While Pawar spoke publicly in favor of a greater measure of socialism in the policies pursued by the state and national party, he carefully muted any criticism of persons in power in the state.

Dharia, according to some of his critics, saw in this situation an opportunity to move closer to Mrs. Gandhi. He publicly criticized the Maharashtra government under Chief Minister Naik for its slowness in bringing about economic reforms and even called for the Chief Minister to step down. This was considered a heresy

25. One prominent state politician suggested that the Forum was useful to several politicians, including Pawar and Vasantrao Patil, as an instrument of personal ambition. This element, he indicated, presented a list of ninety names at the time decisions were being made about MLA candidates. As he asserted, "Of the ninety names proposed by the Forum, fifty got tickets. People thought the Forum would be a catalytic agent for change, but they became disenchanted with it when it began to appear that it was merely a springboard for the ambitions of some leaders."

to the local party faithful and diminished Dharia's already feeble ability to command a following among Congressmen even in his own urban constituency. [26]

Typical of the kind of maneuvering that occurred during this period was the effort by Mrs. Gandhi to launch a national campaign for new and more extensive land reforms. The state leadership of Maharashtra took up this challenge (unlike many other states) and, after an elaborate series of activities brought forward a new law which left matters substantially where they had been before; some persons interviewed suggested that the changes had actually made it possible for people to own more land under certain conditions. Since, as one prominent political leader suggested, the stimulus to the policy change had been political, it was only fair that the response be equally political. The symbolic appearance of change was given while little actual change occurred.

Late in 1971, in preparation for the 1972 state elections, further efforts to encourage dissidence within the MPCC were allegedly stimulated by Mrs. Gandhi's lieutenants, if not by Mrs. Gandhi herself. The major vehicle for this was the encouragement given to S. B. Chavan of Marathwada to challenge the Chavan-Naik leadership of the party on grounds that his region had been inequitably treated over the years. [27] S. B. Chavan drew to his standard other dissidents in the MPCC: some individuals who did not like the policies which the Naik government had pursued in respect to the increasing power of the heads of cooperative institutions (a matter we will review in greater detail in chapter 8); a few

26. Dharia was then serving as Minister for Planning in the central government. His hopes for local leadership in Poona City were dashed in late 1972 when his local supporters were defeated in a test of strength over the selection of a City Congress president by a candidate loyal to the Chavan-Naik group. He was dismissed by Mrs. Gandhi in March 1975 when he sought to effect a reconciliation between Mrs. Gandhi and Jayaprakash Narayan. *New York Times,* 5 March 1975.

27. The economic backwardness of Marathwada is readily indicated by comparison with Poona division. Electricity consumption in 1961 was 110 million kilowatt hours in Poona division as compared to only 3 in Marathwada. Factory employment per 1,000 population was 8.9 to 2.3 and road mileage per 100 square miles was 29.2 to 7.4. Literacy rates were 29.3 percent of total population in the Poona division to 16.3 percent in Marathwada. Sandra McLaren, "Co-operative Marketing Societies: Case Studies in Marathwada," *Economic and Political Weekly,* 28 September 1974, pp. A-81-A-91. The figures in her article are derived from the Maharashtra Development Council, *Report on Economic Problems of Marathwada,* 1965.

individual entrepreneurs, like Mohite, who allegedly saw an opportunity for themselves, at least in the long run. (If a man from Marathwada was given a chance to serve a term, as part of the agreement reached in the course of the Samyukta Maharashtra agitation for rotation among the three major regions of the state, then Mohite would still be young enough to hope that it would be his turn when western Maharashtra received the draw again.)

Through the interventions of the national party leadership under Mrs. Gandhi, S. B. Chavan's supporters were given a prominent place in the MPCC Parliamentary Board.[28] However, during actual negotiations for nominations, the forces opposed to the Y. B. Chavan group found themselves relatively ineffective in turning their representation into legislative seats. Chavan and Naik and their followers were able to play various individual dissidents off against one another. Since the dissidents were themselves deeply implicated in the existing leadership structure, it was all the easier to absorb many of their demands. Thus, while Mrs. Gandhi had made her point by winning her followers a place in the top state leadership, she could not maneuver their domination. Additional advantages were available to her, however, since she controlled the AICC's Parliamentary Board, which was responsible for finalizing state nominations. Even there, she finally showed restraint in trying to tackle Y. B. Chavan head-on.

Thus, the national Parliamentary Board initially tried to establish its own domination over the situation by designating a man presumably loyal to Mrs. Gandhi (D. P. Mishra from Madhya Pradesh), to "scrutinize" the final list of nominations submitted to the AICC from Maharashtra. Through several days of maneuver, the MPCC and AICC representatives jockeyed for a set of accommodations acceptable to both. In several instances from Kolhapur, for example, local dissidents managed to work their way up to New Delhi before their cases were finally resolved; in Poona, too, final decisions in cases of conflict were not left for either the DCC or the MPCC. By the time a final list was achieved, however, the

28. As a result of lengthy negotiations, Naik agreed to add two S. B. Chavan supporters to the board. *Indian Express,* 7 January 1972. However, the *Times of India,* 28 January 1972, cited S. B. Chavan's expression of dissatisfaction to the Prime Minister that the list which had emerged from negotiations in the AICC Parliamentary Board did not include a number of his supporters. Also see, "And So to Delhi . . ." *Economic and Political Weekly,* 22 January 1972, pp. 143-144.

Chavan-Naik group had emerged perhaps with not as much as it would have liked but clearly in command of the state situation. The majority of decisions at the national level were simply ratifications of choices made below.

Despite the publicity given these conflicts, there was no noticeable impact of party divisions on electoral results. The Congress won 222 of 267 seats in the Maharashtra Assembly. This victory was all the more impressive considering that it involved major successes in urban areas, like Bombay and Poona, where the party had always faced significant opposition from parties which were unable to spread their followings into the countryside. Sixteen of the non-Congress seats went to "independents," many of whom were Congressmen who had been refused tickets during the negotiating for party nominations.

While the election confirmed the priority of the Congress in Maharashtra, issues of Cabinet making and reorganization of the Congress soon emerged to provide new opportunities for infighting among the ambitious. For a time, there were rumors of differences between Y. B. Chavan and Naik as the latter seemed to move closer to Mrs. Gandhi. Indeed, a few informants asserted that Mrs. Gandhi had been trying to woo Naik away from Chavan ever since the presidential elections of 1969. It was apparently Mrs. Gandhi's preference that kept Naik in position in 1972 even while other chief ministers were being replaced around the country.

It is the practice of Congress chief ministers to submit their lists of potential ministers to the national party leadership. When the original list of ministers was submitted to Mrs. Gandhi (without full consultation with Y. B. Chavan), it included the name of S. B. Chavan as Deputy Chief Minister. The idea was dropped, however, when it was opposed by both Y. B. Chavan and Vasantrao Patil, although on different grounds. Patil allegedly feared that this would be the basis for S. B. Chavan to stake a claim to the succession. (It was widely rumored that Naik would continue in his position as Chief Minister only for a short time in order to complete ten years in office.) Y. B. Chavan, it is said, argued against the formal designation of a Deputy Chief Minister because such a designation had caused difficulties in the past both in state and national politics. The rest of the list of ministers was also carefully culled, and several prospective candidates, including Rajaram Patil (Vasantrao Patil's major rival in Sangli district) and D. H. Jagtap, Chavan's son-in-law, were dropped by Mrs. Gandhi.

(In the former case, the decision allegedly was greeted with some unhappiness on the part of the Chief Minister.)

The most surprising addition to the list of potential ministers was Vasantrao (Dada) Patil. Although Patil had been president of the MPCC for five years, an MLA from 1952 to 1967, and one of the most prominent leaders of the cooperative movement in the state, he had never taken much interest in a governmental position.[29] Indeed, at the time of his selection he did not even hold a seat in the Maharashtra State Assembly, which was the normal launching pad for ministers. Instead, he was a member of the much weaker Legislative Council. While Patil was widely respected for the role he had played in the freedom movement and for his cooperative activities, he was not the kind of material of which Maharashtra ministers were normally made. As one usually knowledgeable informant indicated:

> It is not clear exactly how Dada became a minister. Rajni Patel [President of the BPCC] was either used by the Chief Minister or he put forward the idea himself that Dada should be taken up in the Cabinet. When the leaders of Maharashtra were called to Delhi to consult with Mrs. Gandhi about the list of ministers, the name of Dada was brought up several times but she did not seem very enthusiastic. . . . People were surprised that she was not so enthusiastic about it. Actually with Rajaram Patil out, Balasaheb Desai out, and D. H. Jagtap also dropped from the ministry, Dada was one of the few leaders from western Maharashtra taken up. Mohite and Pawar were the others, but they could not be seen as leaders in the same light.[30]

Becoming Minister for Irrigation and Power, a major Cabinet position, and deputy leader of the legislative Congress party along with S. B. Chavan (who remained in the Cabinet as second in rank to Naik) might have been regarded as a high achievement, but there were apparently some questions in Patil's mind. Immediately after his selection, he confessed certain doubts to those close to

29. Patil did not contest for MLA in 1972 since there was little expectation he would join the Ministry.

30. Pawar's addition to the Cabinet was also a last-moment arrangement. He was not on the initial list submitted to the Prime Minister. According to one MPCC informant, he was added at the eleventh hour when Chavan made a phone call to Naik. Pawar was being used, some informants suggest, as a potential challenger to Mohite in western Maharashtra. There has been no great friendship between the two men, despite the leftist ideological appeals that both men employ.

him. As one confidant reported, "He felt that he did not know English and had no governmental experience. He has a speech problem that makes it difficult for him to talk in the Assembly. He was also afraid that taking such a position would make enemies for him and few friends." He had good grounds for such fears.

Interestingly enough, another informant suggested that the ministerial bait extended to Patil was by no means the temptation that it might have been to others:

> Rather than strengthening Dada's position, his being taken up in the Cabinet may have been a way of weakening him. He had to give up his position as MPCC president, a position which he had made stronger. He also gave up his post as chairman of the State Marketing Federation and his chairmanship of the Maharashtra State Cooperative Bank. Furthermore, he lost out to Rajni Patel in control of the Rashtriya Mill Mazdoor Sangh [the major textile workers' union in Bombay]. He lost all these places of power to become only one among many ministers.[31]

Mrs. Gandhi and Maharashtra Politics: Round II

When Vasantrao Patil became a minister in March 1972, there was a considerable struggle over the selection of his successor as president of the MPCC. One of the reasons for Naik's strategic position in state politics was that he was a non-Maratha from Vidarbha, whereas many of the other top leaders were Marathas. When Mrs. Gandhi intervened in the process of selecting a new MPCC president, it soon became clear that she wanted someone who was independent of the Naik-Chavan group and, preferably, a Maratha who might develop his own independent following in western Maharashtra. Thus, when Naik suggested the name of another non-Maratha from Vidarbha, she turned him down. She also rejected V. N. Gadgil's name after it was put forward; in this case, the argument was that Gadgil (a Brahman) would simply duplicate the non-Maratha contribution of Naik. Along the way, Patil offered to continue, but Mrs. Gandhi insisted that he had served long enough as president. Finally, after six months of haggling, the name of P. K. Sawant was raised and Mrs. Gandhi

31. Though Patil's men were ousted from control of the Rashtriya Mill Mazdoor Sangh, they fought back by forming their own Mumbai (Bombay) Mill Mazdoor Sangh early in 1973. Interestingly enough, this effort was backed by the Shiv Sena. *Statesman,* 6 April 1973; *Times of India,* 10 April 1973. This contest further embittered relations between the leaderships of the MPCC and the BPCC, relationships which have always been difficult.

agreed. Sawant became acting president of the MPCC in September 1972.[32]

With reference to Mrs. Gandhi's behavior, one interviewee commented, "Not only did she feel that she must have a Maratha, but she also wanted someone not associated so strongly with the Chavan group. She felt she had let down the other group which had supported her and that she needed to show her favor toward them."

Though Naik was willing to go along with the choice of Sawant, Patil was quite opposed to it. At first, there was some notion that this would be only a temporary appointment, since party elections, which had been postponed from 1970, were finally to be held in late 1972. However, at the final stage of those elections the state and national leadership agreed to retain Sawant as president. This sat so badly with Patil that he threatened to resign his ministry in protest. He was finally convinced to remain, but this contretemps contributed to a growing uneasiness between Naik and Patil, an uneasiness which was available for exploitation by others.

Sawant is an elder statesman of the party and actually senior to Y. B. Chavan in terms of age and party activity.[33] Though he

32. According to one published story, Naik suggested Rajaram Patil as one possibility, a name which obviously caused Vasantrao Patil considerable unhappiness. It was rejected by Mrs. Gandhi. As the writer notes, "Though Naik had not included Sawant in his Cabinet after the elections, he was prepared to support him for the party presidentship so as to contain Vasantrao Patil who has never hit it off with Sawant. . . . Vasantrao Patil and his faction in the party may be counted on to be at loggerheads with Sawant who has the support of men like Y. J. Mohite. . . . This fits in very well with the Prime Minister's objective of keeping the party in Maharashtra divided and preventing the rise of any single powerful leader." "Dividing to Rule," *Economic and Political Weekly*, 9 September 1972, pp. 1803-1804.

33. At the time that Chavan left the Maharashtra government to become Minister for Defense, Sawant was the candidate of the BPCC for the chief ministership. His main rival was Balasaheb Desai. However, neither man had sufficient following to assure himself a definite claim to the post. There was also some feeling that the position should go to someone from Vidarbha. While Vasantrao Naik's name was mentioned, M. S. Kannamwar, an elderly compromise candidate from that region, was selected. In November 1963, Kannamwar died suddenly, and jockeying between Desai and Sawant began again. Rather than side with either, Chavan and the national party leadership intervened on behalf of Naik, who was regarded as independent of the Sawant-Desai factional quarrels. *Link*, 15 December 1963, p. 13.

has represented constituencies in the State Assembly from Ratna-giri district since 1946, he has also taken an active role in the union movement in Bombay City and has been on occasion associated with the BPCC leadership in these activities. His differ-ences with Patil may have stemmed, in fact, from earlier conflicts over leadership in the major textile mill union in Bombay where both had sought support.

More than most Congressmen, Sawant verbalized an interest in rebuilding the Congress in a way that would associate an ideologically committed cadre element with the non-electoral activities of the party—a proposal that the central party leadership had been advancing rhetorically since Mrs. Gandhi's electoral vic-tory of 1971 but had done little to follow up. Three months after his formal installation as president in December 1972, however, Sawant was still trying to select a full complement of secretaries for the MPCC. In particular, there was a deadlock between himself and the Chief Minister over the choice of a party secretary to represent Vidarbha. The Chief Minister's choice—the man who had been Naik's first preference for MPCC president—was un-acceptable to Sawant and it took several months to overcome that disagreement.

The alignment of Sawant with Rajni Patel, head of the BPCC, also provided an incentive for the state government and MPCC leadership to embarrass the BPCC during elections for the Bombay Municipal Corporation in 1973. It was expected that the Congress would do well in those elections following its substantial legislative victories throughout India during 1972. Yet the party lost the municipal elections, and the Shiv Sena managed to lead a coalition of groups that took control of major offices in the new city government.[34]

This was an embarrassment to Patel but also caused some difficulty for Naik, since allegations about the state government's support to the Shiv Sena had been common in the press and in political gossip for a decade. Without the power to directly con-front Naik, however, leaders within the BPCC focused their com-

34. As one journal noted, "Through his tactics of overtly appearing to support Rajni Patel and covertly opposing him, the Chief Minister has not only inflicted some crushing political defeats on the BPCC President but has also discredited the latter among his own followers." "Congress Debacle," *Economic and Political Weekly,* 17 March 1973, pp. 541-542. Also see D. F. Karaka, "Did Naik Finance the Shiv Sena?" *Current,* 24 March 1973, p. 1.

plaints against dissidents within the BPCC, most notably the Education Minister, A. N. Namjoshi. Namjoshi, who had assumed that position only after the 1972 elections, was replaced in November 1974 as part of a Cabinet reorganization. [35]

That reorganization was thought to have made Naik's position more secure in state politics. One journalist attributed Naik's continuation in office at the time to his situation as a non-Maratha in a state where a number of Marathas were competing for the opportunity to become chief minister. In particular, the reporter singled out S. B. Chavan, Y. J. Mohite, and Vasantrao Patil as the main contenders for the succession to Naik, but, as he noted, "Y. B. Chavan, himself a Maratha, . . . does not much care for any of the three major Maratha contenders for the chief minister-ship. No doubt he is also apprehensive that a Maratha Chief Minister might pose a serious threat to his leadership of the state Congress." [36]

For whatever reasons, Mrs. Gandhi apparently decided in February 1975 to meet her earlier promises of support. Newspaper reports published on February 13 found Sawant in Delhi along with S. B. Chavan to consult with the national Congress President, D. K. Borooah. Among those consulted on the change were two prominent figures from the Muslim community in Maharashtra and a man who had been described only three months earlier as a "protégé" of Y. B. Chavan. Within a few days, Naik stepped aside and S. B. Chavan was unanimously elected the new Chief Minister of Maharashtra. Reviewing the events which had led up to the change, a reporter for the *Times of India* treated the national decision-making process as one in which Y. B. Chavan had figured only tangentially. [37] With Sawant, Rajni Patel, and S. B. Chavan all pleading for a change in the chief ministership, the Prime Minister was apparently finally willing to move. Her action may have been aided by an indication from Vasantrao Patil that he was no longer interested in being considered as a possible successor to Naik and would support S. B. Chavan. What the implications of the new structure of leadership in Maharashtra are for the state party organization and, more particularly, for the continued influence of

35. *Times of India*, 8 November 1974.
36. "Maharashtra: Shifting Deadline," *Economic and Political Weekly*, 9 November 1974, p. 1880.
37. *Times of India*, 24 February 1975.

Y. B. Chavan in state and national politics remains to be seen, particularly given the state of emergency declared by Mrs. Gandhi later in the year.

THE USES OF POLICY IN AMBITIONAL STRUGGLES

For the most part, the struggle for the succession in Maharashtra did not spill over into issues of public policy. Certain traditional symbolic issues were conjured up, such as demands for equity in treatment for Marathwada and the desirability of representing Marathas in the position of chief minister, but only during the brief flurry over land reforms and the period of activity on the part of the Socialist Forum during 1971-1972 did ideological issues surface.

While ambitional contests are rarely framed in terms of ideological considerations, many of the conflicts over more pragmatic policy changes in Maharashtra do implicate political actors striving for personal advantage in state politics. One case of interest in that respect was the struggle between Vasantrao Naik and Vasantrao Patil over the provision of irrigation facilities to parts of Kolhapur and Sangli districts. The case drew attention in the press because it bore on the conflicts which had emerged between Naik and Patil over ascendancy within the Congress organization and in the eventual succession to Naik. From our perspective, it is also an interesting case because Kolhapur politicians were so deeply involved.

As noted in the last chapter, Kolhapur had long felt itself underrepresented in the benefits distributed among districts, despite its relatively prosperous economic condition. For a number of years, the political leadership of the district, on behalf of the bigger farmers, had been demanding more irrigation facilities.[38] In 1973, complaints about the lack of speed with which various schemes for irrigation had been implemented were highlighted when the state began to feel the impact of a severe drought. Although the drought was so bad that more extensive irrigation facilities would not have been of immediate help, the district

38. Government leadership is decidedly defensive about the slowness with which even the limited irrigation potential of the state has been exploited, but it insists that finances and technical expertise have been important barriers to irrigation development.

leadership in Kolhapur and the dissident group in neighboring Sangli complained bitterly of past failures on the part of the state government. Because he was Minister for Irrigation (or because he was a highly visible political leader), Vasantrao Patil became the special target of these attacks.

Some of the points of attack were petty. One MLA from Kolhapur, for example, blamed Patil for spending more time making tours to inaugurate new buildings and attend weddings than he spent at work on his ministerial responsibilities. More serious were the public meetings and demonstrations which were fomented against Patil's decisions. Thus, an MLA from Kolhapur, who was aligned with Patil's opponents in Sangli, took an active stand in favor of a particular irrigation project for Kolhapur district, which had been in the planning stage for many years but had been held in abeyance by the state government and, most recently, by Patil. Patil had indicated a preference for other projects which, allegedly, favored his own district. The Congress MLA in question received the support of Kumbhar and of independent MLAs from the district in demanding that immediate action be taken in favor of the Kolhapur project.

In early March 1973, a large meeting was held in the affected area (in the northeast and central part of the district). It quickly became clear that the organizers had seized on a politically popular demand. Though some District Congress leaders, notably Udaisingh Gaikwad, did not want to offend Patil openly, most indicated their support for the demand that the project be taken up immediately. Patil agreed to visit the site in early March and at that time promised to begin work by October 31, but there was some feeling that this was a stalling tactic on his part. Thus, despite the promise and because of the political appeal of the issue, a local "action committee" began an agitation as a vehicle both to embarrass Patil and to bring about pressure for speedier action. Demonstrations were organized in April and May demanding immediate pursuit of the project; some Congress MLAs threatened to resign on the issue if work was not begun by March 31.[39]

As an aspect of their activity, a delegation of Kolhapur MLAs visited the Chief Minister. Their threatened actions were stemmed

___

39. As a leader of the Kolhapur zilla parishad noted, "Those who still hope to become ministers would stay away from the protest. The leader is really the chairman of the Bidri sugar factory and the members of that board. They are also being helped by Kumbhar, who is mixing everywhere as usual."

by a promise from Naik to visit the district himself and review matters with local leaders. Such an action constituted an unspoken indication by Naik that he lacked full confidence in Patil's decision-making capabilities. Rumors of threats by Patil to resign on the issue were widely publicized.[40] Part of the dispute involved a technical issue: the use of flow-irrigation systems as opposed to lift-irrigation arrangements. Apparently, Patil argued in favor of lift irrigation, which would make a quicker political impact and be less expensive to implement in the short run than a flow-irrigation system. The latter would take time to carry out but would be capable of transporting more water to a greater number of farmers. To deal with the matter, Naik set up a subcommittee within the Cabinet to review some of the decisions in dispute, while agitations continued to be organized in Kolhapur and threats of such agitations developed in Sangli.[41] Under this pressure, the Chief Minister announced on May 12, 1973, that the main demands of the Kolhapur "action committee" had been conceded.[42]

The final plan, as released by Naik after a Cabinet meeting on May 17, reflected a victory for the Kolhapur people, although certain modifications had been made in the original scheme.[43] How soon actual work would begin on the project was not clear from the statement. What was clear was that Naik had pressed his advantage over Patil to embarrass the latter. That may account for the fact that Patil subsequently became a more serious supporter

40. The issue was exploited particularly by *Blitz*, which apparently saw the matter as another way of both undermining the Naik government and attacking Patil. "Naik Cabinet Cracks," *Blitz*, 24 March and 7 April 1973.

41. In Sangli, the attack was led (as one might anticipate) by Rajaram Patil, who insisted that Vasantrao Patil was putting the state's money into the wrong project at the wrong place. The debate reached the floor of the State Assembly, where Rajaram complained that the site for the storage area had been changed to a new location which would be incapable of holding the same capacity of water. The political aspects of the debate became clouded by technical problems related to the relative costs to the farmer of the two competing types of irrigation systems and of the probable speed of completion of either type. *Times of India*, 22 and 23 March 1973; "Politics of an Irrigation Project," *Economic and Political Weekly*, 30 June 1973, p. 1129. The latter piece identifies Ratnappa Kumbhar as one of those associated with Rajaram Patil in opposing the plan preferred by Vasantrao Patil. Some of the technical aspects of the debate are reviewed in B. K. Vaidya, "Feud in Congress Hits Irrigation Schemes," *Times of India*, 11 July 1973.

42. *Times of India*, 13 May 1973.

43. *Times of India*, 18 May 1973.

of the move to replace Naik, though how serious a contender he himself was at any time is not known. It is instructive about the relationship between Patil and Naik that one report reviewing the Cabinet reorganization of late 1974 noted that the selection of Ratnappa Kumbhar as Minister of State for Home and Publicity in the Naik government was part of a strategy to bring into the government known opponents of those who were contenders for the chief ministership. [44] Yet in the twists and turns of Maharashtra politics, the new Chief Minister, S. B. Chavan, who took over in 1975, retained men like Mohite, Pawar, and Patil in the Cabinet while promoting Kumbhar to full ministerial status as Minister for Food and Civil Supplies.

This brief example of the relationship between politics and policy should prepare the reader for the chapters which follow, for they illustrate in greater detail how proposals for change which claim professional or technical standing are frequently enmeshed in political considerations. However, the character of those political considerations varies from a generalized concern with the collective benefits due non-Brahmans in educational institutions to struggles for personal political and economic advantage at work in the debate over reform in the cooperative sector.

44. "Maharashtra: Shifting Deadline," *Economic and Political Weekly*, 9 November 1974, p. 1880.

SIX

The Ends and Means of Educational Policy

Members of the local political elite in Poona and Kolhapur are regularly drawn into the stream of educational politics. If a person is engaged in panchayati raj, he or she may be called upon by constituents to provide additional primary schools; the local leader may also try to enhance his prestige by helping to found a secondary school or college in the area. Since the organization, accreditation, and extension of financial aid to educational institutions require a series of interactions with the state educational bureaucracy, politics is frequently associated with the process by which schools are brought to the countryside.

To attribute great influence to local politicians alone in such matters may be giving them too much credit. State government leaders and functional specialists at the state and national level also have favored a rapid expansion of rural-based educational institutions; local politicians have been only one among several forces working in that direction. Expansion has occurred without great concern for the effects of that expansion upon the newly educated and without regard for the appropriate trade-offs between quality and quantity. It is only as the consequence of a realization by certain state politicians and functional specialists that resources may have been misallocated in education that questions have begun to be raised about the proper direction of educational development.

Issues of such scope are rarely debated within the arenas of local politics except in reaction to initiatives undertaken by the state government. In chapter 9, we will examine a debate concerning the merit of continuing to assign a role in the administration of primary education to local governments. For the most part, that conflict was distinct from the ones discussed in the present chapter. Here we deal with efforts by certain elements within the state leadership to formulate proposals for change in the educational patterns of Maharashtra.

Institutionalization of the Educational Sector

The state of Maharashtra directly supports most of the costs of primary education in rural areas and indirectly administers primary schools through the zilla parishads. In recent years, it has also underwritten an increasingly large share of the expenses of secondary schools. Since 1966-1967, it has covered virtually 100 percent of both teachers' salaries and school rents.[1] Such support has provided an incentive for private education societies to organize and run secondary schools and, more recently, colleges. (Colleges recover 60 to 70 percent of their operating costs from government grants.)

The existence of private managements in secondary education is by no means peculiar to Maharashtra; indeed, in many of the other Indian states such managements are predominantly associated with sectarian groups—religious communities; castes; ethnic associations.[2] While a few sectarian managements are to be found in urban areas of the state, the relatively homogeneous character of the Maharashtrian countryside, with its economic and political domination by the Maratha community, has tended to work toward an educational pattern which does not really reflect sectarian concerns. Or more properly put, it *no longer* reflects sectarian concerns, for, as we noted earlier, the first part of this century witnessed a struggle in western Maharashtra for political and socioeconomic ascendancy between Brahmans and non-Brahmans.

1. In computing payments, grants are reduced according to tuition fees charged. Managements are also expected to contribute 1 percent of total costs in urban areas and 2.5 percent in rural areas to their own expenses. Though these might be considered small amounts, several informants complained that they were difficult to collect. This reflects the degree to which many of the "private" societies actually are highly dependent financially on government for their survival.

2. In Kerala, for example, education societies run by Christians, Muslims, and different Hindu castes have played a major role in the educational politics of the state. In Karnataka, too, sectarianism has been an important factor associated with the founding of educational institutions. On Karnataka, see Glynn Wood, "Planning, Local Interest and Higher Education in an Indian State" (Ph.D. diss., Massachusetts Institute of Technology, 1969); and T. N. Madan and B. G. Halpar, "Caste and Community in the Private and Public Education of Mysore State," in Susanne Hoeber Rudolph and Lloyd I. Rudolph, eds'., *Education and Politics in India* (Delhi: Oxford University Press, 1972), pp. 121-147.

Under the British, the Brahmans—particularly those residing in urban areas and those who could afford to maintain their children in the cities while they were being educated—were able to derive the greatest benefits from education, and they employed that educational advantage to play a disproportionate role in the political life of the region. It was out of the non-Brahman movement at the turn of the century that a thirst for education for the bahujan samaj began to appear. At first, the Maratha nobility in princely states like Baroda and Kolhapur were responsible for stimulating an increase in educational opportunities for non-Brahmans. They extended financial support and their personal prestige to societies founded to promote non-Brahman education. The Maharaja of Kolhapur, Shahu, for example, not only aided the establishment of schools in his realm but encouraged attendance by granting aid to various low-status communities to run residential hostels where students from the state and from other parts of India might live while attending schools located in the prince's capital city.[3]

The impact of private education societies in the countryside is essentially a post-independence phenomenon. Most of the earlier non-Brahman institutions were located in urban areas and served a middle- or high-status clientele. In western Maharashtra, one of the more interesting educational movements for mass education was spurred by the activities of a single man, Bhaurao Patil.[4]

Born in 1886 in Satara district, Patil was sent to the Rajaram High School in neighboring Kolhapur in 1902. There he enrolled in the Jain boarding hostel sponsored by the royal administration. After living in Kolhapur for seven years, Patil returned to Satara, where he became a salesman. In 1919, he took time away from

3. The earliest education societies in western India were founded by Brahmans. Though such educational institutions admitted high-status non-Brahmans, relatively few made use of those institutions. One of the attractions of Kolhapur at the turn of the century was that schools were run by and for non-Brahmans under royal patronage. With the founding of the Shivaji Maratha Society in 1917 in Poona—a society which received the encouragement of the Maratha aristocracy—educational institutions for non-Brahmans began to develop more rapidly in Bombay State itself. In that connection, see Gail Omvedt, "Non-Brahmans and Nationalists in Poona," *Economic and Political Weekly,* Annual Number, February 1974, pp. 207-209.

4. For the details of Patil's life, see Anjilvel V. Matthew, *Karmaveer Bhaurao Patil* (Satara: Rayat Shikshan Saunstha, 1957).

business to start a boarding hostel in a village near the town of Karad in Satara (the town with which Y. B. Chavan has been most closely identified). Eventually, this led to the formation of an education society which became known as the *Rayat Shikshan Saunstha* (Peasants Education Society).

The Saunstha grew slowly until independence, when Bombay State began to underwrite an expansion in education. The state government decided to absorb all rural primary schools offering the first to fourth grades under the administration of district school boards. At the same time, it extended financial support to private societies offering the higher primary standards and secondary education. With the impetus of government financial support, the Saunstha spread until it now operates over three hundred secondary schools and eighteen colleges in twelve districts of western Maharashtra. Bhaurao Patil died in 1959, but the Saunstha continues to run an impressive educational establishment. Its stature is aided by the fact that the president of the Saunstha since Patil's death has been Y. B. Chavan. However, the Saunstha is not Chavan's political instrument. His position is largely honorific.[5] Indeed, Patil, who was intensely devoted to the regional and parochial interests of Maharashtrian non-Brahmans, held views which prevented him from ever being close to Chavan. Still, shortly before his death, Chavan agreed to Patil's request that he associate himself with the Saunstha.

In his later years, Patil's rather authoritarian domination of the Saunstha was contested by one of the younger members of the organization, G. D. Salunke. When it became obvious in 1955 that Patil would not yield a portion of his authority in the Saunstha to others, Salunke left the organization to form his own educational society—the Vivekananda Society. By 1970, that society claimed in the neighborhood of two hundred secondary schools in the region. As in the case of the Saunstha, most of these are in the rural areas and middle-range towns of Maharashtra rather than in the big cities.[6]

5. The Saunstha's basic decisions are made by a management body dominated by "life-members," teacher-administrators who have dedicated their lives to the society. While such life-memberships were originally positions of social service, abuses associated with life-memberships in some societies have led recently to scrutiny of the practice by the state government.

6. Such societies are not peculiar to western Maharashtra. One based in Vidarbha, the Shri Shivaji Education Society, operates 126 institutions from

Because of the quarrels within the Saunstha which led to the creation of the Vivekananda Society, there has been little affection lost between the two organizations. Their differences have sometimes spilled over into political life. Thus, one spokesman for the older organization went so far as to argue that the more recent society was created with the encouragement of state Congress party leaders because Bhaurao Patil was known to be an active supporter of the Samyukta Maharashtra movement and a sympathizer of the PWP. According to this informant:

> At the district level the educational inspectors, at the state level the Directorate of Education and the ministers ganged up to patronize the Vivekananda Society. They granted funds and they were quite lenient about letting the Society start schools in areas where our schools were already running even if this went against the rule that there was to be no new high school within five to six miles of an existing one. Instead, the government allowed the Vivekananda Society to open schools within one or one and one-half miles of existing schools. This gave rise to unhealthy competition between the two societies.[7]

Healthy or not, the competition has had its ramifications in state and local politics, particularly in Satara district, where the Rayat Shikshan Saunstha has had its home base and the Vivekananda Society has operated many of its educational institutions. (Its headquarters are located in Kolhapur.)

Even if it was true that the Vivekananda Society was more closely associated with the Congress leadership before the creation of Maharashtra, the situation changed after 1960. With the entry of many non-Brahman local leaders into the Congress, the Saunstha acquired or consolidated friendships in leading Congress circles including, most notably, Balasaheb Desai. Desai served as

---

its headquarters in Amravati District. Robert G. Wirsing, "Associational 'Micro-Arenas' in Indian Urban Politics," *Asian Survey* 13 (April 1973): 414-415.

7. After reading an earlier draft of the present chapter, an informant long associated with the Vivekananda Society replied that the Director of Education had not favored the Society: "It was just a time when the government was strongly in favor of educational expansion and was allowing any group seeking to start a school to take it up. Both the Saunstha and the Vivekananda Society took maximum advantage of the situation. . . . At that time people actually thought the Saunstha was on the way down and that Vivekananda was growing and vigorous and had the brighter future so they would approach Salunke to help start schools. . . . The Education Department simply yielded to public pressure in these matters."

Education Minister during a period when policies were adopted which favored the entry of non-Brahmans into a more active role in the making of educational policy in the state.[8] There were those interviewees who saw in Desai's approach to politics an attempt to arouse rural non-Brahman interests against the urban (especially Brahman) elites which had dominated educational policy in the past. Indeed, one leading educator described Desai as a representative of the "PWP element within the Congress." Despite his personal attachment to the Saunstha,[9] when Chavan became nominal president of the Saunstha in 1960, Desai (allegedly out of a personal pique with that organization) accepted the presidency of the Vivekananda Society.[10]

While the Saunstha remained strong enough to ride out political storms and to take a leading part in the events discussed in the next section, the Vivekananda Society found itself in considerable difficulty in the late 1960s. A case of misappropriation of funds intended for the payment of teachers' salaries in some of its institutions in Satara district led to governmental inquiries and provided an opportunity for local politicians in that district to launch attacks on the management of the Society.

Those attacks were part of the factional conflicts within Satara politics as much as they were the result of a concern for the educational questions involved. Especially because the disputes involved actors in his home district, Y. B. Chavan personally intervened and attempted to arbitrate both the managerial and the political questions raised. Despite these efforts, a series of court

8. One of the more controversial steps taken during Desai's tenure as Minister for Education was the decision to start a new university based in Kolhapur, Shivaji University. Some informants saw this as an effort by the new state government to subvert the traditional domination of non-Marathas in Poona and Bombay universities. Contrary to practices in those older institutions, Chavan and Desai intervened directly to appoint the first chief administrative officer—the vice-chancellor—for the institution. Their appointee, Appasaheb Pawar, had been the first Maratha to serve in the highest bureaucratic position in the State Education Department, Director of Education. Pawar was himself a member of the economic elite of Kolhapur; his sister was the widow of Vasantrao Bagal.

9. Desai claimed that he had given Patil considerable assistance in starting schools in Satara district when Desai was president of the District Local Board in the 1940s. Interview, D. S. Desai, 18 February 1973.

10. He resigned from the presidency, however, before the events discussed below became public.

cases followed, as well as fitful attempts by the state government to intervene, but, as late as 1973, an uncertain situation existed with respect to the future of the Vivekananda Society.[11]

Because of experiences with the Vivekananda Society and the influence exercised by the Rayat Shikshan Saunstha in the controversies of 1968-1970, state officials (including both political and administrative actors involved in education) began to favor a degree of decentralization of the major education societies, at least down to the district level. In this they received the support of some local leaders (including leaders of localized societies) who regarded the big societies as insensitive to local needs and attitudes. The stated goal was to involve local persons more actively in the management of such institutions; the often implicit goal was to remove an element which officials, in particular, were beginning to regard as a blockage to major reforms in the educational system. The Minister for Education in 1970 stressed the former motive in his comments on the need for reform, "The main problem is that the private schools are not always responsive and must be made to be more responsive to the community and to be real community centers." [12] As a result of such motives, the state government attempted to impose regulations in 1972 to require that no new institutions be started by societies which already operated more than ten secondary schools in a district. [13] It was uncertain in 1973 how effective these regulations would be.

While large private education societies are enmeshed in state policy making, the character of participation by smaller societies varies. For secondary schools run by one-school societies, politics is a highly localized affair. Politicians who participate in small

11. One sympathizer of the Society attributed the problems of that organization to its pattern of growth: "It grew so rapidly between 1955 and 1965 that some of its gains could not be consolidated. Some of the faults of Bhaurao also began to come out in Salunke. Workers had to refer too many decisions to Salunke himself."

12. Interview with M. D. Chaudhari, Minister for Education, July 1, 1970. This view was also expressed by Mrs. Prabha Rao, Minister of State for Education, in an interview on January 30, 1973: "It is our feeling that the local people should take some initiative in the education field. If a big society going beyond the border of a district comes up, it is a way in which local initiative is reduced."

13. There was some doubt that the regulation was politically enforceable. The new Education Minister, installed in April 1972, also seemed less interested than his predecessor in pressing the issue.

societies may represent the interests of those institutions in political arenas, but the institutions are not major political actors in their own right.[14] On the other hand, the few large private societies are almost precluded from taking an active interest in each locality's politics, but they do have a great concern about keeping on good terms with major political leaders and in achieving desired state policies. Between the two extremes of size are those education societies with several schools, largely confined to one district or overlapping into a second district, which may choose either approach.

An example of a medium-range society is the one operated by the politicians who dominate the Poona Congress. Members of the District Local Board founded the Poona District Education Society (DES) in 1941; it was originally concerned with promoting primary education, but that level was later turned over to the District School Board. The DES opened its first secondary school in 1956 and by 1970 ran thirty-eight schools, offering standards eight to eleven. More recently, the Poona DES has also entered into the field of higher education by starting a college in a part of the district where it already operated six high schools. ·

Although Shankarrao Bhelke served as president of the DES for nine years and was followed by Mamasaheb Mohol (who served for seven), the retired local administrator who acted as the operational head of the DES insisted, "None of the local politicians interfere in the work of the society. Mostly they leave us alone. When they come to me about particular problems, of course, I talk to them."[15] According to this informant, villagers were often the ones who took the initiative in organizing schools:

> If villagers want us to start a school, the village panchayat writes to us to open a school in their area. That means that we rely on the elders of the village for support and if anything special needs to be done, we ask

14. Until 1972, private managements were not active as a corporate group, but since then the Saunstha has taken the lead in trying to form an association of private managements to demand larger grants from government for the operation of colleges. Local organizers of such institutions experience particular difficulty with the heavy costs which must be absorbed in construction and equipment before government recognition is accorded and operating grants begin to flow.

15. Several young men interviewed for positions in the schools of the DES—interviews held on the premises of the zilla parishad—were inclined to believe that political connections made a significant difference in getting appointments. It was impossible to validate this notion.

the village panchayat. We try to stay above village conflicts. If the villagers want a school we may ask them for help on such things as furniture, though now with larger equipment grants from the state government we don't need as much help on this as formerly.

The type of local stimulus cited here is frequently mentioned by those who have become involved in the development of schools in the countryside in the last few years. As opposed to the experience of the big educational societies and their dedicated founders, who were themselves often the key stimuli to the introduction of education into rural areas, an increasing number of secondary schools have been founded more recently as the direct outgrowth of local demands and politicians' responses to those demands.

Under normal circumstances, few politicians take an interest in matters of curriculum or teaching methods. Their interests are more in the tangible and intangible rewards of association with the administration of an educational institution. Tangible rewards include influence in matters of teacher recruitment, participation in spending government grants, and the control of contracts for the supply of services to the schools. Thus, charges are occasionally raised against the managements of private societies (and against the politicians and non-politicians associated with them) on matters such as: misuse of government funds; padding of attendance records in order to gain larger government grants; misappropriation of money from the societies; forcing teachers to work in political campaigns; making teachers' appointments contingent on the payment of "kickbacks" on salaries paid by the state government.

Nevertheless, there is no reason to assume that these are the most common motives for involvement in the work of private education societies. Being associated with the founding of a school, for instance, in itself lends prestige which can be employed for political purposes. On some occasions, too, members of the public may turn to established politicians, or to local economic or social notables, whom they hope will have the kind of access to state educational administrators and politicians necessary to assure the recognition and financial support required to operate a new school. [16] Pressures are put on the ambitious local politician by his

16. In several cases that I examined, a local politician seemed to be only one of several leading local figures sitting on a board of management and not

constituents, therefore, to expedite the creation of new educational institutions, and his success may be used as a standard of judgment in continuing public support to him in other matters.

It is difficult to determine how widespread abuses are. Cases of mismanagement by private education societies are regularly cited on the floor of the state legislature. Informants in Poona and Kolhapur—politicians, teachers, and educational administrators—readily expressed their concern about the existence of such malpractices in education. Yet, as ready as they were to admit to these problems, most were also eager to stress that rapid expansion of educational opportunities had been worth the price.

Political connections are likely to grow even more important in the future since the competition to gain government "recognition" for the establishment of new schools appears to be getting sharper. According to the Director of Education for Maharashtra, in 1969 the state government sanctioned the start of about two hundred new secondary schools, out of well over four hundred requests submitted. In granting permission and subsequently providing financial aid, he asserted, the government employed criteria such as the available population for a school in the designated area and the administrative and financial capacities of those involved in the management of the education society. With the increase in government financial aid, however, greater efforts are now being made to supervise the process; at the same time, as one teacher-member of the Vidhan Parishad remarked, [17] there is a growing

necessarily the dominant one. Thus, education societies do not seem to be quite the single-minded political instruments in rural Maharashtra that they are, for example, in a state like Uttar Pradesh. See Harold Gould, "Educational Structures and Political Processes in Faizabad District, Uttar Pradesh," in Rudolph and Rudolph, *Education and Politics*, pp. 94-120.

17. The indirectly elected membership of the upper house of the Maharashtra legislature (Vidhan Parishad) includes seven seats elected from special teachers' constituencies. Because teaching has traditionally been a Brahman occupation, there has been a tendency for Brahmans to be elected to those seats. The four representatives from western Maharashtra and Bombay in 1970 claimed to be independents, but their political inclinations were known to be toward the Brahman-dominated Jan Sangh. The man quoted in the text noted that there was a certain deference paid in the body to teacher-members on educational affairs. He contrasted this with the situation in the popularly elected lower house (Vidhan Sabha) and reflected his view of the membership of that body when he commented, "The general masses are illiterate and their representatives really represent the masses in this respect."

tendency to favor Congressmen more than opposition politicians in the political competition to open schools:

> Five or six years back anybody who wanted to get a school could form a society and approach the government. While he had to get formal sanction to proceed, this was fairly automatic. Now, . . . the Congress makes sure its own men get the benefit. No doubt there is a race for political power involved but there is also the other side to this question. Our people have been illiterate for so many generations. Now they want education. An old man from a village comes to me and says he is illiterate and that he does not know or understand what it is we are teaching his son, yet he is keen to turn his son over to us and will tell us even to beat him if we need to in order to get him educated. As a result of this feeling, every panchayat and every *sarpanch* [village headman] thinks it is part of his duty to start a school.

The most significant aspect of societies formed to serve the educational needs of rural clienteles may be in the subtle changes they are inducing in the countryside. Secondary and higher education are no longer the urban phenomena that they were before independence.[18] The new institutions have become the basis for the emergence of an urbanizing force in a rural setting. As a result, a moderately educated population is being produced in rural Maharashtra that owes little to personal experiences in the big cities. Difficulties may still arise, as several parents of rural-educated children indicated, when their children find that outlets in the countryside are too limited and they choose to move to the city *after* their educations.

However, there seem to be several counter-trends in progress, including the movement back to the countryside of a younger generation of rural-based politicians who have been educated in cities like Poona and Kolhapur; they return to build political careers which include the promotion of educational institutions in their home areas. Their efforts are now beginning to be supplemented by those of the rural-educated. Furthermore, the creation of rural secondary and collegiate institutions has drawn into the countryside teachers (whose own origins may have been either urban or rural). They utilize their urban experiences to promote a

18. Thus, the earlier image of Poona City as a center for education in western India has been somewhat altered. Data indicate that by 1969-1970, 188 of the 291 private secondary schools in the district were located outside of the city.

growing sense of political awareness and efficacy at least among the better-off peasants—those who are able to absorb the financial costs of going without their children's labor contribution to the family. It is this group, in particular, that has provided support to the new style of education, for it sees such a route as the best one for giving its children some exposure to the larger world while keeping them reasonably close to the family hearth. This is an attitude not too distant in flavor from the popular support that exists in the United States for community or junior colleges as contrasted with cosmopolitan universities.

It may also be useful to deal briefly with the situation of teachers working in private education societies. There appears to be a certain ambivalence toward government on the part of such teachers. On matters of salary and problems of job security, they clearly desire the protection provided by association with the government bureaucracy. Thus, they succeeded in 1970 in having the government legislate direct payment of their salaries through local banks or post offices rather than allowing the payment of salaries to be routed through school managements. Several managers complained at the time that such a practice would result in the private managements losing teachers' loyalty to their particular society, a loyalty they felt it important to preserve. The teachers, however, recalled past instances of non-payment of salaries. The change was also spurred by cases where managements had diverted funds to other uses or, more rarely, where a member of the management had simply made off with the money (as was alleged to have been the case in the Vivekananda Society).

In terms of job security, tenure rules have frequently been flouted by the managers of private education societies. One union spokesman suggested that some societies maintained "floating staffs." Thus, while government rules require tenure after two years, such societies economized by dismissing teachers after two years of service and only later (before the new term began) rehiring the old employees as new staff. Given the scarcity of employment in India, teachers were subject to considerable intimidation in such matters. According to one informant, who was associated with a small society,

> The salary scale is fixed by the state government and one advances through the ranks as long as you stay in the same society. If you go to a new society, then you must fix your pay scale again. One man I know

was ordered to go to _____ by his society and was told that if he refused his seniority would be lowered. In another society, there was a teacher of about twenty years' experience and a newcomer who was a relative of one of the managers. When the government announced its new policy by which teachers [who did not have college degrees] could be deputed to finish their B.Ed.s, both people applied. The person related to the management was given the chance and the other was kept aside. There are many such cases in the way institutions maintained by private societies are run.[19]

Yet, despite experiences of this kind, which might have been expected to result in teachers favoring the abolition of private societies, there was little enthusiasm for such a step. Thus, a teachers' association leader opposed "governmentalization" of secondary schools "because private managements allow for a variety of thinking to be maintained." He went on to comment:

We must safeguard the individuality of the teacher as well as of the managements. . . . Presently managements can direct staffs to follow different outlooks because they have choices of teachers and the teachers have choices of the way they may approach teaching. A teacher is not a machine. Private managements, at least in principle, protect the educational process, though at present too many managements are more interested in their working as managements than they are in imparting education to pupils.[20]

Utimately, most of those interviewed on the subject (including leading politicians) were prepared to rely on democratic processes to curb the excesses of private managements rather than to move toward outright operation of the secondary schools by government.[21]

19. Indicative of the search for autonomy associated with educational institutionalization, the same interviewee advocated the creation of educational "corporations" to operate school systems independent of either the state government or private managements.

20. Interview, Vasudeo Palande, Secretary of the Secondary Teachers Association of Poona City, 25 January 1973.

21. Abolition of private education societies would run into legal difficulty, however, since the Constitution of India assures minority groups that they will be permitted to maintain their own educational institutions. While aimed principally at the Muslims, other groups could make use of this legal provision. The central government could, of course, amend the Constitution to deal with this problem as it has with others.

In this section, I have attempted to identify some of the features of the educational system that has grown up in Maharashtra as a result of the policies adopted in the first two decades after independence. On the whole, the state government has taken the view that most efforts to deal with the problems detailed here must involve changes in performance standards which emanate from changes in public attitudes rather than from the mere passage of legislation. In many instances, the Education Department already has the formal authority to take actions for change on its own. In a later section we will deal with some recent changes the state government has taken on the basis of such authority rather than as a result of a new legislative mandate. Before doing so, we will examine in some detail an educational conflict which arose during 1968. It illustrates how educational policy is formulated and acted upon within the Maharashtrian political system and how, at least in such cases, the preferences of local elites can force the reformulation of policy in ways contrary to these originally proposed by spokesmen of the state government.

The White Paper Debate

While the Constitution of India reserves to the states effective control in the field of education, the Union Government attempts to encourage educational development through such devices as the manipulation of grants-in-aid and through recommendations for reform of the content and organization of education. In the latter connection, the government of India appointed, in July 1964, a commission—generally known by its chairman's name as the Kothari Commission—to enunciate plans for the future of Indian education. The Commission's report appeared in June 1966, with recommendations for both short-term and long-term reform.

States responded in different ways. In the case of Maharashtra, the Commission's work was followed closely by leading educators and its recommendations carefully reviewed by the state's Education Department. Unlike states where the Education Ministry is not considered a position of high prestige or the minister is not inclined by intellect or ambition to take an active interest in the subject matter of his portfolio, Maharashtra was fortunate in having a man, M. D. Chaudhari, who came to his position in 1964 with considerable dedication to the field. [22] He appeared before the Kothari Commission, himself, and maintained contact with members of that body, including the Secretary-Member of the Commission, J. P. Naik. Naik was a Maharashtrian who had served many years in educational institutions in the state before he became an education advisor to the national government. [23] Along with the recommendations of the Kothari Commission and the advice provided by Naik, Chaudhari drew heavily from the ideas of certain senior officials in his department in thinking through proposals for educational change in Maharashtra. [24]

After the report of the Kothari Commission appeared, and particularly after the elections of early 1967 swept the Congress

22. The Minister's father gained a reputation for his activities in the field of education during the Gandhian period. Chaudhari himself was educated in Nagpur and attracted to Gandhi's ashram at Wardha for a time. He continues to have a personal interest in education and is the leader of an educational society in his home district, Jalgaon. In state politics, he was considered close to Vasantrao Naik and was mentioned occasionally as a possible successor to Naik by persons close to the Chief Minister.

23. J. P. Naik was born in Kolhapur in 1907 and was educated there. During the 1930s he became active in the civil disobedience movement in British India. In 1940, he served in Kolhapur as an education advisor to the princely regime and in 1942 became Development Secretary for the state. He left Kolhapur in 1949 to set up his own educational institution in Bombay, but in 1952 he returned to the district to head Mouni Vidyapeeth, an educational institution founded by V. T. Patil. In 1959, Naik assumed his position in the central government. As Secretary-Member, he played a major role in the formulation of the proposals of the Kothari Commission.

Naik's wife, Chitra, also has established a major reputation in educational affairs. After training as a teacher, she became a provincial inspector of education. She rose through the educational bureaucracy of Bombay and Maharashtra to become in 1964 Director of the State Institute of Education, a training center for the educational system. In 1972 she was appointed Director of Education for Maharashtra, the senior functional position in the Education Department.

24. Department officials were not unanimous in their support of the Minister's initiative. Some feared that their own personal prerogatives as educational authorities might be brought into question; others felt a public debate over education might constrain future actions on the part of the bureaucracy and further politicize a field already subject to political supervision. Allegedly, one senior official, a man who came from a wealthy landlord family in Vidarbha, used some of his personal connections in that region to arouse opposition to certain of the proposals.

back to power in Maharashtra, Chaudhari, as Minister for Education, set to work to put together a plan for educational development for the next fifteen to twenty years. Seven or eight sessions were held with J. P. Naik, and others in the educational system (mainly from among functional specialists within the bureaucracy), over a period of three to four months. There was little effort during this preparatory period to involve special interest groups, such as private education societies or teachers' organizations, in the process. Indeed, few attempts were made even to inform ministerial personnel, other than the Deputy Minister for Education, or members of the legislature about what was going on.

The Minister's consultations led to a tentative draft based on the minutes of his meetings with his small circle of advisors. His confidence in the course they were following was apparently buoyed by the reception the proposals elicited when brought before the Cabinet. As a matter of routine, the Chief Minister appointed a high-level committee within the Cabinet to consider the document. Several suggestions for changes from within the subcommittee were accepted—a few, as we shall see, which Chaudhari and his advisors later regretted. On the whole, amendments of the Cabinet subcommittee led to easy ratification of the plan by the full body and submission to the State Legislative Assembly of the Draft White Paper in April 1968. In the Congress party meeting that immediately preceded the Assembly debate, there was little negative reaction. A more substantial debate there might have alerted Chaudhari and his associates to the existence of major problems. They did anticipate some opposition to particular items, such as their attempt to introduce uniformity into the pattern of secondary and collegiate education in the three major regions of the state, but they felt so strongly about the need to introduce such a change that they were willing to press ahead on that presumably controversial issue.[25]

25. In western Maharashtra, the pattern was one of eleven years of primary and secondary education. In Vidarbha the same course of study was ten years. In both regions, a distinct pre-collegiate year has preceded three years of college. The government proposed a ten-year program to be followed by a two-year pre-collegiate course and three years of collegiate training. As the White Paper contended, somewhat hopefully, "The standard to be reached at the end of the new class X will compare favourably with that now reached at the end of standard X in Vidarbha or class XI in Western

Many of the features of the White Paper were non-controversial, though members of both houses of the state legislature were voluble with advice for specific emendations. Along with its effort at introducing uniformity into the educational system throughout the state, there was considerable interest expressed by the government in modernizing curriculums and introducing courses of study which would be more closely related to "work-experiences" and to the "manpower needs" of Indian society. The general goal was to move away from the liberal arts emphasis characteristic of existing curriculums. The White Paper also expressed the interest of the state government in upgrading the quality of teaching, both by increasing formal requirements (while underwriting the costs of in-service training for teachers) and, more significantly, by improving the content of teachers' training courses. The need for better textbooks developed under closer government supervision; the provision of additional educational equipment; better and more service-oriented supervision of teachers by the state inspectional agency—all of these and other matters were topics touched upon by the White Paper which elicited little political debate.

Although qualitative improvement in teaching and revision of the content of curriculums were goals that were strongly emphasized, the White Paper also explicitly recognized a need to continue the expansion of educational facilities—something the critics of the White Paper subsequently tended to ignore. Admittedly, Chaudhari and his advisors sought some way by which the rapid expansion in advanced educational institutions could be brought under sufficient control to allow the professional educators an opportunity to improve the quality of education, but they were not about to restrict access to education. Indeed, one of the recommendations made (and since followed up) constituted a concession to the education societies. The White Paper declared it to be the intention of the state government to encourage secondary schools to offer grades five through seven. Because the skills of teachers recruited by the private societies were generally acknowledged to be of a higher quality than those of government-

Maharashtra." Government of Maharashtra, *White Paper (Draft), Outlining the Educational Reconstruction Proposed to be Undertaken During the Next 15-20 Years, With Special Reference to the New Fourth Five-Year Plan (1969-74) for Maharashtra State* (Bombay, 1968), p. 5.

employed teachers, the White Paper proposed to spur the private societies to expand in this area:

> The standards of education necessarily improve when classes V-VII are attached to secondary schools because better teachers, better facilities and better atmosphere are available. It.is, therefore, proposed that all secondary schools, whether urban or rural, should be permitted, subject to prescribed conditions, to conduct classes V-VII as primary classes without charging fees. A suitable system of grants-in-aid will be devised for the purpose.[26]

At the same time, the Education Minister committed the government to pursuing a more rational plan of establishing secondary schools so that one would be available for a base population of about eight thousand within three to five miles of the home of every child.

While comments on these sections of the White Paper were reasonably restrained, a wave of controversy surrounded other features of the recommendations. Opposition parties and some rural-based elements within the Congress drew upon what Chaudhari and his advisors later conceded were ambiguities of language to launch a general attack on the overall intent of the document. At the heart of this dispute were various proposals which, in the eyes of these opponents, struck an inappropriate balance between "quantity" and "quality" in education. Another issue which drew their fire was the question of the appropriate timing for the introduction of English into the educational process.

Quantity Versus Quality

Both the quality-versus-quantity issue and the debate over English were stirred by the fears of rural-based non-Brahman members of the Assembly that efforts were being made by the Brahman-dominated educational bureaucracy to close those doors to educational opportunity and social equality which had only recently been opened. Nowhere was this view reflected more vehemently than in the campaign jointly organized by the PWP

26. Ibid., pp. 15-16. State authorities were having some difficulty in 1973 in effecting the transition because zilla parishads were reluctant to give up their higher primary grades. As a result, both public and private educational institutions were offering those grades. The state government might have moved unilaterally on the matter but evidenced fear of entering into direct confrontation with local governments and their spokesmen in the legislature.

and the Rayat Shikshan Saunstha against the White Paper, a campaign encouraged by rural-based politicians from within the Congress.[27]

It had always been the policy of the Saunstha to place mass education ahead of attempts to apply qualitative standards to the educational process. A Brahman MLC noted, rather acidly, that Bhaurao Patil, founder of the Saunstha, "was not much concerned with quality in education. He was the kind of person who used to say to people, 'You produce children and we will take care of them.' "

Thus, the Saunstha leadership, already somewhat affronted by not having been consulted during the formulation of the White Paper, reacted against what they took to be an attack on mass education. [28] One of their most active teacher-managers described their course of action:

> In fighting it, we worked closely with N. D. Patil, MLC from Sangli. He had founded a college in his area and was a former professor of economics. He is in the PWP and is General Secretary of the party and leader of the opposition in the Legislative Council. With him, we raised an agitation against the White Paper. As a professor, I could not go out and campaign on the issue, but N. D. Patil organized forty meetings in Marathwada and Nagpur. I myself organized opposition in Satara. We began by holding meetings in some of the bigger villages in Satara district and then in district places like Dhulia, Kolhapur, and Sangli. A preparatory meeting was held in . . . Bombay in July and then the main meeting was held in Kolhapur in November [before the issue was discussed on the floor of the State Assembly]. By this process, public opinion was mobilized.

The proponents of the White Paper saw little in it to arouse the ire of the PWP and its allies. Among those allies was an important element in the Congress, led by Balasaheb Desai, which

27. One MLC suggested that the course of discussion was critically affected by the fact that Chaudhari was not a Maratha, but instead a member of the high-status Leva Patil community. As he stated, "If the White Paper had been presented by a Maratha like _____, the reaction to it would have been softer. Chaudhari did not handle the matter in the right way, but his background was also against him."

28. A spokesman of the organization stated rather resentfully, "Usually it is only the managements from the city areas who are invited [to sit with the ministry in decision making] but not from the rural areas. It was just that one morning in April 1968, the White Paper descended on us."

both shared some of the fears of the PWP and hoped to capitalize
on the embarrassment the debate might cause to Chief Minister
Naik, who stood behind Chaudhari. The opposition seized on
various passages in the White Paper to attack the course of action
the Minister appeared to be espousing. [29] They responded
strongly, for example, to a sentence in the document which
suggested that "in view of the limited resources available, admissions to higher secondary and university education will have to be
carefully regulated," though the next sentence went on to soften
that declaration: "Admissions, therefore, will be made with due
regard to the natural talents of the students, their achievements at
earlier stages and principles of social justice."[30]

Considerable objection was also raised to a section which
referred to the introduction of "advanced" and "ordinary" curriculums in grades eight to eleven. [31] Those schools already having
more developed facilities and better-qualified teachers would be in
a better position, opponents concluded, to offer the "advanced"
curriculum—presumed to qualify the student for college entrance.
Since rural schools continue for the most part to be at a disadvantage in attracting better teachers and supporting the kinds of
activities which are assumed to be associated with better education, the rural representatives saw their constituents consigned to a

29. When asked for his views on the White Paper, Desai remarked, "In the
name of merit, [Chaudhari] would have excluded from education all those
people who had been uneducated for so many generations. What was to
happen to them? ... We need mass education still. ... Villagers need all
possible facilities but the government threatened to withdraw them." Balasaheb Desai, interview, 18 February 1973. Desai had considerable dislike for
many of the bureaucrats whom he had found uncooperative during his years
in the government, "They come from a different class and their attitudes are
hard to change."

30. Government of Maharashtra, *White Paper,* p. 19.

31. As the section reads, in part: "For classes VIII-X and again in classes
XI-XII, curricula will be framed, as recommended by the Education Commission, at the ordinary (0) and advanced (A) levels. Special conditions will be
prescribed for teaching the curriculum at (A) level and only those schools
which satisfy the conditions will be allowed to teach it. A school will be free
to provide the (A) level curriculum in one or more subjects of its choice. ...
In addition, good schools will also be encouraged to and assisted to try out
experiments on their own." Ibid., p. 6. Opponents feared that "good schools"
would be delimited to include mainly the urban schools and that few rural
secondary schools would be in a position to take advantage of the "advanced" option.

future in which they might progress to "ordinary" curriculums at the secondary level but would experience considerable difficulty in gaining admission to college.

Those responsible for formulation of the White Paper disclaimed any such intent. In the case of the advanced and ordinary curriculums, for example, Chaudhari insisted:

> What we intended was to gradually catch up with the advanced countries in fifteen or twenty years by preparing new curriculums and implementing them and other innovations in stages. It would be a continuous process of modernizing and advancing the quality of the curriculum by introducing these experiments in some classes and gradually improving other classes. Unfortunately, the drafting of the paper in that section was bad and the nomenclature of the English system, with its "advanced" and "ordinary" courses, which mark off the college-bound from the rest of the population, was used. People interpreted it as a selection system, which was not intended.[32]

As for the reference to "regulated" admissions to advanced education, no such wording was included in the original draft of the White Paper, but the sentence was added to the document by the Cabinet subcommittee as a call for some economy in the expansion of higher education. Indeed, one educator who was involved in the drafting process indicated that the original words employed by the subcommittee were "selective admissions." Such terminology was rightly seen to be politically provocative and so officials in the educational bureaucracy replaced "selective" with "regulated," which indicated (at least to them) that despite low grades, some persons from the most backward communities and some low-income applicants might gain admission to colleges on a basis other than grades.

As already noted, the White Paper made reference to the goal of linking education more directly to societal needs, including employment requirements. The opposition pointed to this as evidence of a plan for restrictiveness on the part of the government. The government's intention, they asserted, was to grant admissions, particularly to higher education, only in proportion to the existence of employment opportunities. [33] The "actual" intention of the White Paper's authors was stated by one:

32. Interview, 1 July 1970.
33. The concerns of the opponents of the White Paper were touched off by a section which reads, "Education beyond class X will be regulated by

We felt that education should be more closely related to life, but people misinterpreted our intention to mean that there would be no education if there were no jobs. At the moment, there is no real alternative to educational expansion. We suggested that at the higher secondary level there should be more diversified occupational preparation for the absorption of persons into jobs. Maybe this would take away the need of young people to crowd into arts colleges. . . . It is a helpless kind of crowding now. . . . Many of them are simply wasting their time because they have almost no alternative in the form of a job.

The position of the opposition was stated in an interview with a prominent figure in the Rayat Shikshan Saunstha:

The intention of the White Paper went beyond a mere consideration of new curriculums. It is true that the Minister was very apologetic in debate but we feel definitely that quantity is more important than quality. . . . Students are still going without primary and secondary education in this state. No doubt, we are producing many third-class graduates, but that is still some advance on the former situation. They do swell the ranks of the unemployed, but that is probably better than remaining unemployed and, in the village wasting their time distilling illicit liquor. . . . The result is high unemployment among the educated in India, but the fault is in the whole educational pattern and in the present organization of society.

(He was hesitant to suggest, however, where reform in the educational pattern properly was to begin.) Indeed, a number of interviewees who opposed any restriction on educational opportunity made the point that given the character of the Indian economy, the decision was really only between educated unemployment and uneducated unemployment.

The Use of English

In addition to the storm raised about the quantity-versus-quality issue, [34] much attention was given in public debate and in

---

man-power needs or employment opportunities (including opportunities for self-employment which will be emphasized and developed) and the availability of resources in terms of teachers, materials, and money." Government of Maharashtra, *White Paper*, p. 21.

34. Significantly, a plan to develop *vidya niketans*—residential schools at which especially talented boys from rural backgrounds are given training in science and mathematics in a setting akin to the British "public" school— aroused little rural opposition. What criticism there was involved complaints about expense rather than about the elitism involved. This indicates that an emphasis on quality was not in itself unacceptable to rural elites as long as quality was not associated with favor shown to urban or high-caste groups.

the legislature to the timing of the introduction of English. Originally, Chaudhari proposed that English be made compulsory from the fifth standard, but under the influence of his colleagues in the Cabinet, this was changed to make English compulsory from the eighth standard. A reference to language study in grades five to seven was changed to make only Hindi compulsory. The government extended an assurance that facilities for studying English would be made available from fifth standard to those students interested in studying it on an optional basis. The reasons for this change, it was suggested to me, included matters of additional expense, the burden compulsory English would place on those students not going on to secondary or collegiate education who would never move in an English-speaking environment, and the lack of an adequate number of teachers who knew English sufficiently well to teach it from the fifth standard. (Indeed, one of the reasons the Minister wished to attach higher primary grades to secondary schools was that the more proficient teachers of English were already to be found teaching in those secondary schools.)

While the Ministry expected some reaction on the language issue, no matter how the proposal was phrased, the question proved more explosive than anticipated. The explosion also came from an unexpected direction. The language issue in India is, of course, an especially complex and volatile one. [35] No single language suffices as mother-tongue, educational medium, and means of national communication all in one. In Maharashtra, which was created on the basis of the identification of the population with the Marathi language and culture, the regional language might well be adequate for primary education for the vast majority of the population and for their functioning in society, though linguistic minorities within the state continue to insist on the right to educate their children in their own mother-tongues. However, the imperatives of national policy led to the formulation of a national "three-language" policy in 1955—a policy reiterated in 1965 in the wake of language riots—in which not only the mother-tongue but also Hindi and English (the latter as a concession to the anti-Hindi South) were to be taught as part of precollegiate education. The policy followed in Maharashtra of introducing Hindi as a com-

35. See, for example, Jyotindra Das Gupta, *Language Conflict and National Development* (Berkeley and Los Angeles: University of California Press, 1970); and Baldev Raj Nayar, *National Communication and Language Policy in India* (New York: Praeger, 1969).

pulsory language from the fifth standard produced little opposition, but the place and timing of English were open to differences of opinion.[36]

English had been removed as a requirement from primary education in 1946 when the Congress came to power in Bombay. At that time, the Gandhian Chief Minister of the state, B. G. Kher, decided that the continued study of English constituted a badge of inferiority. In time, educators and politicians came to regret the decision. The comments of one educator are typical:

> Many people applauded then, but they are now reaping the problems from it. Maharashtra is now one of the weakest states in India in respect to English. If a hundred people are selected in an all-India competitive examination, not one or two are from Maharashtra.

Not only was there a widespread feeling in 1968 that Maharashtra had fallen behind other states in the competition to win employment in the central government,[37] but there was also a simmering fear among the upwardly mobile rural non-Brahmans that urban Brahmans could afford to or would stint in order to send their children to urban schools that offered strong English programs or all academic studies in the English medium. For the rural middle class, the proposal to make English compulsory only from the eighth standard was viewed as another way of keeping their children behind in the educational race. Therefore, quite unexpectedly, non-Brahman spokesmen insisted that English be made compulsory from the fifth standard so that their own children might be assured of equal opportunity.

36. Nayar, *National Communication*, pp. 152-163, is particularly useful for his history of the three-language formula and the vagaries that formula has undergone since it was originally put forward. Kamat states the issue quite bluntly: "While official thinking at the Centre still clings to the three-language formula, it was, in fact, never accepted in practice by the Hindi-speaking north and has now been unceremoniously rejected by Tamil Nadu in the south. There is no firm policy or practice on the teaching of English in schools and its role in higher education." A. R. Kamat, "The Educational Situation," *Economic and Political Weekly*, 24 June 1972, pp. 1230-1231.

37. Access to positions in the central government so concerned the leaders of Maharashtra that a commission chaired by the Vice-Chancellor of Shivaji University was formed by the state government to make recommendations on the subject. The commission favored the creation of a few centers of special training in the state where students might be coached in taking the national examinations.

Thus, both the quality-versus-quantity issue and the English language issue sprang from the fears of rural representatives that, except for the few upper-middle-class rural non-Brahmans who could afford to send their children to schools offering English in the city, most rural non-Brahmans were likely to remain disadvantaged. A Brahman educator, who had great sympathy for the concerns of the non-Brahmans, commented on this:

> There is a strong feeling among the non-Brahmans and particularly the Marathas that Brahmans have had all possible chances to learn English and this has allowed them to dominate. They occupy government posts and dominate in such key professions as the law. That makes a lot of people dependent on their pleasure and preferences. Since there is still a feeling that a knowledge of English has given the Brahmans vast power, others felt they would get the same advantages if they learned English.

Despite the intensity of these educational disputes, it should be stressed that the issues actually were largely symbolic. For the vast majority of the adult population—a population which has gotten little beyond the stage of illiteracy and whose children (in the aggregate) are in an only slightly better position—the debate was little more than a rhetorical exchange. Yet, only a few "leftist" politicians questioned the expenditure of energy on a debate over the study of English and college selectivity; that debate took place at a time when many of the primary schools in rural Maharashtra were one-teacher schools, where undereducated and undertrained teachers offered classes to four or more standards, and when in a few areas peripatetic schools still existed which required teachers to go to one village for a few days a week and to another village on other days.

Yet, it is consistent with the character of politics in Maharashtra, where a relatively small class of upwardly mobile non-Brahman farmers has constituted the most politically influential segment of the population, that a substantial amount of time in the state legislature was focused on the issue of making English compulsory from the fifth standard. It is even greater testimony to the political influence of the representatives of this rural elite that the government was forced to retreat from its original position. The White Paper, which had been issued as a draft for public discussion, was considerably revised by Chaudhari and his advisors, and a new Policy Statement was issued in February 1970. Controversial proposals offensive to the rural elite were either eliminated entirely or considerably watered down. The "original intent" of other sections was clarified. Thus, in place of the reference to "regulated" admissions to higher education, there were now several sections accenting the need to provide greater educational opportunities for all on the basis of both "innate intelligence"—which apparently went beyond performance in formal schooling—and "social justice."

Furthermore, a new paragraph was inserted which stated, "The seats and scholarships in professional and technical institutions will be distributed among school clusters which will be formed on the basis of population and the number of students in each such cluster." [38] This proposal would constitute a further blow to Brahman representation in such professions as engineering and medicine, for it might well mean that entry into medical and engineering schools would be based not on academic merit but on principles of regional representation. Those principles might well favor non-Brahman and non-urbanized populations as against the highly urbanized Brahmans. [39] Finally, as expected, the new Policy Statement declared that both Hindi and English would be "obligatory" in Marathi-medium schools from fifth standard.

38. Government of Maharashtra, Education Department, *Policy Statement on Educational Reconstruction in Maharashtra, 23 February 1970* (Bombay-Government Central Press, 1970), p. 11. As the former Education Minister explained, "Up to now entry was given on the basis of 'merit,' but merit was so defined as to amount to favoring those who came from urban middle-class families. We tried to combine the two—merit and natural talent—by assuming that talent is equal across all groups of people. . . . The general approach was accepted by the Cabinet but the plan has not been implemented. The problem is to do it in such a way as to not cause injustice to anyone." Interview, M. D. Chaudhari, 21 February 1973.

39. Though entrance into government-run medical colleges is regulated according to examination results, private medical colleges throughout India have been permitted to admit students of lower quality as long as they pay "capitation" fees. In Maharashtra, only one of the dozen medical colleges charged such a fee, but this charge has been the subject of some controversy. *Times of India*, 6 August 1970. While entry into medical education was the most expensive, by 1973 the problem of access to professional education was so generally acute that an investigation was required into the money-making activities of a teacher-training college run by a former deputy minister of Maharashtra. His college was accused of charging heavy entrance fees for admission to the B.Ed. course despite state rules to the contrary. The situation in Karnataka in the use of capitation fees has been described by Wood, "Planning, Local Interest and Higher Education."

FOLLOW-UP TO THE WHITE PAPER

Only slightly chastened by their experiences with "public opinion," the educational leadership of the state government returned to the work of reorganizing education in Maharashtra. A completely revised curriculum, placing a new emphasis on science and mathematics, is gradually being introduced at the secondary school level. As one educational bureaucrat suggested, "It is a rather tough one and is the one that would have been introduced as the 'advanced' curriculum if we had been permitted to test it out." He volunteered that it had been circulated to MLAs, MLCs, teachers associations, and headmasters. Efforts to introduce "work experience" were also being tried on an experimental basis in 1972-1973 with an expectation that such programs would be offered across the state from eighth standard in 1973-1974. As the same bureaucrat pointed out:

> It is not only our intention to train students to work with their hands but to give them some management orientation and some feeling for the use of science. There is some occupational orientation but it is not really training for a job. Rather, it is a way of concerning the student with productivity and getting him to think of ways to get good results with little expenditure.

Spokesmen for teachers and politicians were wary about these innovations, though many were hopeful that problems that were being experienced would be overcome. One such problem was finding a way to cope with the change-over itself, particularly for those students prepared under the older curriculum who might find themselves in difficulty if they failed the standardized state examination. [40] Another problem was meeting the need for teacher training or retraining. The mechanics of such changes have been difficult for the bureaucracy to handle, and questions about the rewards and punishments associated with such preparations are regularly heard. However, as compared to most Indian states, the government of Maharashtra has continued to evidence an intellec-

---

40. As *The Indian Express,* 7 March 1973, noted, confusion surrounded the situation of students who failed in ninth standard in that academic year. It was not clear whether they would be required to take ninth standard for a second time under the old curriculum or under the new.

tual interest in educational matters, if not always a major financial commitment.[41]

It was with some reluctance that M. D. Chaudhari agreed to head the Finance Ministry after the reorganization of the Maharashtra Cabinet in 1972. Most of his policies were reasserted in the months after the new Minister for Education, A. N. Namjoshi, took over.[42] The only noticeable difference was a greater immediate attention to the formulation of a new university act for the state. There was also an effort made to bring forward a new act which would more clearly define the rights and responsibilities of teachers, particularly in private schools. Work on that act, which would have replaced an often-amended code, had been completed as early as 1969, but conflicts between managements and teachers over the terms of the act continued to work against government action. As one teacher suggested, "There are big groups, particularly in the rural areas, who are less interested in education than in running education societies. They feared proposals for restrictions on private managements and therefore opposed bringing forward the act." In the same vein, a Jan Sangh-oriented MLC remarked, "Many MLAs have their own institutions and benefit from them. If there were an act it might be easier to take effective action against managements that act in an irregular fashion."

It was during Namjoshi's tenure that some of the transitional problems of implementing the new curriculum became most apparent. Thus, the new pattern had forced the state government to make alterations in preparations for the SSC (Secondary School

41. The former Education Minister was quite proud of the fact that he had managed to increase state expenditures on education from 17 to 21 percent of the overall budget during his years in office. Interview, M. D. Chaudhari, Minister for Finance, 21 February 1973. Given the relatively low expenditures on education, it is not surprising that national and state promises of achieving universal primary education are constantly being pushed into the distant future.

42. Namjoshi was a former professor of pharmacology and active in the faculty and governance committees of Bombay University. He was also a leader of the faction within the BPCC opposed to Rajni Patel. A non-Brahman educator was quick to note that Namjoshi was a Brahman—"the only Brahman in the current Cabinet"—and also a Bombay man. Namjoshi's tenure as Education Minister ended in late 1974 when he was summarily removed from the Cabinet. The *Times of India,* 8 November 1974, alludes to the role of the national party leadership in backing Patel against Namjoshi in the conflict within the Bombay Congress organization.

Certificate) examinations—the SSC constituting the final certification of completion of the secondary school course and the accepted qualification for admission to college. With the addition of English, mathematics, and science to the curriculum, as one official noted, "The Secretary of the Department decided that the SSC system should be changed so that it would be sufficient to pass in five subjects and only a minimum of some kind would be required in two other subjects." This policy was announced by the new minister in early 1973. There were immediate protests against the announcement. On the one side were those who felt that a distinction should be made between students planning to go to college and those who would complete their educations with secondary school. On the other were members of the SSC Board, the body responsible for overseeing the organization and administration of the examination, who complained that such a policy would have the effect of dissuading students from studying English in the rural areas. As one informant complained, "Suddenly we were back in the old debate. . . . The SSC Board members said a good new curriculum had been made and they went to the Chief Minister with their complaint. As a result, the policy announced by the new Minister was retained but it was agreed that the minimum required in those areas not passed would still be rather high." In my interviews in early 1973, it seemed apparent that considerable confusion reigned among policy makers and policy administrators about what the new rules were to be and when they were actually to go into effect.

CONCLUSIONS

Among the strands of specific educational policies over which men have contended in Maharashtra—to what extent students in rural areas should be provided with educational opportunities equivalent to those living in urban areas; whether English should be made compulsory in the advanced primary grades or be required only in higher grades; what role private education societies should play in the educational system; and whether there should be greater selectivity in higher education—certain contending political principles are evident.

On one side are those who espouse bureaucratic or universalistic standards in modernizing the educational process. These individuals—who include those particularly associated with the educational administration of the state and some leading politicians—are by no means dogmatists insisting on "one right way" to solve India's educational problems. Nor are they intentionally advocates of an elitist style of education, though they do aspire to "rationalization" of education in keeping with what they see as the long-range interests of the nation. As one writer has indicated in his comments on the White Paper:

> It is difficult to believe that a mushroom growth of colleges all over the state will serve any useful purpose. Despite generous spoon-feeding by the state government and by the University Grants Commission,[43] a majority of them will be barely viable. . . . The point for consideration is whether in the present state of the village economy there are sufficient occupational outlets for the graduate sons of [rural] men to be absorbed. It is certain that most of them will regard it as an affront to their newly acquired dignity to return to the so-called humble but rewarding professions of their fathers. . . . Their migration to overcrowded cities where unemployment is already rife, will only deepen their frustration and resentment.[44]

On the other side are those who represent the growing voice in public policy of the relatively well-off rural middle class. They are able and willing to employ the symbols of egalitarianism to oppose moves toward restrictiveness in access to educational opportunities.

To posit the existence of such opposing forces in the case of the public policy process we have described in this chapter is perhaps to oversimplify the situation. For the two "sides"—if they really exist—are conducting their debate within the framework of many common assumptions. Both reject an educational future in which traditional or inherited advantages circumscribe educational opportunities; neither advocates a purely achievement-oriented educational system. Nor does either speak for the kind of radical egalitarianism which might involve a leveling of social groups.

As a result of these common attitudes, there has been some room for innovations in educational practices in Maharashtra. Those changes emerge at the confluence of goals which proceed

43. The University Grants Commission is a central government body modeled on a British agency with similar functions of overseeing the operations of and providing funding to institutions of higher education.

44. V. B. Kulkarni, "A Blueprint for Education—II," *Indian Express,* 22 May 1970.

from the slightly different premises of the educational "establish-ment" and that stratum of the population most active in public life. Thus, political spokesmen of the rural population have attempted not so much to shape the content of education as to make certain that those who administer the system and shape its content are sufficiently sensitive to the needs of that small seg-ment of the population which lives in rural areas under conditions perhaps of intellectual scarcity but with the advantages of eco-nomic surplus. They are less concerned than the bureaucrats with the long-range problems their exercise of political influence may be causing.

Now, at least, the approaches of the educational administra-tor and the politician appear to be only marginally in conflict.[45] The politicians have left considerable room to the functional specialists for experimentation in curriculums and to government bureaucrats in the operation of the educational system. Once access to education has been assured, as it now has been for the politically influential rural interests, such interests are willing to support those innovations which give their offspring all the bene-fits and all the incentives available through urban education. Neither they nor the administrators are a force for massive restruc-turing of educational organization or content.

At the same time, Maharashtra's political leadership has re-flected neither the will nor the capacity to effect major changes in the educational system. Universal education, even at the primary level, remains a remote hope for the future.[46] Such innovations as

45. Kamat, "The Educational Situation," notes an emerging conflict be-tween the two forces. He argues that neither is capable of or eager to operate the educational system entirely on its own. This keeps them working to-gether. I would argue that the antagonisms are neither as deep nor the ideological differences as mutually exclusive as he suggests. With the entry of more rural-born civil servants into higher echelons of the administration, it is probable that what tensions presently exist will also decrease.

46. One speaker during the Vidhan Parishad debate on the White Paper noted that the percentage of the educational budget invested in Maharashtra in primary education was only 31.3 percent of the total. As Kamat, ibid., p. 1235, writes, "The proposal for diverting substantial funds from higher (and even secondary) education to primary education . . . has much to com-mend it on grounds of equity, if it could be practicable. . . . There is, however, little likelihood of the proposed policy change being accepted by the political leadership of the country. . . . Although the super elite may not vigorously resist a policy of making secondary and higher education expen-

are advocated by the Education Ministry seem to deal most directly with the problems of those who are already the audience for educational opportunity. Scholarships continue to be provided for the ex-untouchables and for students from families of low income, though some who qualify for those benefits actually may be from middle-class families who misrepresent their incomes. Nevertheless, educational opportunities *are* being provided to persons from the most backward sections of Maharashtrian society, though those who are in a position to take advantage of such opportunities are relatively few in number and their entry into the educated class is not likely to contribute to a radical reorganization of political or economic life. For many students from impoverished families, as one educator asserted, college becomes "almost like a welfare service."

In the kind of political order that India has thus far constructed, the economically backward students' responses are hardly surprising, for they precisely reflect the kind of "socialism" that operates in Indian society more generally. It is a system in which strategically placed groups, as well as individual political entrepreneurs, strive to manipulate the political order to their own particular advantage. Very few persons have the inclination to expend the time or the energy to consider the social costs of the policies which are being pursued. When plans are developed, they may arouse considerable public controversy, but such controversy has little to do with reshaping the fundamental political and social realities of Indian society. Indeed, the greatest effect of the educational debate in Maharashtra may have been simply to insure that rural politicians be regularly included among those interests which must be consulted in the future with respect to policy making and policy implementation in the field of education.

---

sive—since many in it are already buying expensive education (which, by the way, is also extensively subsidized) and may welcome the 'cleansing' operation which the new policy will perform—the common elite, both the less affluent sections of the older elite and the newer regional section of rural stock, will oppose it tooth and nail. The reason is quite clear. It will deny them their continuance in the elite or bar them from entry to the elite class even at the common level and an opportunity to rise up to join the super elite, a dream which many of them entertain."

SEVEN

The Cooperative Movement I:
Structures of Power

The role played by cooperative societies in rural Maharashtra has contributed to the enhancement of commercial agriculture in the state. Not only are cooperatives not a vehicle for promoting egalitarianism, they probably have had the opposite effect.[1] Those farmers who are deemed "credit-worthy" (mainly the larger market-oriented producers) receive most of the benefits of those societal resources invested in the cooperatives, while the marginal farmer and landless laborer receive at best only a minor proportion of the benefits. For the most part, too, local societies are dominated by the more substantial farmers of an area, who use them to further both their economic and political advantage.

This chapter examines the politics of the cooperative movement in Maharashtra, beginning with an account of the structure of power within the cooperative sector at subdistrict and district levels. Here, as elsewhere in this study, we are as much concerned with how a local political actor becomes involved in building a political career by providing benefits as a patron to his neighbors and prospective followers (in this case, through the cooperatives) as we are with the nature of organization and the areas of conflict within the sector itself. As part of the discussion, we will need to consider the roles of primary societies, taluka cooperative organizations, and processing cooperatives—particularly sugar factories.

1. The perspective of the more articulate functional specialists associated with the cooperative sector is regularly expressed in the writings of W. C. Shrishrimal, who is Managing Director of the Maharashtra State Cooperative Bank and also chairman of the editorial board of the *Maharashtra Cooperative Quarterly*, the publication of the Maharashtra State Cooperative Union (the educational outlet of the cooperatives). In an editorial in the July 1970 issue of the *Quarterly* Shrishrimal wrote, "The elimination of disparity in growth and inequality in income and wealth are primarily functions of planned Government action. Cooperation should only be an instrument of helping Government policy. It cannot, by itself, undertake the responsibility for such a colossal task" (pp. iii-iv).

In the next chapter, we will examine two sets of proposals for reform which have been introduced in the past few years. These proposals resulted from a recognition of certain operational defects within the existing cooperative structure, but they also reflected a growing concern about the system of power that had been developing in Maharashtra based on the control of cooperative institutions.

COOPERATIVE POWER STRUCTURES

Of a total of nearly forty thousand cooperative societies in 1970 in Maharashtra, over twenty thousand were primary agricultural societies (village societies that deal with the DCCBs and marketing societies) organized to provide credit to farmers living in the state's nearly thirty-six thousand villages.[2] Only about 27 percent of these societies included all farmers in the villages covered. According to the Minister for Cooperation, Y. J. Mohite, small-holders (those with fewer than five acres) have tended to be excluded from membership in primary credit societies: 35 percent of all primary societies include less than 25 percent of potential small-holders as members; 21 percent cover between 26 and 50 percent, and the remaining 44 percent cover 51 to 100 percent of the small-holders. As he wrote, "The benefits of cooperative credit have not only not gone to small-holders, but have come to be monopolized by a class of cultivators who can be called the middle and higher groups."[3]

Thus, while almost every villager is within the vicinity of a primary agricultural society, the population actually served by those societies is considerably smaller than the potential coverage would suggest. According to one estimate, there were 3.56 million members of primary societies in late 1970.[4] If one calculates that each membership represents a family unit of five (including both

2. These figures come from the *Maharashtra Cooperative Quarterly*. According to the *Quarterly* there were 20,124 primary agricultural societies in Maharashtra in 1970. Of the others, some were urban-oriented, including 2,767 societies involved in consumer credit and 6,064 cooperative housing societies. *Maharashtra Cooperative Quarterly* 54 (January 1971): 235-240.

3. Y. J. Mohite, *The Cooperative Movement in Maharashtra State: A Reappraisal,* Government of Maharashtra (Bombay: Government Central Press, 16 April 1970), p. vi (hereafter referred to as *Cooperative Reappraisal*).

4. *Maharashtra Cooperative Quarterly* 54 (January 1971): 240.

aged and minor dependents) this might bring the figure of those served by primary societies up to nearly 18 million of about 35 million persons residing in rural places in Maharashtra.[5] Among the districts of the state, Kolhapur is perhaps the most "cooperativized," since it has the largest membership in proportion to rural population;[6] in contrast, Poona falls at about the state average.

In the rush to spread the economic and political benefits of the cooperative movement, many small societies were created which had difficulty sustaining themselves. According to bureaucratic criteria employed by the government of India to measure "viability"—the ability to maintain the services of a full-time secretary, pay for office accommodations, build up reserves, and distribute dividends to members—many primary societies fall short of viability. Indeed, according to Mohite, only 12 percent are viable: "Each state was allowed to determine the quantum of business to make the society viable. According to this criterion, therefore, 17,616 of 20,090 societies established so far have remained economically a drain and it is a matter of time before a large number of them reach the stage of liquidation or winding up."[7]

This concern for economic viability is associated with the political viability of many societies. The increase in the number of village-level societies as well as their economic difficulties have been encouraged by rivalries among villages and among leaders in the same village. In the first instance, leaders of smaller villages have sought their own societies when they felt that leaders from larger villages with whom they shared a cooperative were not

5. Thirty-five million is the figure for the rural population of Maharashtra according to the 1971 Census. Membership figures are complicated by the fact that more than one member of a family may belong to a cooperative society. That may be the case, in particular, where family land is legally divided in order to conform to the land reform law.

6. For a useful history and description of the cooperatives in Kolhapur, see S. L. Shirodkar, "Cooperatives in Kolhapur District" (Ph.D. diss., Poona University, 1967).

7. Mohite, *Cooperative Reappraisal,* p. vi. Since the thrust of Mohite's argument was in part to make a case for consolidation of some of the smaller societies, he may have been applying the criteria for viability somewhat harshly. One journal reported that of 18,786 local societies in 1973, 225 were closed and 524 were operating at a loss. "Maharashtra II: Cooperatives: The True Story," *Economic and Political Weekly,* 29 September 1973, p. 1956.

treating them equitably. Within a village, conflicts have sometimes become so severe that it is difficult for a society to function at all; in some cases, the faction that dominated used the society's resources to benefit its own followers but denied opportunities (including membership) to its rivals.

Some sense of the role of cooperative institutions and their place in local politics may be gathered from case materials. The selection of the case studies provided below is purely arbitrary, but they do reveal the range of cooperative activities in which local political actors, including administrative personnel, have become implicated. In the first two instances, I also have chosen cases which highlight aspects of the activities of major leaders in district politics.

Case 1

K. is the vice-chairman of the panchayat samiti in a particularly backward section of Poona district. He inherited fifteen acres of dry land from his father, five of which were subsequently irrigated. He also maintains a small herd of cattle on fodder grown on his land. Though there has been some effort to organize a dairy cooperative in his locality, there does not seem to be much enthusiasm on his part for such a venture, since the prices offered for milk are about the same from private dealers as from cooperatives.

The primary agricultural society in K.'s village has 255 members. Though he helped to found it in 1960, he did not hold any formal position until 1969, when he was asked to take over for a director ruled ineligible when he was found to be in substantial debt to the society. As this informant admits, the society is not in good condition because it has had difficulty collecting outstanding debts. Poor collection procedures were further exacerbated by weather conditions during 1969 and 1970. As a result, the society recovered only 26 percent of outstanding loans due in 1969-1970.

K. devoted considerable energy after 1960 to helping to popularize the cooperative movement in his taluka. His contacts allowed him to take a leading role in organizing a taluka purchase and sales union in 1968. (His small taluka was previously joined to a larger neighbor for the purpose but received separate status in that year.) K. was elected a director of the union and continues to work with it. Though his taluka union is not formally associated with the District Purchase and Sales Union (the marketing body dominated by the Kakades), the district body does provide the taluka union with supplies of certain items, such as fertilizers, which are distributed to farmers through the primary societies.

The board of directors of the taluka union is elected by secret ballot by representatives of each primary society eligible to vote, plus representatives of individual members who are not members of primary societies. In addition, representatives of the DCCB and the District Purchase and Sales Union are selected to sit with them. In 1970, K. claimed, the Kakade forces had seven seats to the six on the taluka body held by the group in the Poona District Congress led by Mamasaheb Mohol. Nevertheless, he insisted, these political differences had little effect on the actual working of the body.[8]

In addition to sitting on his village agricultural society's board of directors and on the board of the taluka purchase and sales union, K. had recently served as chairman of his taluka's supervising union for two years. That body was responsible for the appointment, assignment, and supervision of the performances of primary society secretaries in the taluka.[9] Again, two political groups were present. In the 1970 election, the Mohol group managed to dominate. Thus, the two taluka-level cooperative institutions had different political complexions.

In reviewing the position of cooperative organizations in the taluka, K. conceded that there were many problems. He estimated that of the thirty-two societies in the taluka, at least ten were in serious financial difficulty and another ten were potentially in trouble.

> There is a tendency among the farmers not to repay their loans and when questions are raised they always make counter-propaganda. For example, if a crop fails they may blame it on the chemicals in the fertilizers given them through the societies. The ten societies in heavy

8. Interestingly enough, this informant was the only Jan Sangh member of the board of directors of the taluka sangh. He was a Brahman, which he felt limited his ambitions to non-governmental fields like the cooperatives.

9. In addition to these duties, the supervising unions were given the job of certifying that the records forwarded by society secretaries to the DCCBs were in order with respect to such matters as the crops under cultivation, the acreage for which loans were being claimed, and the financial condition of the local society. Since village records are in considerable question throughout Maharashtra (and in India, as a whole), much of this certification appears to be based on guesswork.

arrears have not been liquidated yet, but they are in the process. . . .
Only now is the supervising union taking strict action against the
societies. . . . With the help of the police *patil* [a village officer, who is
usually a villager of some local standing], they go to a person and make
him pay. If he does not, they confiscate his property. Quite a few cases
of this kind have occurred. The situation improves as cases are acted
upon in a village, because others then come forward to pay their
arrears.[10]

Case 2

R. V. is a farmer with twelve acres of land in Shirol taluka,
Kolhapur. He grows sugarcane and rice on two acres which are
irrigated by wells. On the rest, his crops include jowar and pea-
nuts. His family acquired their land from local absentee (Brahman)
landlords at the time of the tenancy reforms. Previously, his father
had owned only eight acres, but by 1970 the family (which
includes three older brothers) held over fifty acres among them.
The four men's holdings were legally separate.

Though R. V. grew only about one acre of sugarcane, he was
a member of the new Datta sugar factory initiated under the
leadership of Dattajirao Kadam and a local Lingayat leader. Both
the Kadam group and the one led by Ratnappa Kumbhar, a major
figure in Shirol taluka politics, had sought to sign up members for
their proposed factories in the area from the approximately fifty
villages designated as the potential base of supply for the new
facility. R. V. chose to go with Kadam. As he noted, rather
laconically, "Most of those who supported Kumbhar will be excluded. They will now have to come to us for shares. There may
still be a few shares available and there would not be any partiality
against them."

R. V. had participated in the formation of the primary credit
society in his village in 1950. From 1950 to 1962, he served as
secretary of that society, an administrative position for which his
seventh standard education qualified him. He resigned as secretary
in 1962 when he received the Congress ticket for the zilla pari-

10. Leaders of the Maharashtra State Cooperative Bank attribute the
problem of overdues mainly to unfavorable monsoons or fluctuations in the
prices of commodities. Still, Vasantrao Patil, speaking as chairman of the
State Bank at its Sixtieth Annual Meeting on December 18, 1971, conceded
that of the system's 53,000 defaulters, 4,500 (8 percent) accounted for 36
percent of the total overdues. These were the borrowers of Rs. 2,000 or more
each, who might have been expected to ride out economic difficulties best.
Speech (reprint) (Bombay: Maharashtra State Cooperative Bank), p. 5.

shad. He was defeated in that contest, but he did serve as head of his village government from 1958 to 1966.

As a supporter of the group opposed to Kumbhar in the taluka, R. V. was selected as a member of the board of directors of his taluka supervising union in 1962 and was elected chairman in 1964. In the following year, his group lost its majority in that body with the defection of two members. Recalling his own experiences as chairman and as someone generally familiar with the work of the forty-eight primary agricultural societies and fourteen other cooperative societies in the taluka, R. V. supported recommendations for change in the structure of relations between supervising unions and other cooperative institutions.

> It would be better if the functions of the union were given to the banks. Now, the chairman of the union tends to think in terms of his own group. ... If the working of societies belonging to your *gat* [group] is not proper, then you don't take many steps against them, but you act against those of the opposition group. The supervising unions are in a position to recommend loans to societies. If a society does not belong to your group, you always try to push it down.

R. V.'s own village society was making a profit in 1970 after several years of losses. In addition to its responsibility for extending and collecting loans from the farmers, it ran a fair-price shop, selling grain as the local agent of the state government, and it also engaged in the distribution of fertilizers. The society received fertilizers from either the taluka sangh or the District Purchase and Sales Union and distributed them as part of the loan system which provides for granting agricultural borrowers a portion of their loans in kind rather than in cash.

At the time of the interview, the Kumbhar group controlled the supervising union of the taluka and also ran a local cooperative marketing body specializing in tobacco, an important crop in that particular area. As R. V. noted with respect to the connection between village and taluka and/or district politics, "Everything is decided on the basis of who controls the gram panchayat and the society at the village level. If the majority in these bodies is with Kumbhar, the village will go to Kumbhar."

Case 3

The administrative structure of subdistrict institutions varied, but it may be useful to add a few notes on such structures and the kinds of actors who operated within them.

Like a number of lower-level bureaucrats whom I interviewed, S. N. had drifted first into government service and then into the cooperative sector. Educated up to tenth standard in Poona, he worked for a decade as a clerk in various state government offices and then in the office of his native village's gram panchayat. In 1960, he shifted to the cooperative society of his village and became assistant secretary to the society. He formalized his role in the cooperative sector by taking a three-month course leading to a "lower" diploma in cooperation, and later, he received a "higher" diploma on the basis of a six-month course. After this training, he was assigned to a village where he then served for seven years.

S. N. had been selected for his present position by the local taluka supervising union on the basis of an application. The main considerations, he indicated, had been his educational qualifications and recommendations. The most important recommendations come from secretaries of societies, since many of the applicants to such positions are persons who have held lower positions in other societies.

> Reports on the work of these people is sent to the heads of the societies regularly. I send reports now on the persons working under me to the supervising union and to the chairman of the society.... [In making the appointments elsewhere of such persons], the supervising union not only consults me but they respect my choices.

The supervising union appoints and suspends secretaries; the primary societies do not have any formal role in either action. However, as this informant noted, the chairman of a society can object to a particular choice on an informal basis "since, being in the same taluka, he is well aware of the persons working here." (Most appointments are made from within a taluka and there is no transfer system exceeding the taluka's boundaries. This was especially attractive to persons who wished to remain in contact with their families or personal lands.) Appointments sometimes involved "politics"—attempts by chairmen to get their own men made secretaries. In our informant's estimation this happened in "only" 30 to 40 percent of the cases.

The society which S. N. served had about five hundred members. In a normal year, S. N. calculated, about two hundred members would borrow from it. While approximately eleven hundred farmers fell within the jurisdiction of the society, two hundred rented out their lands on temporary leases, so that only nine hundred were really potential members of the society. Loans normally ranged from Rs. 9,000 down to Rs. 200, depending on the size of holdings and the kinds of crops raised.

The society held memberships ("shares") in the DCCB and the taluka and district purchase and sales unions. One of the directors of the primary society was designated as its representative to the general body of the taluka sangh and participated in the election of directors of that body.

Societies like the one managed by S. N. receive their financing on the basis of authorizations made by the DCCB. DCCBs made loans out of funds granted to them by the Maharashtra State Central Cooperative Bank. In turn, they lent to the primary societies at 6 percent interest, and the societies lent to their members at 9 percent, thus profiting from the difference.

In response to questions about the misbehavior of secretaries in some societies, S. N. remarked:

> The management of many societies is often careless. Being uneducated and illiterate as many of them are now, they merely press their thumbs to whatever the secretary writes. There is no room for misappropriations as far as loans are concerned since these are reviewed by the [DCCB] but in other areas of business there is much scope. For example, in the selling of fertilizers, the secretaries may not keep correct accounts and put the money in their own pockets. . . . [Unfortunately], the supervisors merely make reports and send them by mail and they wait long periods for explanations to be made to the questions raised.

Among those supervisors interviewed, one reported that there had been two or three cases against secretaries in his taluka in the previous year. As he explained the process of bringing charges, "We issue notices to the secretaries and to the two persons who have stood surety for them. If the secretary or the surety does not pay the arrears owed, we file a criminal case. We have done that in a couple of cases and the secretaries involved were given six months in jail."[11]

11. Secretaries are often forgiven their "mistakes" rather than being prosecuted. Thus, one supervisor recalled a case in which a secretary had been transferred three times because he engaged in "small misappropriations" before he was finally prosecuted.

Other Cases

Another supervisor was posted to a taluka union in Kolhapur district which has experienced considerable political difficulties in recent years. Because of perpetual quarrels between the Congress forces and the CPI elements in the taluka (the only taluka where the latter has an important following in the cooperative field), the union was suspended for a year. The Congress group had managed to control the board in the past, but in the year prior to suspension there was a vote for the election of the board taken by raising hands. As the supervisor recalled:

> Members would be shifting back and forth and changing their votes. So finally an administrator was brought in by the government . . . and he ran the union for a year. Then in [the next year] a regular closed-ballot election was held and the [CPI] group was elected. This year three-year terms have been introduced and all those elected were Communists. There were some kidnappings . . . taking away for three or four days, but no murders.[12]

We have not yet discussed those individuals who staff the taluka purchase and sales unions, though mention has been made of some of the functions of those bodies. As the manager of one such union explained:

> The purchase and sales unions do not give loans. If the [DCCB] extends a credit to a farmer [through his village society], he would get it [partly] in seeds and manure mixture. . . . The bank advances the loan to us and we pay them back. It is not required that the farmer pay back his loans by marketing his goods through us, but the local society must recover his loan somehow.

A major purpose of the taluka sanghs—the marketing of the farmers' goods—has only been partially realized.[13] Sugar factories perform a marketing function in handling their members' cane. In

12. What is sometimes referred to as "kidnapping" involves taking a voter away from the immediate scene so he cannot be approached by the opposition side. Often those kidnappings are organized as outings with the expenses borne by the political group involved. Although political conflict did occasionally result in violence, murders were not as common as the statement quoted might seem to suggest.

13. For a careful review of marketing societies in Marathwada, see Sandra McLaren, "Co-operative Marketing Societies: Case Studies in Marathwada," *Economic and Political Weekly*, 28 September 1974, pp. A-82-A-91.

Kolhapur district both the District Union and the taluka sanghs help in the collection and marketing of jaggery. In contrast to this practice, for most fruits and vegetables the private merchant still plays a considerable role. In this respect, a manager of one taluka sangh identified the kind of action he felt should be taken in marketing in his area.

> The government should undertake the monopoly procurement of . . . groundnuts [peanuts]. We could then compete with the private merchants in groundnuts. . . . [Now] we can help the farmer to get good prices [but] there is a limit to the funds available to us. Private merchants can store the nuts. . . . The union is not presently in a position to hold on to them during the period when the prices are low. Government procurement would help maintain an even price. Some big merchants play games with the prices. . . . The farmers need to give their goods at the proper time and the [sangh] needs to be in a position to purchase them.

Finally, in the smaller towns and urban centers of Maharashtra (though not in the larger cities), the principle of regulated markets has been widely accepted. Market committees composed of farmer representatives, local merchants, cooperative society spokesmen, and government officials are responsible, as the Minister for Cooperation has written, for helping

> to improve the standard of marketing services, to keep the farmers and traders fully and promptly informed about the market trends, to establish equity in the bargaining power between the agriculturists and the traders, promoting mutual confidence, preventing malpractices, and giving a fair deal to the farmers.[14]

As of mid-1970, there were 346 regulated local markets in Maharashtra. Although these markets are not organized along the lines of other cooperative institutions, their involvement in the process has led them to be included in the thinking of those state leaders concerned with the further growth of the cooperative sector. Thus, the Minister for Cooperation has attempted to develop plans for further integration of local markets with the cooperative system.

14. Mohite, *Cooperative Reappraisal,* p. 76.

Less Successful Cooperative Societies

Little has been said, thus far, about a wide range of activities organized in the cooperative sector which are generally less significant in the investment calculations of the medium- and large-scale farmer than those credit and marketing operations discussed in the last section. These activities include poultries, piggeries, and dairies, as well as "industrial" (artisan), consumer, and labor team cooperatives—the last consisting mainly of tribal or other low-status groups contracting out as a team for work on construction or other labor-intensive projects. On the whole, efforts in these various areas have not been markedly successful, though performances range from respectable (in the case of at least a few of the dairy cooperatives) to disastrous (in the case of a state government experiment in piggeries). In part, difficulties have arisen because these special-function societies have had available to them neither the technical expertise nor the managerial skills necessary to handle their affairs properly. In other instances, failures have been attributable to ill-prepared rural populations or to certain value and behavior patterns ingrained in the Indian culture.

Thus, the man who was chairman of the federation of industrial cooperative societies in Poona district, and, as a result, a member of the DCCB, complained that the bulk of rural credit was going to the producers of cane and other major commercial crops while little effort was being made to seriously encourage artisan societies. However, he conceded that most of the district's 214 industrial cooperatives were unable to compete in the marketplace.

> Many grow out of artisan traditions and are old-fashioned in their operations. . . . We have found it difficult to evolve schemes for these societies which are really successful. If there is one *chappal* [sandal] maker for each few villages, it is very hard to organize them into a workable cooperative system. Even many of the weavers, who are geographically concentrated, find it difficult to compete with mill-made cloth. They are slow to adapt to new designs.

The experiences with poultries have been equally disheartening. One informant, the manager of a cooperative poultry initiated by the Warna sugar factory, recounted a series of difficulties which the state government had experienced in trying to encourage poultry development in Maharashtra. In 1965, the government created fourteen poultry development blocks in various parts of the state, each consisting of 100 villages in an area covering approximately forty square miles. As project officer to one of these blocks, this informant was responsible for supplying chicks and feed to those who entered the scheme. All loans were made in kind. As he recalled:

> [People] thought that poultry required no care and so were not interested in the bother and expense that the development officers were trying to promote. . . . They did not take proper medical care. . . . They would simply collect the eggs laid by their *deshi* [country] hens and supply them to the government.

In 1969, he came to the Warna poultry to help save an enterprise which had been through difficult times. In part, the government's involvement represented a desire not to lose the substantial investment that it already had made in providing half the capital for the enterprise. Although the poultry was technically a cooperative, as the manager noted, its 142 members really had no responsibility for its operations:

> Originally, the idea was to have one central facility to hatch eggs, rear the chicks up to two months, and then supply them to the farmers. We were also supposed to supply feed to the farmers, medicine, and veterinary aid to collect the eggs. But since the centralized unit came into a loss, the society dropped the idea of individual units and will continue with the central unit only. No one was interested in taking up the poultry business after the failure anyway.

Even in this case, where some success may now have been achieved, the immediate effect on the countryside was limited. The poultry facility did give employment to thirty local people, but the original purpose of providing alternative rural employment to marginal farmers or to the landless in order to supplement their meager incomes has not been well served. For most persons from this class the risks are too great and the profit potential of the poultry business is limited. As my informant pointed out, "Either you need a large cooperative facility to succeed or a one-man business with a minimum of 100 birds. The bigger the farm, the bigger the profit margin."

Perhaps the least successful societies have been the piggery cooperatives. The state government advanced large sums of money to provide the organizers of such societies with pigs of good stock, appropriate feed, and a proper medical and technical support structure.[15]

There were serious difficulties with the project from a technical aspect. The profit margin, once all costs were taken into account, was very small—perhaps 2 percent on sales. There were also major marketing problems. Since pork is not a common Indian food, most of what demand existed was in Bombay City. There was relatively little demand in districts like Kolhapur, where many of the cooperatives were located. (More than half the pigs slaughtered under the scheme were products of Kolhapur cooperatives.) In response to the expected demand from Bombay City, the government constructed a large bacon-packing plant in north Bombay to which the pigs were shipped from Kolhapur. This involved costs of shipping and related activities.

By 1970, only two of the twenty-two societies originally funded in Kolhapur district were making any profit, and even these were operating on the margins of success. The major issue was proper management. Many societies seem to have been funded largely for the back-door profits to be made from their failure; such profits would come from misappropriations or from the liquidation of the society itself, for the government assumed the costs of failure and the persons responsible absorbed few of the risks. Thus, when the first society in Kolhapur was liquidated in 1968-1969, the chairman (a local film star) and his friends celebrated by inviting various local people, including politicians, to a party. As one observer noted, "The success of this liquidation so pleased other chairmen that they assumed they could also get away with it." After this first "successful" failure, therefore, not only were there others but there was a sudden interest in starting piggeries among persons who had absolutely no interest in raising pigs. A man who had worked with the piggery federation in Kolhapur district described some of the local operations:

> Some farmers will take grain or chaff from their own land to feed the pigs and sell the special feed on the market. They pocket the money gained from selling the government feed. They also get loans for *godowns* [storage facilities] and they use the godowns for their own

15. Originally this support was given in the form of a large cash grant. The pattern was changed as soon as the government realized how dangerous such a procedure was.

farms, rather than as intended, for the pigs. In one place, a farmer has turned the godown into housing for his tenants and charges them rent for it. Piggeries can bring a profit but that requires more work than most chairmen and secretaries are willing to expend.

The situation finally became so financially and politically embarrassing to the state government that in mid-1970 it sent an enquiry officer who was less willing than his predecessor to allow easy liquidations. As a result, there has been some change.

> Previously, the chairman and secretary of a society would take whatever profits they could out of the society and then would call a veterinarian whom they might bribe to certify that there were so many live pigs and that their health was all right. Then after many of them would die from malnutrition, the veterinarian would certify that they had died of an unspecified pig disease. Then the chairman and the secretary would apply for liquidation. An inquiry would be made and they might bribe the official some amount to allow the society to liquidate. . . . The new enquiry officer posted here is a more determined and dedicated person and it is not so easy to do anymore.[16]

On the whole, then, a variety of difficulties have prevented the successful development of cooperative societies outside the basic structure of agricultural credit and marketing.[17] Even within

16. The first phase of piggery cooperative activity ended in Kolhapur district with the conviction of the chairman and the secretary of a cooperative piggery on a charge of "getting a sum of Rs. 1,600 for breeding pigs which were non-existent." The chairman was sentenced to two years in prison and fined Rs. 100; the secretary was sentenced to one month and also fined Rs. 100. *Times of India,* 28 May 1970. A review of cooperatives cited in "Maharashtra II: Cooperatives: The True Story," *Economic and Political Weekly,* 29 September 1973, p. 1956, reported that only eight of eighty-six piggery societies were functioning in 1973.

17. In addition to those activities already mentioned, efforts to organize farming on a cooperative basis in Maharashtra have been predominantly unsuccessful. Mohite devotes a section in his *Cooperative Reappraisal* to the problems of farming cooperatives. As of June 1969, he reported, there were 376 Joint Farming Societies and 858 Collective Farming Societies in Maharashtra with a total membership of 28,704. Of the 1,234 societies, 558 were losing money, 270 were making a profit, and 406 were breaking even (p. 211). In "Maharashtra II: Cooperatives: The True Story," (see n. 16) the total figure given is 941 societies initiated, with only 380 of those still in operation as of mid-1973. Such ventures have usually been organized among Scheduled Caste or tribal peoples who are granted poor quality land by the state government out of reserves or are given the marginal land which has

those fields, as we have already noted, many shortcomings exist. Still, a few processing societies have achieved a measure of success. The Ichalkaranji spinning mills are such an instance, and, as we shall see, they are serving as a model for development elsewhere in Maharashtra. Another major thrust for rural economic development in western Maharashtra has come from the cooperative sugar factories. In the following section, we will consider the economic and political roles of such agro-industries.

THE ECONOMICS AND POLITICS OF PROCESSING INDUSTRIES

The Sugar Factories

Since so much said about the operation of the cooperative sugar factories of Maharashtra is self-congratulatory, it may be useful to begin a discussion of that sector's development with the comments of a PWP leader critical of the movement:

> The only successes have been in the sugar factories, which produce goods for a protected market. I am from Sangli district and I know some of the projects run by [Vasantrao] Dada Patil that have failed. He started a solvent extract plant to take oil from groundnuts and make various things. That factory has run into *lakhs* of rupees in losses. The cooperative poultry he started has also failed.... Only sugar has succeeded, and that is not due to the skills of the cooperative leaders but to the way the sugar industry has been protected since 1932. They have benefited from the operations of the tariff. No sugar is imported into India.... I am not against the use of tariffs, but how long is it necessary to nurse the baby?

Sugar production is also cushioned internally by a system of guaranteed prices based on government levies intended to return a "remunerative" price to the producer.[18] Although private sugar

---

resulted from the limited land reforms that have occurred in the state. They have been provided with little in the way of managerial skills or with the finances to make them successful. (Indeed, it has been possible to point to their failure as "evidence" of the unworkability of cooperative farming generally.)

18. There is a continuous debate in India about the economics of the sugar industry and particularly about the pricing system. Discussions of the questions involved may be found scattered throughout the various issues of *Economic and Political Weekly*. See, for example, S. G. Sathe, "The Un-Sweet Compulsions," 10 July 1971, pp. 1371-1372; and anon., "Time for Full Decontrol," 13 November 1971, p. 2297.

factories have existed since the 1930s, the government of India has made it a policy for the last decade to discourage the expansion of these private factories and to authorize the opening of new factories only in the cooperative sector.[19] In the last few years there has been some talk of taking the further step of nationalizing the cooperative factories, thus depriving the farmer-members of their dividends, but there is little indication that the government is likely to move in this direction, especially as long as sugar growers continue to have the political influence they presently do.

There has been a considerable fluctuation throughout India in sugar production over the last decade—a matter that deeply affects the interests of the sugar cooperative politicians of Maharashtra. In 1965-1966, the nation produced 35.4 lakh tons of sugar; there was a slump in 1967-1968 to 22.48, which resulted in price increases and consequently a great interest in producing cane. As a result, production rose again to 35 lakh tons in 1968-1969 and to a record 42.6 in 1969-1970. Part of the rise and fall in availability of sugar was due to central policies of assured prices. The government of India, particularly during periods of low production, has purchased a substantial proportion of the cane production under a levy system that covered as much as 70 percent of output. The remainder has gone into the free market. When production exceeded expectations in 1969-1970, the government made some effort to reduce the amount of sugar requisitioned and then later to decontrol a larger share, presumably contributing to a subsequent drop in production.[20]

19. The private factory in Kolhapur was started in 1933 through a combine of private business interests and the princely regime. In Poona, the only private factory is run by the Walchand business group, which also operates a factory in Ahmednagar district. When the company saw the direction state government policy was headed, it switched its prime interest from the production of sugar to the production of machinery. As a result, the company has been the major supplier of sugar manufacturing machinery for fourteen of the factories built in the cooperative sector in the last decade.

20. Supplies were so great in 1970-1971 that the central government removed all controls from the industry on May 25 of that year. When the war with Pakistan broke out in December 1971, controls were temporarily reimposed. Subsequently, there was a conflict within the industry, with the private factories preferring the freedom associated with decontrol and the cooperatives wanting the protection associated with an assured price. The latter won out, and statutory controls were reimposed from July 1, 1972.

Though the government of India fixes a minimum price, that price depends on an average yield per ton of raw cane. Areas of the country vary widely in their productivity because of soil and water conditions, with the result that while the price may be reasonable for areas with high recovery rates, it may not be as remunerative in areas of low recovery since the costs of production may remain about the same. As a result, many factories have entered into ancillary activities which seek to cushion fluctuations in market prices. Thus, there was considerable support for the effort in 1970 (which was eventually successful) to abolish prohibition in Maharashtra. This would allow for the use of the by-products of the sugar factories in the manufacture of liquor.

In matters of state and national policy making, the sugar factories maintain a vigorous presence. The Maharashtra Cooperative Sugar Factories Federation acts as the representative of the factories in the cooperative sector in dealing with the government, while the Deccan Sugar Merchants Association acts as the agent of the private factories. There are occasions when the two cooperate to pressure the central government for greater recognition of the demands of Maharashtra as compared to the interests of states, like Bihar and Uttar Pradesh, where sugar is processed largely by private factories. Maharashtra feels that undue preference has been given to these states at a time when it and southern states are much more productive in cane.[21] This has been a constant point of argument on the part of state political leaders in making a case for additional cooperative factories in the state. However, as one state government official conceded, "Unless the irrigation potential of Maharashtra is properly tapped, we may have reached a saturation point with factories in the state because we are already bringing into production lands of a marginal character and the result is lower productivity in those areas."

It may be useful at this point to describe the operations of a typical sugar factory in the cooperative sector. Theur, which is

21. Yields in Uttar Pradesh and Bihar are only 15.8 and 12.7 tons per acre respectively, compared to 25.6 tons per acre in Maharashtra, 32.8 in Tamil Nadu, 36.1 in Andhra Pradesh, and 33.3 in Karnataka. As one writer has noted, "Added to this is the fact that sugar factories in UP and Bihar . . . were set up some 30 to 40 years ago. . . . These are now obsolete, many of them are not able to raise their average crushing capacity of 900 tons per day." B. Krishna, "Sugar—A Bitter Crisis," *The Illustrated Weekly of India*, 4 February 1973, p. 8.

located near Poona City in Haveli taluka, is politically dominated by Annasaheb Magar, MLA and sometime District Congress president. It is a new factory led by some of the biggest commercial farmers in the area. The factory had 2,700 farmer-members who owned 5,300 shares and cultivated 4,000 acres of cane land. When and if irrigation schemes are further developed for the area, it is expected that the acreage covered by the factory will increase to 12,000.

To put together the capital necessary to organize the factory, the leaders of the Theur installation needed about Rs. 2.48 *crores* (about $1.9 million). They raised Rs. 57 lakhs from members, received a loan from the state government of Rs. 25 lakhs in the form of share capital, a large loan of Rs. 1.17 crores from the Industrial Finance Corporation (an all-India body), and a loan of Rs. 49 lakhs from the Life Insurance Corporation of India. Of the Rs. 2.48 crores, Rs. 1.45 crores went for plant equipment and the rest for construction and initial operating expenses.

Though factory members are personally financed by the DCCBs, factories vary in their use of cooperative lending facilities for their operating expenses. Some take medium-term loans from the DCCBs; others (particularly those led by persons who are not on good political terms with their local DCCBs) may draw on loans directly from the State Central Cooperative Bank. More recently, some have sought the help of the nationalized banks.[22]

Most factories maintain substantial numbers of bullock carts and trucks, which they employ in bringing their members' cane to the factory. (Non-members must use their own means to get their cane to the factory.) Employees of the factory, including substantial seasonal labor recruited from other districts on a contract basis, assist farmers in harvesting and transporting the cane.[23] In

22. Though relationships between the sugar factories and the cooperative banking system were generally cordial, a note of conflict was sounded by Vasantrao Patil in 1970. Addressing the Tenth Conference of District Central Banks, Patil complained that some sugar factories were collecting on advances made to members before they collected loans due the primary credit societies. He also characterized as a "retrograde step" and "a new disease" the "practice of giving precedence for the purpose of recovery to loans of nationalized banks over those of cooperatives." Speech of the Chairman, 7 March 1970, mimeographed (Bombay: Maharashtra State Cooperative Bank) p. 9.

23. The Theur factory imported its contract labor from Ahmednagar and Bhir districts. One informant insisted that there was a shortage of skilled

all, Theur employed 3,500 people as seasonal labor. (It takes a team of three to service each bullock cart—one to cut the cane, another to stack it, and a third to actually transport it from the field to the checkpoint of the factory where it is weighed and entered into the crushing process.) In addition to seasonal labor, the factory maintains a year-round clerical and mechanical crew of 200 people, thus providing an important additional source of local employment.

In order to raise sugar crops, it is generally estimated that a sugar farmer requires Rs. 2,000 to 2,500 per acre to cover his costs of production. These funds are provided by the DCCBs to the primary societies in the villages. Rather than the societies being responsible for the collection of outstanding loans, however, the loans are deducted from the prices received by the factory from the government and from free sales managed by the factory through the taluka or district purchase and sales unions.

While many small farmers are members of the sugar factories, those who are in a position to dominate their operations are usually the big landowners and leading politicians of a territory.[24] Initially, arrangements need to be made with the central and state governments to acquire the authorization for starting such large enterprises. Political standing is undoubtedly helpful. It is necessary for a group to be organized to raise the local part of the share capital and to sign up farmer-members. There was no rush to engage in these activities in the early period of cooperative organization until it became apparent that cooperative sugar factories could contribute to the economic development of an area and to the economic and political advantage of their leaders. In many

---

labor in Poona district for the kinds of work that contract labor was capable of doing. Contracting is heavily implicated in politics and there are charges of exploitation of low-status laborers by the contractors. Key directors in some factories are alleged to receive political contributions for help in getting such contracts.

24. According to data gathered by the Maharashtra Cooperative Sugar Factories Federation, there were 100,518 members in the thirty sugar factories in operation in the state during the 1970-1971 crushing season. Of these, 51.4 percent owned one acre of cane or less, and another 23.2 percent only one to two acres. This says nothing about the number of members of one family who may hold memberships. Even taking the figures as correct, one government official asserted that the predominant political group in most factories comes from the 1.6 percent of the members who own ten or more acres of cane.

cases, those who organized the factories are still its leaders. In other instances, however, management positions have shifted with each new factory election.

An interesting case is "the one that got away" from the Kumbhar group. As early as 1961, Kumbhar attempted to organize a factory in Shirol taluka to add to the Panchaganga factory in Hatkanangale, which he controls. (He has continuously represented Shirol taluka in the State Assembly since 1962 and has exercised influence in the cooperatives and local government of the area.) According to an interesting document produced by Kumbhar's supporters, the initial meeting to organize the new factory was called in January 1961.[25] Leaders of primary societies, leaders of local government bodies, and other citizens were present. A proposal was formulated and submitted to the central government in December 1962. By that point a group led by Dattajirao Kadam had set itself up as a competitor demanding recognition for its own Datta sugar factory scheme covering essentially the same area.

For the next year, endless correspondence between the Kumbhar group and the government of India was conducted in which the latter kept insisting on submission of further information. Finally, in January 1965, administrative officials from the central ministries of food, agriculture, and cooperation visited the area. Their recommendations were not made public. Indeed, it was not until June 1966 that it was revealed that the Shirol factory proposed by Kumbhar was included in a list of twenty factories supported by the Maharashtra government. However, the Deputy Minister for Food and Agriculture of the central government, Annasaheb Shinde,[26] asserted that the proposal was unacceptable because the area did not have adequate cane potential. The central government was also experiencing severe economic setbacks in 1965-1966 and was unwilling to expend the industrial finance

25. These events are recounted in *Important Events and Salient Features,* a brochure privately circulated by backers of the "Proposed Shirol Taluka Sahakari Sakhar Karkhana [Cooperative Sugar Factory]," published in May 1968. No one interviewed from the opposing side denied the general account of events presented below.

26. Shinde was not exactly an innocent bystander with respect to the sugar politics of Maharashtra. He represented the leading sugar-producing district in Maharashtra (Ahmednager) in Parliament and previously had been chairman of the Maharashtra Cooperative Sugar Factories Federation.

necessary to accelerate the number of factories at the rate the Maharashtra government would have liked.[27]

The debate was stirred up anew in February 1968, when Kumbhar wrote to Shinde inquiring about the status of the project and was told that no application had ever been received officially. Further correspondence by the Kumbhar group with the Minister of State for Cooperation in the central government led them to believe that they ought to make a fresh effort to organize a factory under new rules then being developed by the government of India. Thus, in early 1968, efforts were mounted to sign up prospective members and submit plans, including evidence to support the argument that cane in the target area was sufficient to provide a steady supply to the factory.

According to the Kumbhar group, their proposal was recommended by Chief Minister Naik to the government of India in April 1968. There was a feeling among Kumbhar people at that point of having achieved a definite victory over the Datta group. With visions of sugar plums dancing in their heads, the Kumbhar group wrote to the Directorate of Sugar in New Delhi, in May 1968, to tell them that they had succeeded in raising Rs. 50 lakhs in share capital from local cane growers. Two weeks after that letter was written, however, a Kumbhar representative visiting New Delhi was shocked to discover that the Datta factory had been given higher priority by the government of Maharashtra. New approaches were made by the Kumbhar people to the state government but to no avail. The influence of the Kadam forces was too great. In 1969, the Datta group was duly authorized by the national government to develop a factory in Shirol serving fifty-

---

27. Maharashtra has been more aggressive than most states in pressing the central government for additional licensing of sugar factories. Indeed, in 1971-1972, Maharashtra became the leading sugar-producing state in India. Of 31 lakh tons produced in the country in that year, 10.1 were produced in Maharashtra. Of this amount, 7.9 lakh tons were from the state's cooperatives. Whereas only 27 percent of sugarcane goes for sugar production on an all-India basis, in Maharashtra the figure is 55 percent. These data came from "A Note on the Cooperative Sugar Factories in Maharashtra State," provided by officials of the Maharashtra Cooperative Sugar Factories Federation. A major reason for Maharashtra's share of national sugar production rising so markedly in 1971-1972, however, was that farmers in Uttar Pradesh switched to jaggery (raw sugar) in that particular year as contrasted to the refined sugar produced by the factories. I want to thank Mr. S. P. Marathe, Manager of the Federation, for his help in providing these data and those cited in n. 24.

two villages from that taluka and six from neighboring Sangli district. Kadam conceded that in gaining recognition, "all state-level ministers as well as union ministers were approached in the matter."[28] By 1973, the factory was in operation under Kadam's leadership.

Like Datta, a number of cooperative sugar factories are the undisputed domains of a few individual political leaders or particular large-scale agricultural families. Such is the case with most of the first set of factories in Kolhapur, which included Panchaganga (founded by Ratnappa Kumbhar), Warna (started and still controlled by the Kore family), and Bhogawati (which was dominated from its founding to late 1973 by the Kaulaukar-Patils).[29]

Some factories, however, have been subject to quite intense political jockeying since their founding.[30] One such factory, Kumbhi-Kasari in Kolhapur district, was registered in 1960 and started its first crushing in 1963. Among those associated with the factory was D. C. Narke. Narke's family were large landholders in one of the talukas affected by the factory. Originally, he was one of the directors of the Warna factory, even though his own property did not fall within the territory covered by that factory. In his own words,

> Kore made a special application to the Registrar to include my village in his area, so I could help in raising the capital for the factory. We were friends and he wanted my help. My village is twenty-four miles from Warna, but the factory provided me with transport for only twelve miles while I was a member. That was from 1957 to 1962.[31]

28. Interview, Dattajirao Kadam, 13 September 1970.
29. "Maharashtra: Battle for Sugar Co-operatives," *Economic and Political Weekly*, 8 December 1973, p. 2166. That piece reviews contests for control of the thirty-nine cooperative sugar factories in the state but reports, in particular, efforts by Vasantrao Patil to capture control of those factories in Sangli and Satara districts associated with Rajaram Patil, Y. J. Mohite, and Balasaheb Desai. All of these efforts by Patil failed.
30. For useful studies of the internal politics of cooperative sugar factories in Ahmednagar district, see B. S. Baviskar, "Cooperatives and Politics," *Economic and Political Weekly*, 23 March 1968, pp. 490-495; and "Cooperatives and Caste in Maharashtra: A Case Study," *Sociological Bulletin* 18 (September 1969): 148-166. On the politics of one of the sugar factories in Baramati taluka of Poona district, see Donald W. Attwood, "Political Entrepreneurs and Political Development: Two Villages and a Taluka in Western India" (Ph.D. diss., McGill University, 1974).
31. Interview, D. C. Narke, 20 October 1970.

While he was personally associated with the Kores, Narke was not directly involved in the political factionalism of the district nor was he active in building a political career outside the factory.

Still, as a large landowner, he was interested in starting a factory in his home area. He experienced some opposition from the Shresti group in the Congress, but he and his associates did manage to organize a group of members by 1960 and to build a factory. Over the years, his group has generally managed to control the board of directors. Of the eleven seats elected by members in 1967, for example, Narke's group won seven and the other major group four, but in that year his control began to be challenged. Some members of his group were won away and joined the opposition to elect their own chairman for a year. In 1969 the Narke group backed one of the few politically active figures on the board for chairman and managed to regain their seven to four margin of control. Later, the chairman and Narke quarreled. With new elections approaching in 1970, Narke was concerned about his ability to retain influence in the factory.

Narke's comments on the employment practices in the factory indicate one aspect of his differences with the chairman. As he remarked in the same interview,

> The chairman's group controls the appointments of servants and the use of vehicles. We advertise and for technical posts take people from the outside, but for minor posts we take people locally. That is where politics sometimes comes in. . . . [As a result of the actions of the current chairman], suddenly there has been an addition of 100 laborers before the election, so our employment is now [excessive]. The economic position of the factory suffers as a result of such practices.

Though there was an attempt to compromise some of the emerging differences between Narke and the chairman before the factory elections, this effort failed. Instead, there were three groups in the field: one headed by Narke; another led by the chairman; and a third group associated jointly with the MLA from one of the talukas in the factory area and with a man of considerable influence in another taluka. Both leaders of the third group sat on the board of the DCCB, and the non-MLA was also the representative of the DCCB on the board of Kumbhi-Kasari—a practice not uncommon in the system of interlocking directorates characteristic of the cooperative sector.

Responding to a question in the same interview about the fact that the factory was not running any ancillary activities, Narke revealed several interesting features about his approach.

I have tried to run the factory like a business. We are not in social work. The only area in which we do mix with some social work is in encouraging irrigation projects. . . . I *am* dedicated to making sure, however, that the factory is not turned into a political platform. We must save it from the political leaders.

The incumbent chairman, although he had supported Narke for chairman in 1967, complained that Narke was a "hindrance to development work in the factory," which was the reason he cited for turning his support to another man for chairman in 1968-1969: "We wanted to take up various schemes like a dairy, college, and hospital, but Narke insisted on taking a conservative approach. Actually, it is possible to run the factory without a board, but the board is useful for undertaking a social approach to the needs of the area."[32]

To further confuse the situation, the MLA associated with the third group was a long-time enemy of a sitting MLA from another taluka who was a close friend of the chairman. Though the second MLA was not a member of the sugar factory, he feared that if his rival gained any influence in the factory his own position in district politics might be damaged. He, therefore, entered the fray: "As MLA I have to be interested in what is happening in my taluka and I have to have a certain interest in who controls the sugar factory. If I ignored such activities, I would be out of office."

The election in 1970, therefore, involved a long and complicated ballot on which the names of forty-nine individuals were listed, each man with his own symbol. Beyond three sets of candidates associated with each of the three main slates, there were independents contesting for seats on the sugar factory board. As one group leader commented:

This time everyone wanted to be on the board and we were not able to accommodate their demands so they stood as independents. In some

32. This activist posture is clearly evident in factories like Warna and Panchaganga. Thus, in "A Short Note" (a mimeographed set of pages put out by the factory management) on the working of the Panchaganga factory, a list of ancillary activities includes sponsoring a cooperative spinning mill projected at 25,000 spindles, planning for a distillery, joining together with three other cooperatives in developing a paper factory, proposing a chemical fertilizer plant, and investing in the improvement of transportation systems in the area of the factory, both by contributing to road improvements and to vehicles for transporting cane. The factory also has taken considerable interest in the educational arrangements in its area. Similar activities have been undertaken by the Warna factory.

cases, someone may have instigated them to stand. . . . There is much
personal ambition among them in being on the board. It has much to
do with village politics. . . . A man sees someone else from his village
standing and feels it is a matter of prestige not to allow the other man
to get above him. Many of the candidates who stood as independents
were hungry for prestige.

There is no reason to assume that the same consideration did not
affect the thinking of those on the major panels, although the
arenas toward which their behavior was oriented may have gone
considerably beyond village politics.

In the end, there was a large turnout of members activated by
the various factions and independents. A huge tent was erected on
the factory grounds and polling booths were placed at appropriate
points within the tent. Employees of the factory were posted to
count the ballots under the watchful eye of candidate representatives. Depending on whom one asked, the results were interpreted
slightly differently, but clearly the Narke group emerged with at
least a majority of six out of the eleven directors. Three seats were
won by the followers of the MLA slate, only one by a supporter of
the sitting chairman, and one by an independent. The victory of
the Narke group represented an endorsement of a group within the
factory less involved in the politics of the district and state than
the others.

In contrast to the situation at Kumbhi-Kasari, the conflicts at
the Bidri factory have been among persons otherwise busily engaged in wider political arenas. Indeed, the situation at Bidri was
one of multiparty and multifactional contention amidst conflicts
for personal advantage.

As elsewhere, managerial personnel of the factory complained about the entrance of politics into employment practices:

> We asked the board to authorize the hiring of technically qualified
> people like wiremen but instead we get the kind of people that the
> board wants to favor politically. Each director insists on getting at least
> ten appointments. . . . In some cases, the people recommended . . . are
> not really in need of labor at all, so they do not work. . . . A person
> might be appointed politically and then spend his time sitting with the
> director discussing politics. . . . As a result of these political appoint-
> ments we spend Rs. 3-4 lakhs more on salary annually than we should.

Because of political differences among the potential founders, who included men from the PSP, CPI, and PWP, there

had been some difficulty getting initial authorization for the factory. This difficulty was overcome with the aid of V. T. Patil. Patil became the recognized "organizer" of the factory and the chairman of the ad hoc body which helped collect the necessary funds and completed the preparatory work for the factory. In 1962 the first election by factory members was held for the new board. In that election, two groups emerged. They were divided evenly (five to five) between those favoring V. T. Patil and those against him. The eleventh member of the elected body was Hindurao Patil, who represented not the farmer-members but the small number of local societies which held some shares in the factory. The group opposed to V. T. Patil managed to win the chairmanship by throwing their backing to Hindurao Patil for that position.

In 1964, the chairmanship changed again. The man selected had been associated with V. T. Patil in the previous year's factory election. He served as chairman only until 1965. In 1965, Hindurao Patil's supporters in the general membership managed to win all the seats on the factory board. By that time, Hindurao (who had begun as a Kumbhar supporter) had clearly identified himself with the Shresti group in the DCC and was in a position to employ their support to favor his men in the factory. This led to a series of conflicts, including battles over the role played by the administrative head of the factory, the managing director. A period of internal disorder ended in 1968 when the slate opposed to Hindurao Patil elected its own followers to all the seats on the board. That group continued to maintain its control of the factory into 1973.[33] The chairman noted with some consternation that in 1970 the DCCB had attempted to designate Hindurao Patil—who was by then vice-president of the DCC and a major leader in both the DCCB and the DLDB—to a seat on the Bidri board as the representative of the DCCB but "we simply refused to have him." As he explained, "It is up to us to reject such nominees and if the bank does not like it, it can complain to the Registrar and he might intervene."[34]

33. "Maharashtra: Battle for Sugar Co-operatives," *Economic and Political Weekly*, 8 December 1973, p. 2166. In late 1973, the Hindurao Patil group regained control of the factory.

34. The Registrar is the highest bureaucrat of the Department of Cooperation in the state.

Though the chairman was vaguely a supporter of the Congress himself, in.1970 the board included men of various political stripe: four Congressmen, one from the PWP, one from the SSP, one from the CPI, and four independents (including a Kumbhar man).

Several informants suggested that the instability that existed in the Congress politics of the talukas affected by the factory owed something to the role played by shifts in leadership at Bidri. Even when Congress candidates had the upper hand in contests for MLA, dissident Congressmen might seek the support of those non-Congressmen associated with the factory to boost their own political ambitions. In this connection, one board member made a point developed by others:

> It is natural that the people elected in the factory elections worked at the village level thereafter to help their supporters get elected to local societies and the gram panchayats. The panchayat samiti in my taluka was all Congress in 1967 because the Congress candidates got the help of the factory board directors here.

The Spinning and Weaving Mills

Another major processing industry in Kolhapur is composed of spinning and weaving factories centered in Ichalkaranji. Almost all the looms for weaving are privately owned, but the owners have banded together to provide themselves with financing, a reliable supply of yarn, and a measure of distributional coordination. Although an association of powerloom owners was put together as early as 1938, there were difficulties organizing such activities through the cooperative sector. Gandhians in the Congress wished to preserve weaving as a cottage industry and favored handloom production over the output of powerlooms, which became increasingly popular after World War I. On the other hand, the large private textile mills in Bombay State's biggest cities (Bombay and Ahmedabad) sought to discourage the growth of an alternative form of the textile industry.

Despite this two-pronged opposition, a Powerloom Inquiry Committee appointed by the Bombay State government in 1955 recommended the formation of cooperative spinning mills. No action was taken, however, until shortly after the new state of Maharashtra was formed in 1960. The Chavan government decided to encourage such industries and gave its support to the creation of the first spinning mill in the cooperative sector, the Deccan Cooperative Spinning Mills, located at Ichalkaranji.[35] The first chairman and vice-chairman of that body, respectively, were A. G. Kulkarni and Dattajirao Kadam. Among the directors was Anantrao Bhide. Kulkarni and Kadam held their posts for nearly a decade, until Bhide became chairman in 1970.[36]

In addition to encouraging the development of spinning mills, the leaders of Ichalkaranji attempted to develop some premarketing capacity. For that reason, Bhide, Kadam, and their associates organized the Yeshwant Cooperative Processing Society to collect and process members' cloth from the woven strips into the proper condition for marketing. The society is not a marketing agent, however, and members arrange for their cloth to be disposed of in the private market as they see fit.

Viewed in its entirety, Ichalkaranji is a company town run by leaders who pride themselves on their attitudes of enlightened paternalism toward the workers.[37] Recruitment of workers is itself part of an interesting political process. Thus, the 800 employees in the Deccan Spinning Mill were hired on the basis of political (more particularly, Congress party) recommendations. One leader described the process:

> There are about thirty ward leaders [of the Congress] and we also have contacts through the party into the various villages. We get recommendations for employees through those people. A person will fill out a form we maintain at the party offices and seek the help of his ward leader, and they will give the forms to the chief of the City Congress Committee, who sends these to our factory office.

Asked whether such a procedure affected the character of relations between management and labor, he responded:

35. This information comes from interview materials and from "A Brochure on the Powerloom Industry at Ichalkaranji," put out by the Deccan Cooperative Spinning Mills, Ltd. The "Brochure" was issued in conjunction with the inauguration of the mill by the President of India on November 18, 1962.

36. By 1970, the spinning mill had loans of Rs. 82 lakhs outstanding to the Industrial Finance Corporation and Rs. 48 lakhs to the Kolhapur DCCB. Kadam sat on the board of the DCCB at the time to represent the processing industries of the district.

37. The scope for union activity is rather limited since salary scales are set by the national government. For one study of union politics in a cooperative sugar factory, see B. S. Baviskar, "Union Politics and Management Politics," *Indian Journal of Industrial Relations* 3 (January 1968): 300-315.

There were some inefficiencies in this system at the beginning but we have held that once a man is taken on, if the manager wants to take any action against him, we will not interfere. . . . We have not had any complaints [in recent years] about this.

To complete the description of the basic structure of the cooperative system, the next section briefly examines the organization of credit and marketing institutions at district and state levels.

Major Credit and Marketing Structures

There is no need to repeat here the history of political conflicts within district credit and marketing organizations, but it may be helpful to examine in more detail the organization and operation of the three major institutions, the DCCBs, the DLDBs, and the district marketing societies.

The DCCBS

The most important of the three sets of institutions is the district central cooperative banks (DCCBs), which deal with the distribution of short-term (one-year) and medium-term (up to three years) credit. They are presided over by elected boards of directors in association with an appointed managing director or general manager.[38]

In the case of Poona district, the board has consisted in recent years of twenty-one members: thirteen directors elected for three-year terms by the representatives of societies in the thirteen talukas; four seats filled by representatives of various cooperative societies in which the bank had an interest (sugar factories; smaller processing societies, like oil mills; industrial (artisan) societies; dairies); two nominees (one each from the Maharashtra State Central Cooperative Bank and the DLDB); the managing director; and one member representing the few remaining individual members who held shares in the bank before the reorganization of the cooperative sector.

38. The term employed for the official and his power vary with the district. In Poona, the managing director is counted as a full-fledged member of the board; in Kolhapur he is not, even though the incumbent at the time of the study played a major role in directing its activities.

In Poona and Kolhapur districts, the managerial staff has been headed by an individual deputed by the state bank, though this need not be the practice. In 1970 the two men had long experience in the cooperative banking sector and regarded themselves as professionals in the administration of their banking staffs of approximately five hundred persons in each district. The banks maintained central offices in the largest city of the district, but part of their staffs manned the numerous branches operated in the towns and large villages. These branches handled much of the paperwork referred to them by the secretaries of the primary credit societies and supervising unions. Though the DCCBs are involved in more than serving the agricultural credit needs of the primary societies, that is their main business. Thus, in Kolhapur, of Rs. 14 crores lent in 1969-1970, only Rs. 4 crores went into non-agricultural loans, and part of these went to agriculturally related enterprises, like factories manufacturing granulated fertilizers, or to industries like the spinning and weaving mills. In Kolhapur, as compared to Poona, the bank has been relatively inactive in providing short-term credit for the sugar factories. This was not for want of trying but rather a consequence of the political situation in the district. As an official of the bank explained:

> We are in the process of taking over the short-term financing of the Datta factory. We originally approached some of the older factories . . . [but] they would not accept the idea. All those factories are run by people of different political views from the directors of the bank. Kumbhar and Kore have no place on the board and would prefer to remain aloof from its operation. But it is not those factories alone. . . . We have been able to convince Datta to allow us to handle the temporary finance . . . necessary between the time that the cultivator brings his cane to the factory and the end of the season when the accounts are closed [and the factory receives actual payment for its sugar].

Though these officials acknowledged the existence of political pressures, they insisted that relatively few of the bank's decisions were seriously affected by politics. Credit is not extended to individual borrowers but to primary credit societies on the basis of plans drawn up by their secretaries. The branches of the DCCB scrutinize these plans and send them to the DCCB for ratification.

The board then reviews that recommendation, taking into account the general level of bank resources; that may mean reducing the primary societies' requests by some standard percentage. Where an old district bank exists with a solid capital position it may draw upon its own resources to extend credit, but the state apex bank is available to lend money and most banks will turn to that source rather than depend entirely on share capital or savings accumulated from individual accounts maintained by the banks.[39]

The managerial staff admits the existence of some political leverage, which directors occasionally attempt to utilize.

> [A] society which applies for a loan of Rs. 2 lakhs may be found to be worth only Rs. 1 lakh in loans, but the chairman or the vice-chairman may ask that help be given that society, so it will receive the larger amount. On the other hand, a proposal may also come for Rs. 2 lakhs and the society in question may be a strong one, but the workers in that society may be the political opponents of some of the board members. Then the board may delay action or postpone action or deny the loan. Such cases are comparatively few, however.

While top managerial staff claimed they were not drawn into most political quarrels, they did express a desire that election procedures be regularized. Like most cooperative institutions, the DCCBs were technically the judges of their own elections. This caused considerable difficulty. Disputes would wind up in a special system of cooperative arbitration courts, but these proved inadequate in dealing with such conflicts. The result was that quarrels within the cooperatives (particularly about elections) eventually filtered into the regular judicial system but only after tedious procedures which kept the direction of some institutions uncertain while cases were pending.

Though their managements claimed the DCCBs were operated with efficiency, recovery rates on loans were uneven. Managers, like politicians, attributed poor recoveries to inadequate rainfall, particularly in Poona district, where less than 10 percent of the agricultural land is irrigated. Others suggested that some

---

39. The state apex bank, in turn, may borrow from the Reserve Bank of India at 3 percent for short-term agricultural loans and at 3.5 percent for medium-term loans. The Maharashtra bank does not need to depend as heavily on the Reserve Bank as the apex banks of some other states. In 1970, it had its own capital of about Rs. 15 crores and legal authority to raise additional capital in the money market of Bombay.

credit—especially that given to small farmers—tended to be diverted into consumption needs rather than being used for agricultural purposes. Yet, at the same time, poor recoveries were also blamed on big farmers who failed to repay their loans because of their political positions. Both in Poona and Kolhapur districts, the overwhelming percentage of credit went to a small proportion of farmers. Since an acre of sugarcane may absorb Rs. 2,000-2,500 in credit as compared to Rs. 80 for an acre of wheat, the big sugarcane growers were alleged to be reaping most of the benefits of banking credit.

In Poona district, recoveries for the year ending June 30, 1972, amounted to only 62.8 percent, and it was likely that repayments on loans for 1972-1973 (a year marked by drought) would be lower. Even in a good year (1969-1970), however, the DCCB had managed to collect only 67 percent of its outstanding loans. In such cases, new loans were not given to defaulters, but this did not prevent the accumulation of additional bad debts by other borrowers.

An official of the apex bank insisted that many of the defaults were technical rather than substantive. He pointed to the need for a farmer to meet his debts by a specific date in order that he not be considered in technical default. In fact, many loans were repaid after the date required but were not included in the calculation of repayments. Whether this was the actual case or not, he was relatively philosophical about the problem:

> Defaults are of several types: those which are due to the vagaries of nature; cases where the crop is good but the prices fall. [In the second case,] the man has invested the money but is unable to cover his other costs. In such a case, some is reinvested in his agriculture even when some may be used for personal consumption. . . . Recalcitrant defaulters constitute no more than 20 percent of the defaulters. The problem of reaching them is not really one so much of organization but may arise from local problems like feuds in the primary society or local politics. . . . But even these defaults are generally cleared up the next year; they are not bad debts.

On the whole, managerial personnel associated with the DCCBs were supportive of the institutional arrangements within which they operated. Both administrative personnel and politicians active in the district and state banks based their arguments on grounds having nothing to do (at least explicitly) with political criteria. Rather, as we shall see in the next chapter, they attributed political motives to the advocates of change.

The District Land Development Banks

Critics of the use of land development banks as a means of granting long-term loans (up to ten years) for investment in machinery and capital projects, like wells and irrigation schemes, complained in 1970 that their pattern of operation was a perverted form of cooperative organization because membership was itself a direct function of a state of indebtedness. Unlike the system of credit that had grown up around the DCCBs, the essential unit of the DLDB pattern has not been the village primary society. Membership in a DLDB consists of little more than an amount deducted as share capital from the loan made by the bank. Since individual borrowers formed the principal base of these bodies, they also constituted the electorate for selection of their boards of directors. Indeed, being a borrower has been one of the requirements for running for the board.

The DLDBs were more the creatures of the state bank than the DCCBs. Few DLDBs built up any resources to operate autonomously. What funds they had went directly into loans. As compared to the DCCBs, which might lend Rs. 14-16 crores a year, the land development banks in Kolhapur and Poona districts made annual loans of about Rs. 1.25 crores essentially by passing on funds appropriated to them by the State Land Development Bank. As a result, their administrative leadership complained much more about the inadequacy of funds than did their colleagues in the DCCBs. This deficiency may have also contributed to a greater air of politicization surrounding loan decisions. Though some administrative personnel insisted that the credit pattern was clearly laid down by the state body, others (including some politicians) spoke about the political aspects of the lending policy:

> [When] the cooperatives began to make money available to local persons to develop their land, there was a sudden flow of resources into areas where credit had always been scarce. There was then a considerable misutilization of funds. . . . Some [political leaders] took undue advantage. . . . They were able to make additional money for themselves and their followers by making loans on the condition that borrowers buy their goods from certain distributors who might be themselves, their relatives, or their friends. In some cases, they got their

followers to invest in pump sets or electric motors even where . . . electricity had not come to the area. [Perhaps] the leader promised it would come at the time of the loan.

Despite their financial difficulties, the DLDBs in Poona and Kolhapur were important financial agencies in 1970, with staffs of 150-160 people each and branches in the various talukas. Loans were arranged on the basis of the property value of the land owned by the borrower; in effect, as the earlier title of the state apex body (State Land Mortgage Bank) had indicated, individuals obtained mortgages on their land in return for credit.[40]

An effort has been made by the apex institution to maintain a recovery rate of 85 percent. Despite this goal, state officials conceded that in 1969-1970—a good year by Maharashtra's agricultural standards—recoveries were running at only 75 percent. In 1970-1971, this decreased to 50 percent, and it was probable that the results for 1971-1972 would be even worse. One difficulty the DLDBs experienced was that recoveries were not linked to the procurement system as they were in the case of loans to growers of sugarcane who belonged to sugar factories. There was also some feeling that adequate action was not being taken against rich defaulters. One administrator in the apex institution spoke directly to that concern:

> Strong steps should be taken against . . . those who could afford to repay their loans but who with the help of their political friends have found means of getting around proper payments. Unfortunately, I have discovered that among them are some MLAs, MLCs, and even one former deputy minister. Perhaps we will be able to collect now that he is not in the Cabinet.

Despite the complaints about their functioning, the DLDBs of Poona and Kolhapur were regarded as relatively successful compared to some districts in Marathwada and Vidarbha. An official in the apex body made the following assessment, "Of twenty-six banks, eighteen [have been] going on reasonably well and could be improved with only a little effort, like the removal of

40. Though most borrowers are individuals, the DLDBs do make loans to groups of farmers for lift-irrigation schemes. In 1968-1969, however, the Kolhapur DLDB made only 400 group loans as compared to nearly 17,000 individual loans. Interview, N. A. Khot, Chief Executive Officer, Kolhapur District Land Development Bank, 24 May 1970.

three or four leaders from each bank." He counted Kolhapur as an example of one such bank.[41]

Marketing Societies

The State Marketing Federation of Maharashtra is the apex organization for taluka sanghs in the procurement of certain basic commodities and their distribution to members. After the state government of Maharashtra legislated monopoly procurement of jowar and paddy, the Marketing Federation became its agent for the collection of those grains. It also handles sugar distribution. The Federation became involved as the marketing agent for cotton when a scheme of monopoly procurement was adopted in August 1972, though the future of that program is uncertain.[42] In addition, the Federation was until 1970 the sole agent of the state government in the distribution of fertilizers. In 1970, however, the availability of fertilizers and the effective pressure of private interests led to decontrol of fertilizer distribution with the result that the Federation was competing with private agents in the field. Until hybrid seeds became readily available after 1967, the Federation also acted as procurement and distribution agent in that sector. More recently, the responsibility has been handed over to the zilla parishads.

The members of the Federation were the district and taluka bodies. There were no individual members. The Federation's board of thirty-one directors included representatives of the districts (outside Bombay), the Registrar of Cooperatives, a representative of the sugar factories, and a representative of the State Cooperative Bank. In November 1971, the man elected chairman of the Federation by the other members of the board was Ratnappa Kumbhar, who was the representative of the sugar factories. The representative of Poona district was Mugatrao Kakade; a Kumbhar supporter was the representative of taluka and district marketing societies from Kolhapur.

While the Marketing Federation is closely tied to the structure of government policy in food and agriculture, it is nominally

41. According to the *37th Annual Report: 1971-72* of the Maharashtra State Cooperative Land Development Bank, at least seven district banks were in various stages of receivership.

42. For an interesting account of the problems of that scheme, see "Maharashtra: Monopoly Procurement Scheme in Jeopardy," *Economic and Political Weekly*, 2 August 1975, pp. 1144-1145.

part of the network of institutions organized in the cooperative sector. As with other apex institutions, administrators insisted the Federation was not directly affected by politics. Occasionally, a director might attempt to favor his own district in the allocation of projects but, as one informant noted, "To win out he has to have fairly substantial grounds to convince the other members who would also like the project in their own areas."

At lower levels, however, informants asserted that marketing organizations were subject to political and administrative short-comings:

> We try to advise the taluka sanghs in their working and depute managers to those societies when we find them in hopeless condition. Only yesterday, we received a report from a man who had recently been deputed to one society. When he arrived, he found that everything owned by the society had been sold off. At lower levels, there are also so many fights among groups.

In most of its operations, the Federation relies on agents, who may be either the district or taluka sanghs, to procure items like sugar, cotton, or designated foodgrains. Working with government officials, these agents deliver the goods to designated outlets which are usually the fair-price shops run by taluka sanghs or by primary societies under government auspices.

While the Federation and affiliated local bodies figured in the procurement and distributional chain, district and taluka sanghs conducted additional activities. The Shetkari Sahakari Sangh of Kolhapur was connected to both the apex body and to taluka sanghs on a commodity-by-commodity basis, but its operations were legally autonomous from both. With over sixty branches in the district, the Sangh employed 650 persons to service the 571 societies and 22,000 individuals who were its members.[43] The Sangh played a leading role as a marketing agent for farmers in jaggery. In 1970, it was also the monopoly distributor in much of the district for sugar. Among its other activities, it ran six chemist shops—giving the Sangh control of 60 percent of the medicine business in Kolhapur City—cloth shops, two petrol pumps, and a machine shop. It also was a distribution agent for fuel oils, iron, steel, and cement. In April 1968, the Sangh began its own fer-

---

43. S. L. Shirodkar, "Shetkari Sahakari Sangh Ltd., Kolhapur: A Great Cooperative Enterprise" (privately printed by that organization, n.d.,) p. 3.

tilizer factory to produce manure mixtures and by 1970 distributed half the fertilizer used in the district. As a result of these
activities the society had an annual turnover of Rs. 15 crores. With
working capital of Rs. 1.16 crores in 1969, the Sangh was in a
good position to chart its own course. In contrast, most taluka
sanghs in Kolhapur were only marginally viable and depended for
economic survival on their commissions from governmentally related programs. They also relied on the Sangh for the acquisition
of certain goods.

The almost worshipful regard shown toward the Shetkari
Sahakari Sangh in Kolhapur contrasts with the more sectarian view
of the Poona District Purchase and Sales Union. That body was
clearly an adjunct of the Kakade family, and the relationship of
the various taluka sanghs with it depended on the kinds of political relationships involved. Thus, the closest ties were with the Nira
Canal Societies Purchase and Sales Union located at Baramati.
Established in 1926 to service the villages along the Nira Canal and
dominated since the 1950s by the Kakades, the body dealt regularly with the district organization, though it was not technically
subordinate to it any more than other taluka organizations were.

In the case of Haveli taluka—where the taluka sangh was
dominated by Annasaheb Magar and his associates—there was little
contact with the district unit. For some talukas (Purandhar, Sirur,
Dhond) the district organization acted as an agent for purchasing
sugar and distributing it to the taluka sanghs. Elsewhere, relations
were more politically conditioned. As one of the Kakades' associates in the District Union described the situation in two talukas:

> Ambegaon and Junnar also operate largely on their own, but if they
> need certain things like kerosene or electric motors they may come to
> us. For political reasons, they might not buy, but for the same political
> reasons we might not wish to help them. There is always a tussle in the
> political field and naturally there is some contention in the cooperative
> field. But people look to the group which is serving them best so each
> group seeks to attract the heart of the people.

Like the Shetkari Sahakari Sangh in Kolhapur, the District
Purchase and Sales Union in Poona dealt in the jaggery market.
The manager of the Poona organization commented:

> If the farmer brings his jaggery to a private merchant, he is charged rent
> for storage, interest on credit extended, etc. If he comes to us, there is

no rent for storage. He gets an advance of 70 percent on total value and can also get seeds and fertilizers from us. . . . If he is not in a position to buy fertilizers from us, we sell them on credit, but we do require that he bring his produce to us for sale.

The details presented on cooperative structures and their operations indicate the variety of activities which had been effected in rural Maharashtra by the institutionalization of cooperatives during the 1960s. In stimulating such institutional development, state policy makers also created the conditions for affecting the power structure of rural Maharashtra. In reaction against certain features of the system they had themselves created, state leadership began late in the decade to search for ways to bring the new political institutions under political control. The actual reforms that have been introduced are rather limited in scope; as in education, much of the debate has seemed to be a symbolic, rather than substantive, challenge to the system of power distributions that has emerged in the past fifteen years. Yet, political actors seemed genuinely swept up in the evolving debate. The proposals for change, the arguments advanced on both sides, and the results up to mid-April 1973 form the subject matter of the next chapter.

EIGHT

The Cooperative Movement II:
Efforts at Reform

While the state government and the Congress party of Maharashtra encouraged the growth of the cooperative sector and employed it both to spur economic development in the countryside and to build the political base of the Congress, by 1967 it was becoming increasingly apparent to Y. B. Chavan and Vasantrao Naik, among other leaders, that reforms were necessary.

Four considerations seem to have weighed in their thinking. First, the burgeoning of cooperative institutions in the previous decade had allowed certain abuses to arise in the operation of some cooperatives. Many cooperative leaders were willing to concede as much.

A second factor which figured in the calculations of state leaders was the maintenance of support for the party and government from a generation of younger political activists emerging in the countryside. As Naik, the Chief Minister, indicated, "We wanted to give new blood a chance to come up. That is why we felt no one should stick to a post in the cooperatives."[1] Although Naik was notably reluctant to give up his own position as Chief Minister (until forced out in 1975), he and Chavan foresaw dangers that might arise to the party if opportunities for mobility in the cooperative movement were denied to young persons of promise. The problem was either to create additional opportunities or to distribute existing opportunities in ways that seemed to promise further mobility.

Thirdly, there was the feeling that leaders of the cooperative movement (particularly in western Maharashtra) might be capable of mounting a serious challenge to the major figures in the state leadership. Thus, another reason for attempting to reform the cooperative movement was to lessen the ability of the "coopera-

1. Interview, Vasantrao Naik, 14 March 1973.

tive kings" to use their positions to direct political challenges against Naik and Chavan.

A larger perspective growing out of the last two points would accentuate the fourth consideration: a need to maintain the flexibility of the Congress party as a political organization sensitive to a variety of strata of the population. There was apparently a fear that if the leadership of the cooperatives gained too great an influence in the party organization it would weaken the appeal of the party and, therefore, the base of the government among urban and rural non-landed interests. Up to 1967, Chavan's organization had been notably successful in its attempts to portray itself as responsive to almost all segments of the electorate (except, perhaps, urban middle-class Brahmans). As long as Chavan maintained a wide base of support in his own state, he would be able to preserve his national image as an alternative should Mrs. Gandhi falter. Within the state, too, by maintaining a broad coalition of support for the party and government, Chavan and Naik were assuring themselves that they need not be dependent on any narrow group of interests for their own political survival.

THE FIRST ROUND OF REFORMS

These considerations came to a head following the elections of 1967. Interestingly enough, the man chosen as Minister for Cooperation at that time was Vinayakrao Patil, who left his position as president of the MPCC to assume the post. Patil was by no means a major figure in Maharashtra politics. Hailing from Marathwada, he owed his party post almost entirely to Chavan and Naik. Indeed, he was regarded as a particularly loyal follower of the latter. At the same time that Patil assumed the position of Minister for Cooperation, the state leadership continued to evidence friendliness toward the cooperative movement by the choice of his successor, Vasantrao Patil of Sangli district.

Vasantrao Patil was among the best known figures in the cooperative movement in Maharashtra. In his own district, he was the founder of one sugar factory and a major figure in many other cooperative institutions; he had held key state-level positions in the cooperative movement. Yet, Patil had not built his career only within cooperatives. He had been associated with Chavan in nationalist activities in 1942, and he had been active for many years in the MPCC, including having served as a secretary of the party. From 1952 to 1967, he was also an MLA. Above all, Patil was known for his personal loyalty to Chavan, a loyalty which was sorely tested by the events surrounding Vinayakrao Patil's proposals for reform.

Despite Vasantrao Patil's centrality to the politics of Maharashtra and to a number of major cooperative institutions, he was not consulted in the formulation of the proposals brought forward by Vinayakrao Patil in early 1968. On the contrary, he saw the reforms as aimed at himself and those like him who had worked to build up the cooperatives of the state.

> The cooperative movement began as a economic movement, but it had given some people active in it some political influence. There was a fear on the part of some political leaders that men in the cooperative movement were becoming too powerful. Some reforms were necessary, no doubt. But most of the differences involved politics. Actually, I look at the way in which men work in the cooperatives as being a good thing. They devote themselves to the economic betterment of the public.[2]

The principal feature of the bill introduced in the form of amendments to the Maharashtra Cooperative Societies Act of 1960 was to limit to one the number of cooperative societies that a person might chair at any one time at each of three "levels" of cooperative organization.[3] Nor was it desirable, the Minister stipulated, that a person should combine more than two major posts at a time or chair a particular society for more than six consecutive years. This rule was to go into effect immediately for those who had already served such terms. The amendments included a provision that elections be controlled by an agency independent of the particular cooperative institution involved; another provided that the Registrar play a larger role in issuing rules for the

2. Interview, Vasantrao (Dada) Patil, 17 February 1973.
3. Category I included all statewide societies; Category II comprehended "societies, the area of operation of which does not extend to the whole of the state . . . but extends to one or more districts; or . . . is less than a district, but the authorized share capital of which is more than Rs. 10 lakhs;" and Category III covered societies active in one or more talukas or with a share capital of between Rs. 5 lakhs and Rs. 10 lakhs. Maharashtra Act XVII of 1969, section 12. The complicated language of Category II was intended to incorporate sugar factories.

operation of cooperatives.[4] These last items as well as the overall thrust of the amendments revealed an intention on the part of the state government to bring the cooperative sector more firmly under governmental control.

The response of cooperative leaders was typified by the comments on the proposed amendments made by W. C. Shrishrimal, Managing Director of the Maharashtra State Central Cooperative Bank. Shrishrimal argued that limiting the terms of service of chairmen would mean the loss to major institutions of "the guidance of senior experienced and veteran cooperators and leaders."[5] In support of his argument, he quoted D. R. Gadgil—who had been instrumental in promoting the cooperative movement since the 1930s—as having said,

> There may be some failings in the movement, but the workers in the field are more aware of them than the critics. I am therefore of the opinion that in cooperation we must attach more importance to the discipline and conventions we establish than to legislative measures.[6]

The proposed changes in office holding were more symbolic than substantive, since powerful leaders need not have held all positions themselves but might pass some on to relatives or reliable

4. Other features of the bill included rules that (1) persons might not serve on the DLDBs who were doing business with those bodies or whose relatives were providing goods on the basis of DLDB loans; (2) elections in the larger cooperative societies (more than Rs. 5 lakhs in share capital) would be held under the supervision of the district collector; (3) terms for the boards of large societies would be increased to three years where such provisions did not already exist in the society's by-laws; (4) members of boards of directors would have to publish a record of loans taken by themselves or given to their relatives; and (5) the Registrar of Cooperatives could on his own authority intervene to take action for recovery of arrears from societies.

5. W. C. Shrishrimal, "Amendment to the Cooperative Law in Maharashtra and the Future of [the] Cooperative Movement," *Maharashtra Cooperative Quarterly* 13 (October 1969): 135.

6. Ibid., 136. Gadgil was then serving as Deputy Chairman of the Planning Commission. (The Prime Minister was Chairman.) Gadgil had taken issue with these reform proposals at a meeting of Congress legislators and cooperative activists at which Y. B. Chavan presided. At the same meeting, certain cooperative leaders made known their special distaste for the feature of the act which empowered the Registrar, a government bureaucrat, to issue directives to societies. They preferred at least that such powers be reserved to the state government over which they were able to exercise some political influence. *Link,* 13 July 1969.

political associates.[7] Still, those who regarded themselves as being under attack saw that part of the bill as a major step toward curbing their influence. Men who otherwise were actively engaged in Congress party politics and government now wrapped the flag of cooperative sector autonomy around themselves by asserting a need to preserve the "cooperative spirit"—a spirit which had long passed out of many sections of the movement, particularly after the state and national governments had begun to pour public resources into cooperatives.

The bill prepared by Vinayakrao Patil was submitted to the State Assembly in March 1969. Patil, who had been in poor health for some time, died before the Assembly could take action on the measure. With the support of the Cabinet, the Minister of State for Cooperation, S. B. Patil (from Poona district), shepherded the measure through the legislative process. In his opening remarks to the Assembly, he emphasized that a major purpose of the amendments was to remove a blockage in the cooperative sector which threatened to prevent new leadership from emerging.

When the Assembly met to discuss the amendments in early April 1969, speakers in favor of the amendments were vehement in their denunciation of the way cooperatives were functioning. Uddhavrao Patil of the PWP, leader of the opposition in the Assembly, saw the bill chiefly as the government's response to the challenge raised by the "new rich," a class that the government had itself created, but he went on to argue that the changes proposed were only marginal to the real problems of the sector.[8]

In contrast, Dnaneshwar Khaire (from Poona) characterized the measure as "revolutionary." His remarks emphasized the need to remedy the financial situations of the many societies in default and to correct the misappropriations and malpractices which were common to the movement. He maintained that some of the bigger societies had become the monopoly of a handful of rich people who derived the principal benefits. In the process, contests for cooperative banks and sugar factories had become politicized.

7. In Kolhapur, the Ichalkaranji leadership responded to the amendments by having A. G. Kulkarni and Dattajirao Kadam resign from their positions with the Deccan Cooperative Spinning Mills, but Kadam continued to serve as chairman of the Datta sugar factory and as an effective force in other cooperative institutions.

8. *Times of India,* 4 April 1969.

Another speaker from Poona district, Annasaheb Magar, assured activists in the cooperative sector that the bill was not aimed at particular leaders but was intended to train a "second line" of leaders to whom the cooperatives would eventually be handed.[9]

The Congress MLAs who spoke in the Assembly were largely those committed to the bill; those opposed were active in private. At an MPCC meeting held just prior to the initiation of the legislative debate, Vasantrao Patil announced that he intended to resign all of his posts except that of MPCC president in protest. Patil, Ratnappa Kumbhar, and an MLA aligned with Kumbhar all spoke against the bill in that meeting. They insisted that offices should be open to whomever the people wished to elect. On the other hand, Khaire and Sharad Pawar were prominent among those who demanded early action against persons who monopolized the cooperative field. According to press reports, the Chief Minister showed some hesitancy in pressing forward on the bill because of the evident opposition of powerful party figures, but young MLAs like Pawar and Khaire insisted on action. [10]

Despite the threats by the MPCC President, the bill passed the Assembly in early April. Vasantrao Patil, who had threatened for a time also to resign as MPCC president, was persuaded to withdraw that threat.

In reviewing the implications of the amendments, one journal suggested that the bill sought to remove the "closed door" policies prevailing in the movement.

> First, by choking, through its monopoly of influential positions in the cooperative movement, a major channel of upward mobility within the Congress, [the leadership of the movement] has given rise to widespread discontent among ambitious young men in the lower reaches of the party. Second, since the cooperative movement is most developed in western Maharashtra, Congressmen from other parts of the State, like Marathwada and Vidarbha, have grown weary of the influence of the cooperators over the party and the government. [11]

The cooperative leaders did not give in so easily. They argued that insistence on limited terms discriminated against them since

9. *Times of India,* 5 April 1969.
10. *Sakal,* 3 April 1969.
11. "Flushing Out the Bosses," *Economic and Political Weekly,* 1 April 1969, p. 604.

such rules were not applied to ministers or MLAs. [12] There were others within the cooperative movement who held, consistent with what they argued was the true spirit of the cooperative movement, that the government should stay out of their affairs as much as possible. On the other hand, defenders of government intervention insisted that it had involved itself only to correct what were generally regarded as defects.[13]

Pressures from cooperative interests were mounted to change the mind of the Chief Minister. In July 1969, Naik capitulated. He called a meeting of cooperative leaders, MLAs, and certain MPCC members to discuss the new law. Out of these meetings came a decision to maintain the new amendments on the books but to hold their application in abeyance pending a full review of the working of the Cooperative Societies Act. A delay in appointing a successor to Vinayakrao Patil kept that review in limbo for some time. It was not until October 1969 that Y. J. Mohite was chosen Minister for Cooperation.

THE SECOND ROUND OF PROPOSALS

Mohite, as we noted in chapter 5, joined the Congress in 1960 after a decade of association with leftist parties, particularly the PWP and its offshoots. Although he was deeply rooted in the rich peasantry and involved with the establishment and management of a sugar factory, Mohite has been a persistent critic of the way the cooperative sphere has operated. Thus, he was quite explicit in his support for government involvement in the sector's operations:

12. Supporters of the amendments suggested that the notion of limited terms was not so important as the assurance of democratic procedures in cooperative elections. One informant indicated that the proposal about limiting terms actually had been added at the last minute. Khaire was one of those who felt that terms of service had attracted more attention in the public debate than was warranted. Interview, 7 April 1970.

13. As the *Times of India* noted editorially on July 9, 1969, "The main argument of the old guard against the new restrictions is that they are in office because they have been elected to it by members who have implicit faith in them. But the fact is that under the old election rules chairmen of societies also functioned as returning officers. What is more, in the event of an electoral dispute between those already in office and other contestants the expenses of the former were charged to their societies while those of the latter came out of their own pockets. All this had tended to perpetuate the hegemony of the old guard."

When we accepted planned development and cooperatives as instrumentalities of rural reconstruction in this country, we also accepted state participation in the cooperative movement. The government advances share capital to the cooperative societies and makes capital investments in the movement and therefore has a right to oversee the working of cooperatives. [14]

Once in office, Mohite spent several months preparing a substantial review of the cooperative movement, which he brought forward in April 1970 as a personal set of proposals for change. As he remarked in the same interview;

When I came into the ministry, I already knew many of the defects in the movement since I had been working in it for many years. I was not on the district bank but I had much to do with it as a borrower in connection with lift-irrigation societies, the sugar factory, and primary cooperative societies with which I have been involved.

It was out of this experience that most of the proposals came, although some of them reflected recommendations which had been put forward by various central and state committees during the preceding decade. Like Chaudhari's actions in formulating proposals for educational reform, Mohite proceeded without extensive consultations. His administrative subordinates did assist Mohite in gathering specific data, but the only formal consultations he held were in technical areas where the advice of specialists (in such fields as dairy and fishery cooperatives) was sought.

The document published by Mohite never attained the status of a Cabinet statement (white paper). It did represent the Minister's efforts to arouse public discussion. That it did, for after its release there were a series of lectures, seminars, and newspaper articles throughout Maharashtra which constituted an open debate over the organization of the cooperative sector. Follow-up actions have been piecemeal; in many cases, the Minister's proposals have simply been allowed to die a quiet death.

Mohite's study made only passing reference to the previous amendments. While affirming his intention to enforce the amendments, he proposed a "small alteration" in the amendment which had caused the most debate. He announced his intention to interpret the six-year limit on chairmanships as a prospective rather than a retrospective limitation. As he wrote, "This will serve

14. Interview, Y. J. Mohite, 30 June 1970.

the intention of [government] by discouraging monopolistic ten-
dencies in the future and at the same time remove a large degree of
bitterness . . . amongst the cooperative field workers."[15]

The major features of Mohite's paper involved proposals to
reorganize the credit and marketing aspects of the cooperative
sector. Indeed, several interviewees who approached his proposals
in political terms suggested that unlike Vinayakrao Patil's amendments, which had been aimed at those who dominated the cooperative sugar factories, Mohite's proposals represented an effort to
undercut those who controlled the DCCBs.

Whether true or not, the central feature of the Minister's
paper—at least in terms of the public attention it received—was a
proposal to create taluka banks which would largely replace the
lending, supervisory, and regulatory functions of the DCCBs. (The
DCCBs would continue to dispense industrial credit.) It would be
necessary, however, to combine two or more talukas in some
places in order to create "viable" units.[16] These new taluka banks
would incorporate the functions previously performed by taluka
supervising unions in order to better regulate the behavior of
primary society secretaries. Along with bringing tighter supervision
to bear on society secretaries, the Minister hoped to curb the
financial and administrative difficulties of some of the smaller
primary societies by consolidating them into larger and more
economically viable multivillage societies.[17]

Mohite also proposed to strengthen another taluka-level institution at the expense of district bodies; he recommended that
marketing societies be reorganized into a two-tier system, in which

15. Y. J. Mohite, *The Cooperative Movement in Maharashtra State: A
Reappraisal,* Government of Maharashtra (Bombay: Government Central
Press, 16 April 1970), p. 241 (hereafter referred to as *Cooperative Reappraisal*). The Minister also makes reference there to difficulties which had
arisen with respect to government supervision of society elections. In March
1971, legislation was passed making the six-year rule prospective, a new
system of resolving election disputes was introduced, and the Registar's
power to issue directives to societies was removed and vested in the state
government. *Times of India,* 17 March 1971.

16. Among the 36 talukas (out of 230 in the state) that Mohite saw as
hard-core problems were 7 from Poona district. In contrast, only one taluka
(the smallest) was regarded as potentially "non-viable" in Kolhapur district.

17. No follow-up action has been taken on this proposal. Indeed, pressures are great from village leaders to proliferate primary societies rather than
to consolidate them.

the State Marketing Federation would become a more explicitly federal body dealing directly and exclusively with the taluka sanghs. It was Mohite's intention to eliminate the district units entirely.

The proposal for the abolition of supervising unions seemed to meet with almost universal approval from persons I interviewed—even from some persons controlling those bodies. However, almost every other item put forward by the Minister ran into opposition. Much of that opposition was verbally grounded on technical considerations, but clearly the overwhelming political reaction among active cooperators was a source of resistance to major changes. As a result, those alterations which have been introduced since the Minister's paper was issued in 1970 have appeared on an issue-by-issue basis and in forms which have sometimes varied greatly from what the Minister originally proposed. In sum, while leaders of the government won their point—by insisting that the cooperative movement recognize its subordination to government policy—local cooperative leaders won many of the particular battles.

In terms of specific policy outcomes, by early 1973: (1) the proposal for taluka banks appeared to be dead; (2) the government had ceased to provide direct credit to district marketing organizations, but those bodies continued to function in districts like Poona and Kolhapur and still were called upon for assistance in the performance of some government functions; (3) supervising unions were gutted, but instead of creating a direct association between the DCCBs or the proposed taluka banks and the secretarial staffs of primary societies, a new intermediate system was created with resultant dissatisfaction on all sides; (4) district land development banks (DLDBs) had been suspended entirely (whether their suspension was a temporary measure or a permanent decision depended on the views of the person one interviewed); and (5) a debate which had been simmering since 1969 over the relative responsibilities of the nationalized banks and lending institutions in the cooperative sector had come to a boil. While the last two items did not arise directly out of Mohite's proposals, they will be considered as part of this account of recent efforts to make alterations in the cooperative system of Maharashtra. A sixth item will also be included in our survey of recent cooperative conflicts: an attempt by the state government to regulate the urban agricultural markets of Maharashtra. This battle was actually fought before Mohite came into office, but it is an interesting case of Maharashtrian politics at work. Like some of the other points of conflict, it is by no means clear who won, who lost, or whether it was a draw.

Before turning to a consideration of each of these items, several points need to be made. First, the battle lines which seemed in the process of crystallization in 1969 became much less certain by 1970. While the supremacy of the state government was recognized, it did not choose to press its initial "victory" very far. The new Minister's concession on the six-year rule represented a significant symbolic retreat, if not an exercise in outright capitulation, on the part of the government—though not on Mohite's part, for it conformed to a view that he personally had held even during the earlier debate. On the other hand, Mohite's appointment was not in any sense the product of direct intervention by the cooperative sector or by leaders like Vasantrao Patil—if both of those gentlemen are to be believed—nor did Patil take part in the formulation of the new Minister's proposals.

This leads to a second major point. Once Mohite opened the question of cooperative reorganization, he went much beyond the kind of amendments put forward by Vinayakrao Patil. His proposals were mechanical or administrative in nature—not political or controversial policy recommendations. They brought to light numerous differences even among actors within the cooperative movement over what the proper structure should be. Clearly, cooperative leaders wished to preserve their own enclaves, but there was little agreement on specifics. Persons who might agree in their opposition to the creation of taluka banks could easily disagree about other features of the Minister's plan.

The Taluka Bank Proposal

Mohite's proposals placed in question the role of the DCCBs. As he later remarked:

> Because the members of the [DCCBs] are powerful people in their areas, they have taken mostly to speaking about that matter. . . . My proposal is to keep the three-tier structure but to alter some of its activities. Now the district banks do both the normal credit business connected with agricultural loans and loans to processing industries. . . . The operations of the local societies need closer supervision. . . . Supervision from the district place is not possible. If each taluka has its own

bank, there is also the possibility of lowering the interest rates since the Reserve Bank gives a lower rate for crop loans than for other loans. The district banks charge more because they need to cover their overhead for all loans. . . . Closeness will also make it easier to see that there are no problems of overdues. On the district level no one really knows who hasn't repaid his loan. There may be some public pressure at the local level when the taluka banks are in operation for the borrowers to repay. [18]

All of these arguments by the Minister were greeted by a good deal of skepticism from other leaders. Vasantrao Patil pointed to two major defects in the proposal: taluka banks would not be economically independent; equally important, "they would only become additional centers of politics." [19] In the latter connection, a number of interviewees traced their opposition to the taluka bank concept to the way it might implicate the cooperative credit system even more deeply in politics. At least at the district level, they argued, directors could check each other. When loans were not granted or were given in amounts sharply reduced from the request, the taluka's representative could always blame the management or his colleagues on the board. If responsibilities were placed with taluka bodies, administrative officials and boards of directors would be both more accessible to political pressure and more tempted to manipulate the lending system for their political advantage.

Opposition to the taluka bank proposal was grounded on historical experience as well as on projected administrative considerations. Thus, various informants pointed to failures of similar units elsewhere in India, including Vidarbha, where such banks had existed until 1960. As W. C. Shrishrimal remarked, "The cooperative banks at the district level are the most feasible unit. . . . Economic growth requires the kind of strength that cannot be gotten by depending on smaller institutions. Such a proposal would lead to making every institution weak." [20]

The General Manager of the Kolhapur DCCB also reacted against the proposal for the creation of taluka banks. In his view, the Minister, who had stressed the possible reduction in interest charges that might flow from reorganization, was improperly associating two different matters.

18. Interview, Y. J. Mohite, 30 June 1970.
19. Interview, Vasantrao Patil, 17 February 1973.
20. Interview, W. C. Shrishrimal, 14 December 1970.

> The system as it presently exists in credit is of three tiers (state, district, village) and the proposed system is also of three tiers. . . . The middle level would still remain. A reduction in the interest rate could be carried out even under the present structure. . . . We could also increase the number of branches and, in fact, we are doing so. [21]

To a suggestion by Mohite that creation of taluka banks would be in keeping with the general spirit of democratic decentralization, the General Manager responded, "As it is, the present directors are elected by the representatives of societies in each taluka so it is not as if there is no scope for participation at present." He suggested, nevertheless, that it would be quite reasonable to set up advisory committees in association with the branches of the DCCBs.

To the charge that there were considerable delays in processing loan applications, he acknowledged that it took an average of three months in Kolhapur but asserted that the situation was not quite as bad as it looked:

> Orders have been given to the inspectors at the local level to give fresh credit as an advance up to 75 percent of the loan required immediately to those farmers who repay their previous loans. Thus, only 25 percent of the loan is actually given after the program of the relevant society is approved.

One of the principal factors that may have killed the taluka bank proposal was that there existed an important group of political leaders—those associated with the DCCBs—who could be mobilized to express their opposition (generally stated on technical grounds) to the proposal, [22] whereas Mohite never made any

21. Interview, K. V. Joshi, 21 September 1970.
22. The *Proceedings of the Tenth Conference of District Central Banks,* held in Bombay on March 7, 1970 (even before the new proposals of the Minister for Cooperation were officially released), revealed the uniformity of opposition which existed among DCCB chairmen. Typical were the comments of the influential chairman of the Satara DCCB; his remarks were paraphrased in the following way: "He expressed . . . his fear that systematic attempts were being made in the capital to weaken the Cooperative Movement in Maharashtra and wondered if the present scheme was nothing but a part of such attempts. [He] agreed that the rate of interest should be lowered but wanted the matter to be discussed in advance. He also wanted the shortcomings in the existing system to be proved beforehand. The organization of taluka banks would only create more seats of power with all the attendant evils" (p. 6).

real effort to locate and mobilize a support group behind it. Politicians with district responsibilities either were strongly opposed to the idea or rather dubious that it would have the effects predicted. One Poona DCCB board member who attributed the proposal entirely to political motives argued, "The government wants to curb the district leadership which now controls the district banks. The leadership of the cooperatives have become political leaders because of their handling of large sums of money." Others had mixed feelings. As a Poona MLA remarked:

> The proposal . . . has both merits and demerits. The merit is that the banks will be closer to the people. They will be able to render service more quickly and with less expense. The demerit is that their closeness will allow more controversies and factions to develop.

Among those politicians who were taluka- or village-oriented, there was a bit more support for taluka banks, but there tended to be some confusion, if not total ignorance, over the substance of the proposals. As a result, there was no effective element spurring action in support of the taluka banking system, whereas powerful actors were opposed to it both on political and technical grounds.

By 1973, Mohite had conceded defeat on this item in his proposals, but he felt nevertheless that he had won a small victory as a result:

> Those in the DCCBs were able to take political advantage of their positions in those banks [to oppose taluka banks]. . . . Ultimately, Naik and Chavan thought they needed to preserve the support of the leaders at the district level so they forced me to drop the change. . . . In return for not destroying the existing district bank structure, Naik and Chavan . . . agreed that some of the powers presently located in the district banks with respect to the granting of loans for non-agricultural cooperatives should be separated from the work of the bank in the area of agricultural finance. . . . Twenty percent of the reserves of the banks would be devoted to this item, and special directors would be elected to the bank who would be concerned with this non-agricultural sector.[23]

This new pattern had not yet gone into effect in early 1973, but those interviewed on the subject were generally responsive to the idea. The Managing Director of the Poona DCCB indicated that his bank had already appointed five inspectors under an

23. Interview, Y. J. Mohite, 17 February 1973.

assistant manager to deal with industrial cooperatives. However, allocations were still very small.

Supervising Unions

In contrast to the opposition that Mohite aroused with his proposal for taluka banks, there was general support for a serious reconsideration of the taluka supervising union structure. The Minister's original proposal envisioned abolishing the supervising unions entirely, absorbing their secretaries into the staffs of the taluka banks, and making the taluka banks directly responsible for supervision of the primary societies.

With the likelihood of retention of the DCCBs, district and State Bank officials generally favored making the secretaries servants of the DCCBs. This was in accordance with suggestions that had been made by the national Gorwala Commission and earlier state committees which had reviewed the operations of cooperative institutions. As Vasantrao Patil remarked:

> Previously, the taluka supervising unions were in the hands of taluka politicians who used to handle the salaries for the secretaries and make decisions about transfers. Those unions were weak and the secretaries were taking undue advantage of the situation. There was a conference and then a resolution was passed about 1962. I was on the committee set up as a result of the resolution and we suggested that secretaries should be under a different organization. [24]

Despite Patil's reference to "taluka politicians," politicians who played an active role in their taluka supervising unions felt no particular need to preserve them. In contrast, a number of politicians whose interests were district- or state-oriented expressed some reluctance about abolishing them. In part, this was related to the character of the interviewee's particular relations with his own DCCB. Thus, as we might expect, Ratnappa Kumbhar was not receptive to the proposal.

> The powers over the secretaries should be left to taluka bodies. Some people felt that in a small area there was more interference from small people. I feel the bank that distributes finance should not also direct the secretaries. If they want influence over the behavior of the societies, they have their own inspectors, but it is not necessary to control appointments and transfers. This will only centralize power in the

24. Interview, Vasantrao Patil, 17 February 1973.

hands of a few people in the district. A man who lends money with the authority over how that money is used would get great power. [25]

At the same time, there was a general feeling that the quality of secretaries and supervision over them required upgrading. Balasaheb Kaulaukar-Patil, whose men controlled the supervising union in his home taluka even as he himself represented the taluka on the DCCB, argued for DCCB control of secretaries.

> The kinds of people who are taken up as secretaries at the village level are not always efficient persons, while some societies are handling Rs. 8 lakhs a year now in transactions. The secretaries should also be more qualified persons. With all the graduates now available, some of those should become secretaries. [26]

Others who had influence at the district level, however, were less certain about the desirability of centralizing control over the cooperative societies. V. K. Chavan-Patil, for example, favored retention of the local character of primary societies.

> Secretaries may have been paid only Rs. 70-80 [per month], but that was not so bad for someone who had only a Marathi fourth-standard education, and most of the positions were only part-time. They would look after their farming the rest of the time. Most secretaries did not have [much] work to do. . . . The secretaries should not be [put] under the control of the bank. If the chairman of the bank is a good man, then it is all right, but if he is not, then many problems will follow. [27]

The Minister was well aware of the political problems involved in creating a district system of control of society secretaries.

> Previously there was a proposal to put the secretaries under the district banks in a district cadre, but some people feared that the way the cooperators operated, some might form political groups among the secretaries. The secretaries who might not mind being transferred around their own talukas objected to district level transfers. . . . Their salaries are already meager and to introduce district service would make things even more difficult for them. At the taluka level, as part of a common cadre responsible to the bank, they would be in a better position to recover loans. [28]

25. Interview, Ratnappa Kumbhar, 28 February 1973.
26. Interview, Balasaheb Kaulaukar-Patil, 7 February 1973.
27. Interview, V. K. Chavan-Patil, 7 February 1973.
28. Interview, Y. J. Mohite, 17 February 1973.

Nevertheless, when the taluka bank notion was aborted, Mohite returned to the earlier proposal for creation of a district cadre. Significantly, the form his proposal took avoided giving direct authority to the DCCB. Instead, a body midway between the DCCB and the Cooperation Department of the state government was created, with the DCCB chairman acting as head and the district deputy registrar (a state government bureaucrat assigned to the district to oversee the operation of cooperatives) as secretary. By early 1973, the system had been in operation for nearly a year, but informants in Poona and Kolhapur, in the state government, and in the state bank were all displeased with it, though their reasons for opposing it varied considerably.

Powerful individuals in district cooperative activity sat on the body. In addition to the chairman of the DCCB, its members included the chairman of the DLDB, the chairman of the district cooperative board (the training wing of the cooperative movement in each district), and the chairman of the cooperative committee of the zilla parishad. Still, there was a feeling among many informants that the effective power lay with the state-appointed district deputy registrar. Some complained that this contributed to further "governmentalization" of the cooperative movement. Informants described the pattern that had emerged as a stalemate in which the deputy registrar and the leaders of local cooperative institutions spent their time trying to out-maneuver each other. A typical reaction was that of the man who had been chairman of the Kolhapur board at the time the new organization was introduced; he saw the problem as one of "dual authorities," with politicians being expected to exercise some authority but being constantly checked by officials: "If one finds people doing bad things in the societies, then hang them for their misdeeds, but give those who work properly a free hand to run their societies."

Several informants also reported on the unsatisfactory position in which many primary society secretaries found themselves. One DCCB official remarked:

> The trouble . . . is that neither the chairman nor the deputy registrar really have time to look after the system. It is hard for [the latter] to do with all his other duties. At the same time, the secretaries remain low paid, making Rs. 150 to 300 at most. They get none of the benefits of the regular bank employees. Furthermore, they can now be moved anywhere in the district. . . . Many secretaries are unhappy, but because

the employment situation is so poor they are not willing to resign. We could easily accommodate them within our own cadre. . . . More important, there really has been no improvement in the strength or control of the secretaries. . . . The deputy registrar tends to intervene . . . as little as possible because of his other work. The managements of the societies are often of little use because many are ignorant.

Both Poona and Kolhapur DCCBs had registered complaints against the new system with the apex bank and the state government. Indeed, Poona was showing open resistance in early 1973 to paying its share of the costs of running the cadre system. Under the original formula, the state government was to bear 50 percent of the deficit of the system and the apex bank and the DCCB were to divide the other 50 percent equally. Both the state government and the apex bank had paid their shares in the first year, but the board of the Poona DCCB was simply sitting out all requests that it hand over Rs. 28 lakhs of its own funds for the operation of a system which it found objectionable.

As a result of such resistance, the question of organization of the district cadre was reopened for examination. In late 1972 a committee was created by the state government headed by Vasantrao Kore, the chairman of the Warna sugar factory in Kolhapur, to inquire into the working of the district cadre system and to develop an appropriate salary schedule for society secretaries. One member of that committee commented on the "halfway" step which had been taken in the creation of the district cadre system:

The district deputy registrar is only supposed to be the secretary, but he is the one empowered to call meetings and some have never convened such meetings. . . . It is necessary that the secretary of the board feel responsible to the chairman or the system will not work properly. The deputy registrars are doing nothing and the board chairmen even less. That is why the Kore committee was set up.[29]

As of late March 1973, it was not certain how this problem would be resolved. The Kore Committee's recommendations about salary schedules for primary society secretaries were made known in April. Whereas many secretaries previously had been receiving no more than Rs. 80 per month, the Committee recommended an increase to a flat Rs. 125. The union claiming to represent 13,000 of the 20,000 primary society secretaries in the state responded to

29. Interview, W. C. Shrishrimal, 11 March 1973.

this proposal with a call for a strike. The union spokesman made it clear that his members wanted salaries in line with those of primary school teachers, *talatis* (lower-level government officials responsible for maintaining land records), and *gram sevaks* (village-level development workers). This was part of a general desire "to be treated as government servants."[30]

The Marketing Proposals

On the whole, the Minister's proposals for the reorganization of the crop-loan system elicited the greatest attention because political interests within the existing cooperative system would have been affected most deeply by those proposals. In Mohite's own eyes, however, the most important aspect of his work touched on developing a more comprehensive and better integrated system for marketing the farmer's products. As of June 30, 1969, he reported, the state had 24 district marketing federations and 316 primary marketing societies (mainly taluka bodies), but 3 of the district bodies and 106 of the primary bodies were in debt. The total business of the sector was skewed toward the provision of agricultural inputs to farmers and supplying goods to consumers. Excluding foodgrains marketed under government schemes of monopoly procurement, only 8 percent of the total marketable surplus of the state was being handled by cooperatives.[31]

The Minister sought to alter this situation radically. He set out an elaborate scheme for encouraging the development of cooperative processing and marketing facilities. The cooperative marketing system would move into cotton procurement; ginning and pressing societies would be refinanced or created to service this sector. Similarly, groundnut (peanut) oil crushing mills in the cooperative sector would be upgraded by developing a procurement scheme for groundnut production.[32] In the case of textile

30. The nature of the interim recommendations is reported in the *Times of India,* 11 May 1973, and the reaction to it in the *Times of India,* 28 June 1973. Part of the conflict may have arisen out of the competition between two unions seeking to represent the secretaries.

31. Mohite, *Cooperative Reappraisal,* p. 86.

32. Ibid., p. 91. Though the state government had authorized ninety-nine ginning and pressing societies, by 1968-1969 only sixty-four were in operation and forty-one of these were running at a loss. Similarly, of ninety-seven groundnut oil mills authorized, forty-two were in actual operation, and thirty-seven were making no profit. Mohite argued, "One of the essential

production, too, a pattern of linkages to spinning and sizing facilities would be developed. Referring extensively to the report of a committee which employed the Ichalkaranji experience as its model, Mohite noted:

> The Kogekar Committee on the Cotton Textile Industry of Maharashtra (1968) observed that one of the important factors contributing to the remarkable success of the Deccan Cooperative Spinning Mills at Ichalkaranji has been the success of linking between the mills and the consumers of the yarn who are either handloom or powerloom owners, the existence of a ready local demand for yarn and the production of fine and superfine counts.... Some of the cooperative mills in Vidarbha complain that they had to sell the yarn at distant places ... in the absence of a powerloom centre nearby.... It is, therefore, felt necessary to promote the establishment of cotton powerlooms in [the] Vidarbha and Marathwada regions. [33]

In addition to initiating monopoly procurement of cotton, the state government in 1972 created a Maharashtra State Power Loom Corporation with Rs. 1 crore as equity. A nominated board of representatives from powerloom centers was created, with Anantrao Bhide of Kolhapur as the representative of Ichalkaranji. Bhide was subsequently chosen chairman of the state body. As he explained the situation of the trade in 1973:

> Previously the weavers were at the mercy of the Marwaris, who dominated the business and would cheat them. We are trying to remove the Marwaris from the trade.... The corporation would also try to handle problems related to marketing cloth.[34]

The major responsibility of the Corporation, as Bhide perceived it, was to coordinate processing and marketing functions throughout the state, including designating areas for the construction of additional spinning and sizing facilities.

Aside from specialized processing and marketing facilities, Mohite was interested in developing a general marketing structure which would link credit and marketing more tightly. In part, he hoped that such linkage would assure the cooperative sector of

reasons for the state of affairs is the failure to establish an organic link between the marketing societies dealing in raw material and the processing societies." Ibid., p. 91.

33. Ibid., p. 122.

34. Interview, Anantrao Bhide, 6 March 1973.

better performance in collecting overdues on loans. The system introduced in the case of sugar had worked well and he anticipated that it could be expanded to other processing and marketing areas.

The Minister saw a need to move general marketing organizations away from a major concern with selling inputs to a greater emphasis on marketing the resultant products. Part of the confusion, he felt, lay in the dispersion of responsibility for the distribution of inputs. Thus, while the government distributed fertilizers through the district marketing organizations, the State Marketing Federation was active in handling certain seeds and distributing oil and electric pumps. Insecticides and pesticides were bought by the Department of Agriculture of the state government and distributed by the zilla parishads. Instead of these proliferating agencies for different inputs, the Marketing Federation would carry out all supervision and coordination of input distributions at the state level, whereas the "taluka sales purchase unions [would] be eminently suitable for appointment as wholesalers for such distribution" at the local level. [35]

In this connection, district marketing bodies were to be "decooperativized" by the withdrawal of the government's investment of share capital—a sum of about Rs. 50 lakhs in 1970—from those bodies. That share capital would be transferred to the taluka bodies. The district organizations (if they managed to survive the experience) would not be permitted to open additional branches without the specific permission of the government. Even with respect to the Kolhapur body, Mohite remarked, "Organizations like the Shetkari Sahakari Sangh . . . are like private companies. They are making a huge profit on government concessions, and some of them have formed a clique now."[36]

Despite Mohite's hostility, the district bodies in Poona and Kolhapur survived reasonably well into 1973. The Kolhapur body, in fact, seemed to be thriving. It had depended very little on direct government investment in share capital in the past, and its many ancillary businesses provided a cushion against the withdrawal of government patronage. Indeed, neither the Shetkari Sangh nor the Poona organization had experienced any substantial drop in activity. The only loss had been a technical one—loss of representation on the board of the apex body. In Poona, the district

35. Mohite, *Cooperative Reappraisal,* p. 94.
36. Interview, Y. J. Mohite, 30 June 1970.

body had been converted into a public corporation calling itself the Poona District Agro-Industrial Cooperative Society. As one Kakade remarked, "Right now it is performing the same functions as the previous organization. . . . We did this on our own because we expected that the state would terminate the connection."[37]

The Manager of the Shetkari Sangh insisted that the state's plans for circumventing the district bodies had largely failed. An official of the Poona DCCB seemed to be of the same view.

> Two parts of a loan are made to a farmer: in cash and in kind. It is one of the conditions of the loan that the farmer must buy fertilizer through a purchase sales union. Sometimes this is not possible through the taluka unit so he must seek the help of the district body. We do continue to allow some credit to the District Union for such things as storage charges and operations of its fertilizer plant. Most of their finance comes, however, from the Bank of Maharashtra [a nationalized bank]. . . . Previously the [Sharad] Pawar group was in power in the [DCCB] so there was some denial of credit to the Purchase and Sales Union. Now [with Babulal Kakade serving as the chairman of the Bank] the situation has changed.

Despite the suggestion that the position of the district marketing societies had changed little from before, Mohite argued in 1973 that some progress was being made in the direction he had sought:

> I wanted a two-tier marketing system and we are moving towards that, though we have not abolished the district marketing organizations. However, in our procurement policies—as in cotton procurement—we are using only the state and taluka bodies as agents. We are also not providing any share capital to district organizations. If an organization is strong like the Shetkari Sangh I have no objection to its continuation. . . . Where [taluka] purchase and sales unions are not strong, we are reorganizing them. In others, we are establishing them for the first time.[38]

No action had been taken on another proposal which appeared in Mohite's paper which would have further strengthened the taluka sanghs by combining their agricultural marketing functions with consumer cooperative societies. Mohite's 1970 paper complained about the "haphazard growth" of the consumer coop-

---

37. Interview, Sambhaji Kakade, 3 February 1973.
38. Interview, Y. J. Mohite, 17 February 1973.

erative movement.[39] He proposed that consumer societies continue to function in urban areas while the taluka sanghs absorb the
rural functions, thus further integrating production, processing,
and marketing with the taluka unit. Had the taluka bank concept
been adopted, of course, it would have confirmed the taluka as the
crucial unit for much of the economic activity of the state and
enhanced its importance politically. For the time being, though
the cooperative sector continues to expand into new areas like
cotton procurement and the textile industry, attempts to stan-
dardize the basic unit of cooperative organization as the taluka
largely have been abandoned.

The Poona Market Issue

As part of his general effort to better regulate the marketing
pattern in Maharashtra, Mohite proposed to move for greater
control over the agricultural produce markets of the state.[40]
Maharashtra was already maintaining regulated local markets in
most of the small towns and cities of the state, but the government's efforts encountered resistance in the major terminal (central) markets of the cities of Bombay and Poona.

The major issue in Poona City was whether wholesale merchants (dalals) dealing with the farmers in vegetables and fruits
were behaving properly in the prices they were giving the farmer.
The merchants were accused of using faulty weights and of adding
various concealed service levies, but the brunt of the attack was
directed against the *hatta* (hand) method by which the merchant
bargained on an individual basis with each farmer to reach an
agreed selling price. Those who opposed the method charged that
it was subject to deceptions on the merchant's part and that the
uneducated farmer was likely to be the victim of a process akin to
gambling in entering negotiations with the wholesale merchant. In
its place, the opponents of the hatta method advocated a system
of open auctions regulated by the government.

These efforts at government regulation met with stiff resistance from dalals. Some degree of regulation already existed in
jaggery as early as 1957. In Poona, there were also regulated
markets in condiments and cattle. The last bastion of resistance,

39. Mohite, *Cooperative Reappraisal*, p. 98.
40. Ibid., pp. 79-81.

however, were the merchants dealing in such produce as potatoes, onions, oranges, and bananas.

The principal market of Poona City, which serves as a major wholesale market for the district, has been in its present location since 1866. Its operations (including the rental arrangements for stalls) fall within the jurisdiction of the municipal corporation. Because many of the dalals are active in Congress politics in the city, the interests of the market have been carefully attended to. In 1967, for example, a new shed costing Rs. 10 lakhs was completed at the expense of the city, thereby extending the size and facilities of the market. Spaces were rented to the merchants at relatively low rates.

Although a market committee with the purpose of regulating Poona's market was authorized to go into action as early as 1960, a series of court cases and other legal maneuvers slowed the procedure. Leading farmers from near Poona City, including Anna-saheb Magar and Sakharam Sanas, were active in pursuing the matter. [41] Sanas did so even though his own brother was a leading dalal.

The smoldering issue broke into open conflict in early January 1968, when the Agricultural Produce Market Committee (on which both Magar and Sanas served) issued orders making the terms of the Market Act applicable to Poona's central market from January 26, thereby abolishing the hatta method in favor of an open auction system requiring all dalals to be licensed by the committee.[42] The day before the scheduled inaugural ceremonies,

41. *Sakal*, 30 January 1968, charged that farmers lost 25 to 30 percent of the amount properly due them because of the hatta system. The estimate was taken from a letter sent by Sakharam Sanas to Vinayakrao Patil. One informant estimated that the cost of marketing jaggery, which operated in a regulated market, was Rs. 10 per Rs. 100 of goods sold, whereas in fruits and vegetables this went to Rs. 30 because of hidden charges levied by dalals.

42. One relatively neutral observer associated with the Poona market suggested that farmers would benefit because all transactions would be recorded and "the dalal would not be able to maintain two sets of records—one for the [retail] merchant and one for the farmer." However, the auction system would have its problems, he suggested. It might be effective for much of the year, but in the peak season it might be cumbersome, especially if proper storage facilities were not available to handle commodities unsold on a particular day. It was on the latter point that the dalals publicly based their opposition to regulation.

however, representatives of the merchants met with the Chief
Minister and the Minister for Cooperation, Vinayakrao Patil, and
convinced them not to pursue the matter, at least for the time
being.[43]

Their argument was that it was unfair to institute regulation
of the market in Poona when the same regulations were not yet in
effect in the city of Bombay. They expressed a fear that produce
might be diverted to the Bombay market if regulation was not
instituted in both markets simultaneously. They also insisted that
the new system of setting prices would lead to considerable
spoilage.

As soon as their complaints were heard, orders were issued by
Chief Minister Naik to stop the Poona Agricultural Market Committee from implementing the Market Act. Because the formal
orders were not received on the same day, the committee proceeded with its preparations for the inaugural ceremonies almost
until the appointed hour. Members of the committee were extremely unhappy and embarrassed that after prolonged efforts to
overcome various roadblocks set up by the dalals—efforts that
originally had the backing of the government—they had lost the
government's support. To make matters worse, the dalals had
engaged in a campaign of personal vituperation against members of
the Market Committee prior to the government's last-minute decision to retreat.[44]

Partly to save face, Vinayakrao Patil appointed a three-man
committee, which included Shivajirao Kale (then chairman of the
Poona DCCB), a dalal active in the City Congress, and an educator-
politician. They were supposed to look into the problems associated with implementing the Market Act in Poona. Although local
newspapers continued to attack the use of the hatta method with
regularity, little came of the committee's activities. Non-regulation

43. *Sakal*, 26 January 1968. Among those representing the dalals in this
meeting were: Shankarrao Ursal; Baburao Sanas (brother of Sakharam);
Namdeorao Mate (a former City Congress president); a prominent MLC from
Poona City; and a relative of Khaire's.

44. The inaugural arch erected for the occasion was torn down during the
night and signs defaced or stolen. Several days before the planned inauguration, Sakharam Sanas and Magar were recipients of a package containing
symbols attacking their masculinity and a letter, which read, in part: "The
Committee will not be able to do anything on the twenty-sixth. We have great
influence." *Sakal*, 27 January 1968.

continued to be the rule. Nevertheless, the dalal who served on the investigatory committee insisted that there had been notable changes in the market over the years since proposals for regulation were first broached because of the increasing information available both to the dalals and the farmers through newspapers, the radio, and the truckers who carried information from one market to another.

In his study, the new Minister for Cooperation reaffirmed the principle of regulation.[45] Farmer spokesmen, like Magar and S. B. Patil, insisted that the Act should have been applied to Poona.[46] After 1970, however, the matter stood in abeyance until the wholesale market was moved to an area on the edge of the city—a move that was being directed by the Poona Market Committee (and which has been accepted by the merchants, albeit reluctantly). At the new site it would be possible to have cold storage facilities so that perishable commodities would not depend so much on quick sale. In the view of men like Khaire, who were caught in the middle between dalal backgrounds and the need for political support in the rural areas, there was simply not enough space at the market to carry on sales in a few hours: "Now farmers have no space to keep their goods so they are not really in a position to bargain. Neither is it really the fault of the traders who have been in the business for generations. They have experience in prices. There is simply supply and demand in the present system."[47]

Mamasaheb Mohol, the leading figure in the Poona DCC, pointed up a more explicitly political aspect of the case:

> Magar was very active in pushing the Market Act but some influential market people did not want it. They were too powerful to oppose and they have to be listened to within party circles. The dalals would be affected by the Act. Such controversies are natural in any organization as the business interests would be affected. . . . It is better that the

45. Mohite in his *Cooperative Reappraisal* noted that the Bombay market demonstrated the same resistance as the one in Poona. He commented on delays in Bombay where the responsibility for moving the main market to the outskirts had been given to the municipal corporation: "The reason for the tardiness is probably the fact that it is not the object of the Corporation Act to ensure a fair deal to the growers and fair practices in marketing" (p. 80).

46. Interview, S. B. Patil, 29 June 1970.

47. Interview, Dnaneshwar Khaire, 7 April 1970.

merchants should be convinced of the desirability of the Act rather
than forcing it on them.[48]

Mohol may have put his finger on the style of the Maharashtra
government in this matter as well as in others when he suggested
that "merchants should be convinced of the desirability of the Act
rather than forcing it on them." Much the same was the case of
the taluka banks, except there the district and state politicians in
the cooperative movement were the ones who were not convinced.

At the same time, it should be recognized that the interests
engaged on what I have called the "farmer" side may have been
narrower than they seem at first glance. As matters stand, the
significant producers for a large central market like the one in
Poona constitute a relatively small proportion even of the market-
oriented farmers. The biggest ones among them are increasingly
able to bargain on an equal footing with the dalals. No doubt, the
dalals were able to exercise considerable influence in the past over
the urban markets, but it is generally agreed that more recently
they have responded to changes in the market situation by reducing their previously exorbitant profits. Moves toward state trading
or to tighter regulation of sales of various commodities are likely
to further restrict the freedom of action of the dalals in the
wholesale commodity market, whether those restrictions come
through formal governmental regulation or through the operation
of existing market forces.

The District Land Development Banks Takeover

All of the cases discussed thus far—defeat of the taluka
banks; creation of a district cadre for primary society secretaries;
efforts to reorganize the purchase and sales unions; and regulation
of the central market in Poona—involved lengthy bargaining
among a variety of actors based in state, district, and local institutions. By that standard, a decision taken in early 1973 to "abolish" DLDBs appeared uncharacteristically peremptory.

In 1970, Mohite had made no reference in his report to the
functioning of DLDBs while referring at great length to almost
every other conceivable aspect of the cooperative movement.[49]
When questioned in 1973 about this, he remarked:

48. Interview, N. S. (Mamasaheb) Mohol, 18 March 1970.
49. The cooperative sugar factories are mentioned in the Mohite paper
only in passing. They, too, received little attention in terms of proposals for
change.

Strictly speaking, the land development banks are not part of the cooperative movement. The funds are raised by floating debentures and those debentures are purchased by various bodies, like the Life Insurance Corporation, the Reserve Bank, and the government. Then loans are made on the basis of the funds available. Under the circumstances, it is a strange system to make the banks locally responsible to those persons who are its borrowers.[50]

For the most part, politicians and officials active in the cooperative sector were unhappy about the decision to abolish the DLDBs. As in other cases, they accepted the decision "in principle" but then moved to alter it in a way that would least affect the organized cooperative interests of the state.

Apparently, the action was the result of negotiations between the central government and the state government of Maharashtra, on the one hand, and the World Bank, on the other. The latter agency was interested in seeing improvement in integrated planning for land development in the state and tied a large loan to Maharashtra to the performance of the state in recovering loans on capital investments in agricultural land.[51] In 1973, governmental leaders were clearly sensitive to the possible charge that their decision to supersede the district agencies was "dictated" by the World Bank. What they did admit is that the World Bank made its loan contingent on submitting a plan which would demonstrate ways of improving the viability of the system. An aspect of the plan developed by the state government was to merge the district units into the operations of the State Land Development Bank beginning in January 1973. Existing units would continue to function but simply as branches of the apex body.

At the time of my interviews in early 1973, there was clearly a struggle going on over the future of the superseded district units. The strongest proponent of permanent incorporation of the DLDBs into the apex body among those interviewed was a high official in the apex bank. He described his reasons:

50. Interview, Y. J. Mohite, 17 February 1973.
51. Loans from the World Bank totaling Rs. 45.36 crores were being negotiated in 1971-1972. These would have covered such projects as construction of tubewells, improvement of existing wells, additional lift-irrigation facilities, and land improvement programs. The government of Maharashtra was also involved in trying to promote Bank support for a major hydrological survey. Maharashtra State Cooperative Land Development Bank, *37th Annual Report: 1971-72*, pp. 7-9.

Corruption can be tolerated if it works toward efficiency, speeding up development, but it is intolerable when it contributes to inefficiency and waste. . . . All the orders we issued about the ways in which loans were to be made were flouted by these [local] chaps. As a result the state government—I played a role in insisting on the need for such a shift—has decided that the federal structure in this area should be abolished and that we must try to deliver the goods by some other means.

Recalling the process by which the takeover had taken place, the same official continued:

Some members of our board of directors grumbled at the new policy but there has not been much resentment expressed. . . . There was not really much discussion in the Assembly when the matter came up. That is the advantage of a monolithic party government at the state level.

As previous materials indicate, this interpretation involved a serious misjudgment of the organization of political influence in Maharashtra.

Even though this key official and some other informants assumed that absorption of the DLDBs by the apex bank was to be a permanent feature of the cooperative landscape in Maharashtra, other informants were considerably less certain. Thus, one major official in the Cooperation Department of the state government admitted his uncertainty about the future:

Because of practical problems in their working and the slow pace of growth of those institutions recently, we thought there might be some temporary action to use the unitary system for a short time. It is not intended as a permanent measure. One of the things we want to do is to use the chance offered to develop a plan . . . for both short- and long-term credit throughout the state.

Others active in the cooperative sector acknowledged that the previous system had a number of faults and that the time of supersession might be used to reorganize credit arrangements. Vasantrao Patil, for example, advocated combining the functions of the DLDBs with those of the DCCBs; [52] officials, however, argued this was impossible under the existing structure of credit, which made the former dependent on the Reserve Bank in a quite different fashion from the DCCBs, which had their own members and independent resources.

52. Interview, Vasantrao Patil, 17 February 1973.

By March 1973, it was becoming apparent that bureaucratic visions of permanent supersession were being erased. Politicians— including those in the presumably rubber-stamp Assembly to which the informant quoted above made reference—may have played a part in altering that situation. According to an official of the Maharashtra State Central Cooperative Bank:

> Though there was some notion originally of superseding [the district units] permanently, I think it would last for only two years. . . . What began as a recentralization activity was stopped from going that far by the Assembly. As a result, the apex continues to include representatives from the twenty-five districts along with ten government representatives and the government is [likely to nominate] local advisory committees which, in effect, will restore the boards of the previous bodies. This indicates the continuing hold of the cooperative movement among the majority of the population. The Chief Minister and his Cabinet have concurred in recognizing some of the shortcomings but we must have the courage to accept those mistakes and go on with working the institutions.[53]

The Chief Minister, when interviewed, conceded that the decision to supersede had been taken in order to conform with a condition set by the World Bank that the recovery rate of the land development bank system be increased to 75 percent—a rate that was possible under normal conditions but difficult to achieve in the face of three years of scarcity. He stressed that the action was definitely temporary in character. [54] Judging from his comments and those of Vasantrao Patil, there is little likelihood that other activities presently organized under cover of cooperative participation will follow the direction taken in this case, even if only temporarily. In this particular instance, as in others, local political actors based in cooperative institutions apparently were able to modify a decision which two or three months earlier might well have gone in the direction of more centralized and governmentally related control.

The Role of the Nationalized Banks

A battle was shaping up in early 1973 with respect to relations between the nationalized and the cooperative banks. As early as Mohite's 1970 survey, it was evident that a potential for

53. Interview, W. C. Shrishrimal, 11 March 1973.
54. Interview, Vasantrao Naik, 14 March 1973.

strain existed in that relationship. In particular, Mohite feared that commercial banks might enter into crop-linked agricultural credit—an area he felt the existing credit structure could handle well enough on its own.[55]

As some informants described the situation that had developed by 1973, there was open competition between the nationalized banks and cooperative banks for agricultural investment. For a time, good credit risks were in a particularly fortunate position because a lack of coordination between the two sectors allowed for some duplication of credit; i.e., some farmers borrowed money from both based on the same crops. (Allegedly, a few of these then used the funds as the basis for carrying on money-lending in their villages. They were able, therefore, to invest part in their crops, repay the loans, and make a sizable non-agricultural profit at the same time.) There were complaints, as well, that the nationalized banks weakened the cooperative structure by making loans to the bigger farmers and best risks while leaving the cooperatives with the riskier loans.

Attempts at proper coordination had been feeble. Some effort had been made to avoid loan duplication by arranging for banks to exchange information on loans made. The central government as early as 1970 designated a nationalized bank in each district as the "lead bank" in organizing a coordination committee to oversee the activities of the two sets of institutions. Informants were generally dissatisfied with the performance of these committees.

A senior bureaucrat in the Cooperation Department described the situation in 1973:

> Up to now the nationalized banks have been left pretty much to themselves. Now we are involved in a systematic evaluation exercise. This does not mean that the nationalized banks will replace the cooperatives in any major way. They do not have the same branch network and the local knowledge that the cooperatives have painfully built up. In some ways the cooperative agencies may not be as strong financially but they have the grassroots contacts with the people.... Fundamentally, as a banking system the Maharashtra system is working well, unlike Rajasthan, Assam, and some other states.... Even in Marathwada, where some of the greatest problems exist, we are now handling oil seeds and cotton in the cooperative sector, and this is likely to assure a stable base for the [DCCBs] in the years ahead.... The

55. Mohite, *Cooperative Reappraisal*, p. 27.

working of the linkage system has proven beneficial there, and the benefits in Vidarbha of cotton procurement are even greater.

Despite the assurance reflected in this statement, many leaders of the cooperative sector in Poona and Kolhapur were nervous about the possibility that the nationalized banks might move into the economic territory they had carved out for themselves. Such a concern was evident in the comments of a prominent official in the Kolhapur DCCB:

> The total need of the district for credit would be about Rs. 14 crores. . . . Many of the remaining people are self-supporting. Yet the government is so anxious to take advantage of the funds available through the nationalized banks that they are willing to divert the fruits of nationalization and undermine the fruits of [cooperative] independence. . . . Our chairman is to see the Minister . . . to try to persuade him at least to exclude Kolhapur from the working of the proposed system.

Opposition to a plan of the government to create district committees to survey the credit "gap" that existed—committees consisting largely of officials—was expressed by a key officer of the Poona DCCB, who outlined the situation there:

> It is the intent of the government to allot some areas to the nationalized banks. The precise areas remain to be defined. We can only cover 50 percent of the members of the present societies. The government thinks all these farmers wish to borrow, but we say this is wrong. . . . The gap is estimated, for example, on the basis of the notion that if the total agriculturists in an area are 100 and only 20 are members of the society, then some means must be found to reach the others with finance. . . .
> If the board of the [DCCB] had its way, no societies would be given to the nationalized banks. They would prefer that the nationalized banks simply tap those persons who are not members of any society. . . . We took this view to the Cooperation Minister and insisted we could handle our own funds for the farmers.

An earlier proposal had been that the nationalized banks take over defaulters, but as one cooperative figure conceded, "Who would agree to [allow a] takeover either [of] defaulters, or non-defaulters alone?" Should the nationalized banks take over the bigger farmers with their larger credit demands, as some suggested, this would leave the cooperative banks in a less stable position. The Managing Director of the apex bank made his opposition to such an idea clear: "Our money is at stake and like every banking enterprise we need to maintain overall viability. There is no sin in our being managed on a businesslike basis."[56] It was his feeling that the nationalized banks might well get involved in activities ancillary to the crop-loan system but supportive of it—by giving aid to the digging of wells, to lift-irrigation schemes, and to loans for machinery.[57]

Despite the fears expressed by DCCB board members in Poona and Kolhapur, a senior official in the Cooperation Department denied in March 1973 that any definite plan for takeover of some of the primary societies from the cooperative sector had actually been formulated. He insisted, in fact, that many of the fears of local cooperative leaders were premature: "The Chief Minister is anxious that there be no upset to the working of such institutions as are going on well." Thus, it was apparent that even in what was presumed by cooperative leaders to be "enemy" territory there was considerable sensitivity to the prerogatives of the existing cooperative "establishment." Though the official was unwilling to specify the likely recommendations to be produced by a high-level committee then at work, he assured me that few items would upset the cooperative leadership despite the anticipatory opposition that was being whipped up by them.[58]

OVERVIEW

The last chapter and the present one taken in conjunction are intended to perform four functions in the larger narrative of this

56. Interview, W. C. Shrishrimal, 11 March 1973.

57. Mohite, *Cooperative Reappraisal*, p. 28, lists eleven investment areas where the commercial banks might be of assistance. These included providing credit for purchasing equipment for dairy cooperatives, supplying poultry and poultry equipment, and making loans to marketing and processing societies.

58. A letter critical of the scheme allegedly favored by the state government written by noted economist V. M. Dandekar was published in the *Maharashtra Times*, 13 March 1973. Dandekar assumed that the government had already made plans to allocate a certain number of weaker cooperative societies in each district to the nationalized banks. Though less critical of government plans than some cooperative society leaders, Dandekar's letter reflected concern about preserving the integrity of the cooperative sector. Officials in the Cooperation Department hastened to deny that any plan for a takeover of cooperative societies had been developed.

volume. First, they have provided considerable detailed information on the structure and functioning of cooperative institutions in the state of Maharashtra, a subject which has received only limited attention by political scientists. Second, I sought to suggest the extent to which cooperative units of activity are integrated into both the economic and the political life of rural Maharashtra. Third, I have attempted to show how various issues related to the operation of the cooperative movement have emerged and been handled both at the state level and in the districts of Kolhapur and Poona. Finally, as part of this examination of local politics and policy making, I believe I have demonstrated that politicians based in local cooperative institutions play a major role in the policymaking process in the state of Maharashtra, particularly where their own interests are immediately affected.

It is the last point that is most central to the present study. For whether policies were initiated as a result of the guidance provided by the central government or the preferences of officials or responsible office-holders within the state government, spokesmen of the cooperative sector have exercised a significant veto over the policies actually enforced. In speaking of the cooperative sector, of course, I have not distinguished too finely between local cooperators and those with statewide responsibilities. Indeed, it would be difficult to do so, since such identifications are not mutually exclusive. Rather, a Vasantrao Patil or a Ratnappa Kumbhar is both a state and a local leader of the cooperative sector.

It is notable how readily local political influence was translatable into influence in state policy making in Maharashtra during the period reviewed. This is evident in each of the seven case studies discussed. Clearly, local leaders working with state cooperative figures, like Vasantrao Patil, and assorted cooperative sector subject-matter specialists, like W. C. Shrishrimal, brought about the delay in application of the six-year rule for holding office in cooperative institutions. When a new minister was appointed, however direct or indirect Patil's influence in the selection (and it should not be forgotten that he was MPCC president at the time), the choice of Mohite assured that the rule would be applied only prospectively. In other cases of conflict between the government and the cooperatives, compromises were generally effected. Rarely did state and local cooperative leaders come away from those encounters in total defeat.

On the contrary, in the case of the taluka banks, the Mohite plan was defeated by state and district cooperative leaders; while a "potential interest group" may have existed, there was little evidence that the Minister was able to stir support for his plan from that source. Indeed, it was not certain that taluka-level actors even recognized the opportunities that were being made available to them. More likely, they were so tightly integrated into existing structures of power in the cooperative sector—structures which bound district and taluka together—that it would have been difficult for them to disentangle themselves from the grip of that web. In some cases, of course, district leaders were where they were because they played a major role in taluka cooperative life; in other instances, the scope of their ambitions may have intervened to prevent actors from limiting their horizons to the taluka. Thus, there was apparently little incentive to rally to the support of a plan which would have enhanced the status of the taluka as compared with the district. Perhaps most taluka political actors simply felt that it was worth playing for the larger stakes of district politics than accepting the rewards that might go with an enhanced role for the taluka in the cooperative credit field.

This may also explain why there was so little resistance to the idea of developing a district cadre for primary society secretaries. Here, it was apparently the fear of the state government that the power of district cooperative leaders (particularly those associated with the DCCBs) would be further enhanced that resulted in a halfway-house solution. It is notable that both the administrative problems associated with the district cadre system and effective political pressures mounted by district interests were forcing the government in early 1973 to reconsider the plan.

In another area—the organization of the marketing system— outcomes remained uncertain. Where relatively strong district bodies existed, as in Poona and Kolhapur, an effort to move them aside had only minimal effect. The taluka sanghs remained in 1973 much the same weak bodies they had been in 1970. They were still dependent for much of their survival upon linkages to government programs. The failure to upgrade the status of the marketing units at the taluka level may also reflect an ability on the part of the merchant community to maintain an influence over the political process, an influence that was even more evident in the conflict in Poona City over the control of the central fruit and vegetable market. While merchants influenced such political decisions, they were only one of several contending interests in the state and by no means the dominant one. Furthermore, given the identification of local political leaders with *both* the large commercial farmers and the merchants, potential cleavages were blurred by the political process conducted under Congress auspices.[59] Whatever influence merchants may have exercised in encouraging the slowness of the government in moving into the major urban markets, merchants (particularly in Vidarbha) bitterly protested the losses they expected to suffer as a result of cotton procurement through governmental agencies. Yet in that case, as in others, the government was willing and able to move ahead.[60]

The influence of local political forces centered in cooperative institutions is again suggested by reactions to recent policy processes involving the reorganization of the land development bank system and attempts to integrate the activities of the nationalized banks with the cooperative banking system. In both instances, external factors (the possibility of a sizable World Bank loan, in the first case; pressure from the central government to siphon the resources of the nationalized banks into agricultural investment, in the second) spurred the state government to take actions which seemed to bespeak an unusually autonomous character in respect to the existing cooperative structure. There, as in the other case studies, an initiative was taken by the state government speaking on behalf of the larger society as contrasted to the cooperative

59. Thus, I have severe reservations about the picture of ideological and material cleavages developed by Mary C. Carras in *The Dynamics of Indian Political Factions: A Study of District Councils in the State of Maharashtra* (New York and Cambridge: Cambridge University Press, 1972). For a more detailed critique of her approach, see my "Sources of District Congress Factionalism in Maharashtra," *Economic and Political Weekly,* 19 August 1972, pp. 1725-1746.

60. A report on the experience of the state government with monopoly procurement of the cotton crop in Maharashtra may be found in "Maharashtra: Monopoly Procurement Scheme in Jeopardy," *Economic and Political Weekly,* 2 August 1975, pp. 1144-1145. That article notes that monopoly procurement appeared to stimulate growth of the cotton crop (from 12 lakh bales on the average prior to 1974 to 17 lakh bales in 1974-1975). However, the high production resulted in a glut on the market and a reluctance on the part of the Reserve Bank to continue financing a guaranteed price to farmers.

sector whose spokesmen were presumably more narrowly based. Yet, in each instance, the "special interests" represented by the latter were apparently in the process of wielding considerable influence in modifying the original direction of the actions taken by the government.

The growth of the cooperative movement and its integration into the political life of rural Maharashtra raise several questions about economic development and political change in India. Clearly, despite their dependence on the government for resources and the numerous interventions of government in their work, those persons based in cooperative institutions have exercised crucial autonomy in influencing governmental outcomes. In that sense, the cooperative sector—like secondary school managements in the educational sphere—had become institutionalized. One result was that actors making use of the cooperative infrastructure of institutions to advance their economic and political interests were free to be guided by short-range personal or institutional interests, rather than by a concern with the societal impact of their actions.

This is not to imply that the government possessed an unusually large vision of the good of society, but certainly the cooperative actors we have examined had the capacity to influence the government's behavior in such a way that their own narrower sector interests were preserved and enhanced. This contributed to some of the shortcomings of the sector. In addition to the obvious cooperative society frauds, improper elections, and individual profit-making activities disguised as cooperative ventures, there was an argument to be made that the pattern of cooperative investment did not serve the best interests of society because most financing went to big farmers who could have increased their productivity out of other available resources. The marginal farmer or landless laborer received only minor benefits from government investment in the cooperative sector, but as cooperative leaders kept insisting: No one should have made the mistake of confusing the operations of the cooperative movement (at least as it operated in India) with socialism.

If the cooperative movement was not a vehicle for a major restructuring of social and economic arrangements in rural Maharashtra, despite its many defects it introduced an additional force for economic development. Sugar factories in western Maharashtra and credit facilities made available for the purchase of new varieties of seed, fertilizers, and other means of agricultural production spurred a certain level of economic advance in the state. It is true that the government did not take sufficient steps to maximize the investment in major irrigation works necessary to make use of what water there was available in the state. In part, this was a result of central government policies which were slow to force understandings among the states on river water distributions and to authorize the construction of major irrigation projects—some of which had been waiting for central approval for more than a decade. Still, what amount of modest economic development occurred in rural Maharashtra owed part of the credit to cooperative activity.

As materials in these two chapters show, the development of cooperatives not only contributed to the institutionalization of a set of public roles with economic and political autonomy sufficient to influence governmental policy-making processes, but it added to the supply of resources available to local political actors in pursuing ambitions both in state and national politics. The result is that it was rare for state leaders to seek to impose decisions even if they would have wished to do so. Thus, cooperatives contributed to both segmenting and decentralizing political influence in Indian society and to enhancing the influence of those members of local elites incorporated into the process.

While activation of the cooperative movement abetted a pattern of economic and political decentralization in Maharashtra, it did not necessarily encourage a parochialization of politics. People may have stolen from the cooperative societies, as one informant critical of the movement suggested, but they did so in order to buy cars or, more modestly, motorcycles, and the accoutrements of modern living. Even the smallest village primary society, with its ill-educated part-time secretary, was involved in the business of trying to make the best use possible of societal resources to improve agricultural production and personal incomes, at least for a restricted segment of society. Some cooperative societies may have done this badly or without seriousness (as in the case of the Kolhapur piggeries), but those who tapped into the cooperative system were influenced by its concern with economic rationality and investment in agricultural practices. When new hybrids and fertilizers were introduced, the market-oriented farmers and even many of the marginal farmers who produced mainly to support their daily food needs were soon aware of both the costs and the benefits associated with such innovations. Whether or not the cooperative movement (or other forces) was directly responsible for inducing receptivity to modern agricultural practices, the market-oriented Maharashtrian farmer became increasingly tied into a system of commercial agriculture and into the credit system that went with it. Even if some would judge that this is not modernity in the most desirable sense, at least local farmers and politicians seemed willing to make the most of it.

We will return to this matter and to some of the larger issues of political and economic development raised by the materials introduced in these two chapters after we review selected facets of the system of panchayati raj introduced in Maharashtra in 1962 and recommendations for change in that system.

NINE

Panchayati Raj: Preservation of the Status Quo

Governmental reviews of the working of panchayati raj in Maharashtra have resulted in a number of recommendations for changes in minor features of the system, but there was little evidence in 1973 that the state government had any intention of making drastic alterations in a system which served well the interests of both the state Congress leadership and the local political elite. Members of the local elite would have liked greater influence over the delivery of services provided through the zilla parishads and panchayat samitis; many also complained about the limited financial resources made available to them by the state government, though in both Poona and Kolhapur districts the zilla parishad leadership was reluctant to exploit all the potential sources of local income permitted by the state government. On the whole, however, persons in leadership positions in these rural local bodies seemed relatively satisfied with the system that had emerged since the introduction of panchayati raj.

THE POLITICS OF PANCHAYATI RAJ

Relations between the leadership of the state government and the local elite involved in panchayati raj were complicated by the interests of two other sets of actors. First, and less important, were the MLAs. Considerably more significant were members of the state and local bureaucracy.

As noted in chapter 2, the panchayati raj system in Maharashtra was created in such a way as to exclude MLAs from formal participation in either the zilla parishads or the panchayat samitis. The result was that some MLAs felt challenged by local officeholders who were able to exercise direct influence over the delivery of goods and services to the same constituents. An MLA who did not have great influence in his district Congress organization, in cooperative institutions in his home taluka, or in other organizations was thought to be at a disadvantage when vying for political influence with an office-holder in the zilla parishad or panchayat samiti. He might still exercise influence through his connections with state ministers or key state government bureaucrats, but this influence was clearly less direct than the kind of political leverage exercised by an office-holder in one of the local government bodies. On the other hand, where an MLA was a minister, an important Congress leader, or held a set of institutional connections in the cooperative realm, he might well have been able to wield considerable influence over the behavior of members of his local panchayat samiti. In such instances, he might be consulted regularly on actions they took, or his lieutenants serving on such bodies would act to serve his personal and political interests. This situation was rather rare in the high-conflict politics of Kolhapur, but was somewhat more common in Poona district.

Despite whatever challenges they may have felt from political actors in panchayati raj institutions, very few members of the state legislature actually advocated dismantling the system. Of approximately twenty-five MLAs, MLCs, and former state legislators interviewed in 1970 and 1973,[1] only two indicated such extreme dissatisfaction with the practice of panchayati raj that they were prepared to abandon the institution entirely.[2] Other respondents favored the principles behind panchayati raj, but they varied considerably in their reactions to the actual operation of local government institutions.

Among these respondents were a group of about seven legislators who argued that the kinds of local leadership which had come into panchayati raj bodies had fallen considerably short of

1. There are difficulties involved in categorizing these respondents as part of a fixed survey population because they included ex-MLAs, MLAs who served both in 1970 and 1973, and some who held office during only one of those years. Several of the newer MLAs were persons who had held panchayati raj positions recently. In the case of one man who was a zilla parishad committee chairman when he was interviewed in 1970 and an MLA by 1973, the later attitudes he expressed about panchayati raj were clearly less favorable than his earlier views. In the other instances of persons who were re-interviewed, attitudes were relatively consistent.

2. One Poona MLC based his opposition on the money "wasted" on salaries and fringe benefits provided to office-holders in panchayati raj institutions. The other man saw the system as little more than a way of paying off politically influential Congressmen or finding a way for the politically ambitious to keep busy.

the ideal which panchayati raj was meant to stimulate. Several thought it might be necessary to impose an educational requirement; others toyed with that idea but conceded that it was basically undemocratic.[3] When questioned about possible changes in power, most of the seven felt that continued oversight by the state government was necessary. Two argued that a better move was to grant even more power to elected officials so that they

3. In a study of three districts of Maharashtra (Satara, Aurangabad, and Akola), Sirsikar found that 13 percent of those involved in panchayati raj bodies (zilla parishads and panchayat samitis) had college educations, another 25 percent had at least some secondary school education (eighth standard through SSC), and the remainder had only some primary education. V. M. Sirsikar, *The Rural Elite in a Developing Society* (New Delhi: Orient Longmans, 1970), p. 42.

Sirsikar does not break down his figures for zilla parishad as opposed to panchayat samiti members. Data made available to me by election officials in Kolhapur district for the 1967 panchayati raj elections show a slightly different pattern for the two levels. Of the 52 zilla parishad members for whom data were available, 48 percent had some college education or higher, another 44 percent had taken some secondary education, and only 8 percent had a seventh standard education or less. This is a remarkably high figure. It contrasts with data collected for 159 of the 160 candidates for the zilla parishad. In that case, comparable figures were 20, 25, and 56 percent, respectively. As for panchayat samiti members, only 4 percent had some college education, 24 percent had attended secondary school, and 72 percent had not proceeded beyond primary education.

Sirsikar does not report education by party. In a study of local recruitment in Chanda district, Robertson found that Congress candidates were better educated than candidates running for opposition parties or as independents. John E. Robertson, "Political Recruitment at the Zilla Parishad Level, Chanda District, Maharashtra" (Paper presented at the Fifth Annual Conference of the Maharashtra Studies Group, Philadelphia, Pa., 5-7 May 1972).

My Kolhapur data indicate a similar tendency for better educated candidates to be more heavily represented among Congress nominees at the zilla parishad level. (Thirty-eight percent of the Congress nominees had college educations in 1967 as against only 12 percent of the non-Congressmen.) About equal proportions (23 and 25 percent) had completed secondary education. At the panchayat samiti level Congressmen were both more heavily represented among those with only primary educations (79 to 69 percent) and those with college education (7 to 2 percent). At least at the zilla parishad level, an argument in favor of an educational qualification for membership does not seem warranted. It should be noted that male literacy in rural Kolhapur in 1961 was only 34.4 percent. Thus, zilla parishad members constituted a distinctly elite group on the educational dimension as on others. (I wish to thank Arun Wagh and Sidney Klein for assisting me in the analysis of the Kolhapur data reported here.)

would be forced into a rapid maturing process, as a result of which they would either successfully manage local government or local institutions would be taken over by the state government. Reflective of this last view are the thoughtful comments of a senior Congressman from Kolhapur district:

> The real intention of panchayati raj was to nourish the local initiative of the people and to get people to participate to a greater extent. Now the bodies involved in panchayati raj do little more than spend the budget they get from government. . . . [Officers] get full remuneration and conveyances. Everything is given to them, but they do not use the opportunity to harness the initiative of the people. . . . There have been so many reservations in imparting local people with real powers. The problem is that [the state government] may feel local people are not using those powers properly. Equally important, people at higher levels do not want to part with their powers because they feel they would lose importance. Thus, they have created local institutions with one hand but they have been reluctant to give more powers to those institutions that they have created.

Of the remaining sixteen respondents, seven were generally satisfied with the existing character of panchayati raj. They neither condemned the existing leadership nor did they offer any specific suggestions for change. Most of these responses came from the less educated and less articulate state legislators. The remaining nine offered only minor suggestions for improvement, most of which involved recommendations for greater local authority or increases in revenue which could be employed more flexibly by local leaders.

This brief review of the attitudes of state legislators reveals no consensus for significant modification in the existing pattern of rural local government. Interviews with political leaders holding responsible positions in the Maharashtra government also indicated no inclination among them to foster major changes. There was some division of opinion, however, about the need for further devolution of powers to local bodies as opposed to maintaining the existing balance. The one instance where public controversy had arisen about the division of powers involved the suggestion that education be withdrawn either entirely or in part from local influence. Nevertheless, state leaders took a generally supportive position in their approach to panchayati raj. As one commented:

> It was only a cautious step that was taken in 1962 [when panchayati raj was introduced]. Now there is a feeling that there should be more

deofficializing of panchayati raj. This could be done without damage. It is true that [office-holders] do occasionally involve themselves in such matters as transfers of officers in the educational field, in particular, but officials tend to complain because they do not want to part with their own powers.

As the last remark indicates, there were some difficulties getting administrators to accept the basic principles behind panchayati raj. Thus, for the most part, those high-status administrators who served in local government bodies on deputation from agencies of the state government preferred close state government oversight of local bodies. Despite their distaste for the political climate in which they found themselves, most administrators learned (sometimes ungracefully) to adjust to their existing situations.

Although local politicians deplored the weakness of their position vis-à-vis the panchayati raj bureaucracy, their complaints against the formal separation of political authority from effective control over the bureaucracy was less profound than one encountered in Indian urban areas. In part, that was because individuals elected to offices in the zilla parishads and panchayat samitis did have a somewhat greater degree of formal authority than those who held equivalent positions in municipal corporations; equally important, they exercised a considerable influence with state political leaders, which allowed them to use informal means to bring pressure upon local administrators to do things which administrators might have preferred not to do.[4]

Nevertheless, a good deal of antagonism existed between administrators and those persons elected to zilla parishads and panchayat samitis. Such antagonism flowed, in part, from the conceptually distinct but operationally overlapping roles assigned by state law to the two sets of actors and, in part, from the distinct intellectual traditions within which the roles operated. Thus, several administrators revealed in interviews the continued

4. For a brief examination of administrator-politician relations in two Indian municipal corporations, see my *The Limited Elite* (Chicago: University of Chicago Press, 1970), pp. 180-209. An interesting study of how politicians may use their formal authority and informal political influence to overcome the great amount of bureaucratic autonomy built into municipal government structures may be found in Roderick Church, "Authority and Influence in Indian Municipal Politics: Administrators and Councillors in Lucknow," *Asian Survey* 13 (April 1973): 421-438.

effect on their thinking of administrative notions of benevolent authoritarianism inherited from British rule. Such attitudes were not simply a function of age, for one of the younger officials saw panchayati raj as a system "to develop the rural areas down to the village level, to make people aware of the things being done for them in the process." While acknowledging a new participatory element, the respondent saw himself as a benefactor of the rural population, whose interests were being badly served by the interference of petty politicians:

> The government machinery should be allowed to work and there should be no intermediary between it and the people. . . . As it is now, the zilla parishads only pass resolutions and otherwise the members spend their time trying to see that their own work is done and that their own areas are helped.

Because "politics" was being imported into panchayati raj, most bureaucrats complained about the pressures which could be brought to bear on them to force actions which went against existing regulations. Thus, one block development officer (BDO) remarked with respect to the means elected members employed:

> They threaten [administrators] with passing resolutions against them which can be an embarrassment to the officers. . . . They are regularly going on tour and taking expenses for those tours, but they do not do any work. . . . If we complain, they pass a resolution in the panchayat samiti against the BDO or other officials. Such a resolution may become a record of our inability to do the work. They also threaten us with transfers and of speaking to the minister or the commissioner against us. Sometimes a BDO will keep quiet but will refuse to do this illegal work.

For their part, local government members attributed a lack of initiative to most officials. Many, they complained, were merely time-servers who were protected by bureaucratic rules which allowed them to move slowly on any of the recommendations put forward by the politicians. A few respondents stressed the class origins of most higher bureaucrats; some of these hinted that the continued representation of Brahmans in the higher civil service accounted for failures in local administrative performance.

For their own part, bureaucrats assigned to panchayati raj institutions did not view such assignments with particular favor. Those who served as BDOs during the initial phases of community development were recruited from subordinate positions in the state revenue service, the same service from which emerge district collectors. (The latter are the officials traditionally responsible for overseeing revenue collection—hence their titles—and maintaining law and order in the districts.) Indeed, they were equivalent in status to *tehsildars,* revenue officials who performed at the taluka level functions analogous to those the collector performs for the district as a whole. Similarly, the chief executive officers (CEOs) of the zilla parishads were equivalent in rank and background to the collectors. Yet, as one such official explained:

> Persons prefer to be collectors rather than CEOs because in zilla parishads you need to work with sixty to seventy people who feel free to call on you day and night to perform services for them. A collector is a more independent individual.... The same president [of a zilla parishad] who will issue orders to a CEO will see nothing wrong in making an application for an appointment with the collector.

As a bird of passage with ambition for further promotion or a posting to a more prestigious location, the CEO (like the BDO) obviously had a stake in assuring that the zilla parishad was administered well, but there were few incentives for him to accord local politicians any greater influence. Behind these government bureaucrats were the institutional loyalties of the vast governmental bureaucracy in Maharashtra. Since the CEO has been a person who either has been recruited through the system of national examinations organized under the Indian Administration Service (IAS) or has risen through the state service and has been promoted into the IAS, he has developed the kinds of skills associated with bureaucratic politics. Even on those occasions, therefore, when local political leaders actually agreed on a policy which ran contrary to the rules that the administrators saw themselves as serving (and such occasions were rare), the CEO or BDO usually could find some support for his position within the regulations of the state bureaucracy or from the responsible minister. There were very few instances, then, when the administrator's appeals to regulations did not win out. In some cases, state ministers felt themselves bound to follow the advice of their departmental administrators; in other cases, the ministers may have had little affection for the particular local politicians who sought their assistance against the CEOs, and they may have seen no political benefit to be gained for themselves by intervening on behalf of those local politicians.

Officials and even some politicians (though mainly those from opposition parties or those not involved in panchayati raj) were frequently critical of the expenditures absorbed by local bodies in providing salaries and allowances to office-holders of the zilla parishads and the panchayat samitis. One former member of a district local board provided some critical comments on expenditures by and for political actors as well as on the bureaucratic costs involved in operating panchayati raj:

> No one on the district local boards used to receive any salaries. Now there are twenty-five presidents and vice-presidents [in Maharashtra] and seventy-five chairmen of subject committees in addition to chairmen of panchayat samitis and vice-chairmen. In addition to set amounts, they also have housing and other allowances. It has contributed to a top-heavy expenditure for administration. . . . There is also too much overlapping of administration in the villages. A village may be visited by the BDO, extension officers, gram sevaks, the artificial insemination officers, someone trying to encourage the production of more milk, etc. All of these people require traveling expenses and they add to the great red tape which exists. . . . One major official in each village who is well paid and well trained and is able to deal with most matters that affect the villager is enough. Decisions would then be quicker.

Relations between officials and elected members were always subject to tension. Petty quarrels were likely to break out over seemingly unimportant matters. Attempts to act in matters which one or the other group saw as an infringement on its formal powers were often special grist for the mills of local controversy.

Several aspects of the relationships between politicians and administrators (both bureaucrats and those I have characterized as functional specialists) in panchayati raj are revealed through an examination of the debate which occurred from 1970 to 1973 over possible reforms in the panchayati raj system. The major focus of that debate was the degree of influence politicians should properly exercise over educational decisions, particularly decisions affecting the transfer of teachers. Along with examining that issue, committees appointed by the state government took under consideration other alterations in the system of local government. As we will see, few of the recommendations that were produced involved serious challenges to the existing balance of political power between the state government and the panchayati raj bodies. Neither did those proposals much affect relationships between local administrators and elected local office-holders. To understand the nature of the proposals which did emerge, however, it is necessary to provide a somewhat more detailed description of the organization and delivery of those administrative services operated through panchayati raj.

The Organization of Local Services

In its political organization, panchayati raj replaced and expanded (through the creation of taluka panchayat samitis) the political infrastructure of rural Maharashtra, which had been marked previously by the existence of district local boards and *gram* (village) panchayat structures.[5] The new political structure took on administrative responsibilities of two kinds: certain activities which previously had been handled directly by state governmental agencies; national investments in community development programs, which were formerly organized in a separate system of community development blocks.

The community development program was introduced on a demonstration basis in 1952. By 1957, the program had taken firm hold and was gradually being extended by the central government to cover much of the nation.[6] As it operated during this period, blocks of approximately sixty-six thousand persons each were created. They were to be provided with a set of developmental services financed largely from central resources. Originally pegged at Rs. 15 lakhs for the first five-year period (stage I), this amount was subsequently reduced to Rs. 12 lakhs as a result of the need to divert resources to defense in the wake of the Chinese war of 1962. After the initial period of five years, each develop-

5. In place of a chief administrative officer recruited locally and clearly subordinate to the will of the members of the district local board, the legislation creating panchayati raj proceeded cautiously by formally separating administrative from political authority at district and subdistrict levels. The head of the district bureaucracy, the CEO, serves up to three years and then moves to another post. As a result of the introduction of this official and the assignment of crucial administrative authority to him (subject to state government supervision), some respondents felt that the zilla parishads were actually weaker than their predecessors.

6. For a review of the history of the community development program, see Sugan Chand Jain, *Community Development and Panchayati Raj in India* (Bombay: Allied Publishers, 1967), esp. pp. 53-76.

ment block was supposed to pass through a second developmental stage of five years in which national funding would amount to an additional Rs. 5 lakhs.[7] Once the span of ten years was completed, each block was to be left to its own resources or those resources made available through state governments. As one senior bureaucrat in the Maharashtra government described the state of the program in mid-1970:

> All the blocks in the state have completed stage I, although somewhat more slowly than originally anticipated. . . . When the schemes were originally started some categorical grants were given but . . . these categories were abandoned and the blocks took the money and spent it where they could. About 200 blocks out of the 425 created in the state are still in stage II and the rest in post-stage II where they are no longer eligible.

The Administrative Staff

The major emphasis of the community development program was on economic development and particularly on agricultural innovation—the demonstration of new techniques and the spread of information about new seeds and fertilizers. Development blocks were also assigned some responsibility for promoting social change with respect to health practices, social relations (especially the improvement of the conditions of the untouchables), and literacy. These activities were to be coordinated within the block by the BDO.[8] Extension officers working under him were responsible for particular functional specializations. To some extent, developmental activities were to be reintegrated at the village level through a single individual, the *gram sevak* (village-level worker) who was assigned to direct services for one or two villages.

Generally, the gram sevak tended to concentrate his efforts in the area of agricultural innovation and in the distribution of those

7. Funds for the second stage did not materialize on the scale originally promised; payments also were strung out over a much longer period than the program initially anticipated.

8. As originally conceived, development blocks were conceptually distinct from traditional administrative units. In practice, the traditional revenue taluka was employed in western Maharashtra as the organizational unit by combining multiples of the average block population in allocating resources. Thus, a revenue taluka might be calculated as containing a certain number of development blocks. Areas in which tribals constituted two-thirds of the population were eligible to receive an additional Rs. 10-15 lakhs above any funds already allocated.

inputs made available through the panchayati raj structures. Other developmental work was left to extension officers for the various specialized services who visited the villages on a regular basis. The situation was complicated in administrative practice by the manner in which extension officers were recruited and maintained in their positions, for most were tied to existing departmental structures at the state level. Only very recently has the state of Maharashtra begun to disentangle service in panchayati raj institutions from state bureaucratic commitments.[9] (We will examine one aspect of this problem and the creation of a district cadre pattern later in this chapter.)

When panchayati raj was introduced, the developmental block was integrated into the new taluka unit. The BDO became the administrative head of taluka services as well as the secretary of the taluka panchayat samiti. As late as 1970, however, about half of the BDOs in Maharashtra were still being recruited through the Revenue Department. Many clearly would have preferred assignments in the regular revenue service as tehsildars. Indeed, among those BDOs interviewed, those from the revenue service were especially likely to complain about the political influence under which they were forced to operate, both as coordinators of local developmental services and as formal subordinates of the elected members of the panchayat samitis.

Along the same lines, one CEO described the role he played in staffing the panchayati raj bureaucracy:

> There are constant pressures on the CEO in connection with such things as appointments, transfers, and promotion. Eleven thousand persons, including teachers, work for the zilla parishad, so the job of the CEO is mostly looking after such complaints as arise from these matters. . . . I have delegated much of my authority in the matter of transfers to subordinate officials—to heads of departments and, within the talukas, to the BDOs. The political pressures then arise at the lower level, but still at the district level the responsibility is on us and I take an interest in major appointments by the district or divisional selection boards. I choose from the selection list provided by those bodies. Even when we do not know the persons listed, the [politicians] often approach us and

9. From early in discussions about the organization of panchayati raj, there was some consideration of the desirability of creating a separate district development cadre of persons involved only in local service, though subject to transfer around the state. Not until 1968, however, did the state government of Maharashtra begin to move in that direction.

try to get to us to post persons whom they know. Our major political difficulties arise in these matters of transfers and postings.

The Indian administrative system, which is ranked into four broad categories, or classes, involves an exquisitely diverse set of recruitment standards (including examinations and educational requirements), a complex pattern of salary scales, and diverse promotional arrangements. (Some aspects of the system may have changed after 1973.) When panchayati raj was initiated, a number of class I officers were assigned from various departments to positions in the zilla parishads in order to direct programs financed by the state government but nominally attached to panchayati raj. In addition to the CEO and a deputy CEO, class I officers included a planning officer, a finance officer (concerned with the accounts of the zilla parishad), and various persons holding technical positions, such as the district education officer, the executive engineer, the district agricultural officer, and the public welfare officer.

These officials, as well as the BDO (who is generally a senior class II official), tended to identify with career patterns in those state departments from which they came. Such state-level administrative identifications provided them with a degree of insulation from local political demands. At the same time, however, their recruitment from distinct state departments bred a degree of insulation from each other. Thus, rather than feeling themselves to be members of a common service with a common set of goals, senior officials were likely to identify themselves as members of a state government department in pursuit of its own functional goals. It has been the unhappy task of the CEO at the district level and of the BDO within each taluka to try to bring some coordination to these activities. Unfortunately, they have been given little flexibility in the handling either of men or programs. The result at least in some cases was stalemate.

The CEO's situation was not necessarily eased by the presence of a deputy CEO, who had his own career interests and over whose selection the CEO had little control. The CEO had substantial formal authority over his deputy; he could report him for insubordination or misconduct. Such extreme actions were generally unnecessary, particularly since each party to the relationship had an interest in not drawing attention to himself. The CEO would not wish to reveal an incapacity to manage his subordinates;

his deputy would not want to risk possible future promotions by openly countermanding orders framed by his superior. Nevertheless, in both of the districts studied, there appeared to be a certain wariness between the two officials.

In addition to the BDOs, class II officials included some of the district and subdistrict functional specialists, such as the deputy engineers (each of whom was responsible for overseeing public works projects in two or three talukas) and certain educational and agricultural officers whose responsibilities extended beyond one taluka.

Extension officers assigned to specialist responsibilities organized at the taluka level belonged generally to class III, but this varied with the particular service and the experience of the official. These lower-level bureaucrats were recruited in different ways—some come from state departments; others were chosen by divisional and district selection boards. In neither the divisional nor the district boards did the CEO have a major voice. The presiding official was either the district collector or the divisional commissioner. Other members of these boards included persons drawn from a panel designated by the state government. [10] In the case of recruitment for positions of a technical or specialized character, the responsible senior class I officer in the district might sit with the district selection board, but this was not always the case. The most important selection process (quantitatively), the one for teachers, involved district recruitment. One district education officer interviewed insisted he was not formally a member of that body, but he did sit with it and reviewed the credentials of the candidates. The chairman of the zilla parishad education committee also took part in that selection process.

Finally, lower-level positions in the general clerical staff (class IV) were filled by a selection board for the zilla parishad in which

10. There are four divisions in Maharashtra consisting of five to eight districts: Bombay Division contains seven districts; Poona division has six; Aurangabad five; and Nagpur eight. The divisional commissioner coordinates the activities of the district collectors in his jurisdiction.

While great effort was made to give recruitment processes the appearance of impartiality, and, no doubt, most administrative recruitment was based purely on objective criteria, the principle of strict impartiality may have been moderated by the fact that appointees to divisional selection boards included persons with political connections.

the CEO or his deputy played a part. In such cases, the district-level specialists and the chairman of the relevant zilla parishad committee were also involved. Once the selection boards compiled their lists of prospective candidates, these names were passed to the responsible technical official and it was his duty to distribute personnel according to the needs indicated by existing staffing authorizations.

Not only was this system ungainly, but no single official or small group of officials had continuing responsibility for managing the overall pattern of transfers or promotions. Furthermore, transferability, which was employed both as punishment and reward, was not consistent from service to service. For persons recruited by the zilla parishad directly, movement might be rare or limited to one taluka. In some cases, various grades of officials recruited by the district selection board might be transferred only within their respective talukas; in other instances their transfers might be district-wide in range. Where the divisional selection board was involved, transfers were more regular and involved movement among the several districts constituting a division. The length of service in a single location also varied with the position and the nature of the recruitment process.

One major problem of any senior official, then, was staying on top of the personnel management responsibilities with which he was charged.[11] Given the complex system of recruitment and conflicting institutional loyalties, higher officials found it difficult to oversee the local delivery of services effectively. The CEO also regularly became involved in trying to resolve disputes within the bureaucracy between technical specialists, on the one hand, and BDOs, on the other. On some occasions, these disputes would involve class I officers assigned to the district headquarters.

A case in point was a dispute that arose because of the attitudes of health professionals. Several with whom I spoke indicated their unhappiness with the status that medical practitioners had been accorded originally under panchayati raj. Positions for extension officers for public health (class III) went

11. Since some promotions require appearing for training courses, the administrative routines of the zilla parishad also involved filing requests for persons to fill positions left vacant during authorized absences. Deaths, illnesses, and other leaves create a constant set of personnel problems to which the official devotes considerable time.

unfilled because few doctors were willing to join a service that assigned them low status and circumscribed their financial rewards. This problem was overcome only partially by a policy of bonding into the service new entrants to the medical profession.[12] To deal with the problem, the rural medical service of Maharashtra was restructured to operate alongside but not quite within the panchayati raj system (at least not at the taluka level). Though this has been done to avoid status conflicts between health professionals and the BDOs, some conflicts still arose. Indicative of the kinds of strains involved are the comments of one senior government functional specialist:

> There is presently some friction at the taluka level between the BDO, who is a non-technical person and in education junior to the doctors assigned as medical officers, and the doctors, who have MBBS degrees. The latter have more prestige, and the BDO occasionally does not recognize this. The medical officer draws his pay from the state, but the lower health staff is paid by the BDO. Sometimes frictions arise in this connection and also from the fact that BDOs sometimes divert some of the medical workers to other responsibilities. We have recommended that all the staff be placed directly under the medical officers. . . . [What may happen now, for example, is that a] sanitary inspector is supposed to tour for twenty days a month but he refuses to submit his records to the medical officer, or he is used for other work by the BDO and the BDO refuses to cooperate with the health officer in the matter. . . . When the medical officer tries to transfer the inspector or to punish him, he may be protected by political leaders or the punishment may be ineffective. . . . Much depends on the personal strength of the medical officers and the relations he has with the CEO. . . . If the CEO is competent and strong, the CEO can take effective action in such matters. If he is weak, he cannot protect the interests of the district health officer.

As a result of such conflicts, one district health officer interviewed favored removing health services (except for family planning) entirely from the panchayati raj system. While stressing that relations varied considerably from place to place, he remarked: "In technical matters I can deal directly with the local health personnel, but if I want to discipline a man I have to go

12. A service bond has been demanded in recent years of any student completing a medical education; it requires the student to agree to work in a rural public health facility. Before 1970, the term of service was one year; in January 1970, the term was increased to two.

through the BDO and sometimes I do not even find out if the problem was acted upon by the BDO." Furthermore, politicians regularly "interfered." Even where his interventions were not effective, a politician might give the impression that he had influence. The result would be that "others complain who don't have influence or cannot claim to have influence . . . particularly . . . in instances where punishments are involved."

Educational Services

A key department in any district is education. In Kolhapur district, for example, 6,700 of the district government's 10,000 employees were associated with the educational staff. In addition to teachers, the district education officer had a small central office staff and each taluka had assigned to it two or three extension officers for education; the extension officers divided responsibilities for inspection of the primary and secondary schools in a given area according to standards established by the state educational bureaucracy.

For the most part, there was a division of labor between administrators and politicians. The educational administrators were quite willing to leave specific decisions about the location of facilities to the politicians while they reserved to themselves the day-to-day administration of educational services. As we indicated in our earlier review of state educational policy, primary and secondary school curriculums were set by state agencies. Thus, the one area where room remained for considerable battle over authority between administrators and politicians was in the responsibility for transferring teachers. An educational administrator put the matter in terms much milder than those used by others:

> The elected people may want certain teachers posted to their own areas, but that is not always possible. Sometimes we cannot give them the teachers they ask for, so problems arise. Sometimes they encourage teachers in their misdeeds, so problems are created in efficiency. Where the teachers posted in a place are not working properly, they must be taken out and others who are willing put in their place. We do what we can, but there is pressure to stop us.

Each district was authorized to transfer approximately 10 percent of its cadre of teachers each year. In both Poona and Kolhapur districts, the share of responsibility for transfers has been divided equally between zilla parishads and taluka panchayat samitis. Typically, a committee would be set up at the taluka level consisting of the BDO, the extension officer for education who was responsible for the particular section of the taluka being reviewed, and the chairman of the panchayat samiti. The same kind of committee existed at the district level; the members were the CEO, the district officer for education, and the elected politician who chaired the education committee. Most teachers were transferred as a result of their own requests; in many instances, they were seeking greater proximity to their native villages, despite state regulations designed to inculcate a more objective perspective on the part of teachers by requiring postings that were no closer than ten and preferably twenty miles from the teacher's native place. Such rules were regularly breached as a result of the requests of teachers and the sympathetic responses of both senior administrators and local politicians. Other teachers were transferred because of complaints from villages or as a form of punishment for misconduct. (On occasion, one faction within a village might assert that the teacher was acting in political collusion with the other group.)

The chairmen of the Education Committees in Poona and Kolhapur districts—each was vice-president of his respective zilla parishad and became president of that body after the 1972 elections—viewed struggles over transfers as requiring firmer rules which would be adhered to both by politicians and administrators. As one remarked:

> Most transfers are made in favor of the teachers who want to be in their own village or at least in their own taluka. . . . In my view, there should be strict rules of appointment including a rule that a person should not be in his own taluka. Lady teachers, in particular, do not like to go to rural areas, but these rules should be made equally applicable to all.

Since teachers constituted the largest single group in the local service, and expenditures on education were nearly half the total of all local budgets,[13] state politicians and educational bureaucrats were engaged in a battle in 1970 over a proposal to remove

13. Of Rs. 68 crores spent through panchayati raj institutions in Maharashtra in 1966-1967, 33.2 crores went to education. Only Rs. 5.8 crores of this amount was raised locally. Government of Maharashtra, Bureau of Economics and Statistics, *Handbook of Basic Statistics for Maharashtra State, 1968* (Bombay: Government Central Press, 1969), p. 82.

the transfer authority from local government influence. There was considerable diversity of opinion both at the state level and in local circles on this issue. A senior political leader in the state reflected the situation in comments made in 1970:

> At some places, the non-officials are very good but the teachers behave badly. . . . At some places the teachers are good but the local politicians interfere in education. It is unfair to blame the situation on one particular local element.

Opinion was equally divided in the districts. In some instances the senior officials were critical of the behavior of teachers, while the elected members of the zilla parishad came to their defense. Thus, in Kolhapur, the education officer remarked:

> Some teachers take advantage of local politics. . . . They do not get to school on time, they do not reside near the schools. They do not follow instructions well. . . . In one case recently a teacher was a director of a lift-irrigation society and an enquiry was made into the society. He was then transferred some distance away but we were pressured into bringing him back. I [reluctantly] gave the decision to bring him back to _____ , but still he is some distance from his previous village.

The few primary school teachers with whom I spoke were reticent on this subject or insisted that they had experienced few political pressures. It may be significant that all but one of those interviewed were located in villages relatively close to their family homes. Despite rules to the contrary, most had also served in the same place for periods exceeding five years. One was quite open about how his brother had approached the chairman of the panchayat samiti to arrange his transfer to a village closer to home. When asked whether his brother had provided any political favors to the chairman in return, the teacher hedged. He replied that his brother and the chairman were old friends and that if his brother had supported the chairman politically that was no concern of his.

Some of the flavor of the situation is suggested by a passage from a study done by Pratima Kale of teachers in Poona district (reaffirming a conventional teachers' perspective):

> The rural teacher's main problem is connected with the power structure of the village community. As a teacher from a rural school said, "Usually the villagers are good to us. But when it comes to village politics, it's all different. If you don't conform to their dominant political ideology, and don't join their political activities, they see to it

that you are fired in no time. There is no democracy here. They always have contacts with the district officers. So your complaints never go beyond that office."[14]

Other Development Services

Compared with the controversy which surrounded the administration of education, other development services were relatively free of public debate. Services varied considerably, however, in the quality and quantity of support they received from local elites. Thus, most politicians were positively oriented to the agricultural services provided through panchayati raj. They were also eager to exploit whatever resources were made available (generally under state categorical grants) for public works like roads, small dams, and local bridges; however, they were by no means satisfied with administrative procedures which they felt caused delays in contracting for and carrying out such work. In contrast, few politicians or bureaucrats involved in local government felt that there was much need for expenditures in promoting cooperatives or rural industries through panchayati raj, particularly in districts like Poona and Kolhapur. There was somewhat greater verbal sympathy for investment in the areas of social welfare and social reform, but the Poona zilla parishad indicated its basic feelings on the subject by not investing any of its own money in such efforts prior to 1969. In that year, the zilla parishad committed a tiny amount to social reform (Rs. 15,000). Kolhapur district, largely because of the personal prodding of the president of the zilla parishad, spent a fairly substantial sum each year (Rs. 2.8 lakhs in 1969-1970) on a variety of schemes, though many members felt such money was wasted.

Agricultural Services—On the whole, local politicians were most sanguine about the progress in agricultural development they associated with panchayati raj. Most members of the zilla parishads and panchayat samitis interviewed were farmers who could report

14. Pratima Kale, "The Career of the Secondary School Teacher in Poona, India," (Ph.D. diss., University of Wisconsin, 1970), pp. 120-121. Kale goes on to suggest a nice analogy to the situation of rural teachers during an earlier period in the United States when the rural or small-town teacher was often recruited from the outside and subject to the mores of the community. As she writes, "With all his educational qualifications he [found] himself in an isolated position among the uneducated landowners who [held] high positions in the power structure of the village community" (p. 121).

their personal experiences with various agricultural methods and with the new seeds and fertilizers promoted by the state and national governments. District officials in charge of agriculture recalled few conflicts in their relations with local politicians. Instead, they cited numerous instances where developmental activities were positively encouraged by those associations. Politicians could often reach villagers more effectively than the extension officer for agriculture or the gram sevak acting on his own.

There was a certain clumsiness to the organization of agricultural services. District and taluka extension officers were often state government employees; gram sevaks operated under them and were locally recruited. However, between the district officers and the extension officers was supposed to be a layer of taluka agricultural officers. Such positions had been difficult to fill. Typically, the issue raised was one of status in the civil service system. In one of the districts studied, five of the twelve positions were empty allegedly because of the disparity between the requirements of the position and its status in the administrative hierarchy. Both these officials and the extension officers for agriculture were rated as class III civil servants, but the higher positions required persons with advanced training in agriculture. Rather than accept appointment to such local government positions, recent graduates of agricultural colleges attempted to attach themselves directly to the specialized services maintained by the state government.[15]

There were other aspects of the administrative organization of agricultural services that raised problems. The gram sevak, who served as the local official for developmental programs, has doubled as the chief administrative officer of his village. Some of the younger men who worked in the service were recruited after secondary school and especially trained for their positions, but the remainder of positions were filled by an older generation of sometimes poorly educated men who served as village secretaries

15. The creation of additional agriculture colleges in Maharashtra in the 1960s promised to correct this situation. A similar situation had existed earlier in the decade with respect to engineers. By 1970, it was possible to fill engineering positions in panchayati raj departments with relative ease. Unfortunately, as in education, where primary school graduation has gradually been replaced by completion of secondary school and more recently by college training for certain teaching positions, a process of credentials.inflation was underway.

prior to panchayati raj. The state attempted to upgrade the skills of the latter group by requiring them to take a special training course, but it was by no means clear that the course had been effective. (Training for a gram sevak consisted of more than instruction related to agriculture, in any case, for he was required to be familiar with the record-keeping procedures of the various governmental agencies with which he came in contact.)

The range of activities of a gram sevak in a larger village is suggested by this list, provided by one who was asked about his work: record-keeping in connection with various schemes for construction of a school and several wells; supervising the installation of street lights and the collection of market taxes when the weekly bazaar was held; answering inquiries from villagers about applying for agricultural loans from the state government; serving as secretary at meetings of the gram panchayat; arranging for the posting of additional teachers to the village school; encouraging family planning and small savings schemes in the village; providing insecticides to persons who were not members of the cooperative societies; and working with the cooperative societies in the popularization of hybrid seeds.[16]

Given such a wide range of responsibilities, the gram sevak was less likely to see himself as a leader in agricultural innovation than as a local support for other agricultural specialists who regularly interacted with the area. The most important of these were the agricultural assistants. Some agricultural assistants had responsibilities for several villages. In addition to those with territorial responsibilities, however, there were functional specialists of agricultural assistant rank. Above the level of agricultural assistants come the extension officers for the taluka, and above them, in turn, the taluka agricultural officer.

As a recent survey of administrative organization in Maharashtra showed, the pattern of agricultural services was awkward. That study drew on an example from a village in Junnar taluka in Poona district where, it noted, all of the following individuals

16. For some gram sevaks agricultural training may be inappropriate; the villages to which they are assigned are more highly urbanized than some entities officially designated as municipalities. The larger urbanized villages have found it beneficial financially to remain gram panchayats because grants from the state government are more generous for certain investments in local public works for rural bodies than is the case for municipalities.

provided services to the same village: an assistant gram sevak;[17] an agricultural assistant for intensive cultivation; an agricultural assistant for dry farming; an agricultural assistant for oil seeds; and an agricultural assistant for potatoes. As the author went on to remark, "With a number of field workers attending to different functions in a group of villages, each field worker has to spend considerable time in covering his relatively wide jurisdiction."[18] This added to the expense of providing agricultural services to the villager and might on occasion subject him to conflicting advice. Furthermore, the report found that many gram sevaks thought they were relieved of their responsibilities for agricultural extension work by the regular presence of one or another of the agricultural assistants.

Public Works—While specific public works projects aroused considerable contention among local politicians, these conflicts had little to do with the organization of the zilla parishad's public works department. State regulations limited locally authorized construction projects to relatively small sums. Larger projects required action by the state bureaucracy. In either case, construction work was contracted out. The major activities of public works officials—an executive engineer at the district level; deputy engineers, who supervised public works activities for two or three talukas; and overseers, who played roles at the taluka level equivalent in status to extension officers—consisted of reviewing plans, organizing the bids on contracts, and maintaining some supervisory check on contracted work as it proceeded.

There were many complaints on the part of politicians about the slowness of the work and the way in which contracts were let, but the local bodies had little direct control over such arrangements. Politicians were likely to suggest that various officials in the service of the public works department were regularly "paid off" as part of the arrangement for a contract. This was one of the

17. At ground level, assistant gram sevaks perform the same services as gram sevaks, but they generally are recruits to the service who previously served as village secretaries. Normally, they do not have the educational qualifications of the gram sevaks. Depending on length of service, however, there may be little difference in salary scales.

18. Shri M. N. Heble, Commissioner for Administrative Reorganization, Government of Maharashtra, *Reorganization of Maharashtra Administration,* vol. 1 (Bombay: Government Central Press, 1971), p. 104 (hereafter referred to as *Heble Report).*

reasons, one informant suggested, that it was so difficult for the zilla parishad to get bidders on many contracts.

The executive engineers in both districts pointed to other reasons: the small amounts involved in contracts let by panchayati raj bodies; the complications and delays in payment; and the technical problems involved in doing construction in some of the remoter areas where the minor works contracted for were to be carried out. Indeed, both department heads pointed to the need to generate a new class of rural contractors for the kind of work being undertaken by local government bodies. As one suggested, this might mean using political connections:

> We may have a project in an interior area for only Rs. 5,000. A big contractor will simply not be interested in involving himself in the time and expense of having to go to some remote area to do such work. . . . Under the circumstances, if anyone shows an interest in pushing a project—even if he is connected with someone in the zilla parishad—we may encourage him for want of someone else. . . . Being a leader of the village at least means that a person may feel some responsibility for seeing that a project is completed.

Since much of the larger construction that went on under the supervision of the staff attached to the zilla parishad involved the utilization of state government funds under specific state planning and development grants, local bodies had to apply for state government approval of plans. This approval was granted on the basis of state priorities, with the result that local governments waited in long lines for major public works investment or attempt to jockey among themselves for favor with the minister and his bureaucracy. The situation was even more constrained where large-scale projects were involved.

Public works officials also had to contend with what they regarded as the improper demands made by politicians. As one district official commented:

> We cannot formulate plans on our own. Various interests come in the way. We are even prevented from punishing bad work. It has happened that I have levied a fine against the bad work done by a contractor and the zilla parishad may set it aside. Once the list of projects is prepared, the responsibility for prosecuting the work should be left to the executive engineers. The present difficulties are the result of political pressures, but they are also built into the zilla parishad code, which requires slowness. Some of the unnecessary steps should be eliminated.

Cooperatives and Rural Industry—One of the missions given to local government officials in the 1962 panchayati raj innovations was to promote and help to register local cooperative societies. Inspection, supervision, and regulation of the cooperative sector were functions left either to the Cooperation Department of the state government or to the cooperative infrastructure itself. With the burgeoning of cooperative institutions, extension officers for cooperatives found little to do. Another area where panchayati raj was weak was in the promotion of rural industries. There the amount of money made available was very small. What industry was started on these small sums derived mainly from traditional handicrafts or artisan skills. Such industry soon foundered for want of adequate capital, a lack of marketing skills, or problems of supply of raw materials. As funds for this purpose withered with the impending conclusion of community development subsidies, local bodies were not much moved to invest substantially in this sector.

At the district level, one official functioned in each of the two districts to coordinate the cooperatives and industries programs. One of those interviewed readily conceded that extension officer positions in the two fields ought to be either consolidated or abolished. With time on their hands, such officers were often called upon by BDOs to play a part in various mobilization schemes promoted by the state or national governments: family planning, small-scale savings, and "grow more food" campaigns. These activities amounted almost to "make-work" projects.

Social Welfare—Finally, in the office of the zilla parishad a social welfare officer, who was a member of the Education Department, was responsible for administering various schemes funded by either the state or the national government to promote educational opportunities for persons from traditionally backward communities and those of low income. He also was supposed to encourage the formation of social organizations for women, young people, and other groups in order to promote intergroup understanding and the advancement of "the backward." At the taluka level, these organizational activities fell within the province of an extension officer for social education. Where such officials continued to exist, they reported low levels of interest in their work among panchayat samiti leaders. However, there were only two regular extension officers for social education left in the whole of

Poona district in 1970 and it was likely that both of them would soon be converted into regular extension officers for education.[19]

Members of the Kolhapur zilla parishad, spurred by the president of that body, had provided funds for various minor social welfare schemes, including extremely limited old-age pensions and grants to the poor for the purchase of bicycles and eyeglasses. Even some of those members who voted for such measures were skeptical about their efficacy. One committee chairman suggested that investment in one village well would have provided more general welfare than all the minor ameliorative schemes generated by the president.

FISCAL CONSTRAINTS ON PANCHAYATI RAJ

As we have already suggested, panchayati raj institutions were highly dependent fiscally on the state government. Of Rs. 62.3 crores provided to local governments in Maharashtra in 1966-1967, Rs. 29 crores were tied to categorical grants, which were highly detailed. Another Rs. 15.8 crores went for planning and block grants, which also involved fairly strict definitions by the state government of the uses to which funds might be put. Finally, part of the remaining funds went to underwrite salaries for personnel associated with the community development program or those sent on deputation from the state government. As a consequence, the amount of "free money" made available to local governments by the government of Maharashtra was meager.

Some funds were generated locally as user charges for services provided by local bodies, but the main source of unrestricted revenue was the local cess levied as a surcharge on land revenue collected by the state government. Land revenue taxation is based on the productivity of land, but reassessment has not been undertaken in western Maharashtra since the 1930s. The state government has returned a substantial portion of the land revenue to local governments and also has permitted zilla parishads to levy a land cess of up to Rs. 1.50 for every rupee of land revenue collected. For political reasons, neither Kolhapur nor Poona politi-

19. Prior to 1970, *gram sevikas* (women village-level workers) functioned to promote social welfare activities, particularly among women. However, that service was being phased out as community development funds to underwrite social change programs were withdrawn from panchayati raj institutions.

cians wished to antagonize their rural constituents by raising the land cess to such a figure.[20] In 1970, both were levying around Rs. 1.20 per rupee of land revenue. As an incentive to local governments, the state did provide equalization grants to districts which had good performance records in levying the land cess, but this did not seem to inspire additional levies in either district.

The zilla parishads were obligated to turn over 30 percent of local cess funds to their panchayat samitis and another 30 percent to their gram panchayats. The gram panchayats had independent sources of income in the form of taxes on various local services, like water, sanitation, and electricity (where such services are provided), as well as house taxes and levies on weekly markets. While this gave the gram panchayats some flexibility in their fiscal arrangements, the situation was very different for the panchayat samitis. Those bodies were totally dependent on whatever funds were passed through to them by the zilla parishads, either as part of zilla parishad schemes or as their share of the local cess. The result is that many complaints were heard from those associated with the panchayat samitis about the fiscal incapacities of those bodies. Part of their dependence was reflected in the fact that the budgets of the panchayat samitis had to be reviewed and approved by the zilla parishad.

Because of the complexity of bureaucratic requirements involved in turning allocations into actual investments, panchayat samitis did not always spend even their budgeted amounts in a given fiscal year. In Kolhapur this led to a major dispute when the zilla parishad decided in 1963 to allocate resources slated for construction projects to panchayat samitis on a project-by-project basis, rather than turning the panchayat samitis' portion of the land cess over to them directly. Leaders at the district level argued that distributing the limited funds on a project basis would permit them to be applied where they could most immediately be put to

20. The additional funds raised when the cess was enhanced were not entirely subject to the discretion of the zilla parishad. At each level of increase, the zilla parishad was obligated to assume certain functions previously administered by the state government. Reluctance to increase the cess also reflected the feeling prevalent, particularly where sugarcane growers were politically influential, that they were already paying high taxes in the form of special water charges and a sugarcane tax which was applied to education by the state government. These taxes were raised locally but not returned proportionally to the localities.

use, rather than allowing unused funds to accumulate. Some of the more active talukas were happy with this arrangement, for during the time the practice was in effect (from about 1964 to 1969), they received more for projects like minor roadwork than might otherwise have been the case. On the other hand, those talukas which did not gain from the practice finally complained to the state government, and in 1969 the matter was decided in favor of the talukas. Not only was the zilla parishad required to turn over all future funds legally owed to the panchayat samitis but they were forced to repay past monies. Several zilla parishad members expected that some panchayat samitis would again accumulate unused funds (especially where local decision making was stalled by factional quarrels within the samiti), while others would be starved for project funds.[21]

Most panchayat samiti members (and particularly the chairmen) complained about the financial constraints on their activities and the narrow definition of authority granted them. As one chairman commented:

> We require more powers so we can handle the village level work more smoothly. Our deputy engineer can sanction work only up to Rs. 20,000. Much red tape is involved in getting the permission of the executive engineer of the zilla parishad for amounts between Rs. 20-50,000.

Complaints about the lack of fiscal autonomy and its dysfunctional consequences for programmatic performance were common also at the district level. Thus, a committee chairman in the Kolhapur zilla parishad detailed how a particular program sponsored by the state government ran into difficulties in his home constituency because of the lack of local discretion:

> Rs. 5 crores of work done under panchayat raj involves using the zilla parishad only as the agency of the state government. These schemes are chalked out by the departments of state government and the rules laid down at that level. This creates problems. In the case of *bandharas* [small dams], for example, Rs. 3,000 has been allocated for each. . . . Usually Rs. 1,500 is contributed by the zilla parishad to the local body

21. The financial position of panchayat samitis also was marginally strengthened by a ruling in 1970 that state funds previously administered through the zilla parishad to finance village approach roads would now go directly to the panchayat samitis rather than being placed in the office of the district's executive engineer.

for this construction. . . . Under present regulations, construction materials need to be brought from Bombay and supplied to the gram panchayats through the zilla parishad. Seventy-five percent of these schemes have been failures because of the rigid rules of the government. We are not allowed to change structures, shapes, or estimates. . . . If the state had given the money directly to the zilla parishad or to the gram panchayats, we could have built the bandharas according to local needs and conditions and achieved our targets much better. . . . We are blamed by the public for such failures, but it is really the fault of the state government and the departments.

Such views were by no means reserved to the elected members of the zilla parishad. Administrators in a number of local government departments also complained about the lack of discretion available to them in moving funds among categories so that they might meet the most pressing needs of the district. As they pointed out, the state allowed little flexibility to any district in deciding what its own priorities were even within a given program. Thus one young BDO remarked:

Some schemes devised by government have been thrust upon [local governments] without consultation. As a result, local people do not execute those schemes properly. . . . Schemes should be available so that if the people of a village really want a well they will come together, contribute some money, and we will give them Rs. 1,000, but the idea of setting a target of a number of wells and giving money away without certainty that people will carry out that work is a waste. . . . There is a tendency on the part of government that there should not be any break in the application of a general pattern even when the ideas they introduce are not workable in a particular place.

PROPOSALS FOR CHANGE

Two reports were commissioned by the government of Maharashtra in recent years which led to recommendations for reforms in panchayati raj. The first was a one-man survey of administrative organization in the state, written by M. N. Heble, a senior civil servant appointed in August 1968 to the newly created position of Commissioner for Administrative Reorganization. Heble's report was released in early 1971. The report dealt with various aspects of state and local administration; it devoted six chapters specifically to district administration and panchayati raj.

The second and somewhat more significant report for our purposes was that of the Evaluation Committee on Panchayati Raj appointed by the state government in February 1970. Its findings and recommendations were also made available in 1971. The eleven-member committee was headed by L. N. Bongirwar, a former civil servant who had more recently assumed the vice-chancellorship of the state's major agricultural university. The Bongirwar Committee was able to proceed expeditiously by drawing upon the findings and some of the recommendations of the Heble Report. However, it went beyond Heble both in collecting data through questionnaires sent to local bodies and by making a series of visits to selected districts. The terms of the Committee's activities were broadly stated. They included not only examination of the administrative aspects of panchayati raj but also questions bearing on the political structure of the system, including modes of election and the "powers and functions of the Subjects Committees and office-bearers of the Zilla Parishads, Panchayat Samitis and Village Panchayats."[22]

A majority of the members of the Committee were persons with backgrounds either in state administration or in educational institutions. Among the four politicians on the body, three were Congressmen; the one non-Congress politician was a woman from the Republican party. As several critics of the Committee's Report subsequently noted, it was a body that guaranteed a generally approving tone for the way the state government had managed panchayati raj. The administrative bias of Committee members may also have been responsible for the fact that the accent of the final report was on administrative proposals. Most of these proposals were essentially minor in character. Thus, despite a summary chapter of recommendations, which covers nearly forty pages, all but a few indicate broad approval of the basic structural arrangements underlying panchayati raj in Maharashtra.

The Bongirwar Committee, following in the footsteps of the Heble Report, recommended abolition of the position of extension officer for cooperatives, a severe cutback of extension officers

22. For the specific assignment given to the Committee, see Government of Maharashtra, Rural Development Department, *Report of the Evaluation Committee on Panchayati Raj* (Bombay: Government Central Press, 1971), pp. 4-5 (hereafter referred to as *Bongirwar Report*).

for industries, and elimination of the women village-level workers
(*gram sevikas*) involved in "social education."[23] While reducing
those positions in the panchayati raj service, the Bongirwar Report
called for the recruitment of an additional 7,710 persons over a
ten-year period to fill positions as gram sevaks. It stressed the need
to recruit trained college graduates for such positions.[24] The
Report also made detailed proposals for a "development service
cadre" which would consist of about seventy-five class I officers,
half of whom would be recruited by examination and half by
promotion of BDOs, to fill positions such as planning officer,
administrative officer for panchayats, and deputy CEO. Class II
would include about three hundred BDOs.[25] As for those class III
officers who were still attached to state government departments,
such as Agriculture and Education, the Committee recommended
that such persons be eligible for promotion in the development
service "if they forego their claim for promotion in their respective parent department."[26] The Committee also called for the
abolition of district and divisional selection boards and their
replacement by a local service commission for recruitment specifically for panchayat raj service.

  With respect to the committees of the zilla parishad, the
Report recommended alterations in the kinds of persons co-opted
to serve alongside elected members on specialized committees. It
commented unfavorably on the practice of co-opting persons who

23. These recommendations merely underscored actions that the state
government was already in the process of taking.
  24. *Bongirwar Report*, p. 51. Heble recommended that agricultural assistants, gram sevaks, and assistant gram sevaks recruited before 1962 be
immediately absorbed into a common gram sevak cadre after due training.
Heble Report, pp. 107-108. The Bongirwar Committee was silent on this
question of reforming the gram sevak system.
  25. The Bongirwar Committee thought it unwise to include the CEO in
the district cadre. They disagreed with a suggestion by Heble that BDOs be
promoted to class I officers. *Bongirwar Report*, pp. 57-58. They did favor a
system by which class I and class II officers should be transferred in consultation with the state government's Department of Rural Development.
  26. Ibid., p. 58. Again, this was a case where the Committee merely
confirmed a policy which the state government was already beginning to
implement. By late 1970, class III officers had been asked to choose between
service in a district cadre or in the state government. Since positions in the
state governments were limited, this meant persons without seniority or
without special technical qualifications would either have to accept district
service or leave the bureaucracy.

did not have technical qualifications to committees where expertise was needed. The Committee reaffirmed a recent policy established by the state government which had created a zilla parishad committee on social welfare. (Members of that committee are drawn from scheduled caste and tribal members of the zilla parishad.) That committee joined the existing committee structure consisting of committees on education, public works, finance, agriculture and cooperatives, and a standing (executive) committee. The Bongirwar Committee also favored the creation of a new committee on animal husbandry and dairying, which would incorporate schemes still being operated through that state government.

While the Report discussed problems of political control, there were few specific recommendations for changes in political structure. The only significant one was a recommendation that taluka panchayat samitis consist of village chairmen or deputy chairmen elected on a broader franchise than previously.[27] Those persons from the taluka elected to the zilla parishad would continue to sit on the panchayat samitis along with certain cooperative officials and others either co-opted to the body or serving there on an ex-officio basis.

On the whole, the Report took for granted the existing separation of political and administrative roles and made it clear that the CEO was to be the superior authority in day-to-day administrative matters. This reaffirmation of faith was tempered by a certain evenhandedness, however, in the way the Committee viewed the performance of politicians in panchayat raj and their relations with the administrative structure. While noting that the panchayati raj system was bringing forward a younger, better-educated leadership drawn predominantly from agricultural backgrounds, it merely expressed regret at the failure of the poorest sections of society to be represented in proportion to numbers. It accepted this as inevitable.

> There is . . . nothing to indicate the growth of proper leadership is being discouraged in the present form of election to the serious disadvantage

27. The Report suggested that candidates for seats on the panchayat samitis (other than zilla parishad and co-opted members) continue to be drawn from the ranks of chairmen and vice-chairmen of gram panchayats. Instead of electing such members through an electoral college consisting only of others of their kind, however, the Bongirwar Committee recommended a popular vote. *Bongirwar Report*, pp. 19-20.

of any particular minority community or the comparatively less afflu-ent people, at least at the village and Panchayat Samiti level.[28]

On the whole, the Committee found local political leaders to be remarkably well informed about existing programs and ener-getic in performing the tasks assigned to them. The most obvious danger to be guarded against was the tendency of local politicians to strain the limits of their authority and to exploit the potential for "a show of power, favouritism and nepotism, if not corrup-tion." The Report attributed this to the "pleasure obtained in interfering with the day-to-day administration . . . as a show of power to the people around or obliging certain functionaries in the executive."[29]

The blame for interference was by no means placed entirely on the politicians, however. The politically attuned members of the Evaluation Committee demonstrated sensitivity to the com-plaints of elected office-holders in panchayati raj institutions. Thus, the Report referred in one place to problems which arose from administrators who had "shown signs of becoming at times, apathetic, irresponsible, bureaucratic and indicative of all disre-spect for the elected leadership."[30] Indeed, one of the bluntest passages in the Report complained of a lack of administrative dynamism. In some cases, the members noted, local administrators had failed "to project themselves as agencies for the welfare of the common man." Indeed, the Report continued,

> The anachronistic, die-hard, bureaucratic, wooden-headed approach appears to linger still in many places, and the imminent danger is that these traits may unwittingly be imbibed by the new entrants as well. This may be one of the reasons why people choose to approach their representatives directly even in respect of matters regarding which substantial relief can, if they so desire, be granted by officials.[31]

The evenhanded tone of the Committee was apparent, as well, in the area where the greatest controversy surrounded its

28. Ibid., p. 152.
29. Ibid., p. 155.
30. Ibid. In the same vein, Heble commented on a process of textbook review which "has all the characteristics of a steeple chase where the number of stages through which the text-book has to pass before it emerges trium-phant is legion." He noted that texts for the final standards "are required to go only through a mere five stages against about eleven which are required for books intended for the lower standards." *Heble Report,* p. 302.
31. *Bongirwar Report,* pp. 218-219.

work—the question of educational reorganization. Teachers organizations, bureaucrats in the Department of Education, and officials in many of the panchayati raj bodies had argued before the Committee either that education should be withdrawn entirely from local bodies or that greater insulation from political interference should be provided. The Report reviewed what it felt to be the major reasons given in support of separation:

> (i) due to the conflicts between officials and non-officials in matters of transfers, postings, punishments, etc. the work of the Education Department has greatly suffered, (ii) since non-officials are preoccupied with matters of transfers of teachers and other staff of the Education Department they are unable to pay proper attention to "development" activities, (iii) there is a decline in the quality of education on account of laxity in inspection, (iv) there is indiscipline in the teaching staff itself, (v) there is general inefficiency and indiscipline on account of the various malpractices in the Zilla Parishads, (vi) the Zilla Parishad leadership is of ordinary calibre and does not have sufficient understanding of the education policies and is unable to solve the myriad problems in this field and pay rational and scientific attention to educational development, (vii) the Panchayati Raj bodies are "election-oriented" and primary teachers have become pliable instruments for election campaigns of the office-bearers.[32]

Despite this impressive list of charges, the Committee did not feel greatly moved by them. Returning education to a bureaucratically dominated home in the state government, it recognized, would be a direct denial of the purposes of panchayati raj. The charges levied by educators and bureaucrats were not entirely warranted, they asserted. "We have found that . . . some of the complaints . . . were highly exaggerated and that in fact the role of the non-official machinery as a watch-dog and policy-maker of the educational organization has been quite beneficial and usefully effective."[33]

While not supporting the withdrawal of education from local influence, the Bongirwar Report did recommend a modest increase in the insulation of educational affairs from the zilla parishad. This was to be done by establishing a body equivalent to the school boards which exist in Maharashtrian cities. Rather than being composed of seven members of the zilla parishad and two co-

32. Ibid., p. 106.
33. Ibid., p. 107.

opted educational specialists (the existing pattern of education committees in the zilla parishads), the new bodies were to consist of thirteen members. Two were to be co-opted on the basis of special qualifications. The remainder were to be elected by members of the zilla parishad both from their own members and from outsiders. While this might permit the zilla parishad to select only from among its own members, the common practice in most cities has been to include some non-members. The Committee felt such a body would be somewhat detached from the general activities of the zilla parishad. The powers vested in the new education committee would remain much like those for the zilla parishad body though with perhaps greater flexibility in setting budgetary needs and personnel policy.

On the controversial issue of transfers, the Bongirwar Committee advocated the retention of a 10 percent annual rate for transfers in a district, with half of that total being assigned to the panchayat samitis for their determination. They continued to assert a role for zilla parishad and panchayati samiti office-bearers in decisions on such transfers. The Committee also supported the practice of posting teachers at least twenty miles from their home villages.[34] Finally, the Report stressed the importance of assuring teachers that they would be assigned to a given location for at least five years, though transfers should be required after seven.[35]

REACTIONS TO THE BONGIRWAR REPORT

Despite the considerable effort that went into the compilation of data for the two reports and the thoughtfulness reflected in the comments of Commissioner Heble and the Evaluation Committee, their recommendations were of limited immediate impact.[36] Most

34. Based on responses from twenty-four districts, the Committee reported that at least 14 percent of all teachers were posted in their home villages. The figures were 16 percent for Poona and 26.8 percent for Kolhapur district. Only Sangli district showed a higher percentage than Kolhapur, and that was a remarkable 39.8 percent. Ibid., p. 303.

35. Ibid., p. 105.

36. At the end of 1970, a number of rules were changed, allowing vice-chairmen of panchayat samitis to serve on zilla parishad committees and permitting greater flexibility to zilla parishads in their assignment of chairmanships in the various committees. *Times of India,* 12 December 1970.

MLAs and zilla parishad members interviewed in early 1973 had not read the Evaluation Committee report, though it had been available for over a year. Many had never heard of its recommendations. The reaction of the president of the Poona zilla parishad was typical, however, of those who were familiar with it:

> [The Committee] generally praised the working of the system and made only recommendations for technical changes. They felt a power of sanctioning works should be taken away from the president, that more money should go to the work of the education committee, such things. But, on the whole, the recommendations were not major. Nothing was done and nothing will be done about changing education. That was a demand of the teachers but nothing will come of it. It is the kind of thing of which the opposition complains, but the opposition is always making complaints and trying to create tensions.

A senior office-holder in Kolhapur offered a generally favorable set of comments on the Report but balanced those with some negative ones:

> Most of the ideas are useful but there are so many economic implications in the running of the zilla parishads [that the Report overlooks]. The Report is mainly concerned with changes in administration. . . . [I]nsufficient money is being given for the discretion of the zilla parishad and the panchayat samitis. Even though the system is more

---

In May 1973, the government announced plans to provide full payment of the salaries of officials associated with the zilla parishads rather than the 75-90 percent grant that had been the standard previously for state employees deputed to the local bodies. The state leadership also affirmed its intention to inaugurate the operation of a state development cadre from August 15. The service, as one report noted, "would include the posts of the chief executive officer, revenue officer, planning officer, engineers, and block development officers." The piece added, "While creating this cadre, the zilla parishad employees would be given due promotions." *Times of India,* 1 May 1973.

Later, in July 1973, the Chief Minister announced that the state government would assume not only the cost of salaries of the new cadre but would cover all costs of the administrative establishment, including travel allowances and other contingent expenditures. He also declared that 1,500 agricultural graduates would be recruited as gram sevaks and trained under a national Planning Commission scheme for the educated employed. Contrary to the recommendations of Commissioner Heble, however, these gram sevaks would be assigned special duties, such as overseeing cotton and sugarcane development. *Times of India,* 6 July 1973.

progressive than in most states, still we have little say in how money is spent. A large part of it simply goes for administration.

Several informants whose political memories went back to the period before the consolidation of district school boards and district local boards were not sanguine about recommendations for what seemed to them a return to the earlier system. A man who had served on the Kolhapur District Local Board and on the state consultative committee for Maharashtra, which established the panchayati raj pattern, remarked:

> After various experiments with district local boards and school boards, we have settled on the present pattern for panchayati raj, and it is a pattern that is being followed more or less throughout India. Some say we should go on making changes but there are always complaints that one can raise with any pattern. When you are trying to execute policy, it is very difficult if you keep changing it all the time.

The Minister of State for Education of Maharashtra, who was interviewed in 1973, expressed a point of view which indicated little likelihood that the state would endorse a major change in the relationship between educational administration and panchayati raj institutions:

> There is no planned move to change the pattern of working [with respect to education]. The people of Maharashtra are so aware of their voice in democracy that they would not let the system come back under official control. They resist interference by officials and insist on a democratic way of administering education. It is impossible to go against their wish.[37]

As best I could determine, the Evaluation Committee was brought into being because the Chief Minister, Vasantrao Naik, who had been involved in the original design of panchayati raj in Maharashtra, decided that a general review was in order. Its activation did not reflect the efforts of any organized set of interest groups in Maharashtrian society nor did any ambitious political leader see it as a vehicle to advance a political career. At the time the Committee was created to conduct its review, there were few overwhelming forces behind proposals for change. No doubt, there were a host of minor dissatisfactions with respect to specific features of the system. More broadly, local politicians felt they did

37. Interview, Mrs. Prabha Rao, 30 January 1973.

not have enough authority; bureaucrats posted to local governments did not like the kind of political influence that politicians were able to exercise. However, few state politicians apparently felt their own interests would be served by expanding the scope of local government powers; if anything, further decentralization of power from the state governments to local government might mean watering down those powers which individual state leaders had fought so hard to capture.

Thus, despite occasional bows to Gandhian sentiments, state leaders were halfhearted in their commitment to "democratic decentralization." Abetted by a state bureaucracy which seemed to distrust local politicians more than it did state political leaders (with whom bureaucrats had learned to work fairly comfortably), the compulsions for structural change were insignificant. Some marginal reforms were introduced, but nothing was done to alter the structural arrangement of basic political or socioeconomic interests in rural Maharashtra, which continued to be served through the panchayati raj system.

TEN

Local Opportunism and National Policy Goals

It may be useful to restate the major themes developed in the course of the present study. First, a large part of our attention has been devoted to a political history of the policy process in Maharashtra over the past twenty years. That examination has revealed how national and state policies in the areas of education, cooperatives, and panchayati raj helped introduce new institutions and new political relationships into rural Maharashtra. Our review of socioeconomic and political changes in a portion of rural India also has been intimately intertwined with a second major theme: how the modified political system of Maharashtra has given considerable scope to ambitious local politicians to use the resources of the new institutions as opportunity structures to further their own personal ends. Political careers drawing on such resources have been based in districts of the state, but the political and policy ramifications of local ambition have radiated to state and national arenas of politics. As an extension of these two themes, a third may be stated: a major consequence of turning societal resources over to local actors on terms significantly influenced by their personal preferences and ambitions has been to make the larger political system increasingly reflective of the interests of an expansive local elite as against the interests of the larger society. The individual reader must judge whether that has been a desirable outcome. In the rest of this chapter, however, I have proceeded on the assumption that it has not been.

By 1973, when field work for the study was completed, it could well be argued that Maharashtrian rural politics represented an effective example of "democratic elitism" at work.[1] A situation existed in which a rather small segment of the population dominated the political mechanisms of the society through their influence over instrumentalities normally associated with political

1. Peter Bachrach, *The Theory of Democratic Elitism* (Boston: Little, Brown, 1967).

democracy: a party system which allowed some scope to new political entrants; competitive elections (albeit, in the case of Maharashtra, ones that were dominated by a single party); and multiple forums for the expression of divergent opinions, most notably through various print media. In addition, public policies verbally supported by state and national leadership were implemented only to the extent that they reflected the preferences of the local elite.

Only marginal influence over the implementation of such policies and in the general deployment of societal resources was exercised by the great majority of the Indian population. It would have required a very different kind of leadership than Mrs. Gandhi and the Chavan-Naik group in Maharashtra were then willing and able to assert to bring about a more equitable distribution of economic resources and of political opportunities and political influence. Instead, most of the actions of leadership worked to strengthen the hands of the expansive elite.

Institutionalizing the Expansive Elite

Creation by the national and state governments of cooperative mechanisms, educational societies, and local government institutions had several consequences. One important effect was to provide the ambitious with resources by which they have been able to enhance their political careers. Insofar as the new institutions were absorbed into the fabric of economic and social relationships in the countryside, they also brought about a new structure of political life. By the standards of some students of political development, most notably Samuel P. Huntington, they appeared to contribute to political development by "institutionalizing" the rural areas. As Huntington treats it, the process of institutionalization is one by which "organizations and procedures acquire value and stability." That seems to be an appropriate description of institution building in Maharashtra. The level of institutionalization of any political system, he goes on to suggest, "can be defined by the adaptability, complexity, autonomy and coherence of its organizations and procedures."[2]

There may be some question about the extent to which the institutions introduced into the Maharashtrian countryside during

2. Samuel P. Huntington, *Political Order in Changing Societies* (New Haven and London: Yale University Press, 1968).

the past two decades conformed specifically to Huntington's four criteria.[3] There is little question, however, that activation of the institutions described in previous chapters introduced complexity into rural life and created a basis for the autonomy of individual political actors. As a result, both locally and at the state and national levels, persons based in a variety of local economic, political, and social organizations struggled to affect processes of policy making and policy implementation.

In comparison with the restricted decision-making processes that existed under the British, of course, the number and complexity of institutional interests represented in politics in the post-independence era increased considerably. New educational institutions, new forms of economic organization and expanded systems of local government provided additional life chances for individuals. It is less certain whether the absolute quantity of opportunities kept pace with population growth or, equally important, whether additional opportunities were distributed to new kinds of actors in the political system or simply divided among members of the prevailing political stratum whose roots were deep in the established leadership of the villages.[4]

However much one may be inclined to paint the process of political participation as an expanding one after 1947 or however

3. Given the uncertainty of language that one encounters in Huntington, it is not always clear what he means by terms like "adaptability" and "coherence." Since he varies between speaking of the characteristics of particular organizations, on the one hand, and the behavior of what may better be treated as systems of institutions, on the other, the application of his terminology to specific cases is difficult to be sure about. It could be argued, for example, that a "complex" institutional system in which numerous individuals and institutions operate in a relatively autonomous fashion is inconsistent with both institutional and societal "coherence." In a rather different fashion, it might be contended that the adaptation of a particular institution to localized circumstances may prove to be in conflict with system-level adaptation. In the present study, it may be the consequences of "successful" local adaptation for national system performance that are at issue. For a discussion of this problem in the case of French politics where "overinstitutionalization" is identified as an important blockage to change, see Mark Kesselman, "Overinstitutionalization and Political Constraint," *Comparative Politics* 36 (October 1970): 21-44.

4. The latter view is adopted in Anthony T. Carter, *Elite Politics in Rural India: Political Stratification and Political Alliances in Western Maharashtra* (Cambridge: Cambridge University Press, 1974); also see Jayant Lele, *Patriarch, Patrons and Pluralists* (unpublished manuscript, 1974).

open one may wish to suggest the expansive elite was to the entry of new individuals into that stratum, it remains clear that a considerable status gap continued to exist between the local elite, which dominated the rewards associated with rural institutionalization, and the vast majority of the rural population. Some members of that larger population—small landholders, tenant farmers, landless laborers, artisans, petty traders—might opt out of the existing rural social order. Some sought equivalent (i.e., low-status) employment in the city; a few took advantage of educational opportunities to rise slightly in the occupational system—mainly, again, in the city. For the most part, however, the configuration of economic positions in rural India has not involved any significant movement since independence.[5]

Thus, while opportunities for some few may have expanded as a result of the institutionalization of the countryside, the total effect was hardly a general movement toward equality of opportunity and even less toward equality of results.[6] In the interstices of new institutional arrangements, individuals might find the means for making advances in personal status. Those who began with such advantages as substantial landholdings, however, probably gained disproportionately from the various institutional and technological innovations that took place.

Although it is true that a few persons of little education, little property, and traditionally low ritual status did manage to gain positions in local institutions like the zilla parishads and panchayat samitis, lacking the social status and the economic and political prerequisites normally associated with such positions, they were generally unable to wield substantial influence. (This was the situation characteristic, in particular, of those tribals, ex-untouchables, and women elected or co-opted to local bodies.)

5. As one economist has written, "In total, there is little support for the proposition that inequalities are narrowing in India; the opposite possibility, that the personal income distribution is widening finds stronger support." Wilfred Malenbaum, *Modern India's Economy* (Columbus, Ohio: Charles E. Merrill, 1971), p. 130.

6. For a discussion of the differences between equality of opportunity and equality of results in the American case, see Daniel Bell, "On Meritocracy and Equality," *The Public Interest* 29 (Fall 1972): 29-68; and Robert Nisbet, "The Pursuit of Equality," *The Public Interest* 35 (Spring 1974): 103-120. The latter is an examination of the more egalitarian approach espoused by John Rawls in *A Theory of Justice* (Cambridge, Mass.: Belknap Press, 1971).

On the whole, such important local institutions tended to be dominated by men who had accumulated considerable local standing through advanced education or through the control of other institutional, economic, or political resources.[7]

No doubt, there were a few individuals in the two districts studied who had risen from quite humble origins to hold positions of local influence, but these few had done so while also acquiring the other correlates of high political status. Their rise may have been helped by the status uncertainties that accompanied the period of nationalist activity and the early years of system change after independence. Thus, for a time the two districts witnessed the emergence of a class of "new men," like Ratnappa Kumbhar, Balasaheb Desai, and Mamasaheb Mohol, who were unusually well placed to exercise influence in the creation and exploitation of new institutions. Having participated in that process, they and other members of the expansive elite subsequently developed patterns of behavior which made entry by others into institutions more difficult.

Thus, despite some flexibility in the system, a strong relationship existed among social standing, economic position, and political leadership in rural Maharashtra. The farmer with a larger piece of land was more likely to invest in new technology, to commercialize his agricultural production, to send his children to college, to improve his standard of living, and to take a hand in the politics of his village and taluka and in his local cooperative institutions. In addition to exercising considerable personal influence over how his less fortunate neighbors gained their livelihoods, he also was able to direct the way they cast their votes in presumably democratic elections.[8]

7. Studies of panchayati raj in Maharashtra which support this point include Jayant Lele, "Theory and Practice of Democratic Politics in Maharashtra" (Paper presented to the Maharashtra Studies Group, Ann Arbor, Mich., 27-29 April 1973); John E. Robertson, "Political Recruitment at the Zilla Parishad Level: Chanda District, Maharashtra" (Paper presented to the Maharashtra Studies Group, Philadelphia, Pa., 5-7 May 1972); Lawrence L. Shrader and Ram Joshi, "Zilla Parishad Elections in Maharashtra and the District Political Elite," *Asian Survey* 3 (March 1973): 143-156; and V. M. Sirsikar, *The Rural Elite in a Developing Society* (New Delhi: Orient Longman, 1970).

8. For Maharashtra, see Lele, *Patriarchs, Patrons and Pluralists*; for other parts of India, see David J. Elkins, *Electoral Participation in a South Asian Context* (Durham, N.C.: Carolina Academic Press, 1975); and John W.

My argument that advantages have flowed in a cumulative fashion to a restricted segment of the rural population of Maharashtra should not be taken to mean that all members of the expansive elite shared exactly the same social spaces in rural society or that they sought to use the resources available to them in precisely the same fashion.[9] A few major political actors, like the Kakades in Poona district or Udaisingh Gaikwad in Kolhapur, controlled over two or three hundred acres under those legal subterfuges commonly employed to counteract even the mild land reforms which have been enacted in Maharashtra.[10] On the other hand, some of the largest landholders in the two districts played only minor roles in politics.

The vast majority of political actors with whom we have dealt had holdings which were rather modest by American standards. Twenty to forty acres was considered a substantial piece of land. What is more significant for our purposes is that such holdings provided them with the means—including both the economic surplus and the leisure time—to engage in political careers. In some instances, this was made possible by the activities of family members who supervised actual farming operations; others looked after the activities of their farm laborers themselves. For the most part, those who took an active part in political life did

---

Gartell, "Development and Social Stratification in India: the Structure of Inequality in Andhra Pradesh" (Ph.D. diss., University of Wisconsin-Madison, 1973). These studies point to some of the social aspects of the voting process.

9. This is one of the issues raised in the debate over community power structures in the United States—the extent to which power resources in particular circumstances are cumulative and reinforcing or, alternately, noncumulative (often meaning specific to particular policy sectors) and societally diffuse. For a useful review of the studies which have treated this problem, see David Ricci, *Community Power and Democratic Theory* (New York: Random House, 1971), esp. pp. 133-135 and 166-170.

10. These laws vary among the regions of Maharashtra and take into account such factors as the amount of irrigated land held (including the source of such irrigation) and the quality of the soils. A variety of legal and political devices have been developed for subverting such laws. A former Minister of Agriculture in the Maharashtra government and more recently MPCC President, P. K. Sawant, conceded that when the major laws were enacted around 1961, the state government anticipated that there would be 1.1 million acres available for redistribution. As it turned out, less than 500,000 acres were obtained and those mainly of a marginal quality. Interview, P. K. Sawant, 18 February 1973. Based on the total cropped area of Maharashtra, this comes to less than 1 percent of the land.

not physically participate in the cultivation of their own lands, though to keep up appearances (and, again, for the sake of the land reform laws), they formally claimed that they maintained an active interest in the management of their land.[11]

The economic means to engage in political activities have been associated with other factors as well. As we noted in earlier chapters, Maharashtra is particularly ill-favored geographically. Among its problems are a lack of irrigation potential, though even the potential available has not been fully exploited. (According to official estimates, only 8 percent of agricultural land was irrigated in 1973; perhaps 25 percent could have been brought under some form of irrigation.[12]) Most agriculture must depend on monsoons, which are unreliable in India. Those farmers served either by flow irrigation, by lift-irrigation schemes, or by irrigation from wells are therefore in a particularly advantageous position. Thus, it is significant that among politicians interviewed in Poona and Kolhapur, a disproportionate number had access to some form of irrigation, at least for a portion of their lands. Irrigable lands or lands with an assured supply of monsoon water make it possible for a farmer to produce a marketable surplus with a relatively small holding of even ten to fifteen acres. Such holdings do require the credit necessary to invest in modern agriculture if they are to maximize

11. One of the major aims of the early land reforms was to remove the absentee landlord from the countryside. In Maharashtra, where the absentee landlord was not as important a factor as in many parts of northern and central India, the law had the effect of formalizing the expulsion of Brahman and other urban-based interests from the countryside. It is my impression that the anti-Brahman riots of 1948 heightened the fears of those Brahmans with rural landholdings sufficiently to make them willing to sell off their claims rather cheaply even before tenancy laws went into effect. Their fears may have been compounded by the leftist-sounding rhetoric of post-independence political actors, including the PWP. In contrast, those Marathas and other non-Brahmans who held fast to their land claims during this period had little to fear from the land tenancy laws. Some interviewers complained to me of having disposed of land (mainly what they assumed was unusable land) in anticipation of land reform before they realized the profit that might come from investment in new technologies or additional irrigation.

12. Maharashtra is among the least irrigated of the Indian states. The percentage of irrigated area to total cropped area is about 7.5 as against 45.6 percent in Tamil Nadu, 44 percent in the Punjab, 27.9 percent in Uttar Pradesh, and an all-India average of 19.5 percent. These figures are from data provided to me in 1973 by personnel of the Maharashtra Land Development Bank.

their profitability. It is in the distribution of credit to acquire necessary "inputs" at low interest rates that cooperative institutions have come to play an especially important economic and political role in the Maharashtrian countryside.

Like other rural elites which have responded positively to the incursions of capitalist methods of agriculture, the expansive elite in rural Maharashtra reacted with enthusiasm to new forms of rural economic organization and to related innovations in technology. Furthermore, it accepted and made use of rural political institutions introduced from above that were more democratic in form (if not always in content) than the kinds of political arrangements that prevailed in rural India earlier. Even as the local elite made room for the ambitions of a few talented men of low status and transformed itself to a degree in order to adapt to political and economic innovations, it worked to constrain the redistributive effects of new programs in order to bend such programs to its own preferences. In a fundamental sense, then, the expansive rural elite has not been an innovative force. Rather, it has been a mechanism for exploiting opportunities induced into the local situation from the outside by nationally and internationally oriented bureaucratic and political elites. This points to a problem that writers like Huntington have tended to overlook in the emphasis they have placed on institutionalization as the route to political development. For institutionalization is a double-edged political weapon, which can stunt political change at a certain level of development rather than foster it.[13]

POLITICAL AMBITION AND OPPORTUNITY STRUCTURES

Research on Indian politics during the past two decades has reflected a certain ambivalence about the uses of power on the part of both political actors and the social scientists who study

13. The argument developed here and in the rest of the chapter represents an attempt to come to terms with both Huntington's understanding of the process of political development and with the comparative rural pre-conditions to revolution stated in Barrington Moore, Jr., *The Social Origins of Dictatorship and Democracy* (Boston: Beacon Press, 1967). Unfortunately, Moore's treatment of the Indian situation is so factually weak (for example, his emphasis on the resistance of the caste system to economic modernization) that it is not a particularly useful empirical guide to analysis of the materials discussed here.

them. Indeed, as part of a general tendency among those social scientists trained in the behavioral mode there has been a notable reluctance, until recently, to come to grips with the human motives which accompany the pursuit of ambition. Thus, political scientists have sought explanations for political behavior primarily in economic factors, cultural identifications, and social origins. Even the father of ambition theory, Harold Lasswell, originally associated the predisposition to political action with various forms of psychopathology.[14]

In a well-known essay, Myron Weiner attributed to Indians a peculiar ambivalence about power.[15] However, I would contend that the Indian culture is no more peculiar in this respect than the American. Anyone familiar with the history of the Progressive movement in the United States and the assault mounted against party organizations at the turn of the century or with recent reforms in the Democratic party should recognize the extent to which there has been a consistent flight both in analysis and life from "politics" and thus from recognition of a contention among men which may be derived, at least in part, from a "nature" which men choose to express through political activity.

Even among those modern political analysts who appreciate that the pursuit of power is part of any social activity that goes on in a nation, there has been a certain unwillingness to recognize the possibility that ambition may assume an independent character of its own. Perhaps the seeking of power has not seemed ethically justifiable in contemporary societies. Certainly, theorists of social-ist societies have been as reluctant as others to treat ambition as an important independent variable in understanding political life. Social science, in the main, has followed the thinking of "modern" men generally in adopting a notion that ambition must necessarily be a means to other ends.[16] Sometimes ambition is seen to be

14. Harold D. Lasswell, *Psychopathology and Politics* (Chicago: University of Chicago Press, 1930); also see his *Power and Personality* (New York: Norton, 1948). For more recent treatments of ambition, see Joseph A. Schlesinger, *Ambition and Politics* (Chicago: Rand-McNally, 1966); and Kenneth Prewitt, *The Recruitment of Political Leaders* (Indianapolis, Ind., and New York: Bobbs-Merrill, 1970).

15. Myron Weiner, "Struggle Against Power: Notes on Indian Political Behaviour," reprinted in his *Political Change in South Asia* (Calcutta: Firma K. L. Mukhopadhyay, 1963), pp. 153-165.

16. It is her treatment of ambition as an unimportant factor in under-standing political factionalism that makes the approach taken by Carras in her

cloaked with what are taken to be ideological trappings; alternately, it is assumed that ambition must be in the service of goals
which will benefit larger collectivities.

This form of antiambitional thinking has certainly had a
strong acceptance in the *rhetoric* of Indian society. Like American
politicians, few Indian politicians profess to assign a prominent
place to ambition in their activities for higher office or for domination over large groups of men or substantial institutional resources. They do recognize the play of such factors in politics, but
that recognition commonly appears in the form of attributing
ambitional motives to their rivals. For the most part, such motives
are evaluated in negative terms.

In focusing on ambition, of course, there is a danger that one
will not take seriously other goals which ambitious actors have
pursued. In the present study, for example, these included: the
collective goal of group status improvement associated with the
non-Brahman movement; the collective symbolic goal of an independent state for speakers of Marathi and those who share in their
culture; and, more problematically, the goal of national development in areas such as education, agricultural investment, and
governmental participation. Although the latter goal was promoted as a way of developing and distributing benefits to society
as a whole, a disproportionate share of these benefits have flowed
to the more ambitious members of society. In recent circumstances, ambition also has been intimately tied to policy goals. In a
sense, it has been the energy as well as the vehicle—the means as
well as part of the end system—by which political and socioeconomic change has been encouraged in the Maharashtrian countryside and elsewhere in rural India.

A major problem for any regime is how to develop and
employ societal structures so as to harness ambition in ways which
support the policy goals sought by leadership and, perhaps more
important, sustain the regime itself. Adaptation of ambition to

---

study of factions in the zilla parishads of Maharashtra ultimately unpersua-
sive. See Mary C. Carras, *The Dynamics of Indian Political Factions* (Cambridge: Cambridge University Press, 1972). For a critique of both the theory
and the findings of that research, see my "Sources of District Congress
Factionalism in Maharashtra," *Economic and Political Weekly,* 19 August
1972, pp. 1725-1746. For one study of the mix of factors that encourage
factionalism, see Paul R. Brass, *Factional Politics in an Indian State: The
Congress Party in Uttar Pradesh* (Berkeley and Los Angeles: University of
California Press, 1965).

societal purposes may take many forms. On the whole, Indian political leaders selected mechanisms for the expression of ambition which asked very little of the ambitious in return. Expanded opportunities in education and in local educational institutions, new structures of credit distribution and agricultural productivity, new forms of rural local government—none of these involved the imposition of radically new values. Rather, such policies built upon the values which already existed among local elites, and their implementation was hedged about by values associated with localism and decentralized political influence which had developed earlier in Indian society. As a result, support among established or aspiring persons from locally dominant socioeconomic and political strata was readily forthcoming, especially once the new institutions began to show signs of carrying both political and personal material value. Insofar as such policies either developed a potential latent in the countryside or drew directly upon existent local leadership, they did not threaten existing social relationships or the interests of most members of the dominant local elites. They also did not involve any reciprocity from local beneficiaries in the form of higher taxes on increased productivity, commitment to further change, or more stringent standards of party loyalty. On the contrary, we have seen a number of instances of local dissidence against state and national leaderships which not only went unpunished but in some cases were rewarded.

Obviously, where a political actor has tied his or her ambitions to the structure of existing opportunities, it is largely unnecessary for him or her to be concerned with a set of ideal possibilities (an "ideology") which he/she feels must be pursued in order to enhance personal prestige or political power. In the circumstances that existed in India until recently, the pattern of democratic elitism fostered a way of thinking among members of the politically active stratum which, for the most part, de-fused radical ideologies by providing opportunities to most ambitious political actors.

Such an assertion admittedly does gloss over, perhaps too readily, the reality of radical movements which appeared in the Indian countryside during the 1960s.[17] Efforts to mobilize the

17. In that connection, see the various contributions to Paul R. Brass and Marcus F. Franda, eds., *Radical Politics in South Asia* (Cambridge, Mass.: MIT Press, 1973).

landless and the marginal farmer met with temporary success in a few areas, but these minor successes were soon suppressed by the use of the military and the police, strongly backed by local elites. The expansive elite thus proved to be a much tougher and better-organized force than had been the case in other societies which have been challenged by radical movements. [18] In a fundamental sense, it provided a conservative substratum for a supposedly liberal national state that had developed in India since independence, a support structure which was rewarded by that state through the investments made in rural economic development and the freedom given to the personal ambitions of its members.

This argument necessarily requires raising an additional theoretical point. While the nature of contemporary Maharashtrian society gave rise to an ambitional system which rewarded the pursuit of individual self-interest, ambition theory must also take account of that kind of ambition which is expressed through the identification of one's self with the interests of a larger collectivity. Throughout this study, no doubt, we have emphasized the behavior of individuals whose primary concern was with their own personal advantage, but in many instances there are also actors present who combine the assertion of personal will (and personal worth) with striving to attain realization of a "cause." From an earlier time, a few figures like Gandhi and Nehru come to mind as exemplars of an ambition which was closely tied to larger social purposes. [19] More recently, many of those radicals associated with

18. In keeping with the model developed by Moore, *Social Origins,* the Indian situation during that period began to take on the characteristics sometimes associated with authoritarian regimes despite its continuing outward appearances of liberalism.

19. It would be interesting, for example, to identify more clearly than has been done the motivational roots of Nehru's resistance to the challenges mounted by Sardar Vallabhhai Patel and his followers to the authority Nehru attempted to wield in the Congress party after independence. A narrative of the events is available in Stanley A. Kochanek, *The Congress Party of India* (Princeton: Princeton University Press, 1968), esp. pp. 27-74. Gandhi's efforts to maintain a personal following during the nationalist movement under the strain of ideological, personal, and regional pressures are suggested in many studies of the period. See, most recently, Judith Brown, *Gandhi's Rise to Power* (Cambridge: Cambridge University Press, 1972). Unfortunately, that study places more emphasis on how Gandhi used power than on his motives for seeking power. Some aspects of that are reflected in the recent psychological studies of Gandhi. Erik Erikson, *Gandhi's Truth* (New

revolutionary movements in pockets of urban and rural India exhibited similar characteristics. (It is problematic whether Indira Gandhi's actions can be viewed in the same light.)

The identification of a cause with one's self is, of course, also a recipe for considerable conflict among leaders and followers. Unfortunately, for the analyst, it is almost impossible to be certain in any given instance how much conflicts over ends or means are derived from differences over doctrinal points as such and how much they are associated with the personal gratification and the self-worth which are achieved through the insistence of leaders upon the inherent superiority of their own policy preferences.[20] For either or both reasons, of course, ideology has a potent capacity for producing and exacerbating conflict. To the extent that the leader embodies a cause, of course, his or her acquisition of a following and the advancement of that cause may be linked to the personal collection and expenditure of power resources.

Whatever one may think of the exceptional cases, most of the Maharashtrian politicians with whom we have been dealing were not leaders in the mold of Gandhi and Nehru or the revolutionists of the 1960s. They were not fighting for a discernible cause. Even Y. B. Chavan was not so much a compelling public figure leading a goal-oriented party as he was a highly respected organizer and conciliator. The scene in Maharashtra might have lent itself to greater ideological appeals as it did elsewhere in India, but few politicians in the state, particularly those in the Congress, made more than passing verbal commitments to a set of articulated goals. Latent in both their behavior and their attitudes was a set of principles, no doubt, but they were rarely enunciated as a coherent ideology.[21] Nevertheless, certain behavioral principles can be

---

York: W. W. Norton, 1969); and Lloyd I. Rudolph and Susanne Hoeber Rudolph, *The Modernity of Tradition* (Chicago: University of Chicago Press, 1967), part 2.

20. On recent conflicts among personalities and among doctrines on the Indian left, see Brass and Franda, *Radical Politics;* Marcus F. Franda, *Radical Politics in West Bengal* (Cambridge, Mass., and London: MIT Press, 1971); and Mohan Ram, *Indian Communism: Split Within a Split* (New Delhi: Vikas Publications, 1969).

21. On the problems of abstracting ideology from behavior and disparate interview materials, see J. David Greenstone and Paul E. Peterson, *Race and Authority in Urban Politics* (New York: Russell Sage Foundation, 1973), esp. pp. 52-162.

attributed to them. The emphasis of those principles was on the desirability of maintaining existing social and economic relations, except where such relations interfered with economic opportunities for the better-placed individual. Land relations were to be maintained as they were; caste relations were to be given perhaps less serious concern than in the past, but social and economic distinctions were maintained or enhanced whenever possible. Above all, the ambitious were to be duly rewarded with the economic and political fruits of their activity.

Despite whatever maldistribution of social and economic opportunities has existed in the countryside, the state political leadership in Maharashtra was fairly skillful at managing the resultant power relations. Sometimes factionalism within the local elite structure grew quite bitter. Yet, state leaders exercised enough restraint on local actors to assure the continuation of the state political system under the leadership of the Congress party. They also provided the system with sufficient flexibility so that frustration of unmet ambitions would not be cumulative. Members of opposition parties were allowed easy entry into the Congress; also, not all institutional positions were held by Congress loyalists.

Thus, even in Kolhapur, where leadership conflicts were frequent, local leaders refrained from trying to carry their ambitional quarrels to the point of demanding a radical restructuring of the system of power in the state or attempting to bring about a change in the terms on which power was distributed between the larger population and the elite. Given the degree of intra-elite consensus that existed, it was possible to accommodate most local political actors within the larger party organization. In cases such as those of Ratnappa Kumbhar and the Kakade family, personal conflicts were too severe to permit local accommodation, but state and national party leaders continued to maintain personal ties to those dissidents. This was possible because so much organizational dissidence was based on ambitional conflicts and not on any fundamental challenge raised against the assumptions of the political system. The personal relationships among Khadilkar, Mohite, and the Kakades indicate how much scope there was within the elite for presumed differences of ideology to operate alongside the sharing of common personal interests.

The inflexibilities of local leadership were also partially compensated for by the sensitivity of responsible leaders of Maharashtra to the need for change, or, at least, the importance of maintaining the appearance of that sensitivity. Thus, interventions by certain state leaders, most notably Y. B. Chavan, seemed to be informed by a desire to keep the channels of ambitional mobility open in the face of attempts by local elites to prevent aspirant elements from gaining access to some additional share of the available political chances. In this respect, in fact, the leadership of the Maharashtra Congress proved itself more adept than most state leaderships in India in distributing opportunities among established local actors, opening opportunities for those persons with appropriate credentials into political life, and creating new opportunity structures when old vehicles for the manifestation of ambition appeared to be overloaded.

Local and state leadership were not consistently anti-egalitarian but their behavior belied any verbal commitment they made to that principle. The nationalist movement initiated a strain toward the expression of egalitarian values, and independence led to the formalization of such ideals in documents like the Indian Constitution. In Maharashtra, few public actors of any stature openly rejected such ideals. However, there was a considerable gap between verbalizing egalitarian goals and putting those goals into practice. In part, there was a current in the system that forced a trade-off between ambition and egalitarianism and came down on the side of the former. Consequently, egalitarian ideology figured in only a minor way in the behavior of the men of ambition who constituted the elite of rural Maharashtra. Instead, those in the Congress party who took part in local politics were keenly aware of the personal benefits to be gained from political participation. Some admitted verbally and others conceded even more by their behavior that they approached such institutions as cooperatives and rural local governments primarily as arenas for ambitious men like themselves to seize personal opportunities. The case of education is more ambiguous than the other two. There, rural politicians seemed to be less exploiters of institutional opportunities than participants in a process which was still tinged with the earlier ideology of the status movement which had pressed for rapid expansion of educational chances among rural non-Brahmans. As a result, the symbolism of educational opportunity was emphasized, but those opportunities which were most likely to flow to the ambitious and well-placed were given special stress.

In these cases, as in others, local leaders were not the creators of ideas. These were generated by subject-matter specialists or by a few individuals in state or national positions of policy leadership who chose, sometimes for reasons of their own ambitions, to espouse particular policy choices which they estimated to be electorally popular or to be useful as the basis for gaining greater support for themselves among the local elite. In some instances, the linkage between ambition and the selection of particular policies may have had an element of social consciousness to it; in other cases, the ambitious national or state politician chose to take whatever policy stand came to hand and to "ride" that position in a way he or she anticipated would enhance his or her political career. What was true of the Indian politician is true of most politicians in liberal political systems: very few advance causes which are not likely to have some personal advantage to themselves.

While there was very little discussion of principles or the theories behind policies in district politics, somewhat more consideration of such matters occurred in arenas of state decision making, and even more at the national level. The homogeneity of political culture in district politics flowed from the fact that, at least in the context of rural Maharashtra, individuals shared common social backgrounds and common experiences in political socialization. (Thus, the somewhat greater diversity of caste backgrounds in Kolhapur and the differences in political socialization experiences under the princely regime and in independent India may account for a slightly greater degree of conflict over ideology there than among Poona politicians.) The largesse of the Congress government of Maharashtra in distributing societal resources to the rural elites may also have lessened the potential for ideological conflict among local actors. Should such resources be diverted to other outlets or more groups within society be made part of the system of benefits, the potential for ideological conflict could be considerably heightened.

One of the reasons that ideology was more apparent in state politics than in district politics was that at the state level more diverse interests had to be considered (including the wide range of urban interests that are present in a relatively urbanized and industrialized state like Maharashtra). The existence of active non-Congress politicians in urban areas drawing their support from diverse interests which were only represented marginally in rural politics contributed to this situation. Such factors were even further magnified in national politics, where issues were most directly posed about where the resources were to come from to provide benefits to underprivileged sectors of society. Diversity of urban and rural interests, overlaid by considerations of regional claims and the representation of an even wider spectrum of ideological parties, contributed to a constant (if sometimes restrained) debate in Parliament and other national arenas over the ends and means of economic and social reconstruction.

While ambition is not always the basis upon which political actors ground their policy positions—and in many situations it is joined to other factors—it contributed significantly to the bewildering pattern of personal and factional alignments that have characterized so much of Indian political life. Thus, institution building in Maharashtra and other regions of India under the aegis of a liberal state served largely to whet the appetites of the ambitious. It remains doubtful how capable the system of liberal politics that prevailed until recently really was of providing a means to meet the needs of the larger society. Perhaps, like Adam Smith's capitalist entrepreneurs, the political entrepreneurs of India supplied some benefits to society as an unintended consequence of their pursuit of personal rewards, but like the practitioners of laissez-faire capitalism, they were little concerned with the inequities which their behavior either maintained or exacerbated. The problem that arose became one of how to make alterations in the political regime that would continue to provide rewards for the ambitious and yet approach problems of public policy with an eye toward greater equity—a goal which had been frequently proclaimed by Indian national leadership but only pursued at the margins of public policy.

INSTITUTIONALIZING CHANGES IN INDIA[22]

It is neither my role nor within my capabilities to draw a blueprint for further political development in India. Rather, in this last section, I wish to discuss some of the problems relevant to the

22. Like the rest of this volume, the following section was originally drafted in early 1975, prior to the Declaration of Emergency in June. The section was revised in March 1976, but the earlier orientation was largely retained. An epilogue follows which takes more recent events directly into account.

present study which the leadership of the nation must still try to resolve if stated regime goals of equality of opportunity and a more equitable share in the social product are to be pursued more seriously than in the past.

Despite their receptiveness to those innovations introduced into rural life by external forces, rural local elites have proven themselves highly insensitive to the long-range consequences of their behavior. Increasingly, they have become a source of institutional restraint, standing in the way of more participatory and more redistributive patterns of political development. [23] As noted earlier, state and national political leadership has sometimes found itself fighting to keep open channels of opportunity that influential local leaders have attempted to consolidate into larger spheres of personal influence. For a time it was possible for local, national, and state leaders to pay off their subordinate clienteles with educational, governmental, and cooperative-related opportunities. Dependents among the general public might be herded to the polls and taught to vote for members of the local elite or candidates supported by that elite in return for minor economic benefits (including retention of jobs), but they remained largely peripheral to the principal ambitional game.

In such circumstances, the use of public policy sectors proved a relatively ineffective instrument for inducing fundamental social change. Furthermore, neither the planning process nor the administrative system responsible for integrating and directing the Indian economy took up the slack. As a result, the political system failed to play an effective role both in substantially increasing national productivity and in redistributing the resources which had accrued to the few sectors of the economy that had prospered.

It was in its failure to implement public policy from an egalitarian orientation that the asymmetry of the Indian political system became most apparent in the 1960s. In the formulation of policies, the national leadership and the leadership of Maharashtra were able to enunciate goals which reflected various shades of

23. In terms employed by some students of comparative politics, the problems which confronted the Indian political system by the 1960s were ones of "participation" and "distribution." For the source and uses of this terminology, see Leonard Binder et al., *Crises and Sequences in Political Development* (Princeton: Princeton University Press, 1971); for the Indian case in particular, see Rajni Kothari, *The Politics of India* (Boston: Little, Brown, 1970).

socialist doctrine. However, when policies were actually to be legislated or implemented, considerable influence could be brought to bear by local elites to assure that public policy was kept in line with their own interests.

The resistance of the expansive elite to change was, of course, selective. At issue was not the maintenance of traditional rural values or social structures as such. The political actors who had come to dominate the new institutions of rural India were "modern" men representing a class of market-oriented farmers. They were better educated than their forebears; many of them had personal ties to one or more urban areas; and they were linked into major networks of state and national communication.[24] At the same time, the non-directive nature of the Indian political system allowed them to pursue their localistic and personal interests rather than forcing them to act in ways which reflected any conscious societal interest. Thus, very few district politicians whom I interviewed took Congress party rhetoric about socialism seriously; or, if they professed to do so, their understanding of socialism usually could be reduced to vague support for humanitarian goals like providing more food, clothing, and shelter to the mass of the population. Among some of the most articulate of these local politicians even Congress-style socialism was unacceptable. For example, the belief was strong that further land reform was undesirable because it would discourage productivity in agriculture.[25] Instead, they equated increased productivity with such desiderata as markets protected by the government, government support of investments in agriculture (including technological innovations), low wages to farm workers, and low taxes—hardly what one would normally characterize as "socialism." If anything, their version of socialism may have pointed them toward support of a form of state socialism in which the government employed

24. Rather than a "crisis in penetration" existing in India (as Binder et al., in *Crises and Sequences,* suggested was the case in other developing nations), the problems were more the result of the successes local elites had achieved in "penetrating" fairly strong national institutions with their own preferences and political influence. It is a situation quite familiar to students of American federalism.

25. Considerable evidence exists that productivity actually is greater on smaller holdings, apparently because of more intensive cultivation. See, for example, Malenbaum, *Modern India's Economy,* pp. 147-152.

the instruments of public policy to serve as the guarantor of elite interests.

Thus, while the Indian political leadership pursued an interventionist economic strategy which was in theoretical contradiction to the political liberalism which the system incorporated into its operations, its interventionism carried few economic or political costs to the beneficiaries of the policies which were promulgated. If anything, public policies involved redistributing resources from urban areas and taxation of the poor (both in the city and the countryside) to benefit the expansive elite, whose activities were subsidized both directly and indirectly by the state and national governments. [26] Increasingly, societal changes were possible only when they accorded with the perceived needs of the expansive local elite, as well as the needs of relevant urban business interests and of certain well-placed members of the professional-bureaucratic class in Indian society. Together these elites constituted a crucial set of actors engaged in power exchanges and in policy-making processes in Maharashtra and in national politics as well. Subject-matter specialists might plead their cases well and receive a warm response as long as their arguments were backed by the ambitions of powerful state or national politicians. In turn, the latter found it difficult to act at all if they had to overcome a solid phalanx of local opposition. Similarly, governmental generalists might be able to affect the course of policy formulation and (more subtly) the processes of implementation, but they were forced to yield the political lead on most substantive matters to others— something they were willing to do as long as their own bureaucratic interests were not severely disturbed.

While, in theory, state and national politicians might have been expected to dominate key decision-making processes in India, their domination in policy matters seemed to be a guarded one. Since they were unwilling, for the most part, to resort to blatant use of force to command acceptance of policy decisions, authority appeared to rest on the consent of the governed. For many policy decisions affecting rural India, however, the relevant "governed" were little more than members of the expansive local elite, although electoral victories required mobilizing larger followings.

26. On this question, see George Rosen, *Democracy and Economic Change in India* (Berkeley and Los Angeles: University of California Press, 1967), esp. pp. 154-194.

At one time (in 1970-1971) it appeared that Mrs. Gandhi might appeal—over the heads of the expansive elite—directly to the mass of the population, which had been left unrewarded in the wake of institutional innovation and growth. For reasons which remain obscure, she did not seize the opportunities provided by temporary international political success (the creation of Bangladesh) and the popularity of her appeals to the poor in the 1971 elections. She failed to develop more effective instrumentalities of politics and administration, which might have supplanted existing mechanisms of policy formulation and policy implementation. Nor was there any evidence of a will or capacity on her part to restructure the political system in a fundamental fashion.

Having invested a good deal of themselves in the existing reward structures, and having been handsomely repaid for that investment, few members of the expansive elite would have rallied to radical causes unless the system were clearly restructured to make the existing set of arrangements threatening to them. The greatest threat, of course, would have been to reduce their political autonomy by "de-institutionalizing" the countryside or setting more rigid criteria for gaining access to the benefits channeled through the existing (or modified) institutions. Instead, local political actors were allowed to proceed on their entrepreneurial way. As a result, they continued to provide a strong base of support for counter-revolutionary activities as evidenced in rural opposition to radical activity. It was only with considerable reluctance, for example, that members of the local elite in Maharashtra eventually extended support to Mrs. Gandhi when she split the Congress in 1970. That demonstration of support owed much to the assurances provided by Chavan that the changes to be introduced by the "new" Congress would not seriously threaten the advantages of the elite.

If the expansive elite has not constituted a vehicle for further social change, alternatives must be considered. The political culture of rural India is such that the massive population will remain discontented but quiet even under the most extreme circumstances. A much more effective means of destroying the rural social structure would be necessary than presently exists if egalitarian ideals were to be promoted successfully. The regime has demonstrated little real interest in that kind of "cultural revolution." The stability that existed in much of the Indian countryside was reinforced by moderate concessions (likely to be more symbolic than substantive) made to individuals or groups aspiring to enter the expansive elite; on occasion, it was necessary for the government to resort to instruments of repression like the prisons, the police, and the army—elements which were employed with increasing regularity during the decade prior to the Emergency—to deal with localized outbursts of radical activity.[27]

Assuming that there was still some capacity among the national political leadership to perceive the condition of Indian society and to act upon it, it would not have been too late to seek some kind of resolution from above. In one form, this might mean identifying and providing assistance to counter-elites in the localities of India to organize against entrenched local interests. It appeared that this was the strategy being contemplated by Mrs. Gandhi in 1971 when her electoral pledges appealed to the educated unemployed and brought forward younger leadership in many of the Indian states in place of the older men who had previously run the Congress organization. However, the initial spirit of change was quickly vitiated when she failed to follow up those pledges to social and political reconstruction through national policy or through an effective reorganization of the Congress party. For example, she toyed briefly with the idea of turning the Congress into a cadre party of a kind more characteristic of movement-regimes, but she then drew back from the implications

27. The increasing employment of coercion by the government to maintain internal political order was becoming a growing source of disaffection among former admirers of Indian democracy by 1975. Not only did India continue to maintain a substantial military force, despite the earlier dismemberment of Pakistan, but it made growing use of military and paramilitary police units in quelling civil disturbances. In 1974, there was also worldwide concern expressed about the great number of political dissidents that had been held in prison for many years without proper legal procedures. On this matter, see "Detention Conditions in West Bengal: Text of Report by Amnesty International," *Economic and Political Weekly,* 21 September 1974, pp. 1611-1618. In a later article referring to that report, which had noted that fifteen to twenty thousand political prisoners were being held in the prisons of West Bengal, the editors noted that "the government cooly countered that the number of 'political prisoners' in the state was precisely 1,609; the rest were simply not defined as political prisoners." "A Matter of Definition," *Economic and Political Weekly,* 23 November 1974, p. 1926. Also see "Kerala: Torture of Political Prisoners," *Economic and Political Weekly,* 7 December 1974, pp. 2009-2011.

of such a strategy, including the costs it might carry in terms of losing the support local elites continued to provide to her as long as her symbolic policy gestures and public rhetoric were not matched by actions.

Yet, evident in Mrs. Gandhi's uncertain behavior was an awareness of the kinds of problems that challenged the political order. For example, the educational system had spawned a generation of educated unemployed who were available for participation in political movements. The leftist tactics of the 1960s proved ineffectual, but under appropriate leadership and given the kinds of ideological appeals that a demagogue (of either the left or the right) might put forward, there was a ready-made audience for radical actions. The ambitional blockages evident in the concentration of power in the hands of the expansive elite only provided additional kindling for such a movement.

As we have seen in the present study, Mrs. Gandhi attempted to exploit a situation marked by considerable internal contradiction. She drew upon the support of factions within the regional and local elites to enhance her personal political authority. At the same time, she condemned the principles of inequality which that elite represented.

Given the strategic control of institutional resources by members of the local elite, and their autonomy as a force in rural politics, major changes in rural India clearly were most likely to come only through a series of cultural and political changes directed from above. One way for Mrs. Gandhi to effect such changes was to attempt to co-opt the movement developed by Jayaprakash Narayan or—more realistically, given the shaky constituency upon which that movement depended—[28] to design a similar movement which would cleanse the political system of the administrative malaise and the uncertainties of policy formulation and policy implementation that characterized it. What was required was a more effective set of organizational weapons at the command of a national leadership responsive to societal needs and capable of converting programmatic goals into implementable policies. It might have involved, for example, developing a new charac-

---

28. On the nature of the backing for the movement led by Narayan, see Rakshat Puri, "India's Opposition Parties Find a Leader," *South Asian Review* 8 (January 1975): 91-95. Also see John R. Wood, "Extra-Parliamentary Opposition in India: An Analysis of Populist Agitations in Gujarat and Bihar," *Pacific Affairs* 48 (Fall 1975): 313-334.

ter for the national Congress party—one more responsive to national goals than to local elites. Some means would also have been needed to change the national bureaucracy in a fashion which would have made it more politically responsible and more seriously concerned with organizing for change than for maintaining law and order and the status quo.

In sum, the Congress party and the governments of India and Maharashtra had been relatively successful in building institutions in the countryside supportive of the regime at low costs in terms of coercion, but that was because so much was given to local elites while asking them for so little in return, except the provision of support to the regime. Unless Mrs. Gandhi was willing to sacrifice the dreams and ambitions of the vast majority of Indian citizens, she was necessarily forced to come to grips with the challenge represented by the expansive elites of rural Maharashtra and other parts of the subcontinent. The costs of continued mismanagement of Indian society otherwise would have continued to mount in the form of poverty and disease and, what is in some ways worse, the misapplication of those limited societal resources which did exist. Such resources were to be found not only in industrial organization and agricultural technology but in the vast amount of human creativity which exists in India in the form of untapped capabilities.

Considerable debate is possible over the most appropriate strategy for political development. While one thinks automatically of political changes which might involve the introduction of a more centralized and ideologically consistent party system or the generation of mechanisms to create a more effective and goal-directed bureaucracy, some pattern of change based on a serious effort to alter the political culture of the countryside on a decentralized basis which would activate non-elites would be preferable. In certain respects, one of the major problems was that the administration of local service systems was overbureaucratized, and that bureaucracy served the interests of the expansive elite rather than being employed in the service of all local persons. One possible solution might have involved finding some means by which existing institutions could be revised to accommodate more effective general participation in their operation, perhaps through a new form of communal responsibility.

Unless something of that sort happened, it was already apparent to observers before 1975 that an increasing expenditure of societal resources would be necessary to support the coercive mechanisms required to keep the system on its uncertain course. At some point, the price of system-maintaining coercion might well have proven to be greater both in terms of human lives and societal resources than the costs of social change. When that happened, India might indeed have been ready for a revolution, cultural or otherwise. For the time being, however, that day does not appear to be upon us. Instead, as we now know, Mrs. Gandhi moved to pre-empt the possibility of radical change.

Epilogue:
The Road Not Taken

On June 26, 1975, Indira Gandhi, acting through the President of India, declared a state of emergency. Prominent opposition leaders were imprisoned, and strict censorship was imposed on the newspapers and journals of the nation. A series of amendments to the Constitution were subsequently accepted by a Parliament deprived of a portion of its opposition members. In effect, those amendments denied due process to political prisoners, largely removed the judicial system from a significant role in the operation of the Constitution, and made it virtually impossible to control the Prime Minister through legal means.

There is no need to review these actions in any detail nor the steps which led up to the Emergency, including the challenge mounted by Jayaprakash Narayan and his amorphous reform movement. Even less need be said of the particular incident, involving a challenge to Mrs. Gandhi's election to Parliament in 1971, which may or may not have been a precipitating event.[1]

What is more significant is what the constitutional coup did not involve. Insofar as can be surmised, the move toward dictatorial rule was made entirely by Mrs. Gandhi and her immediate advisors. There is no evidence that the military played a large role in the matter nor, indeed, that any other set of major national institutions, like the bureaucracy, was at the forefront of the action. It is equally significant that while the regime did effect a series of changes in the operation of the media, the party system, and the judiciary, the fundamental character of social and eco-

---

1. For a useful chronology of events, see Richard Park, "Political Crisis in India, 1975," *Asian Survey* 15 (November 1975): 996-1013; and Norman D. Palmer, "India in 1975: Democracy in Eclipse," *Asian Survey* 16 (February 1976): 95-110. One of the most interesting documents to become available recently is the issue of *Seminar* published for January 1976. See, in particular, Rajni Kothari, "End of an Era," *Seminar* no. 197 (January 1976): 22-28.

nomic organization was not altered. Even in the sphere of political activity, institutions were, for the most part, stifled rather than entirely eliminated. (Exceptions to this were suppression of communal organizations of the militant right, most notably the Rashtriya Swayamsevak Sangh, and the conservative Muslim party, Jamaat-e-Islami-e-Hind.[2])

As she had in the past, on the occasion of policy maneuvers which were essentially responses to political challenges, Mrs. Gandhi issued a Twenty Point Program on July 1, consisting of a collection of reform pledges which had been made by the government or the Congress party over a period of years. These included pledges to end rural indebtedness and indentured labor, promises of land reform and welfare measures to aid the rural poor. As of this writing, there is very little evidence that any of these promised reforms have been seriously undertaken or that the few that have been taken up have had much effect upon the operation of rural society.

Occasional reports, as well as the claims of the government, point to successes on various fronts: a new spirit of commitment on the part of the bureaucracy, perhaps born of fear of the unknown, seems to have improved the quality of public services; the food distribution system appears to be operating more equitably, driving the notorious black market underground; the ravages of inflation have been brought in check, though it is difficult to determine how much of this "success" is due to a good harvest and how much to a new vigor demonstrated by governmental leaders. Whether the corruption previously rampant in the system has been checked is anyone's guess.

As congenial as these improvements in the operation of the political system may be to most Indians, it remains unclear what the long-range implications of recent changes will be. To follow up a theme developed earlier, it might well be argued that India's difficulties were multiplied in the period leading up to the Emergency by an *excess* of stability; that stability was grounded upon an elite consensus which served the institutional interests of

2. Among other groups banned were the splinters of what had been the Communist Party of India (Marxist-Leninist). This official edict was mainly a symbolic act since the organization had already been effectively quashed by 1975 as a result of the imprisonment of its leaders and internal splintering during the previous decade.

important local, state, and national leaders but did not serve the fundamental needs of the vast majority of population living lives barely above the survival line. In such a situation, the stability of the Indian political order might have been an instance of "political decay" of a kind not treated effectively in the writings of Huntington and others—the consequences of an unwillingness on the part of a regime with strong institutions to meet the developmental needs of its society.[3]

Confronted with the challenge represented by strong local elites and the institutions which granted considerable autonomy to them, the regime might have moved in any number of ways. Indeed, one of the things that was most notable about the way in which the Emergency was handled was the ease with which Mrs. Gandhi apparently imposed it. Presumably, she was free to choose the direction subsequent actions would take. (Thus, the military and police seemed to accept her directives with little demurrer, though censorship makes it difficult to be entirely sure of this assertion.) What underground continues to exist is probably more inclined toward the rustling of papers than the clashing of arms. Indeed, for the average citizen the removal of the ebullient voices of the opposition from the front pages of the newspapers may have been more of a relief than a cause for protest. That is especially likely to have been the reaction since so many of the opposition leaders had been so ineffective as policy makers in the past.

3. In this connection, see Mark Kesselman, "Overinstitutionalization and Political Constraint," *Comparative Politics* 3 (October 1970): 21-44. A critique of the high value placed on stability by Huntington and other writers in the comparative politics literature may be found in Kesselman's "Order or Movement?: The Literature of Political Development as Ideology," *World Politics* 26 (October 1973): 139-154. For an examination of the political situation in 1971 that questions the applicability of the Huntington model to India (but for quite different reasons than I have advanced), see L. P. Singh, "Political Development or Political Decay in India?" *Pacific Affairs* 44 (Spring 1971): 65-80. Many writers have been sensitive to the effects that failures in economic performance may have upon the legitimacy of political regimes. In the Indian case, for example, see Rajni Kothari, *Politics in India* (Boston: Little, Brown, 1970), esp. pp. 351-382. In the recent Indian case, however, there is no evidence that there was a direct relationship between low economic performance and the steps taken to obliterate many of the democratic procedures that previously were characteristic of the Indian system of government.

The radical change in political institutions effected from above by Mrs. Gandhi, however, was perhaps most remarkable for its basic conservatism. Aside from the severe repression exercised against the political opposition and the media, the chief products of the change were the minor housekeeping improvements noted earlier. There has been no noticeable effort by the new regime to destroy or even alter the major socioeconomic institutions which existed previously. Thus, much to the point of the argument advanced in the last chapter, there is little evidence that the expansive elite has been checked in any major way except to the extent that it finds it more difficult to exploit political opportunities of the kind previously associated with the electoral system. The federal system has also been retained though it is not clear whether it functions as it did in the past. At least on the surface, the state government of Maharashtra continues to operate under its new chief minister; the central government has not moved directly into the administration of state services, although that is more the case in some other states. Municipal governments have been superseded in many places, but that is hardly unusual.

It should be stressed that the challenge to the Gandhi regime in 1975, such as it was, came essentially from the political right. Calls for cleaner government and jobs for the unemployed could easily have been tolerated within the political system that existed earlier. Indeed, there was little in the program of the movement at odds with what Congressmen had been favoring on public platforms for years. Whether Jayaprakash Narayan's appeals for a radical change in the regime were sufficient grounds to justify the enormous reaction of the Gandhi government is another matter. Yet, in the end, the course taken was essentially system-maintaining.

It would have been misleading to suggest in the text that members of the expansive elite and others who supported the previous regime were inherently democrats; if anything, the argument I have advanced has pointed to the pragmatic nature of most members of that elite. Given the way the system is now operating, one suspects that most individuals in the local elite have adapted to the situation reasonably well. The problem of long-term adaptation may, however, be a more challenging one. Mrs. Gandhi played a skillful game up to 1975 of maintaining verbal if not substantive commitment to the balancing of her policies between the local elites and the majority of the citizens of India. Under the current regime, she appears to have continued that balancing act. How long she can continue to maintain that balance is unclear. Already, some of her actions on the economic front suggest that she may seek to encourage industrial development and perhaps agricultural production at the expense of the distribution of existing resources to the masses. For a time, improvements in the administration of the food supply system and, more generally, in the bureaucratic structure may be a public benefit treated with considerable value by the bulk of the population. For the long haul, however, it is unclear how the regime will respond to the need for more fundamental societal changes.

It is my view that the problems detailed in the present study did not directly create the Emergency; Mrs. Gandhi did that. That may explain why the actions taken by the regime have dealt only peripherally with major problems of equality of opportunity and equity in distribution. To silence the opposition and censor the press may stifle public debate for a time over the course to be taken in dealing with the fundamental issues of Indian society. They hardly constitute a useful first step toward making the regime a more salutary instrument for participatory public policy making or a more effective mechanism of service delivery.

The character of her actions in the wake of the Emergency indicates that Mrs. Gandhi had no more idea of where she was going then than she had in 1970, when she tore the Congress apart without developing an alternative political mechanism to chart a more effective national course, or in 1971, when she promised a new order of benefits to the poor in her campaign to abolish poverty without having any means to deliver upon that promise. The worst possibility is that all that has happened in the past two years is the expression of personal pique by Mrs. Gandhi against a political opposition and a communications industry which did not share her own estimate of her personal worth.

POSTSCRIPT, MAY 1977

During the Emergency and in the election campaign leading to the Congress's national defeat in March 1977, Y. B. Chavan remained a staunch supporter of Mrs. Gandhi. As Minister for External Affairs, however, he was not directly responsible for administering the malodorous policies of the period. Thus, after Mrs. Gandhi's resignation as Prime Minister, Chavan was acceptable as official leader of the Congress in the Lok Sabha.

The Congress's setbacks actually strengthened Chavan's hand within the Maharashtra party. Unlike in the northern states, where the Janata party and its allies swept most of the seats, the party division in Maharashtra was fairly even: of forty-eight seats contested, twenty went to the Congress, nineteen to the Janata itself and the rest to its affiliates—five to the PWP, three to the Communist Party of India (Marxist), and one to a splinter of the Republican party.

The Chief Minister, Shankarrao Chavan had played a prominent role in designating MP candidates and came under immediate attack from the forces supporting Y. B. Chavan. Vasantrao Patil, who had been forced out of the Cabinet in 1976 and at the time had declared his retirement from politics, suddenly re-emerged. Indeed, during the last weeks of the campaign hints surfaced that his wife (and possibly Patil himself) was leaning toward support of the Jagjivan Ram-led Congress for Democracy. By April 9, Shankarrao Chavan could no longer resist the pressures, though he did not actually resign until April 16, when Congress legislators gathered in Bombay to vote for a new Chief Minister. Patil rallied the forces associated with Y. B. Chavan and Vasantrao Naik. The Shankarrao Chavan group and other dissidents consolidated behind the candidacy of Y. J. Mohite. Patil defeated Mohite by a vote of 189 to 88. Congressmen like Mohite, Pawar, Gaikwad and Kumbhar, who had continued to serve in the government during the Emergency, were included in the new government. One party defector was Rajaram Patil, long-time opponent of Vasantrao Patil; he left the Congress to become leader of the Congress for Democracy in the state. Reflecting the fears that haunted the new Chief Minister, a huge state ministry of forty members was created in the hope of heading off other defections to the new parties.

Reaction to the Emergency in the districts was clearly greater in Poona than in Kolhapur. Annasaheb Magar was elected MP from the Khed constituency in place of R. K. Khadilkar, but V. N. Gadgil, then serving as Minister of State for Defense in the national government, was defeated by Sambhaji Kakade. As a leader of the Organization Congress in Maharashtra, Kakade had emerged a prominent figure in the Janata party in the state. Even more prominent in that party was Mohan Dharia. Elected from Poona City, Dharia became a Minister for Commerce in the new Morarji Desai government. In Kolhapur, both Congress candidates were elected. Shankarrao Mane returned to his seat in Kolhapur City; the other victor was not well known in the district at the time of my research.

Index

Administrative Reorganization, Commissioner for. *See* Heble Report

Administrators. *See* Functional specialists; Government bureaucrats; Indian Administrative Service (IAS)

Agra (city), 11

Agricultural Market Act, 253-256

Agricultural marketing, 55-56. *See also* Dalals; Marketing societies; Regulated markets; Taluka sanghs

Agricultural services, 287-290

Agriculture, Department of, 250

Ahmedabad, 218

Ahmednagar district, 53, 207n, 209n, 211n, 213n

AICC. *See* All-India Congress Committee

Akola District, 34n, 271n

All-India Congress Committee (AICC), 32n, 84-85, 142; dispute over Kolhapur DCC, 111; relations with MPCC, 137; conflict over MP candidates, 144; Parliamentary Board (1972), 148-149. *See also* Congress party

Almond, Gabriel A., 3n

Ambedkar, B. R., 35n, 39

Ambegaon taluka, 53, 84, 228

Ambition, 8, 11, 16, 27, 75, 88, 145; theory, 313-315, 316-322; in cooperatives, 44, 230-231, 235; in education, 167-168, 182-184; conflicts derived from, 139-141, 155-158; in Kolhapur, 94, 107-113, 122-123; in sugar factories, 216; policy aspect, 218-221. *See also* Opportunity structures

Anderson, James E., 18n

Andhra Pradesh, 146, 208n

Anti-Brahman riots, 98-99, 110

Anti-Brahmanism, 94, 98-99. *See also* Non-Brahman movement

Arbiter role, 52, 77-78, 129, 130-132. *See also* Chavan, Y. B.; Mohol, N. S. (Mamasaheb)

Assam, 260

Attwood, Donald W., 9n, 63n, 213n

Aurangabad district, 271n

Bachrach, Peter, 5n, 23n, 59n, 306n

Bagal, Madhavrao, 110; background, 94-95; in Praja Parishad, 95-97; opposition to Kolhapur merger, 98-99; in PWP, 100, 101n; in Samyukta Maharashtra, 102

Bagal, Vasantrao, 97, 99, 102n, 164n

Bahujan samaj, 161

Baker, David, 26n

Balbus, Isaac, 6n

Baramati municipality, 80, 81n

Baramati taluka, 53, 55, 228; politics in, 64, 70-71, 213n

Baratz, Morton S., 18n, 59n

Baroda, 161

Baviskar, B. S., 213n, 219n

BDO. *See* Block Development Officer

Belgaum district, 93

Bell, Daniel, 309n

Bhelke, Shankarrao, 166; background, 61-62; in zilla parishad conflicts, 68-69, 72; rivalry over dairy scheme, 69; as chairman of DLDB, 62, 74; decline, 83

Bhide, Anantrao, 119-120, 219, 249

Bhir district, 209n

Bhiwandi, 142

Bhogawati sugar factory, 104, 213

Bhor taluka, 53, 60, 61

Bidri sugar factory, 104, 105n, 156n, 216-217

Bihar, 208

Binder, Leonard, 3n, 323n, 324n

Block Development Officer (BDO), 298; role in panchayati raj, 274,

337